International Finance and Financial Services

INTERNATIONAL FINANCE AND FINANCIAL SERVICES

KRISTIAN L. HAGEN
EDITOR

Nova Science Publishers, Inc.
New York

For permission to use material from this book please contact us:
Telephone 631-231-7269; Fax 631-231-8175
Web Site: http://www.novapublishers.com

Library of Congress Cataloging-in-Publication Data

International finance and financial services / Kristian L. Hagen (editor).
p. cm.
ISBN-13: 978-1-60021-756-2 (hardcover)
ISBN-10: 1-60021-756-7 (hardcover)
1. International finance. 2. Financial services industry. 3. Financial institutions. I. Hagen, Kristian L.
HG3881.I57616 2007
332'.042--dc22

2007045286

Published by Nova Science Publishers, Inc. ✢ New York

CONTENTS

PREFACE

International finance is the branch of economics that studies the dynamics of exchange rates, foreign investment, and how these affect international trade.Financial services is a term used to refer to the services provided by the finance industry. Financial services is also the term used to describe organizations that deal with the management of money and includes merchant banks, credit card companies, consumer finance companies, government sponsored enterprises, and stock brokerages. Financial services is the largest industry (or industry category) in the world, in terms of earning. This new book presents important analyses in these interaction fields.

Chapter 1 - Over the past twenty years, U.S. import prices have become less responsive to the exchange rate. The authors propose that a significant portion of this decline is a result of increased trade integration. To illustrate this effect, the authors develop an open economy DGE model in which trade occurs along both the intensive and extensive margins. The key element the authors introduce into this environment is strategic complementarity in price setting. As a result, a firm's pricing decision depends on the prices set by its competitors. This feature implies that a foreign exporter finds it optimal to vary its markup in response to shocks that change the exchange rate, insulating import prices from exchange rate movements. With increased trade integration, exporters have become more responsive to the prices of their competitors and this change in pricing behavior accounts for a significant portion of the observed decline in the sensitivity of U.S import prices to the exchange rate.

Chapter 2 - The Barro-Gordon inflation bias has provided an influential argument for fixed exchange rate regimes. However, with low inflation rates now widespread, credibility concerns seem no longer relevant. Why give up independent monetary policy to contain an inflation bias that is already under control? The authors argue that credibility problems do not end with the inflation bias and they are a larger drawback for flexible exchange rates than usually thought. Absent commitment, independent monetary policy can induce expectation traps–that is, welfare ranked multiple equilibria–and perverse policy responses to real shocks, i.e., an equilibrium policy response that is welfare inferior to policy inaction. Both possibilities imply that flexible exchange rates feature unnecessary macroeconomic volatility.

Chapter 3 - This paper investigates the volatility transmission mechanism within the European Monetary System (EMS) and concentrates on the German 'Leadership Hypothesis'. The empirical analysis is carried out via short-term interest rates for six European countries, namely Belgium, France, Germany, Italy, the Netherlands, and the United Kingdom, and one outside country, the United States, for the March 1972 to December 2002 period. The results essentially support the idea of a German predominance within the European Monetary System, but not in a strict sense, since Germany's short-term rates are also affected by actions from its European counterparts. When including the U.S. short-term interest rate, neither the German nor the U.S. rates surface as prevalent players in the interest-rate volatility transmission mechanism. This is explained by the fact that during Germany's post-unification era (after July 1990), the EMS and U.S. monetary policies were diverging rather than converging. This is also supported by the fact that the EMS countries (excluding the U.K.) were making serious strides to converge among themselves in preparation for the upcoming monetary union with a single currency. Another notable finding refers to the absence of asymmetric behavior within EMS after Germany's reunification, attributed to the rapid economic convergence of the EMS countries.

Chapter 4 - The economic interpretation of the adjustment cost function in Q theory raises awkward questions. One common justification of adjustment costs is the disruption of production associated with the reorganization of production and the training of workers involved in installing new capital equipment. The problem with this interpretation is that reorganization and training both involve information as an input and might therefore be expected to result in decreasing marginal costs rather than increasing marginal costs.

In this chapter, the authors instead use the Demers (1991) model of uncertainty, irreversibility, and learning to motivate adjustment costs. In this model, irreversibility (in conjunction with the anticipation of receiving information) leads to lower investment levels than in the case of costless disposal of capital. The intuition is straightforward: errors of overinvestment are costly. In the model, irreversibility leads to an endogenous time-varying marginal adjustment cost. Thus, the "parameters" of the adjustment cost function vary over time because changes in expectations of future demand and the degree of uncertainty affect the size and likelihood of excess capital.

In their empirical work, the authors start by taking the Q theory as their null hypothesis; using standard assumptions, it is then possible to estimate the parameters of the adjustment cost function. If the assumptions of the Q model are correct, these parameters should be constant over time.

The authors use three different techniques to estimate the adjustment cost parameters. The first uses linear projections on past information to construct an estimate of the present value of the future stream of revenue from a unit of capital. The second takes advantage of market information: if the stock market is efficient, then the stock market price of a firm reflects the future revenue stream. The third avoids the construction of a present value by focusing on the period-to-period arbitrage condition for the optimal choice of investment.

In order to allow the adjustment cost parameters to vary freely over time, the authors turn to a unique panel data set of 136 U.S. firms for which they have 36 years of data. The authors find that adjustment costs vary substantially over time. Furthermore, their results seem to support the irreversibility cum learning model since there is some evidence that the marginal adjustment cost parameter declines over time: as the firms in their sample mature and form a more precise estimate of the state of demand, the marginal adjustment costs due to irreversibility diminish.

Chapter 5 – The authors analyze the impact of some internal control mechanisms - ownership structure, capital structure and growth opportunities- on earnings management in Chilean firms throughout 1991-2001. Their results are interesting due to the specific characteristics of the corporate system in Chile where investor protection is weak and banks play a prominent role. We find that ownership concentration has a non-linear relation with earnings management, consistent with both the control of directors by main shareholders and the idea of expropriation of minority shareholders by large controlling shareholders. Financial leverage and public debt gives managers incentives to accounting discretion whereas bank debt plays an active role in corporate governance as a control mechanism. Their results also show that earnings are not managed to signal growth opportunities.

Chapter 6 - Globalisation, commonly defined as the increasing market integration, also involves the expansion of multinational enterprises and foreign direct investment (FDI), mostly by such enterprises. This investment is influenced by the comparative tax regimes of host countries. This contribution involves consideration of two types of taxation effect. The first is the effect on the FDI decisions of multinational enterprises of international variations in taxation rates and rules. The second is their effect on intra-firm trade and pricing policy once an MNE establishes a foreign subsidiary. The first aspect involves international fiscal competition and the second entails transfer pricing. Indeed, manipulation of this transfer price is often used to minimise a multinational enterprise fiscal burden. It is argued that fiscal competition is desirable because it maintains welfare in host countries by acting as a disincentive for transfer pricing manipulation.

Chapter 7 - The breeding of an international apparatus to deal with the crucial aspect of world competition policy, as it is anticipated to be finally discussed on the Cancun Ministerial Meeting of the WTO in September 2003. Should this matter be restricted to the WTO context? Is the WTO the proper venue, especially when analyzing the theme from the standpoint of Brazil and other developing countries? There should be any international institution dealing with the matter, or, for instance, an unattended system of bilateral treaties would do? Given the complexity of international, domestic, regional and Third World-specific interests, the criteria of fairness and rationality seem to advise the setting up of an international institution, entirely dedicated to competition matters. It would seem that, if such assumptions are correct, a non-trade entity should be built upon the joint experience of both pre-WTO and post Doha competition collaboration. The authors are not certainly proposing an international institution that should chase and prosecute the international public interest on an autonomous and cavalier fashion. On the contrary, the reality of multilateral negotiation and complex national and regional policies indicate that only a prudent entity, acting in the same, ad hoc, case-by-case basis as the international judicial courts have been hitherto acting, could be of any practical import.

Chapter 8 - Over the last two decades, the development of the European financial market has been influenced by the advances in information technology and finance theory, retreat of state financing, capital flow liberalization, institutionalized savings management, and population maturation. It has also been stimulated by the introduction of the euro as a common currency, and the implementation of a single market. One of the EU‘s key priorities since the beginning of the 1990s, when the idea of a single market was formalized, was to ensure the conditions for the single market for financial services. Efforts to build the single financial market received greater emphasis in the Financial Services Action Plan (FSAP) created in 1999. The importance of the single financial market for the EU's development and the fulfillment of goals specified in the Lisbon declaration are both reflected in the Sapir report. This report explicitly recommends that market financing should be stimulated in the EU in order to increase investment levels in both research and development, and education. In the concluding part of the Sapir report, the role of the single market is also promoted through growth stimulation policies. It has long been proclaimed in financial literature that the financial market development is important for economic growth. The authors present a review of the relevant literature in section two of this chapter. Section three brings an overview of the achieved integration level of the European financial market, and the most important barriers to its implementation. In section four, the authors briefly compare the development of the Slovenian and European financial markets. Section five concludes by summarizing the most important findings.

Chapter 9 - The European Union (EU) is often perceived as lacking legitimacy. Yet, this understanding of EU policymaking is more and more contested through discussion of input and output legitimacy. The paper speaks to this issue by focusing specifically on integration in the financial services sector, particularly the securities industry, and by assessing how the policy process facilitates or impedes the legitimacy of policymaking in this field. By analyzing the Lamfalussy regulatory process, the authors argue that the EU has made important strides in ensuring both output and input legitimacy although there remain gaps in its approach. The legislative agenda of the Financial Services Action Plan was adopted on time and the regulatory process favours consultation with market actors. However, complete implementation of measures across the Union remains a problem as is the inability of end-users and consumers to fully access the policy process.

In: International Finance and Financial Services
Editor: Kristian L. Hagen, pp. 1-38
ISBN: 1-60021-756-7

Chapter 1

TRADE INTEGRATION, COMPETITION, AND THE DECLINE IN EXCHANGE-RATE PASS-THROUGH*

Christopher Gust, Sylvain Leduc†, and Robert J. Vigfusson

ABSTRACT

Over the past twenty years, U.S. import prices have become less responsive to the exchange rate. We propose that a significant portion of this decline is a result of increased trade integration. To illustrate this e ect, we develop an open economy DGE model in which trade occurs along both the intensive and extensive margins. The key element we introduce into this environment is strategic complementarity in price setting. As a result, a firm's pricing decision depends on the prices set by its competitors. This feature implies that a foreign exporter finds it optimal to vary its markup in response to shocks that change the exchange rate, insulating import prices from exchange rate movements. With increased trade integration, exporters have become more responsive to the prices of their competitors and this change in pricing behavior accounts for a significant portion of the observed decline in the sensitivity of U.S import prices to the exchange rate.

Keywords: Pass-Through, Trade Integration, Strategic Complementarity
JEL classification: F15, F41

---

* We thank Jeannine Bailliu, Martin Bodenstein, Jeff Campbell, Luca Dedola, Joe Gagnon, Jordi Galí, Luca Guerrieri, and seminar participants at the Federal Reserve Board, Federal Reserve Bank of Chicago, Bank of Canada, and Université Laval for helpful comments. The views expressed in this paper are solely the responsibility of the authors and should not be interpreted as reflecting the views of the Board of Governors of the Federal Reserve System or of any other person associated with the Federal Reserve System.
† Corresponding Author: Sylvain Leduc, Telephone 202-452-2399, Fax 202-736-5638. Email addresses: christopher.gust@frb.gov, sylvain.leduc@frb.gov, robert.vigfusson@frb.gov

1. Introduction

An important factor influencing trade balance dynamics and the transmission of business cycle across countries is the responsiveness of import prices to exchange-rate movements. To the extent that exchange-rate pass-through to import prices is low, currency fluctuations will be accompanied by small changes in trade prices and quantities, muting the international spillover effects of shocks on domestic activity and prices. As a consequence, exchange-rate pass-through is particularly relevant for monetary policymakers interested in maintaining price stability.[1] Furthermore, in a low pass-through environment, the effects of a dollar depreciation on the trade balance may be limited, which has important ramifications for the ongoing debate concerning how adjustment of the current U.S. trade deficit may be resolved.[2] What is the extent of exchange-rate pass-through (pass-through herein) to import prices? Consistent with the evidence surveyed in Goldberg and Knetter (1997), our estimate of pass-through for the 1980s is roughly 55 percent for the United States. This estimate implies that, following a 10 percent depreciation of the dollar, a foreign exporter selling to the U.S. market would raise its price in the United States by 5.5 percent. In the 1990s, however, we document that there has been a considerable decline in pass-through, as fluctuations in import prices have moderated substantially relative to exchange rate fluctuations.[3] In this paper, we develop a novel approach that links this fall in pass-through to an increase in trade integration spurred by lower tariffs, transport costs, and changes in relative productivities across countries. Following the recent international trade literature, we build a real, open economy model with endogenous entry and exit of exporters so that trade occurs along both the intensive and extensive margins.[4] We study incomplete pass-through building on the work of Kimball (1995) and more recently, Dotsey and King (2005). These papers allow for strategic complementarity in price setting using demand curves for which (the absolute value) of the demand elasticity is increasing in a firm's price relative to the price of its competitors.[5]

This feature implies that a firm's pricing decision depends not only on its marginal cost but also on the prices of its competitors. Because a foreign exporter does not want its price to deviate too far from its competitors, it is optimal for the exporter to increase its markup in response to a dollar appreciation that lowers its costs in dollars. Accordingly, pass-through of exchange-rate changes to import prices is incomplete in an environment with strategic complementarity in price setting.

---

[1] See, for example, Corsetti and Pesenti (2005) and Devereux and Engel (2003), who show how optimal monetary policy depends on the extent of exchange-rate pass-through

[2] See Gust and Sheets (2006) for a discussion of how trade balance dynamics change in a low pass-through environment.

[3] Our empirical evidence is in line with the work of Olivei (2002) and Marazzi, Sheets, and Vigfussen (2005) for the United States. Ihrig, Marazzi, and Rothenberg (2006) also document a fall in pass-through in other G-7 economies, and Otani, Shiratsuka, and Shirota (2003) find a decline in exchange rate pass-through in Japan.

[4] As in Melitz (2003), Ghironi and Melitz (2004), Bergin and Glick (2005), and Alessandria and Choi(2006), we postulate that monopolistically competitive firms face fixed costs of exporting and only a fraction of firms choose to export.

[5] We follow Woodford (2003) and define pricing decisions to be strategic complements if an increase in the prices charged for other goods increases a firm's own optimal price. For a similar approach to modelling the strategic complementarity in an open economy, see Bergin and Feenstra (2001). For a game-theoretic approach, see, for example, Atkeson and Burnstein (2005), Bernard, Eaton, Jensen, and Kortum (2003), or Bodnar, Dumas, and Marston (2002).

It is well known that models with strategic complementarity have incomplete pass-through. Our main contribution is to show that, in a model with strategic complementarity, factors that lead to greater trade integration may reduce pass-through. In our model, lower per-unit trade costs or higher productivity improve the relative competitiveness of a foreign exporter in the domestic market — allowing the foreign firm to increase its relative markup over costs.[6] With strategic complementarity, the foreign exporter's price becomes more responsive to the prices of its competitors as its markup increases, and the firm finds it optimal to vary its markup more and its price less in response to an exchange rate movement, i.e., lower pass-through. In our model, strategic complementarity thus induces an exporter to set a relatively high and variable markup when its costs are lower than its competitors and a low and unresponsive markup when its costs are relatively high. We show that this mechanism has a significant impact on the pricing behavior of exporting firms. In our benchmark calibration, lower trade costs and higher foreign productivity account for about one third of the observed decline in pass-through since the early 1990s.

We also assess the importance of exporters' entry decisions for trade integration and exchange-rate pass-through. With endogenous entry, the model is better able to account for the rise in the U.S. import share over the last 25 years. Similar to Dornbusch (1987), the entry of foreign exporters, other things equal, leads to a rise in exchange-rate pass-through. However, we show that following a reduction in the cost of exporting the effects of markups adjustments that arise only along the intensive margin largely dominate the impact of entry on pass-through.

Another implication of our model is that factors that increase trade integration induce an economy to become more competitive. Because lower trade costs reduce the prices of foreign exports relative to domestic producers, domestic producers lose market share. Strategic complementarity in price setting induces these producers to reduce their markups in response to the decline in the prices of foreign exporters.[7] The approach developed in this paper is thus in line with the view that trade integration has reduced the market power of U.S. producers and squeezed their profit margins.

Finally, to support our theoretical findings, we provide empirical evidence linking the fall in pass-through to lower trade costs. Using industry specific measures of pass-through and trade costs, we show that industries in which the decline in trade costs has been relatively large have also experienced relatively large declines in pass-through.

The paper is organized as follows. The next section presents evidence on the decline in pass-through in the United States, while Section 3 describes the time-series properties of trade costs and documents changes in productivities in di erent regions of the world. The model is described in Section 4, and we relate our statistical measure of pass-through to the model in Section 5. Section 6 discusses the model's calibration and our results are presented in Section 7. The last section concludes.

---

[6] In contrast, markups would be constant for a CES demand curves where there is no strategic complementarity.

[7] This result is consistent with the evidence in Chen, Imbs, and Scott (2004) who estimate that markups have fallen in the European Union since 1990.

2. U.S. Import Prices and the Real Exchange Rate

We first examine the statistical relationship between import prices and the exchange rate and document the increasing disconnect between these variables.

In our analysis, we focus on imports that are included in the end-use categories of automotive products, consumer goods, and capital goods, excluding computers and semiconductors. We will refer to these categories as finished goods, which account for 45 percent of the nominal value of total imports since 1987.

We concentrate on this more narrowly defined measure of import prices for two reasons. First, we exclude import prices of services, computers, and semiconductors because of concerns about price measurement. Prices for services are notoriously hard to measure. In addition, over time, di erent kinds of services have been added to the measured series and thus their composition is particularly unstable. We also exclude computers and semiconductors since their hedonic prices are heavily influenced by rapid increases in technology.

Second, our preferred measure excludes import prices of foods, feeds, beverages, and industrial supplies, because we view our model as less applicable to these categories.[8] In particular, we model the determination of import prices as arising from the decisions of firms that are monopolistic competitors and have the ability to price discriminate across countries. In the context of our model, excluding these goods is sensible since many of these goods are homogeneous and are traded on organized exchanges, so that the extent of monopolistic behavior and price discrimination is limited.

We argue that the decline in pass-through can be understood using a real model and thus focus on real import prices and real exchange rates. Accordingly, we define the real price of imports as the ratio of the finished goods import price deflator to the U.S. CPI deflator. Henceforth we will refer to our relative price index of finished goods as the relative price of imports. For our measure of the real exchange rate, we use the Federal Reserve's real e ective exchange rate, which is constructed from data on nominal exchange rates and consumer price indices for 39 countries.

The top panel of Figure 1 plots the relative price of imports and the real exchange rate (as the inverse of the Federal Reserve's real e ective exchange rate) so that a rise in the real exchange rate denotes a real depreciation of the dollar. Our relative import price index (the solid green line) has fallen over time, reflecting in part that goods' prices have declined relative to the prices of services. To abstract from this trend, the dashed orange line shows the ratio of the price of imported goods to a consumption price index that excludes services.[9] Using this series, it is apparent that real import prices and the real exchange rate in the 1980-2004 period have tended to move closely together, although movements in import prices tend to be dampened relative to the exchange rate. This series also suggests that in the 1990s movements in relative import prices have become more disconnected from movements in real exchange rates. Import prices rose in the 1970s with the dollar's depreciation and also rose sharply in the late 1980s with the large dollar depreciation beginning in 1985. In contrast, import price movements have been much more subdued in the 1990s: even though the dollar

---

[8] Industrial supplies include oil, natural gas, non-fuel primary commodities, such as copper, and more processed items, such as chemicals.

[9] We use NIPA data to apply standard chain-aggregation routines to construct both our deflator for imported finished goods and our deflator of U.S. consumption goods that excludes services.

depreciated in the early 1990s and then appreciated in the latter half of the decade, import prices remained relatively unchanged.

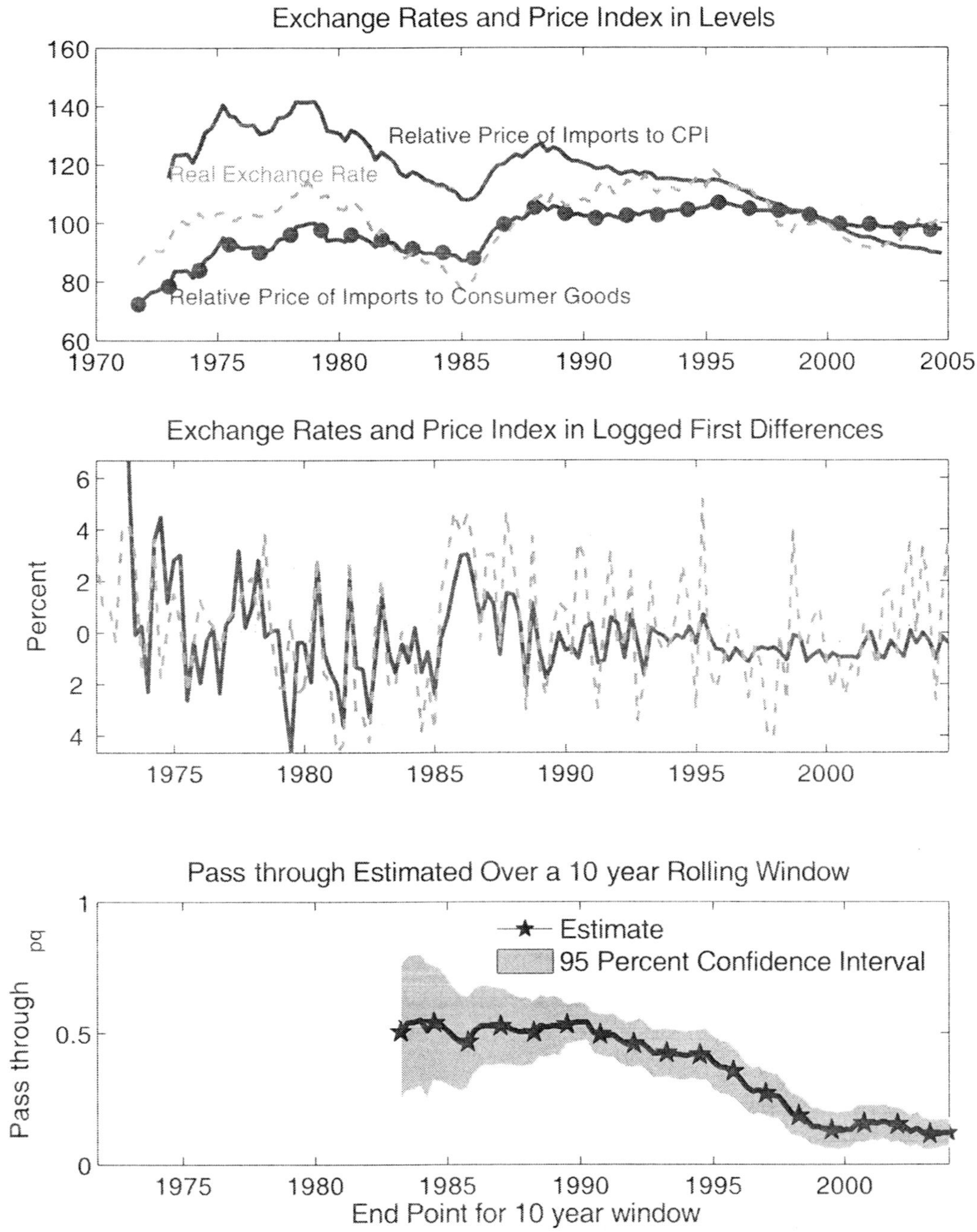

Figure 1. The Real Exchange Rate and Relative Import Prices.

The same basic pattern emerges when we remove the trends in relative prices by examining the series in log-differences. The middle panel of Figure 1 plots the relative price of imports (the solid green line) and the real exchange rate (the dashed orange line) after log-differencing these series. The relative import price, though less volatile than the real exchange rate, is highly correlated with it. Moreover, import price volatility appears to have moderated relative to exchange rate volatility since the late 1980s.

Table 1 summarizes these findings by comparing the volatility and correlation of the relative import price and the real exchange rate over different subsamples. The top panel shows the results for the data in differences and the bottom panel for HP-filtered data. Both the HP-filtered and differenced data show a marked decline in the ratio of the standard deviation of import prices, σ_{p_m}, to the standard deviation of the exchange rate, σ_q, in the latter half of our sample. The correlation of the relative import price with the real exchange rate has declined noticeably as well.

Table 1. Volatility and Correlation of Relative Import Price and Real Exchange Rate[a]

Moment (Differenced)	Full Sample	1980:1-1989:4	1990:1-2004:4
a. $\beta_{p_m,q}$ (a = b*c)	0.35	0.55	0.13
b. σ_{p_m}/σ_q	0.47	0.60	0.25
c. corr (q, p_m)	0.75	0.92	0.51
Moment (HP-Filtered)			
a. $\beta_{p_m,q}$ (a = b*c)	0.46	0.59	0.17
b. σ_{p_m}/σ_q	0.54	0.61	0.29
c. corr (q, p_m)	0.85	0.95	0.60

Another important statistic summarizing the relationship between these two series is:

$$\beta_{p_m,q} = \frac{\mathrm{cov}(p_m, q)}{\sigma_q^2} = corr(p_m, q)\frac{\sigma_{p_m}}{\sigma_q}, \qquad (1)$$

where p_m denotes the relative price of imports and q denotes the real exchange rate. This statistic takes into account the correlation between the two series as well as their relative volatility and can be derived as the estimate from a univariate least squares regression of the real exchange rate on the relative import price. As shown in Table 1, our estimate of $\beta_{p_m,q}$ has declined in the 1990s, reflecting both the decline in the relative volatility of import prices and the lower correlation between the two series. Further evidence of the increasing disconnect between these variable is shown in the bottom panel of Figure 1 which plots estimates of $\beta_{p_m,q}$ for the log-differenced data based on 10-year, rolling windows (The line with stars indicates the point estimate and the shaded region denotes the 95 percent confidence region.) There is a gradual decline in $\beta_{p_m,q}$ beginning in the mid-1980s. We view the decline in $\beta_{p_m,q}$ as a useful way of summarizing the increasing disconnect between the relative import price and the real exchange rate. Our summary statistic, $\beta_{p_m,q}$, is closely related to estimates of pass-through in empirical studies. One notable difference is that these studies typically estimate a specification for import prices with the exchange rate controlling for a number of other factors influencing import prices. A recent paper that follows this approach is Marazzi, Sheets, and Vigfusson (2005), who argue that pass-through of exchange rate changes to import prices has fallen from about 0.5 in the 1980s to a current estimate of 0.2. One reason we choose to use the statistic $\beta_{p_m,q}$ is that it eases comparisons between the model and the data. However, we note that we get comparable estimates to Marazzi, Sheets, and Vigfusson (2005) regarding the change in the relationship between import prices and the exchange rate.[10]

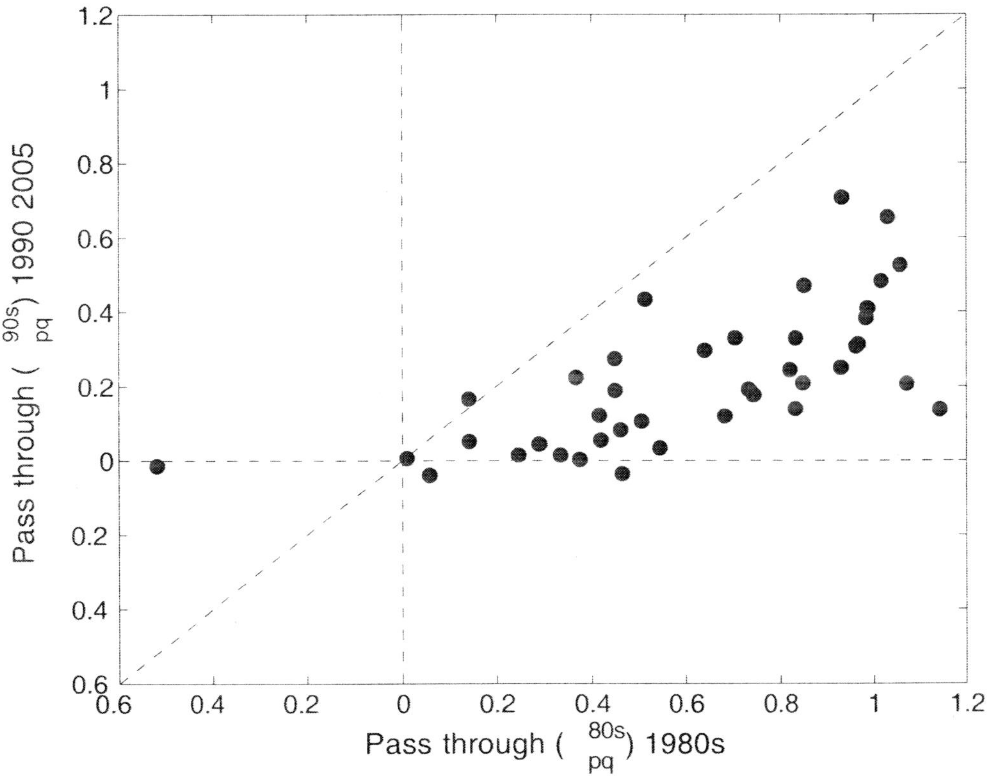

Figure 2. The Change in Pass-Through for Different Finished-Goods Industries.

[10] When estimating pass-through, Marazzi, Sheets, and Vigfussen (2005) control for movements in marginal costs using foreign CPIs and commodity prices. The results are also similar if different control variables are used. For instance, pass-through declines to the same extent when unit labor costs and domestic output are respectively used to control for changes in marginal costs and import demand, as in Campa and Goldberg (2004).

Examining more disaggregated data, we also document that the decline in pass-through is broad-based. For industry *i*, Figure 2 reports our summary statistics, $\beta^{i}_{p_m,q}$, using data in log-differences on prices for each of 40 finished goods industries (a mixture of two- and three-digit SITC industries) and our real exchange rate measure defined earlier. (See the appendix for a description of these industries.) This statistic is computed for two sample periods: pre- and post-1990. As can be seen in Figure 2, most industries have experienced a sizeable decline in $\beta^{i}_{p_m,q}$. Taking a simple average across industries, the mean value of $\beta^{i}_{p_m,q}$ declined almost 40 percentage points, from an industry-average value of 0.61 pre-1990 to a value of 0.22 post-1990.

Overall, the evidence suggests that there has been an increasing disconnect between the price of imported finished goods and the exchange rate.[11]

3. Trade Costs and Productivity

In this section, we address the time series evidence regarding whether tariffs and transport costs have fallen over time as well as discuss the behavior for other forms of trade costs. We also examine the data on changes in the relative productivity of the United States vis-à-vis its trading partners.

Barriers to international trade take many forms, some less tangible than others. Typically, tariffs and transport costs come to mind as factors impeding the flow of goods across countries. However, international trade can also be hindered by the presence of legal and regulatory costs, distribution costs, and institutional and cultural barriers. Although tariffs and transport costs make up only a fraction of overall trade costs, they remain an important factor underlying the movement towards greater trade integration. For instance, Baier and Bergstrand (2001) find that the decline in tariff rates and transport costs played an important role in post-World-War-II expansion in international trade for OECD countries.[12] Data on tariffs and transport costs support the notion that trade costs have been falling over time. For the United States, detailed information on tariffs and transport costs are available from Feenstra (1996) and Feenstra, Romalis, and Schott (2002) who have compiled product-level import data. Using this data, we compute tariffs and transport costs for finished-goods industries from 1980 to 2001. For each available industry, we measure trade costs as the sum of transport costs and tariffs and compute an industry-weighted average trade cost measure. (See the appendix for the details of these calculations.) Figure 3 reports that, over our sample period, the average trade cost across industries fell from 11.1 percent of the custom value of the goods in 1980 to 5.2 percent in 2001. The figure also decomposes our average trade cost measure into its tariffs and transport costs components. It shows that transport costs have declined somewhat since 1980 but that the fall in trade costs has been driven mostly by a reduction in tariffs.

[11] This decline in pass-through is most evident for finished goods. The decline in pass-through for total imports is smaller and less precisely estimated.

[12] The fact that tariff and transport costs have been declining throughout the post-war period yields the implication in our model that, other things equal, exchange-rate pass-through to import prices should have declined throughout the post-war period. Unfortunately, our measure of import prices for finished goods industries does not extend back far enough to investigate this possibility.

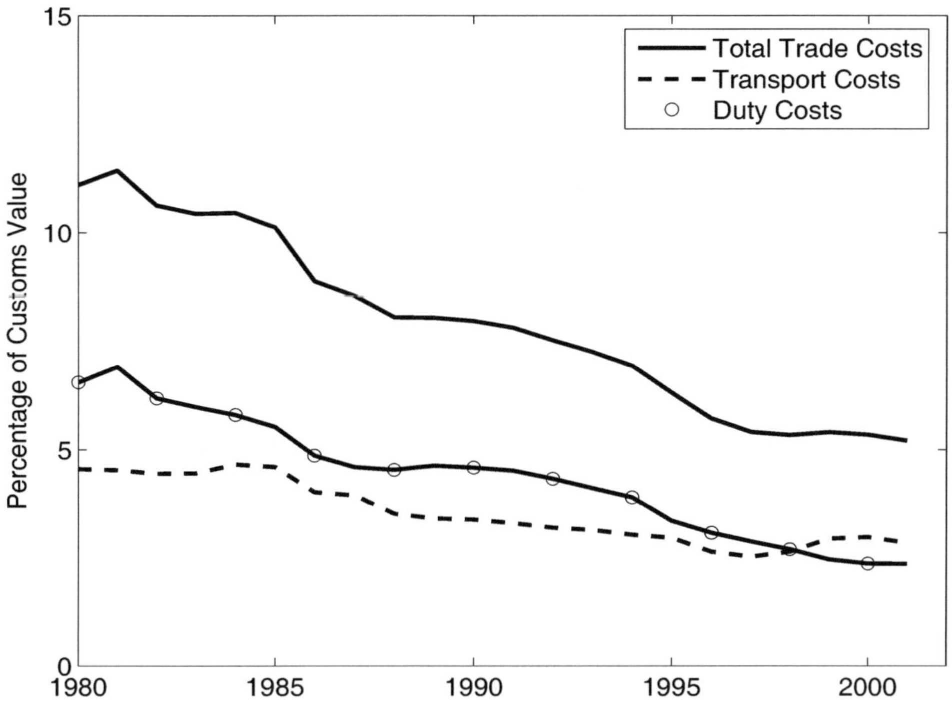

Figure 3. The Decline in Average Transport Costs and Tariffs for U.S. Imported Goods.

Although tariffs and transport costs have the advantage of being relatively easier to quantify, it is more difficult to measure precisely other forms of trade costs, since they are often not directly observable. As a result, researchers infer these costs by estimating gravity models of international trade. This literature finds mixed evidence regarding a possible decline in overall trade costs.[13] As a result, we take a conservative approach and focus only on the evidence regarding transport costs and tariffs.

Since trade integration can also be triggered by improved productivity of exporting firms, we document changes in relative productivity across countries. The top panel of Figure 4 displays the annualized percentage change in GDP per employee for the United States ('US'), its foreign counterpart ('ROW'), and other regions around the world for the 1980-2003 period.[14] These indices are constructed using data on GDP per employee, and the ROW index is based on data for OECD and major developing countries. Growth in GDP per employee outside the United States outpaced U.S. growth largely due to faster productivity growth in developing Asia ('DA'), which includes a number of rapidly-developing countries such as China and South Korea. Productivity growth in Europe ('EU') was roughly on par with growth in the United States, while Japanese ('JA') productivity growth was somewhat faster than in the United States, despite a marked deceleration in Japanese productivity in the 1990s.

[13] Using different datasets and methodologies, Rauch, Coe, Subramanian, Tamirisa, and Bhavnani (1999), Coe (2002), and Brun (2002) find that trade costs have fallen continuously since the 1970s. On the other hand, Frankel (1997) and Berthelon and Freund (2004) find no evidence of a significant decline in trade costs.

[14] Although we would prefer a more disaggregated measure, we focus on productivity at the aggregate level due to data limitations for developing countries.

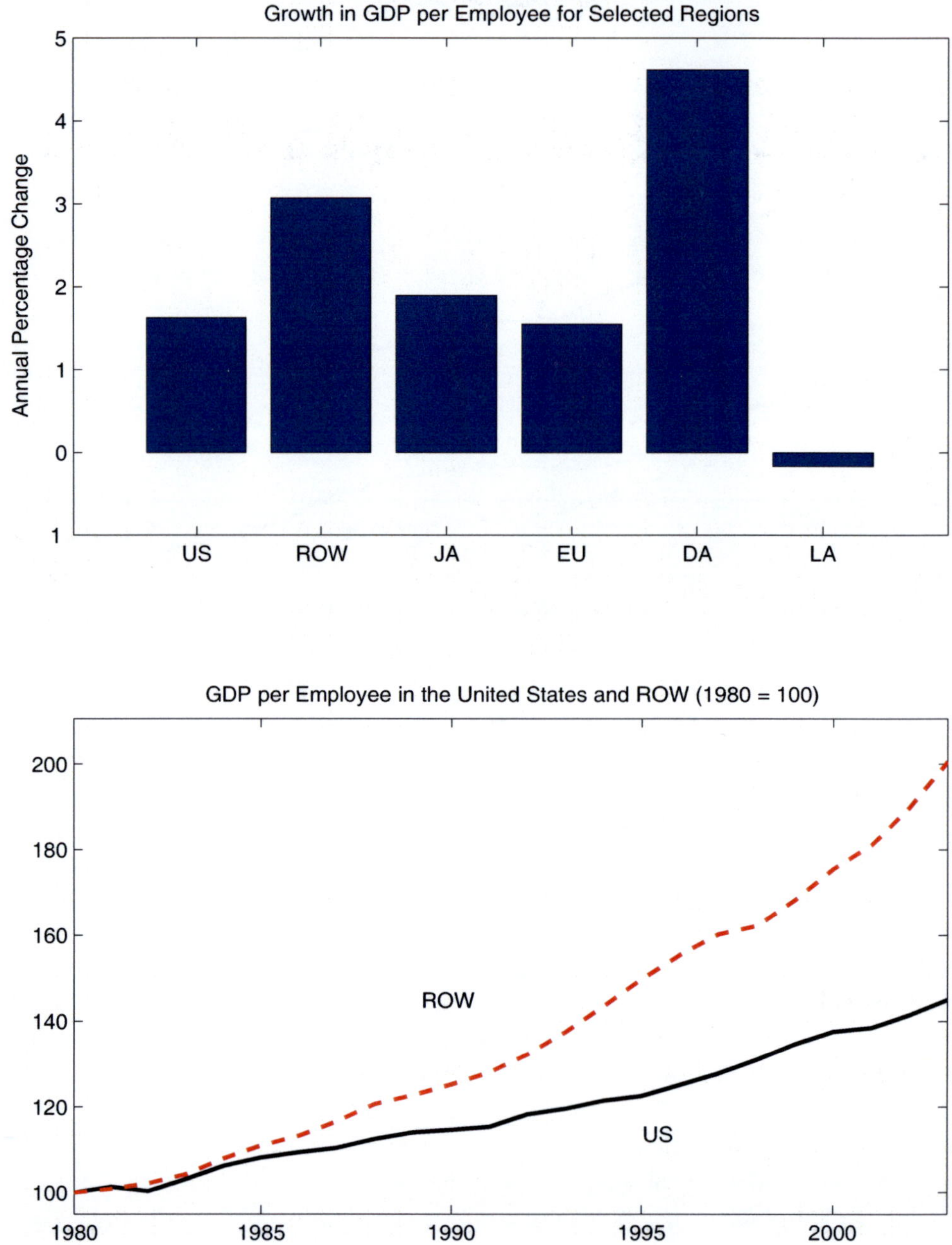

Figure 4. Growth in GDP per Employee in the United States and the Rest of the World Growth in GDP per Employee for Selected Regions.

With foreign labor productivity growth higher than U.S. productivity growth over the last two decades, there has been considerable convergence of foreign productivity to the level of U.S. productivity. The bottom panel of Figure 4 shows that GDP per employee outside the United States roughly doubled over the 1980-2003 period, while U.S. GDP per employee rose about 40 percent over this period. As a consequence, the level of foreign productivity has increased by 40 percent relative to U.S. productivity over the past twenty-five years.

4. THE MODEL

Our model consists of a home and a foreign economy. These two economies have isomorphic structures so in our exposition we focus on describing only the domestic economy. The domestic economy consists of two types of agents: households and firms. Households have utility that depends on the consumption of both domestically-produced goods and imported goods. These goods are purchased from monopolistically competitive firms, who set prices flexibly each period. While the range of goods produced by these firms is exogenously given, the fraction of firms that export is determined endogenously. In particular, because a firm must pay both a fixed and variable cost to export its good, it may choose to sell its good only in the domestic economy. The key element we introduce into this environment is that a firm's demand curve has a non-constant elasticity so that exchange-rate pass-through to import prices may be incomplete.

We abstract from other features such as sticky prices and distribution costs that give rise to incomplete pass-through. We view our approach as largely complementary to these alternatives. For instance, Bergin and Feenstra (2001) have shown that the interaction of demand curves with non-constant elasticities and sticky prices denominated in local currency is helpful in accounting not only for incomplete pass-through but also for the observed volatility and persistence of the exchange rate. Our approach also would complement models that include a distribution sector for traded goods such as Corsetti and Dedola (2005) and Corsetti, Dedola, and Leduc (2005) and results in incomplete pass-through to import prices at both the retail level and the point of entry. Although nominal rigidities or distribution costs imply incomplete pass-through, it is more difficult to account for the decline in pass-through based exclusively on these features. For simplicity and to emphasize the role of trade integration and strategic complementarity in price setting, we therefore choose not to incorporate these elements into our analysis.

4.1 Households

The utility function of the representative household in the home country is

$$E_t \sum_{j=0}^{\infty} \beta^t \left\{ \log(C_{t+j}) - \chi_0 \frac{L_{t+j}^{1+\chi}}{1+\chi} \right\}, \tag{2}$$

where the discount factor β satisfies $0 < \beta < 1$ and E_t is the expectation operator conditional on information available at time t. The period utility function depends on consumption C_t and labor L_t. A household also purchases state-contingent assets b_{t+1} that are traded internationally so that asset markets are complete.

Households receive income from working and an aliquot share of profits of all the domestic firms, Ω_t. In choosing its contingency plans for C_t, L_t, b_{t+1}, a household takes into account its budget constraint at each date:

$$C_t + \int_s p_{bt,t+1} b_{t+1} - b_t = w_t L_t + \Omega_t \tag{3}$$

In equation (3), $w_t = \frac{W_t}{P_t}$ is household's real wage and $p_{bt,t+1}$ denotes the price of an asset that pays one unit of the domestic consumption good in a particular state of nature at date $t+1$. (For convenience, we have suppressed that variables depend on the state of nature.).

4.2 Demand Aggregator

There is a continuum of goods indexed by $i \in [0,1]$ produced in each economy. While a domestic household purchases all of the domestically-produced goods, there are only $i \in [0, \omega_t^*]$ that are available for imports, where ω_t^* denotes the endogenously determined fraction of traded foreign goods. A household chooses domestically-produced goods, $C_{dt}(i)$, and imported goods, $C_{mt}(i)$, to minimize their total expenditures:

$$\left[\int_0^1 P_{dt}(i) C_{dt}(i) di + \int_0^{\omega_t^*} P_{mt}(i) C_{mt}(i) di\right], \tag{4}$$

subject to $D\left(\frac{C_{dt}(i)}{C_t}, \frac{C_{mt}(i)}{C_t}\right) = 1$. In minimizing its expenditures, a household takes the prices of the domestic, $P_{dt}(i)$, and imported goods, $P_{mt}(i)$, as given. (For convenience, we denote these prices in nominal terms, although prices are flexible in the model and we solve only for real variables.) In our model, there are no distribution services required to sell the imported goods to households. Accordingly, $P_{mt}(i)$ denotes both the retail import price for good i and price charged at the point of entry.

The function, $D\left(\frac{C_{dt}(i)}{C_t}, \frac{C_{mt}(i)}{C_t}\right)$, is a household's demand aggregator for producing a unit of C_t and is defined by:

$$D\left(\frac{C_{dt}(i)}{C_t}, \frac{C_{mt}(i)}{C_t}\right) = \left[\frac{1}{1+\omega_t^*} V_{dt}^{\frac{1}{\rho}} + \frac{\omega_t^*}{1+\omega_t^*} V_{mt}^{\frac{1}{\rho}}\right]^{\rho} - \frac{1}{(1+\eta)\gamma} + 1, \tag{5}$$

In this expression, V_{dt} is an aggregator for domestic goods given by:

$$V_{dt} = \int_0^1 \frac{1}{(1+\omega_t^*)(1+\eta)\gamma} \left[(1+\omega_t^*)(1+\eta)\frac{C_{dt}(i)}{C_t} - \eta\right]^{\gamma} di, \tag{6}$$

and V_{mt} is an aggregator for imported goods given by:

$$V_{mt} = \frac{1}{\omega_t^*} \int_0^{\omega_t^*} \frac{1}{(1+\omega_t^*)(1+\eta)\gamma} \left[(1+\omega_t^*)(1+\eta)\frac{C_{mt}(i)}{C_t} - \eta \right]^{\gamma} di. \tag{7}$$

Our demand aggregator adapts the one discussed in Dotsey and King (2005) to an international environment. It shares the central feature that the elasticity of demand is nonconstant (NCES) with $\eta \neq 0$, and the (absolute value of the) demand elasticity can be expressed as an increasing function of a firm's relative price when $\eta < 0$.[15] This feature has proven useful in the sticky price literature, because it helps mitigate a firm's incentive to raise its price after an expansionary monetary shock in the context of a model in which other firms have already preset their prices. It is also consistent with the evidence that firms tend to change their prices more in response to cost increases than decreases (see, for instance, Peltzman (2000)). Another important implication of this aggregator, discussed below, is that exchange-rate pass-through to import prices will be incomplete when the elasticity of demand is increasing in a firm's relative price.

Expenditure minimization by a domestic household implies that the demand curve for an imported good is given by:

$$\frac{C_{mt}(i)}{C_t} = \frac{1}{1+\omega_t^*} \left[\frac{1}{1+\eta} \left(\frac{P_{mt}(i)}{\Gamma_t} \right)^{\frac{1}{\gamma-1}} \left(\frac{P_{mt}}{\Gamma_t} \right)^{\frac{\gamma}{\gamma-\rho}\frac{\rho-1}{\gamma-1}} + \frac{\eta}{1+\eta} \right] \tag{8}$$

In the above, Γ_t is a price index consisting of the prices of a firm's competitors defined as:

$$\Gamma_t = \left[\left(\frac{1}{1+\omega_t^*} \right) P_{dt}^{\frac{\gamma}{\gamma-\rho}} + \left(\frac{\omega_t^*}{1+\omega_t^*} \right) P_{mt}^{\frac{\gamma}{\gamma-\rho}} \right]^{\frac{\gamma-\rho}{\gamma}}, \tag{9}$$

and P_{dt} and P_{mt} are indices of domestic and import prices defined as:

---

[15] When $\eta \neq 0$, our demand aggregator can be thought of as the combination of a Dixit-Stiglitz and Armington aggregator. To see this, note that in this case we can rewrite our aggregator as:

$$C_t = \left(1+\omega_t^*\right) \left[\frac{1}{1+\omega_t^*} C_{dt}^{\frac{\gamma}{\rho}} + \frac{\omega_t^*}{1+\omega_t^*} C_{mt}^{\frac{\gamma}{\rho}} \right]^{\frac{\rho}{\gamma}}$$

where $C_{dt} = \left(\int_0^1 C_{dt}(i)^{\gamma} di \right)^{\frac{1}{\gamma}}$ and $C_{mt} = \left(\frac{1}{\omega_t^*} \int_0^{\omega_t^*} C_{mt}(i)^{\gamma} di \right)^{\frac{1}{\gamma}}$.

Our specification of the demand aggregator also rules out the ``love of variety" effect.

$$P_{dt} = \left(\int_0^1 P_{dt}(i)^{\frac{\gamma}{\gamma-1}} di \right)^{\frac{\gamma-1}{\gamma}} \quad (10)$$

$$P_{mt} = \left(\frac{1}{\omega_t^*} \int_0^{\omega_t^*} P_{mt}(i)^{\frac{\gamma}{\gamma-1}} di \right)^{\frac{\gamma-1}{\gamma}} \quad (11)$$

Expenditure minimization also implies an analogous expression for the demand curve of domestic good *i*, which depends on prices, $P_{dt}(i)$, P_{dt}, and Γ_t.

A property of these demand curves is that the elasticity of substitution between a home and foreign good can differ from the demand elasticity for two home goods. This separate elasticity for goods occurs when $\rho \neq 1$, which gives the model more flexibility to match estimates of the elasticity of substitution between home and foreign tradeables as well as estimates of economy-wide markups. More importantly, when $\eta \neq 0$, the demand curve has an additive linear term, which implies that the elasticity of demand depends on the price of good *i* relative to other prices. It is this feature that helps give rise to incomplete pass-through to import prices and implies that pass-through depends on the economy's structure including the underlying shocks.

The aggregate consumer price level is given by

$$P_t = \frac{1}{1+\eta}\Gamma_t + \frac{\eta}{1+\eta}\left[\frac{1}{1+\omega_t^*} \int_0^1 P_{dt}(i)di + \frac{1}{1+\omega_t^*} \int_0^{\omega_t^*} P_{mt}(i)di \right] \quad (12)$$

From this expression, it is clear that the consumer price level is equal to the competitive pricing bundle, Γ_t, when $\eta = 0$. In general, the consumer price level is the sum of Γ_t with a linear aggregator of prices for individual goods.[16]

4.3 Firms

The production function for firm i is linear in labor so that

$$Y_t(i) = Z_t L_t(i) \quad (13)$$

In the above, Z_t is an aggregate, *iid* technology shock that affects the production function for all firms in the home country. A firm hires labor in a competitive market in which labor is

[16] The consumer price level can be derived from equating equation (4) to $P_t C_t$ and substituting in the relative demand curves. The price Γ_t can be derived from substituting the relative demand curves into equation (5).

completely mobile within a country but immobile across countries. Marginal cost is therefore the same for all firms in the home country so that real marginal cost of firm i is given by $\frac{w_t}{Z_t}$.

Firms in each country are monopolistically competitive and each firm sells its good to households located in its country. Profit maximization implies that a firm chooses to set its price as a markup over marginal cost. As a result, the price of good i in the domestic market satisfies:

$$\frac{P_{dt}(i)}{P_t} = \mu_{dt}(i)\frac{w_t}{Z_t}, \qquad i \in [0,1], \tag{14}$$

with $\mu_{dt}(i) \geq 1$. The markup $\mu_{dt}(i)$ can be expressed as:

$$\mu_{dt}(i) = \mu_{dt} = \left[1 - \frac{1}{|\varepsilon_{dt}|}\right]^{-1} = \left[\gamma + \eta(\gamma-1)\left(\frac{P_{dt}}{\Gamma_t}\right)^{\frac{\rho}{\rho-\gamma}}\right]^{-1} \tag{15}$$

where $|\varepsilon_{dt}|$, is the absolute value of the elasticity of a domestic good given by:

$$|\varepsilon_{dt}| = \left[(\gamma-1)\left(1+\eta\left(\frac{P_{dt}}{\Gamma_t}\right)^{\frac{\rho}{\rho-\gamma}}\right)\right]^{-1} \tag{16}$$

In the above, we have dropped the index *i*, since we restrict our attention to a symmetric equilibrium in which all firms set the same price in the domestic market (i.e., $P_{dt}(i) = P_{dt}$, $\varepsilon_{dt}(i) = \varepsilon_{dt}$ and $\mu_{dt}(i) = \mu_{dt}$.)

Equation (15) shows that a firm's markup depends on the price it sets relative to its competitor's price Γ_t. When the (absolute value of) the demand elasticity is increasing in $\frac{P_{dt}}{\Gamma_t}$, the markup will be a decreasing function of this relative price. Consequently, a firm will respond to a fall in the price of its competitors by lowering its markup and price. A firm finds it desirable to do so, because otherwise it will experience a relatively large fall in its market share. An important exception to this pricing behavior is the CES demand curve in which $\eta = 0$. In this case, a firm's markup does not depend on the relative price of its competitors.

We view our setup with variable markups as a tractable way to capture the strategic complementarity amongst price-setting firms. Although we do not explicitly model strategic behavior using a game-theoretic framework, our setup has similar implications to those of Bodnar, Dumas, and Marston (2002), Bernard, Eaton, Jensen, and Kortum (2003), and Atkeson and Burstein (2005) who model the strategic complementarity that arises between firms through Cournot or Bertrand competition. These alternative setups, like ours, give rise to a markup that is increasing in a firm's market share or decreasing in its price relative to those of its competitors.

Following Melitz (2003), Ghironi and Melitz (2005) and Bergin and Glick (2005), we allow for the endogenous entry and exit of firms into the export market. In particular, we assume that each period a firm faces a fixed and per-unit export cost and decides whether to export or not. Unlike these previous papers, which allow productivity to vary with a good's type, we assume that the fixed cost varies with the variety of the good.[17] In particular, we assume that the fixed cost is given by:

$$f_x(i) = \frac{f_x}{1-\alpha_x i}, \qquad \alpha_x \geq 0, \tag{17}$$

and is paid in units of labor. We view this fixed cost as reflecting the cost to a firm of making consumers aware of its product, setting up a distribution system, and understanding the legal and regulatory environment of a foreign market. It seems reasonable to assume that these costs differ depending on the type of good.

Since an exporter must make its entry decision before the realization of shocks in period t, a firm will choose to export if its expected profits from exporting (appropriately weighted) exceed its fixed cost:

$$E_{t-1}\left[p_{bt-1,t}\left(\pi_{xt}(i) - f_x(i)w_t\right)\right] > 0,, \tag{18}$$

where exporter i's per-unit profits in the foreign market are given by:

$$\pi_{xt}(i) = \left(q_t \frac{P^*_{mt}(i)}{P^*_t} - \frac{D_t w_t}{Z_t}\right) C^*_{mt}(i), \tag{19}$$

In the above, q_t is the real exchange rate expressed in units of the home consumption bundle per units of foreign consumption, $P^*_{mt}(i)$ is the nominal price of home good i denominated in foreign currency, and $C^*_{mt}(i)$ is the demand for home good i by foreign households. (We use a star to denote foreign variables.) Also, D_t is an iceberg shipping cost which we assume to be a stochastic iid process.[18] Finally, our functional form for the fixed

[17] In our environment with variable markups, heterogeneity in the technologies of firms would considerably complicate the analysis, since computing aggregate prices and quantities would involve accounting for a distribution of markups. In contrast, because the fixed cost does not affect a firm's marginal pricing condition, we can still analyze a symmetric equilibrium in which all firms who decide to export choose the same price and markup.

[18] This assumption is not critical for our analysis. We assume that D_t is stochastic mainly to illustrate how pass-through differs depending on the type of shock.

cost implies that only firms on the interval $i \in [0, \omega_t]$ will export their good where the marginal good ω_t satisfies equation (18) as an equality.

Similar to a firm's pricing decision in the domestic market, profit maximization implies that a firm chooses its export price as a markup over marginal cost:

$$q_t \frac{P^*_{mt}(i)}{P^*_t} = \mu^*_{mt}(i) \frac{D_t w_t}{Z_t} \qquad i \in [0, \omega_t] \tag{20}$$

In a symmetric equilibrium, all exporting firms will choose the same price and markup (i.e., $P^*_{mt}(i) = P^*_{mt}$ and $\mu^*_{mt}(i) = \mu^*_{mt}$). An exporter's markup is given by:

$$\mu^*_{mt}(i) = \mu^*_{mt} = \left[1 - \frac{1}{\varepsilon^*_{mt}}\right]^{-1} = \left[\gamma + \eta(\gamma - 1)\left(\frac{P^*_{mt}}{\Gamma^*_t}\right)^{\frac{\rho}{\rho-\gamma}}\right]^{-1} \tag{21}$$

where $|\varepsilon^*_{mt}|$ is the absolute value of the elasticity of a domestic good in the foreign market.

Comparing equations (14) and (20), we note that the law of one price (i.e., $\frac{P^*_{mt}(i)}{P^*_t} q_t = \frac{P_{dt}(i)}{P_t}$) will not hold when $D_t > 1$. In addition, because the demand elasticity can differ across markets (i.e., $\varepsilon_{dt} \neq \varepsilon^*_{mt}$), a firm will optimally choose to price discriminate. It will be able to do so, if the difference between a firm's price in the two markets (expressed in the same currency unit) is less than the cost of shipping the good:

$$\frac{D_t P_{dt}(i)}{P_t} \geq \frac{P^*_{mt}(i)}{P^*_t} q_t \text{ and } \frac{P_{dt}(i)}{P_t} \leq \frac{D^*_t P^*_{mt}(i)}{P^*_t} q_t, \tag{22}$$

where D^*_t denotes the per-unit cost of shipping a good from the foreign economy to the home economy.[19] The first condition ensures that a foreign household can not buy the good for less in the domestic market inclusive of the cost of shipping the good. The second condition ensures that a domestic household can not buy the good for less abroad. Later, we verify that these conditions and their counterparts for the prices set by foreign firms are satisfied.

4.4 Market Clearing

The home economy's aggregate resource constraint can be written as:

---

[19] Implicitly, we have assumed that a household faces the same per-unit cost of shipping the good as a firm and bears no fixed cost in transporting the good. To the extent that households also face fixed costs and larger per-unit shipping costs, their ability to engage in arbitrage is more limited than implied by equations (22).

$$\int_0^1 \frac{C_{dt}(i)}{Z_t} di + \int_0^{\omega_t} \frac{D_t^* C_{mt}^*(i)}{Z_t^*} di + \int_0^{\omega_t} f_x(i) di = L_t \ . \tag{23}$$

Given that we focus on a symmetric equilibrium, we define aggregate output as $Y_t = Z_t L_t$. Finally, we note that the foreign economy has an isomorphic structure to the home economy and differs only in its level of trade costs and technology.

5. Defining Pass-Through

We consider two alternative definitions for import price pass-through. For the first, we define pass-through from the perspective of an individual exporter who views the exchange rate as exogenous. This definition considers how much an individual exporter changes his price in response to a one percent change in the exchange rate, holding constant the other factors a firm takes as given: its marginal cost and the prices of other firms. Letting $p_{mt}(i) = \frac{P_{mt}(i)}{P_t}$ and $\xi_t = \frac{\Gamma_t}{P_t}$ denote the relative price of exporter i and the relative price of its competitors, respectively, a foreign exporter's pricing equation can be written as:

$$p_{mt}(i) = \mu_{mt}(i) D_t^* \frac{w_t^*}{Z_t^*} q_t \ , \tag{24}$$

where $\mu_{mt}(i)$ is given by an analogous expression to equation (21). The direct effect of an exchange rate change on the price of foreign exporter i is given by $\kappa_{mt}(i) = \frac{\partial p_{mt}(i)}{\partial q_t} \frac{q_t}{p_{mt}(i)}$:

$$\kappa_{mt}(i) = \frac{1}{1 - \eta \mu_{mt}(i) \left(\frac{\rho(\gamma - 1)}{\gamma - \rho} \right) \left(\frac{p_{mt}(i)}{\xi_t} \right)^{\frac{\rho}{\rho - \gamma}}} - \frac{1}{1 + \left(\mu_{mt}(i) - 1 \right) \frac{\partial |\varepsilon_{mt}(i)|}{\partial q_t} \frac{p_{mt}(i)}{|\varepsilon_{mt}(i)|}} \tag{25}$$

Because $\kappa_{mt}(i)$ measures only the direct effect of an exchange rate change on an exporter's price, we refer to it as the direct pass-through measure.

From the expression directly after the equality, we can see that if $\eta < 0$ then direct pass-through will be incomplete.[20] In this case, a one percent increase in q_t drives up a foreign exporter's cost when denominated in dollars; however, a firm does not raise its price a full one percent because as the exporter's price rises relative to its competitors, it induces the exporter to accept a lower markup rather than give up market share.

---

[20] With $\eta < 0$ the demand curve is less convex than the CES case.

Alternatively, the expression after the second equality in equation (25) indicates that direct pass-through depends on the level of the markup and the elasticity of the elasticity of demand, $\frac{\partial|\varepsilon_{mt}(i)|}{\partial p_{mt}(i)}\frac{p_{mt}(i)}{|\varepsilon_{mt}(i)|}$. This expression is similar to the one derived by Eichenbaum (2003) in a closed economy context. With $\eta<0$, the elasticity of the elasticity of demand is positive and as a result $\kappa_{mt}(i)<1$.

To facilitate comparisons of our model with the data, in addition to our direct pass-through measure, we also examine our model's implications for the second moment $\beta_{p_m,q}$ previously defined (in log-differences) as:

$$\beta_{p_m,q}=\frac{\operatorname{cov}(\Delta p_{mt},\Delta q_t)}{\operatorname{var}(\Delta q_t)}. \tag{26}$$

The relationship between $\beta_{p_m,q}$ and $\kappa_{mt}(i)$ can be seen by log-linearizing equation (24) around the non-stochastic steady state to write a foreign exporter's pricing decision as:

$$\hat{p}_{mt}=\kappa_m\left(\hat{D}_t^*+\hat{\omega}_t^*-\hat{Z}_t^*+\hat{q}_t\right)+(1-\kappa_m)\hat{\xi}_t. \tag{27}$$

The symbol ^ denotes the log-deviation of a variable from its steady state value and $\kappa_m=\kappa_m(i)$ evaluated at nonstochastic steady state. Using this equation, we can relate $\beta_{p_m,q}$ and κ_m via:

$$\beta_{p_m,q}=\kappa_m+\kappa_m\left[\frac{\operatorname{cov}\left(\Delta\left(\hat{\omega}_t^*-\hat{Z}_t^*\right),\Delta\hat{q}_t\right)}{\operatorname{var}(\Delta\hat{q}_t)}+\frac{\operatorname{cov}\left(\Delta\hat{D}_t^*,\Delta\hat{q}_t\right)}{\operatorname{var}(\Delta\hat{q}_t)}\right]+(1-\kappa_m)\left[\frac{\operatorname{cov}\left(\Delta\hat{\xi}_t,\Delta\hat{q}_t\right)}{\operatorname{var}(\Delta\hat{q}_t)}\right]. \tag{28}$$

According to equation (28), the univariate regression statistic, $\beta_{p_m,q}$, is related to κ_m except that $\beta_{p_m,q}$ takes into account any correlation of the real exchange rate with an exporter's costs and the pricing index of an exporter's competitors that occurs in general equilibrium. Thus, $\beta_{p_m,q}$ takes into account both direct and indirect effects of an exchange rate change on an exporter's price.

In our analysis, we focus on comparing our model results to the data for $\beta_{p_m,q}$ rather than κ_m. This reflects that $\beta_{p_m,q}$ is a second moment that is easily measured in the data. In contrast, measuring κ_m is complicated by finding good measures of marginal costs and the prices of a firm's competitors as well as correctly specifying the equations for estimating κ_m and dealing with the endogeneity of the exchange rate and the prices of other firms.

6. Calibration

In order to investigate the role of trade costs and productivity differentials on pass-through, we log-linearism and solve the model around two different steady states. In the first, the home and foreign economies are identical, and both economies have relatively high trade costs. We call this our benchmark calibration. In the second, we lower trade costs as well as raise the level of foreign productivity, keeping the remaining parameters constant.[21] We call this the 2004 calibration.

The value of η, which governs the curvature of the demand curve, is critical for our analysis. Faced with sparse independent evidence regarding this parameter, we calibrate it as a part of a simulated method of moments procedure. Specifically, we choose η along with the standard deviations of the iid technology and trade cost shocks so that the model's implications for the volatility of output, the ratio of the volatility of relative import prices to the real exchange rate, and the correlation between relative import prices and the real exchange rate match those observed in the 1980-1989 period. In doing so, we constrain the standard deviation of the technology shocks and trade costs shocks to be the same in both countries (i.e., $\sigma_z = \sigma_z^*$ and $\sigma_D = \sigma_{D^*}$). By construction, our model matches the observed value of $\beta_{p_m,q}$ for the 1980s. With η pinned down based on the pre-1990s data, we then examine the fall in $\beta_{p_m,q}$ arising from a fall in trade costs and a higher level of foreign productivity.

Tables 2 show our calibrated value of η as well as the calibrated values of other important parameters of the model. We choose γ to be consistent with an exporter's markup over marginal cost of around 20 percent in the benchmark calibration. We set $\rho = 0.85$, which implies an aggregate trade-price elasticity for the benchmark calibration of 2.[22] The discount factor $\beta = 1.03^{-0.25}$, and the utility function parameter χ is set to 1.5, which implies a Frisch elasticity of labor supply of 2/3. We set χ_0 and χ_o^* to imply $L = L^* = 1$ in the benchmark calibration.

[21] While the level of foreign productivity is actually lower than U.S. productivity, for simplicity we begin with a calibration in which the two economies are identical. This simplification seems reasonable, since our results for the decline in pass-through depend critically on the change in relative productivity in the two countries rather than their initial levels.

[22] We define the aggregate trade-price elasticity by differentiating aggregate import demand:

$$\omega_t^* C_{mt} = \frac{\omega_t^*}{1+\omega_t^*}\left[\frac{1}{1+\eta}\left(\frac{P_{mt}}{\Gamma_t}\right)^{\frac{\rho}{\gamma-\rho}} + \frac{\eta}{1+\eta}\right] C_t$$

with respect to $\frac{P_{mt}}{\Gamma_t}$ holding C_t and ω_t^* constant. With $\rho < 1$ in our benchmark calibration, this aggregate elasticity is lower than the elasticity of demand for individual good i, $\left|\varepsilon_{mt}^*(i)\right|$.

Table 2. Parameter Values and Properties of Calibrated Models

	NCES Demand		CES Calibration
	Benchmark Calibration	2004 Calibration	
ρ	0.85	0.85	1.7
η	-3.05	-3.05	0
γ	1.1	1.1	0.835
β	0.9926	0.9926	0.9926
χ	1.5	1.5	1.5
χ_0	0.79	0.79	0.83
$D = D^*$	1.1	1.05	1.1
Z	1	1	1
Z^*	1	1.35	1
f_x	0.46	0.46	0.37
α_x	2.5	2.5	2.5
$\sigma_z = \sigma_z^*$	0.0178	0.0178	0.0191
$\sigma_D = \sigma_D^*$	0.0094	0.0094	0.008
Home Trade Share	10.0%	14.0%	10.0%
Home Firms' Domestic Markup (μ_d)	1.27	1.24	1.20
Foreign Exporters' Markup (μ_m)	1.20	1.38	1.20
Home Trade-Price Elasticity	-2.0	-1.2	-2.0
Direct Pass-Through (κ_m)	0.48	0.36	1

For the initial levels of technology, we choose $Z = Z^* = 1$. As discussed earlier, foreign technology rose about 40 percent relative to the level of U.S. productivity over the past 25 years. For the 2004 calibration, we choose a more conservative 35 percent increase in relative productivity by setting $Z^* = 1.35$. Consistent with Figure 3, we set $D = D^* = 1.1$ in the benchmark calibration and lowered $D = D^* = 1.05$ in the 2004 calibration.

For the fixed costs of trade we set $f_x = f_x^* = 0.46$ which implies that the import share in the home economy is about 10 percent. Since we assume that trade is balanced in the initial steady state, the foreign economy has the same import share. We choose $\alpha_x = \alpha_x^* = 2.5$ so that after the fall in trade costs and increase in foreign productivity the home country's import share rises about 4 percentage points.

We also compare our benchmark calibration to one with CES preferences (i.e., $\eta = 0$). Table 2 reports the parameter values used for the CES calibration, which were selected in an analogous manner to our benchmark calibration. Table 3 shows that both the CES and benchmark calibration (by construction) match the observed volatility of output and correlation between import prices and the exchange rate in the 1980s. However, only the benchmark calibration with $\eta \neq 0$ has the flexibility to match the observed value of $\beta_{p_m,q}$ in the 1980s. Although the benchmark calibration implies slightly more exchange rate volatility than the CES calibration, both versions of the model understate the amount of volatility relative to the data. Thus, while the NCES demand curves better account for the observed relationship between the relative import price and the real exchange rate, they do not by themselves explain other important aspects of the data emphasized in the international business cycle literature.[23]

Table 3. Selected Moments of Data and Calibrated Models[a]

	Data		Model	Model	Model
Moment	**1980-1989**	**1990-2004**	**Benchmark Calibration**	**2004 Calibration**	**CES Calibration**
a. $\beta_{p_m,q} = \frac{\text{cov}(\Delta q, \Delta p_m)}{\text{var}(\Delta q)}$ **(a = b*c)**	0.55	0.13	0.55	0.40	1.08
b. $\frac{\sigma(\Delta p_m)}{\sigma(\Delta q)}$	0.60	0.25	0.60	0.43	1.17
c. $corr(\Delta q, \Delta p_m)$	0.92	0.51	0.92	0.92	0.92
$\sigma(y^{hp})$	1.74	0.98	1.74	1.71	1.74
$\sigma(q^{hp})$	4.98	2.70	2.79	2.86	2.54

[a] The subscript 'hp' denotes that a variable was transformed using the HP-filter (with $\lambda = 1600$).

7. RESULTS

To gain intuition for our main results, we first illustrate the implications of our setup for pass-through in partial equilibrium. We then demonstrate how our preferred measure of pass-through, $\beta_{p_m,q}$, depends on the economy's shocks. Finally, we discuss our main findings regarding the effects of falling trade costs and higher foreign productivity on pass-through. In doing so, we pay particular attention to the influence of both the intensive and extensive trade margins.

[23] See Bergin and Feenstra (2001) for a discussion of how the interaction of NCES demand curves with sticky prices denominated in local currency can be helpful in accounting for exchange rate dynamics.

7.1 A Partial Equilibrium Explanation for Declining Pass-Through

The upper left panel of Figure 5 plots our calibrated demand curve of import good i and compares it to the CES demand curve. The absolute value of the demand elasticity for good i, $|\varepsilon^*_{mt}(i)|$, is shown in the upper right panel. Our calibrated demand curve is consistent with strategic complementarity in price setting, as the absolute value of the elasticity is increasing in an exporter's relative price. Therefore, an exporter finds it optimal to reduce its markup rather than increase its prices, and, hence, direct pass-through, $\kappa_{mt}(i)$, is incomplete.

Another important implication of our demand curve is that pass-through will fall with a decline in the cost of exporting. Thus, our model will be able to account for a declining pass-through via either a fall in trade costs or a rise in foreign productivity relative to U.S. productivity. We now discuss the intuition for this result.

We begin by noting that foreign exporter i's marginal revenue satisfies:

$$MR_{mt}(i) = \frac{P_{mt}(i)}{\mu_{mt}(i)} = P_{mt}(i)\left[1 - \frac{1}{|\varepsilon_{mt}(i)|}\right] \tag{29}$$

The lower left panel of Figure 5 displays marginal revenue (in logs and scaled by Γ_t) as a function of the relative price $\frac{P_{mt}(i)}{\Gamma_t}$. As a firm increases its price relative to the price of its competitors, marginal revenue exhibits diminishing returns. At a low relative price, the demand elasticity is also low and an increase in exporter i's relative price boosts marginal revenue because of a) the direct effect of the rise in the firm's price and b) the increase in the demand elasticity as an exporter's price rises relative to its competitors. However, as the exporter's relative price increases and the demand elasticity becomes high enough, the latter effect becomes negligible and the increase in marginal revenue is limited to only the direct effect of the increase in price. (As the demand elasticity approaches infinity, a firm is essentially setting its price equal to marginal cost.) Thus, the effect of strategic complementarity in price setting diminishes as the elasticity rises, and, as displayed in the lower right panel of Figure 5, an exporter's markup is more responsive to $\frac{P_{mt}(i)}{\Gamma_t}$ at a low elasticity (i.e., high markup) and less responsive to $\frac{P_{mt}(i)}{\Gamma_t}$ at a high elasticity (i.e., low markup).

A consequence of the concavity of the marginal revenue schedule is that a fall in an exporter's costs will result in a decline in direct pass-through. To illustrate this point, consider the dashed blue line, labeled mc_H, of the lower left panel, which shows the logarithm of the exporter's marginal cost denominated in domestic currency units (also scaled by Γ_t). At this portion of the marginal revenue schedule, a real (exogenous) depreciation of the domestic currency that results in a 3 percent increase in firm i's marginal cost (mc'_H) only results in about a 1 percent increase in a firm's relative price, so that direct pass-through is roughly 33 percent. Now, suppose a fall in trade costs shifts the firm's marginal costs down to mc_L. In this case, a 3 percent real depreciation of the domestic currency increases the exporter's costs from mc_L to mc'_L and results in only about a 0.45 percent increase in relative price, so that direct pass-through is roughly 15 percent. Pass through is lower for a low-cost producer because a cost increase requires a smaller increase in price, since the associated rise in the demand elasticity provides an extra boost to marginal revenue.

In comparison, under CES demand curves direct pass-through of exchange-rate changes will be complete: A two percent home currency depreciation results in a two percent increase in price regardless of an exporter's costs. This reflects the fact that the demand elasticity, and thus the markup, do not vary with a monopolist's relative price.

7.2 The Effects of Different Shocks on Pass-Through

We now show that productivity and trade-cost shocks have different effects on our two measures of pass-through. An important difference between the two measures is that κ_m is independent of the economy's iid shocks, while $\beta_{p_m,q}$ is not. To illustrate this, the second column of Table 4 shows the effects of a one standard deviation increase in home technology for the benchmark calibration. Home technology shocks induce a real depreciation of the home currency (i.e., a rise in q_t) and put upward pressure on the real marginal cost of foreign firms, as foreign labor supply contracts and real wages rise abroad. Import prices at home increase, though by less than the rise in q_t, since foreign exporters react by lowering their markups. Accordingly, our measure of pass-through, $\beta_{p_m,q}$, will be positive following a technology shock, as import prices rise with the real exchange rate.

The implications of a change in trade costs on pass-through differ substantially from those triggered by changes in technology. The third column of the table shows that following an increase in the foreign exporter's per-unit cost D_t^* pass-through will be negative: because of the fall in the demand for foreign goods, the increase in foreign trade costs leads to an appreciation of the domestic currency, while import prices simultaneously rise as the cost of exporting increases. Note that import prices do not rise as much as the increase in foreign real marginal costs since foreign exporters decide to lower their markups.

Overall, our calibration procedure implies that the bulk of the variation in the real exchange rate and the relative import price are driven primarily by technology shocks. As a consequence, the values of $\beta_{p_m,q}$ reported in Table 3 for the benchmark calibration mainly reflect the influence of technology shocks.[24]

---

[24] It is interesting to note that the cyclicality of the domestic producers' markups in the home market depends on the source of the shock. Domestic markups are countercyclical conditional on changes in trade costs faced by home exporters and procyclical with respect to the other shocks. The domestic markup is procyclical unconditionally, reflecting the importance of technology shocks. Incorporating nominal rigidities in domestic prices would imply a countercyclical markup.

Table 4. The Effect of *iid* Shocks for the Benchmark Calibration[a]

	One Standard Deviation Increase in	
Variable	**Home: Technology (Z_t)**	**Foreign: Trade Cost (D_t^*)**
Real Exchange Rate (q_t)	1.39	-0.10
Home Import Price (p_{mt})	0.78	0.41
Foreign Firm's Marginal Cost ($\frac{w_t^*}{Z_t^*}$)	0.23	0.00
Competitive Price Index (ξ_t)	0.02	0.01
Foreign Exporter's Markup (μ_{mt})	-0.84	-0.43

[a] Entries refer to the percent change in a variable relative to its steady state value.

7.3 Trade Integration and Declining Pass-Through

Table 5 shows the effects of lowering trade costs and higher foreign productivity on pass-through and important steady state prices and quantities. The table shows the value of the variables in steady state except for $\beta_{p_m,q}$, which is obtained from log-linearizing the model and computing the population moments of the model's variables given the shock processes. We start by looking at the effects of changing one variable at a time (columns 2, 3 and 5), before analyzing their combined impacts (last column). As shown in the second column, a five percentage point fall in the trade costs of foreign exporters reduces the real marginal cost of exporting (denominated in terms of the home consumption bundle) by 3.5 percent. Note that the fall in foreign exporters' real marginal cost, $qD^* \frac{w^*}{Z^*}$, is less than the decline in D^* as increased demand for the foreign good puts upward pressure on the real exchange rate, q, and on foreign wages. With lower costs, foreign exporters reduce their prices and the home country's import share rises 0.7 percentage point. Because foreign exporters' prices fall relative to their competitors - the domestic firms, they are able to increase their markups and still gain market share. Conversely, the prices for domestic goods rise relative to their competitors, and domestic firms are forced to cut their markups in reaction to stiffer competition from abroad.

Table 5. The Effect of Permanently Lower Trade Costs and Higher Foreign Productivity[a,b]

	Lower D^*	Lower D	Lower D^*, D	Higher Z^*	Higher Z^* Lower D^*, D
Foreign Exporter Trade Cost (D^*)	-5	0	-5	0	-5
Home Exporter Trade Cost (D)	0	-5	-5	0	-5
Foreign Productivity (Z^*)	0	0	0	35	35
Home Import Share	0.7	0.2	0.9	3.3	4.0
Home Firm Markup at Home (μ_d)	-0.3	-0.1	-0.3	-1.4	-1.7
a. Home Import Price (p_m) (a = b+c)	-1.6	-0.3	-1.9	-8.2	-9.9
b. Foreign Exporter's Markup (μ_m)	1.8	0.3	2.2	10.9	13.9
c. Foreign Marginal Cost ($qD^* \frac{w^*}{Z^*}$)	-3.5	-0.7	-4.1	-19.1	-23.8
Real Exchange Rate (q)	1.1	-1.1	0	-17.5	-17.7
Direct Pass-Through (κ_m)	-1.8	-0.4	-2.2	-9.5	-11.6
Pass-Through ($\beta_{p_m,q}$)	-2.3	-0.6	-2.9	-12.5	-14.7

a Entry refers to the log-difference for a variable from its value in the benchmark calibration. For the trade costs, home trade share, κ_m, and $\beta_{p_m,q}$, we report the percentage point difference. For Z^*, we report the arithmetic percentage change instead of the log-difference.
b Row a equals row b plus row c with any discrepancy due to rounding.

With higher markups on foreign goods, the strategic complementarity intensifies and foreign exporters become more willing to vary their markups in response to cost shocks (see the lower left panel of Figure 5). Thus, the 5 percentage point decline in trade costs causes the direct pass-through measure κ_m to fall from 0.48 to 0.462, or 1.8 percentage points. This fall in κ_m also leads to a reduction in our statistical measure of pass-through, $\beta_{p_m,q}$, of 2.3 percentage points. To understand the fall in $\beta_{p_m,q}$, recall that equation (28, reproduced below) implies a fall in κ_m directly lowers $\beta_{p_m,q}$:

$$\beta_{p_m,q} = \kappa_m + \kappa_m \left[\frac{\operatorname{cov}\left(\Delta\left(\hat{\omega}_t^* - \hat{Z}_t^*\right), \Delta\hat{q}_t\right)}{\operatorname{var}\left(\Delta\hat{q}_t\right)} + \frac{\operatorname{cov}\left(\Delta\hat{D}_t^*, \Delta\hat{q}_t\right)}{\operatorname{var}\left(\Delta\hat{q}_t\right)} \right] + \left(1 - \kappa_m\right) \left[\frac{\operatorname{cov}\left(\Delta\hat{\xi}_t, \Delta\hat{q}_t\right)}{\operatorname{var}\left(\Delta\hat{q}_t\right)} \right]$$

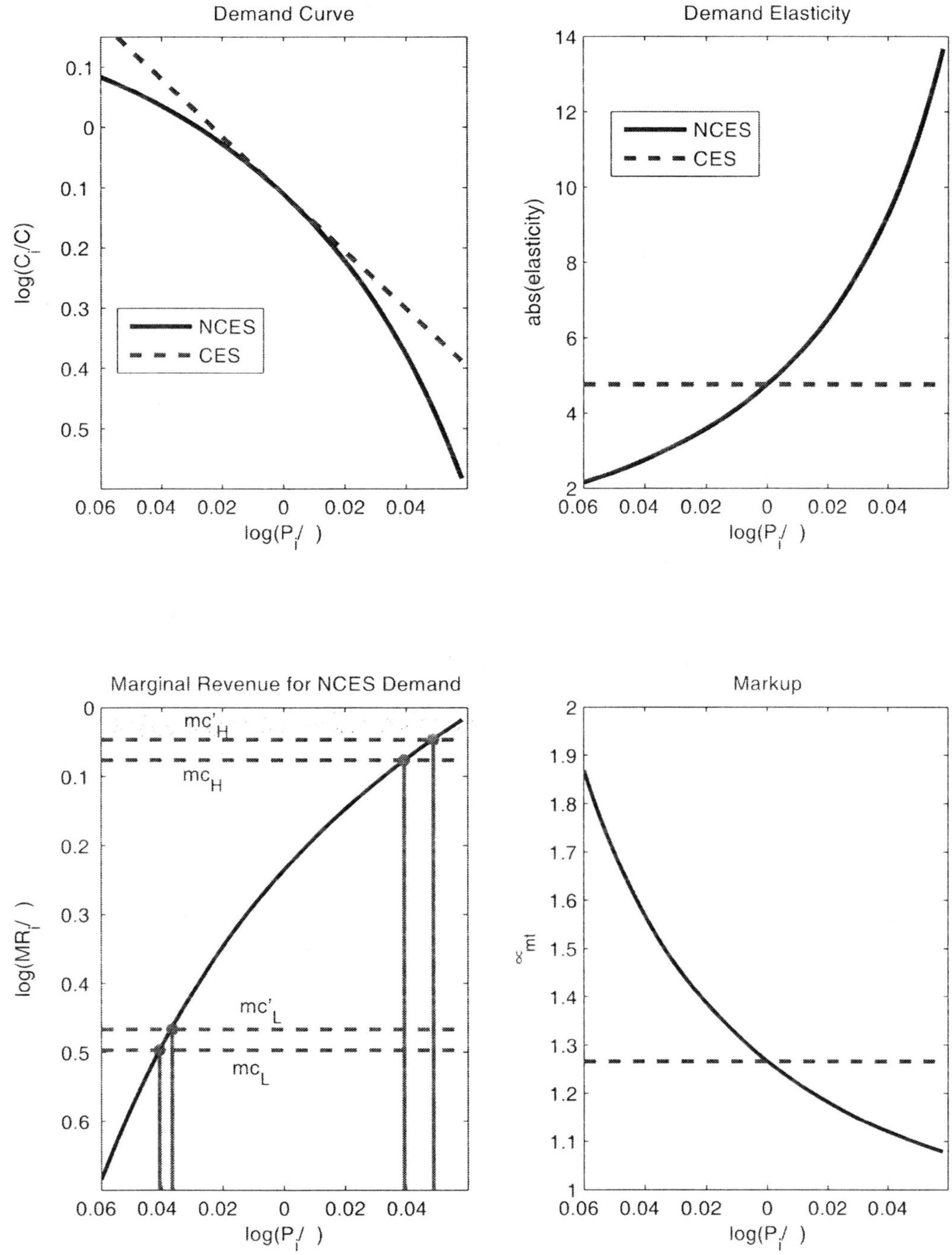

Figure 5. Import Demand and an Exporter's Marginal Revenue Schedule.

Moreover, the decline in κ_m implies that there is less weight on the marginal cost term (the first term in square brackets) and more weight on the price competitiveness term (the second term in square brackets). The marginal cost term is larger than the price competitiveness term because ξ_t has little variation (See Table 4). As a result, a fall in κ_m, by shifting a firm's emphasis in pricing away from cost considerations to considerations of price competitiveness, induces an even larger decline in $\beta_{p_m,q}$.

A fall in D, the trade cost on domestic goods sold to the foreign economy, also lowers pass-through (third column of Table 5). In general equilibrium, increased foreign demand for home goods causes an appreciation of the home currency that reduces the cost of foreign exporters and leads to a fall in pass-through. The appreciation of the currency results in the real cost of foreign exporters (in home currency) falling by 0.7 percent. This decline in costs triggers a fall in foreign exporters' prices relative to prices of domestic goods in the home market. As a result, exporters increase their markups and prices of foreign goods decline only 0.3 percent. At these higher markups, κ_m declines 0.4 percentage point and $\beta_{p_m,q}$ declines 0.6 percentage points.

For simplicity, we calibrated the fall in D and D^* based on transport costs and tariffs for U.S. imports. We view this approach as conservative, since tariff data from the United Nations Conference on Trade and Development (UNCTAD) indicates that import tariffs outside the United States and especially in developing countries have fallen more than in the United States. If we took the UNCTAD data into account, the fall in an exporter's costs would be larger, inducing a more pronounced decline in pass-through.

The fourth column of Table 5 shows the combined effects of lowering trade costs in the home and foreign economies. In this case, foreign exporters' share of the domestic market expands by 0.9 percentage point and our statistical measure of pass-through declines about 3 percentage points.

The fifth column of Table 5 displays the effects of raising the level of foreign productivity by 35 percent. Although there is a substantial increase in foreign real wages in response to the higher level of productivity, marginal costs in foreign currency fall. The foreign currency also depreciates; so, an exporter's marginal cost in home currency units falls almost 19 percent. This large decline in foreign costs allows foreign exporters to both substantially reduce prices and expand their markups at the expense of their domestic competitors. Consequently, the decline in $\beta_{p_m,q}$ is a sizeable 12.5 percentage points.

The last column of Table 5 displays the decline in pass-through from the benchmark calibration to 2004 calibration in which the increase in foreign productivity is combined with the decline in D and D^*. Higher productivity and lower trade costs have a substantial impact on pass-through. Overall, $\beta_{p_m,q}$ falls almost 15 percentage points, which accounts for about one third of the observed decline. The fall in pass-through occurs even though the home market is simultaneously becoming more competitive: markups on domestic goods fall 1.7 percentage points (see Table 2 for a more detailed comparison of the properties of the benchmark and 2004 calibrations). These results broadly capture the view that pass-through has fallen in the United States because of increased foreign competition, which in turn has reduced profit margins of domestic producers in the U.S. market.

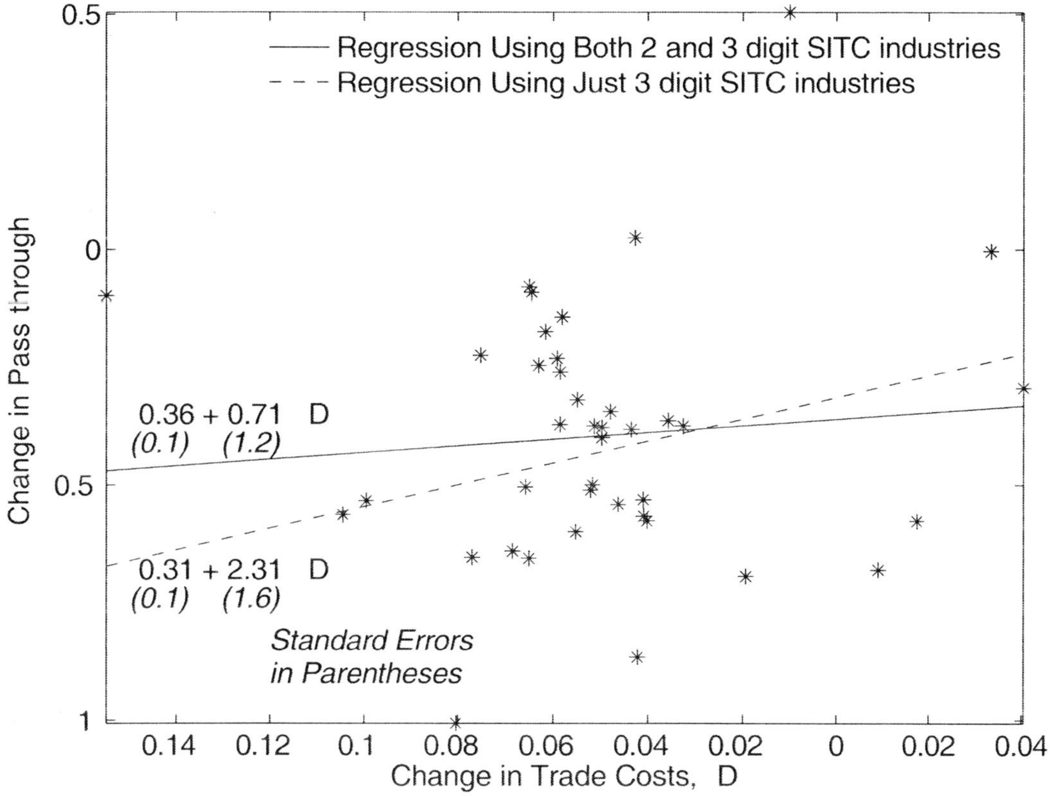

Figure 6. The Relationship Between Pass-Through and Trade Costs Based on Industry-Level Data.

The positive relationship between trade costs and pass-through emphasized in our model is broadly in line with U.S. industry-level data since the early 1980s. Figure 6 relates the changes in industry-specific pass-through (reported in Section 2) to the changes in industry-specific trade cost (discussed in Section 3). The figure indicates that declines in trade costs are correlated with declines in pass-through. As indicated by the solid line, a 1 percentage point decline in trade costs is associated with a 0.7 percentage point decline in pass-through, about the same magnitude as in our benchmark calibration. This estimate is based on data from both 2- and 3-digit industries. Estimation using only the more disaggregated industries implies a slope coefficient of 2.3 (the dashed line).

Although the model is able to explain a significant part of the decline in pass-through, it does not account for the observed decline in the correlation between import prices and the exchange rate. As shown in Table 3, $\beta_{p_m,q}$ has declined due to both falls in the relative volatility of import prices and the correlation of import prices with the exchange rate. In comparison, the model is only able to account for the decline in the relative volatility of import prices. As a result, other factors such as changes in the magnitudes and types of shocks are also important in explaining the decline in pass-through, and we leave a more thorough understanding of the reduced correlation between import prices and the exchange rate to future research.

Finally, we note that with producers engaging in price discrimination, a household might find it profitable to exploit deviations in the law of one price. However, we verified that in the benchmark calibration households have no incentive to do so because deviations from the law of one price (as measured by $|p_d - p_m^* q|$) are less than 10 percent, which is the cost of trading goods across countries. Deviations from the law of one price are less than the level of the trade cost, because a monopolist must take into account the influence of its competitors' prices on its own price setting behavior: in the market where its costs are low, a producer sets a high markup, while in the market where its costs are high, it sets a low markup. Thus, the strategic complementarity in price setting acts to offset deviations from the law of one price arising from the presence of trade costs.

The strategic complementarity also implies that the degree of price discrimination declines in response to a fall in trade costs. Given lower trade costs, a firm increases its markup abroad and lowers it in its own market and, as such, markups converge. These changes in markup, however, do mute the degree to which prices change in response to the fall in trade costs. For example, the 5 percentage point fall in D and D^* only results in about a 2 percentage point convergence in prices. This result is consistent with the evidence that notwithstanding an increase in trade integration, price convergence remained muted in comparison.[25] In comparison, in an economy with constant markups, deviations from the law of one price would decline one-for-one with the fall in trade costs.

7.4 The Impact of Entry on Pass-Through

We now assess the interaction of the intensive and extensive trade margins with the strategic complementarity and their role in accounting for the decline in pass-through. To do this, we consider a version of our model that abstracts from entry altogether and then consider a version in which only foreign exporters make entry decisions. In each case, we consider a fall in domestic and foreign trade costs of 5 percentage points and an increase in foreign productivity of 35 percent.

To better understand the relative importance of the intensive and extensive margins, Figure 7 plots a number of key variables as a function of the number of foreign exporters. We do so for three different cases: the benchmark calibration with relatively high trade costs and low foreign productivity (the dashed blue line), the 2004 calibration with low trade costs and high foreign productivity (the dotted red line), and the 2004 calibration except only foreign exporters make entry decisions (the dashed-dotted green line). The corresponding numerical results to Figure 7 are shown in Table 6.

Consider first the dashed blue lines in each panel. As the number of foreign exporters increases, per-unit profits of export good i decline due to lower demand for each individual good and a decline in an exporter's markup. This markup decline reflects that an increase in the number of foreign exporters drives up wages and production costs in the foreign economy, inducing a real home currency deprecation and a rise in the relative import price, p_m. Conversely, the markups of domestic firms in the domestic market increase.

[25] See Engel and Rogers (2004) and Bergin and Glick (2005). Bergin and Glick (2005) also report puzzling instances in which price dispersion increased over time as barriers to trade fell.

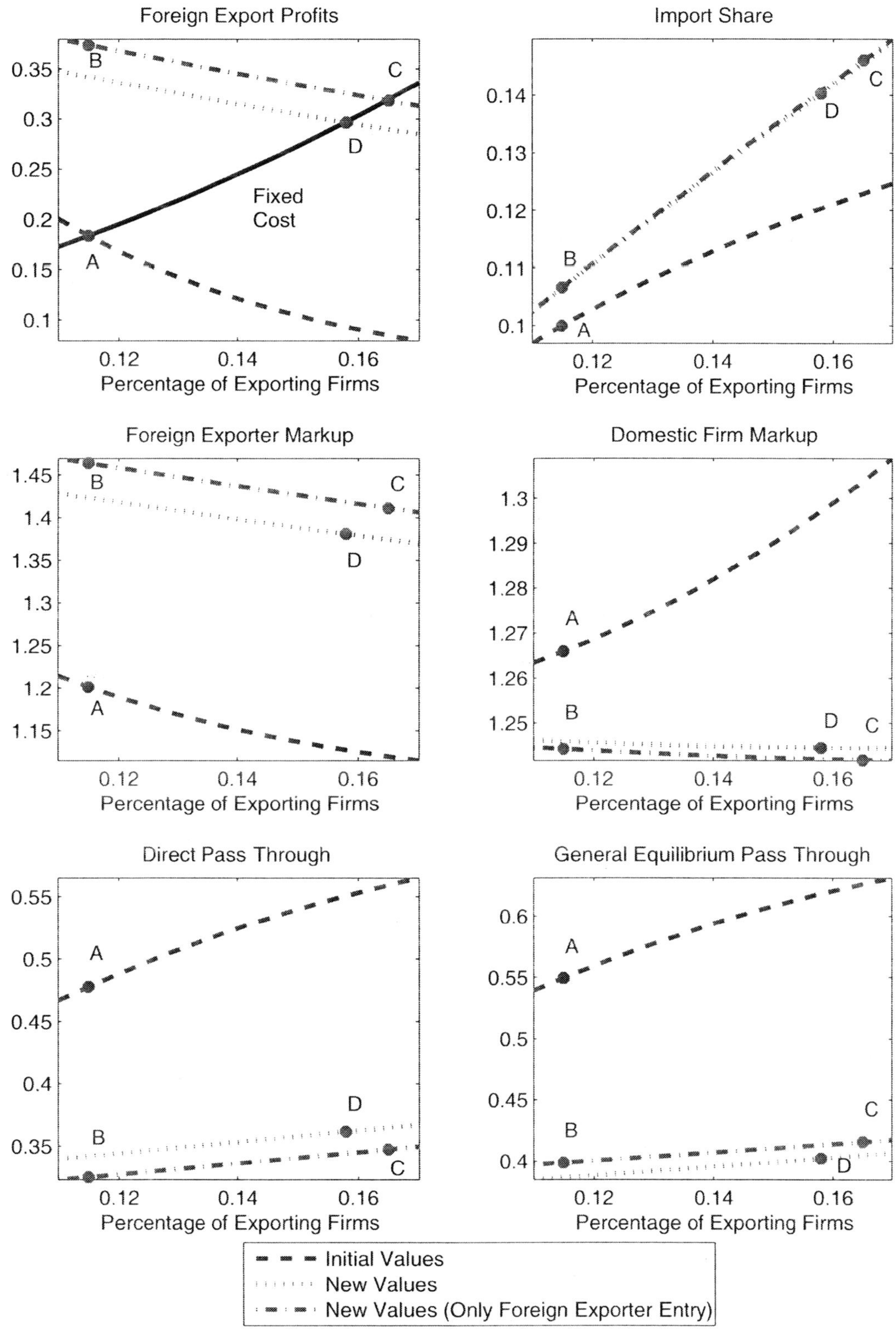

Figure 7. The Effect of the Intensive and Extensive Entry Margins on Pass-Through.

Both measures of pass-through increase as the number of foreign exporters rises. As discussed earlier, this increase reflects that a reduction in an exporter's markup is associated with an increase in direct pass-through, κ_m. Also, an increase in the number of exporters in the domestic economy implies that there are more firms who change their prices in response to exchange-rate movements, which also increases pass-through in general equilibrium, $\beta_{p_m,q}$. Thus, as in Dornbusch (1987), our model implies that other things equal, an increase in the number of foreign exporters leads to higher pass-through of exchange rate changes to import prices.[26]

Returning to the upper left panel, the equilibrium number of foreign exporters in the benchmark calibration is given by point A where per-unit profits intersect with the fixed cost (the solid black line). What happens when we lower trade costs and raise foreign productivity but completely abstract from the extensive trade margin?

The equilibrium shifts from point A to point B, as the fall in export production costs raises the demand for an exporter's good as well as his profits. As shown in the upper right panel, the import share in the home economy also rises from about 10 percent to 10.7 percent. Lower production costs are also associated with an increase in the markups of foreign exporters and, as shown in the second column of Table 6, a decline in pass-through of about 15.1 percentage points. Consequently, most of the decline in pass-through occurs along the intensive trade margin.

Now consider the case in which we allow for the entry of foreign exporters in response to the decline in the cost of exporting. In this case, the equilibrium shifts from point B to point C, as the increase in profits induces more exporters to pay their fixed entry cost. Accordingly, the import share now rises to about 14.6 percent and there is some decline in the markups of foreign exporters. While the two measures of pass-through rise, the effect is small relative to the decline in pass-through associated with the intensive margin.

When we further indigenize home exporters' entry decisions, the equilibrium moves from point C to point D, which corresponds to the last column in Table 6. Since foreign firms are 35 percent more productive than in the initial equilibrium (point A), foreign demand for domestic goods falls and domestic exporters decide to exit the foreign market. Table 6 shows that this reduction in the number of domestic exporters implies a smaller appreciation of the domestic real exchange rate and as a result the profit and markup functions for a foreign exporter shifts down to the red dotted line. At equilibrium point D, foreign exporters markups are smaller and, in turn, the direct measure of pass-through, κ_m, is higher than at point C. Despite this increase in κ_m, $\beta_{p_m,q}$ falls, reflecting that there is less co-movement between the real exchange rate and foreign marginal cost (see equation (28)) with a decline in the number of domestic exporters in the foreign economy.

Overall, we conclude that ceteris paribus a rise in the number of foreign exporters raises pass-through. However, this effect is small relative to the decline in pass-through that results

[26] Our model implies that the import share gained through the intensive margin lowers pass-through, whereas import share gained through the extensive margin increases pass-through. These two effects may help explain the empirical results of Feenstra, Gagnon, and Knetter (1996) for automotive exporters. At low levels of market share, they estimate that pass-through declines as market share increases. Whereas, for a high market share, pass-through rises with an increase in market share. See Alessandria (2004) for an alternative theoretical analysis based on search costs that can also account for the observed U-shaped relationship between market share and pass-through.

from strategic complementarity along the intensive margin in response to factors that increase trade integration.

Table 6. The Effect of Permanently Lower Trade Costs and Higher Foreign Productivity for Alternative Model Versions [a|b]

	Without Entry	With Only Foreign Exporter Entry	With Entry
Foreign Exporter Trade Cost (D^*)	-5	-5	-5
Home Exporter Trade Cost (*D*)	-5	-5	-5
Foreign Productivity (Z^*)	35	35	35
Home Import Share	0.7	4.6	4.0
Home Firm Markup at Home (μ_d)	-1.7	-1.9	-1.7
a. Home Import Price (p_m) **(a = b+c)**	-12.9	-11.0	-9.9
b. Foreign Exporter's Markup (μ_m)	19.8	16.1	13.9
c. Foreign Marginal Cost ($qD^* \frac{w^*}{Z^*}$)	-23.7	-19.2	-17.7
Real Exchange Rate (*q*)	-15.2	-13.0	-11.6
Direct Pass-Through (κ_m)	-15.2	-13.0	-11.6
Pass-Through ($\beta_{p_m,q}$)	-15.1	-13.4	-14.7

a Entry refers to the log-difference for a variable from its value in the benchmark calibration. For the trade costs, home trade share, κ_m, and $\beta_{p_m,q}$, we report the percentage point difference. For Z^*, we report the arithmetic percentage change instead of the log-difference.

b Row a equals row b plus row c with any discrepancy due to rounding.

8. Conclusion

In this paper, we proposed a new explanation for the decline in exchange-rate pass-through to import prices that emphasized the role of trade integration and strategic complementarity. When firms face strategic complementarity in setting prices, a fall in exporters' marginal costs may lower pass-through. Using conservative estimates of declines in per-unit trade costs and increases in foreign productivity, we show that this mechanism is able to account for about one third of the observed decline in pass-through.

To isolate and emphasize the role of strategic complementarity in price setting, we abstracted from another feature that may also lead to a decline in pass-through in response to greater trade integration. Increasing trade in intermediate goods could also lower the responsiveness of import prices to exchange rate fluctuations. In our model, introducing imported intermediate goods should reinforce the effect of trade integration on pass-through, as declining export costs increases their demand. We leave the exploration of this issue to future research.

References

Alessandria, G. (2004). International deviations from the law of on price: the role of search frictions and market share. *International Economic Review 45,* 1263—91.

Alessandria, G. and H. Choi (2006). Do sunk costs of exporting matter for net export dynamics? mimeo, Federal Reserve Bank of Philadelphia.

Atkeson, A. and A. Burstein (2005). Trade costs, pricing to market, and international relative prices. mimeo, University of California at Los Angeles.

Baier, S. L. and J. H. Bergstrand (2001). The growth of world trade: Tariffs, transport costs, and income similarity. *Journal of International Economics 53,* 1—27.

Bergin, P. R. and R. C. Feenstra (2001). Pricing-to-market, staggered contracts, and real exchange rate persistence. *Journal of International Economics 54,* 333—59.

Bergin, P. R. and R. Glick (2005). Tradability, productivity, and understanding international economic integration. National Bureau of Economic Research Working Paper 11637.

Bernard, A. B., J. Eaton, J. B. Jensen, and S. Kortum (2003). Plants and productivity in international trade. *American Economic Review 93,* 1668—90.

Bernard, A. B., J. B. Jensen, and P. K. Schott (2003). Falling trade costs, heterogeneous firms, and industry dynamics. National Bureau of Economic Research Working Paper 9639.

Berthelon, M. and C. Freund (2004). On the conservation of distance in international trade.
World Bank Policy Research Working Paper 3293.

Bodnar, G. M., B. Dumas, and R. D. Marston (2002). Pass through and exposure. *Journal of Finance 57,* 199—231.

Brun, J.-F., C. Carrere, P. Guillaumont, and J. de Melo (2005). Has distance died? evidence from a panel gravity model. *World Bank Economic Review 19,* 99—120.

Campa, J. M. and L. S. Goldberg (2004). Exchange rate pass-through into import prices.
Centre for Economic Policy Research Discussion Papers 4391.

Chen, N., J. Imbs, and A. Scott (2004). Competition, globalization and the decline of inflation. Centre for Economic Policy Research Discussion Papers 4695.

Coe, D. T., A. Subramanian, N. T. Tamirisa, and R. Bhavnani (2002). The missing globalization puzzle. International Monetary Fund Working Paper 02/171.

Corsetti, G. and L. Dedola (2005). A macroeconomic model of international price discrimination. *Journal of International Economics 67,* 129—155.

Corsetti, G., L. Dedola, and S. Leduc (2005). Dsge models of high exchange-rate volatility and low pass-through. Board of Governors of the Federal Reserve System International Finance Discussion Papers 845.

Corsetti, G. and P. Pesenti (2005). International dimensions of optimal monetary policy.
Journal of Monetary Economics 52, 281—305.

Devereux, M. B. and C. Engel (2003). Monetary policy in the open economy revisited: Price setting and exchange rate flexibility. *Review of Economic Studies 70*, 765—783.

Dornbusch, R. (1987). Exchange rates and prices. American Economic Review 77, 93—106.

Dotsey, M. and R. G. King (2005). Implications of state-dependent pricing for dynamic macroeconomic models. *Journal of Monetary Economics 52,* 213—42.

Eichenbaum, M. and J. D. M. Fisher (2004). Evaluating the calvo model of sticky prices. National Bureau of Economic Research Working Paper 10617.

Engel, C. and J. H. Rogers (2004). European product market integration after the euro. *Economic Policy 39,* 347—84.

Feenstra, R. C. (1996). U.s. imports 1972-1994: Data and concordances. National Bureau of Economic Research Working Paper 5515.

Feenstra, R. C., J. E. Gagnon, and M. M. Knetter (1996). Market share and exchange rate pass-through in world automobile trade. *Journal of International Economics 40,* 187—207.

Feenstra, R. C., J. Romalis, and P. Schott (2002). U.s. imports, exports and tari data, 1989-2001. National Bureau of Economic Research Working Paper 9387.

Frankel, J. A. (1997). *Regional Trading Blocs in the World Economic System.* Washington, D.C.: Institute for International Economics.

Ghironi, F. and M. J. Melitz (2005). International trade and macroeconomic dynamics with heterogeneous firms. *Quarterly Journal of Economics 120,* 865—915.

Goldberg, P. K. and M. M. Knetter (1997). Goods prices and exchange rates: What have we learned? *Journal of Economic Literature 35,* 1243—72.

Gust, C. and N. Sheets (2006). The adjustment of global external imbalances: Does partial exchange rate pass-through to trade prices matter? Board of Governors of the Federal Reserve System International Finance Discussion Papers 850.

Ihrig, J. E., M. Marazzi, and A. D. Rothenberg (2006). Exchange-rate pass-through in the g-7 countries. Board of Governors of the Federal Reserve System International Finance Discussion Papers 851.

Kimball, M. S. (1995). The quantitative analytics of the noemonetarist model. *Journal of Money, Credit, and Banking 27,* 1241—77.

Marazzi, M., N. Sheets, and R. J. Vigfusson (2005). Exchange rate pass-through to u.s. import prices: Some new evidence. Board of Governors of the Federal Reserve System International Finance Discussion Papers 833.

Melitz, M. J. (2003). The impact of trade on intra-industry reallocations and aggregate industry productivity. *Econometrica 71,* 1695—1725.

Olivei, G. P. (2002). Exchange rates and the prices of manufacturing products imported into the united states. *Federal Reserve Bank of Boston New England Economic Review* 0, 3—18.

Otani, A., S. Shiratsuka, and T. Shirota (2003). The decline in the exchange rate pass-through: Evidence from Japanese import prices. *Monetary and Economic Studies* 21, 53—81.

Peltzman, S. (2000). Prices rise faster than they fall. *Journal of Political Economy* 108, 466—502.

Rauch, J. E. (1999). Networks versus markets in international trade. *Journal of International Economics 48,* 7—35.

Woodford, M. (2003). *Interest & Prices: Foundations of a Theory of Monetary Policy.* Princeton: Princeton University Press.

DATA APPENDIX

A Trade Costs

We use product-level (ten-digit harmonized system) U.S. import data from U.S. customs' reports to compute a measure of trade costs. We respectively measure transport costs and tariffs using the shares of freight and insurance expenditure, F, and collected duty, T, in terms of customs value of the goods, V, which is the value on which duties are assessed in the United States. Freight expenditure represents Feenstra, Romalis, and Schott (2002)'s measure of Import Charges: "...the aggregate cost of all freight, insurance and other charges (excluding import duties) incurred in bringing the merchandise from alongside the carrier at the port of exportation and placing it alongside the carrier at the first port of entry in the United States." In turn, customs values reflects " ...the value of imports as appraised by the U.S. Customs Service. This value is generally defined as the price actually paid or payable for merchandise when sold for exportation to the United States, excluding U.S. import duties, freight, insurance and other charges incurred in bringing the merchandise to the United States."

$$d_{it} = \frac{T_{it} + F_{it}}{V_{it}}$$

from 1980 to 2001. We then compute an average trade cost measure, d_t, by weighting an industry's trade cost measure by that industry's share of total customs value of finished goods:

$$d_t = \sum_{i=1}^{N} \frac{V_{it}}{\left(\sum_{j=1}^{N} V_{jt}\right)} d_{it}$$

where N is the total number of finished-goods industries.

B Trade Prices

We report results for two different (but related) kinds of trade price indexes. First, we constructed the price index of finished goods as the chain-weighted price deflator constructed for imports of capital goods excluding computers and semiconductors, automotive products and consumer goods. The underlying data comes from the National Income and Product Accounts as reported by the Bureau of Economic Analysis. The price index for consumer goods is likewise based on a chain-weighted aggregation over the NIPA categories of consumer durables and nondurables.

We also reported results using industry-level price indexes for imports of finished goods as classified by two— and three-digit SITC code. We used two-digit industry only when the underlying three-digit industries' price indexes did not begin in the 1980s. These price indexes are published monthly by the Bureau of Labor Statistics. Within finished goods, we reported results for 40 industries. These 40 industries are listed in Table 7.

Table 7. Finished Goods Industries

SITC	Descriptions
54	Medicinal and pharmaceutical products
55	Essential oils; polishing and cleansing preps
625	Tires And Inner Tubes Of Rubber
665	Glassware
666	Pottery
667	Pearls, Precious And Semiprecious Stones, Unworked Or Worked
716	Rotating Electric Plants And Parts
721	Agricultural Machinery (Excluding Tractors) And Parts Thereof
723	Civil Engineering And Contractors'
724	Textile And Leather Machinery, And Parts Thereof
728	Machinery And Equipment Specialized For Particular Industries, And Parts
73	Metalworking machinery
741	Heating And Cooling Equipment And Parts
742	Pumps For Liquids; Liquid Elevators; And Parts Thereof
743	Air And Vacuum Pumps, Compressors, Fans, Centrifuges, And Filtering Apparatus
744	Mechanical Handling Equipment, And Parts Thereof, N.E.S.
745	Nonelectrical Machinery, Tools And Mechanical Apparatus, And Parts
751	Office Machines
761	Television Receivers, Including Monitors, Projectors And Receivers
762	Radio Broadcast Receivers
763	Sound Recorders Or Reproducers; Television Image And Sound Recorders
764	Telecommunications Equipment, N.E.S.; And Parts, N.E.S., And Accessories
771	Electric Power Machinery (Except Rotating Power Machinery) and Parts
773	Equipment For Distributing Electricity, N.E.S.
774	Electro-Diagnostic Apparatus For Medical, Surgical, Dental Or Vet. Use
775	Household Type Electrical
778	Electrical Machinery and Apparatus
781	Motor Cars And Other Motor Vehicles Principally Designed For The Transport
784	Parts And Accessories For Tractors, Motor Cars, And Other Motor Vehicles
81	Prefabricated buildings; plumbing, heat and lighting fixtures
84	Articles of apparel and clothing accessories
85	Footwear
874	Measuring, Checking, Analysing And Controlling Instruments And Apparatus
881	Photographic Apparatus And Equipment, N.E.S.
884	Optical Goods, N.E.S.
885	Watches And Clocks
893	Articles, N.E.S. Of Plastics
894	Baby Carriages, Toys, Games And Sporting Goods
897	Jewelry, Goldsmiths' And
898	Musical Instruments, Parts and Accessories Thereof; Records Tapes

C. Productivity

The productivity indices are constructed using GDP in 1990 U.S. dollars at purchasing power parity. The data are from the Groningen Growth and Development Centre (http://www.ggdc.net). We define labor productivity based on GDP per employee rather than GDP per hour, since the former index allows for greater country coverage. This aggregate is constructed using data on Australia, Austria, Belgium, Canada, Denmark, Finland, France, Germany, Greece, Iceland, Ireland, Italy, Japan, Luxembourg, the Netherlands, New Zealand, Norway, Portugal, Spain, Sweden, Switzerland, Turkey, the United Kingdom, China, India, Indonesia, Malaysia, South Korea, Taiwan, Thailand, Argentina, Brazil, and Mexico. Note that we arrived at a slightly larger productivity differential if we use GDP per hour worked and fewer countries for our foreign aggregate.

In: International Finance and Financial Services
Editor: Kristian L. Hagen, pp. 39-70
ISBN: 1-60021-756-7

Chapter 2

DOES THE TIME INCONSISTENCY PROBLEM MAKE FLEXIBLE EXCHANGE RATES LOOK WORSE THAN YOU THINK?*

Roc Armenter and Martin Bodenstein†

ABSTRACT

The Barro-Gordon inflation bias has provided an influential argument for fixed exchange rate regimes. However, with low inflation rates now widespread, credibility concerns seem no longer relevant. Why give up independent monetary policy to contain an inflation bias that is already under control? We argue that credibility problems do not end with the inflation bias and they are a larger drawback for flexible exchange rates than usually thought. Absent commitment, independent monetary policy can induce expectation traps–that is, welfare ranked multiple equilibria–and perverse policy responses to real shocks, i.e., an equilibrium policy response that is welfare inferior to policy inaction. Both possibilities imply that flexible exchange rates feature unnecessary macroeconomic volatility.

Keywords: Time Inconsistency, Independent Monetary Policy, Exchange Rate Regimes

---

* The authors are grateful to Gadi Barlevy, Christian Broda, Lawrence Christiano, Martin Eichenbaum, Sergio Rebelo, Alexander Wolman, Sevin Yeltekin, and Kei Mu Yi for discussions. In addition, the authors thank seminar participants at the 2002 SED Meeting in New York, the 2002 CEPALES Conference, Northwestern University, the Federal Reserve Bank of New York, the SCIEA meetings at the Board of Governors, Universitat Pompeu i Fabra, University of British Columbia, the 2nd Annual Meeting of German Economists Abroad and the Federal Reserve Bank of Philadelphia. The views expressed in this paper are solely the responsibility of the authors and should not be interpreted as reflecting the views of the Board of Governors of the Federal Reserve System or any other person associated with the Federal Reserve System, or the Federal Reserve Bank of New York.

† Armenter: Federal Reserve Bank of New York, e-mail: roc.armenter@ny.frb.org; Bodenstein: Board of Governors of the Federal Reserve System, e-mail: martin.r.bodenstein@frb.gov.

1. INTRODUCTION

The most influential argument in favor of fixed exchange rates is based on the celebrated inflation bias of Barro and Gordon (1983). A monetary authority that lacks the credibility to commit to a policy, the logic goes, can peg its currency, import the monetary policy of another country with more credible institutions and achieve lower average inflation. Of course, the fixed exchange rate regime has to be credible for this argument to go through–a premise we adopt in this paper. The textbook case against fixed exchange rates follows the lines of the classic Mundell-Fleming analysis. A fixed exchange rate implies no independent monetary policy and therefore no ability to ease real macroeconomic volatility.[1] With low inflation rates widespread these days, the case for fixed exchange rates appears less appealing. For example, Chang and Velasco (2000) concludes that "the credibility consideration seems to be less compelling than it once was for emerging markets." Rogo (2003) has argued that globalization has enhanced the central bank's credibility in fighting inflation.

However, the problems arising from the lack of credibility do not end with the inflation bias. We argue that a flexible exchange rate regime additionally suffers from two independent phenomena associated with the time inconsistency problem: expectation traps and perverse policy responses. Both have been overlooked in the exchange rate regime debate but constitute key drawbacks of flexible exchange rates.

First, the lack of credibility can induce *expectation traps*, i.e., welfare-ranked multiple equilibria.[2] High inflation expectations force the monetary authority to accommodate and the economy can be caught in long spells of high inflation. Moreover, undesirable macroeconomic volatility can arise from spurious shifts in private sector expectations.

Second, we show that the monetary authority overreacts to persistent real shocks. As a result, the equilibrium policy response to these shocks can be worse than policy inaction–we refer to this as *a perverse policy response*. In a fully specified model, real shocks are bound to affect the monetary authority's incentives to inflate beyond expectations–for example, shocks can change the slope of the "Phillips curve." The private sector responds to the changed incentives by updating inflation expectations. In equilibrium, the monetary authority has to react both to the shock and the induced change in inflation expectations. There is no guarantee then that the policy response is close to the optimal one. The lesson from perverse policy responses is that the Mundell-Fleming argument does not carry over to the case of policy without commitment: contrary to the standard view, flexible exchange rates may feature excessive macroeconomic volatility.

We show that expectation traps can be ruled out by a soft exchange rate peg with appropriately chosen bands, without hindering the ability of the monetary authority to respond to macroeconomic shocks. However, a hard peg is required in order to avoid perverse policy responses.

---

[1] Of course there are other persuasive macroeconomic arguments in favor of fixed exchange rates, such as the well known `` fear of floating" of Calvo and Reinhart (2002). See also Devereux and Engel (2003) who argue that an optimal policy with commitment features a fixed exchange rate in the presence of a large degree of local-currency pricing. However, this claim has been recently disputed by Duarte and Obstfeld (2005). See Obstfeld and Rogoff (1996) and references therein for a general discussion.

[2] Chari, Christiano and Eichenbaum (1998) originally introduced the term.

To illustrate both phenomena we present a tractable model of a small open economy that builds upon Armenter and Bodenstein (2004). Nominal rigidities introduce a role for active monetary policy. Combined with monopoly distortions, nominal rigidities also set the stage for optimal monetary policy to be time inconsistent. Furthermore, in order to introduce a cost of inflation we assume that some firms have to borrow the wage bill in advance. We define two policy equilibrium concepts, where monetary policy is endogenously determined as the outcome of a benevolent policymaker. In the analysis of flexible exchange rates, we work with Markov equilibria where the monetary authority has full discretion in setting monetary policy.[3] We define policy equilibria under the constraint of an arbitrary exchange rate regime. The policymaker takes the exchange rate regime as given and it therefore constitutes an exogenously sustained commitment.

Expectation traps arise naturally in the context of monetary policy discretion and lack of credibility.[4] There is a low inflation equilibrium where the monopoly and financial distortions are balanced. The monetary authority has little to gain from further inflation: any sticky price firms' output expansion is nearly o set by the output loss in the financially constrained sector. It is a different scenario when the private sector believes inflation will be high. Since sticky prices are set according to expectations, low actual inflation would imply very high real prices. On the other hand, if high inflation expectations are validated, then the financially constrained firms will be severely distorted.

We find two Markov equilibria in an economy calibrated to match several stylized facts about inflation and openness. The low inflation equilibrium features an inflation rate around 2%, in line with what is an acceptable level of inflation for many countries. However, the second equilibrium features costly high inflation. In our loosely calibrated economy, the high inflation equilibrium raises the costs of the lack of commitment by a factor of three.

We illustrate the perverse policy response phenomenon with a persistent negative terms of trade shock. The shock contracts the sector of tradeables, which makes the whole economy less competitive and therefore it increases the time inconsistency problem. The heightened monopoly distortion raises the incentives of the monetary authority to inflate. In equilibrium, private sector inflation expectations rise, shifting monetary policy away from the optimal response to the shock. In our calibrated economy, the policy response in a Markov equilibrium overshoots the optimal response by a factor of ten. Households prefer no policy response–the outcome under a fixed exchange rate regime–to the Markov equilibrium policy response. Hence, a flexible exchange rate fails to provide the macroeconomic stability which is presumed to be its main virtue.

To the best of our knowledge, the possibility of a perverse policy response has not been discussed in the literature. Our finding, though, is related to the stabilization bias. Clarida, Gali and Gertler (1999) and Svensson (1997), among others, point out that credibility is needed to implement the optimal policy response. However, the literature has not pursued the analysis of stabilization policy in the absence of credibility.

---

[3] We label this equilibrium Markov because we focus on equilibria sustainable in finite horizon economies. This rules out equilibria based in trigger strategies.

[4] There is a growing literature on multiple equilibria with discretionary monetary policy, e.g., Albanesi, Chari, and Christiano (2003), King and Wolman (2004), Armenter and Brodenstein (2004) and Siu (2004). Armenter (2004) characterizes the necessary conditions for the existence of expectation traps and argues that they are very general.

We do not claim, theoretically or empirically, that fixed exchange rates are always welfare superior. First and foremost, fixed exchange rates are not exogenously credible.[5] Nevertheless, the lack of a credible monetary policy is a larger drawback for flexible exchange rates than usually thought. No previous research work has considered the possibility of expectation traps and perverse policy responses. Their omission renders any welfare analysis of exchange rate regimes incomplete.[6] Our analysis implies that we should treat with caution some of the arguments made lately in favor of flexible exchange rates. For example, the observed fall of inflation rates worldwide should not be taken as conclusive evidence that the credibility problem in monetary policy has been solved. All that is needed to be back to high inflation is a shift in inflation expectations. Moreover, larger real volatility does not necessarily make a stronger case for flexible exchange rate regimes either. Summarizing the state of the debate, Frankel (1998) asserts that "if the country is subject to many external disturbances, [...] then it is more likely to want to float its currency." Chang and Velasco (2000) also concludes that the case for exchange-rate flexibility is "especially strong for countries that are often hit by large real shocks from abroad." It is necessary to check that the relevant real shocks do not induce perverse policy responses. If they do, larger real volatility actually makes the case for flexible exchange rates weaker.

The remainder of the paper is organized as follows. In Section 2 we present our model and define the equilibrium concepts. Section 3 discusses expectation traps and Section 4 takes upon the possibility of perverse policy responses. Section 5 concludes. An Appendix, containing several proofs as well as calibration details, is included.

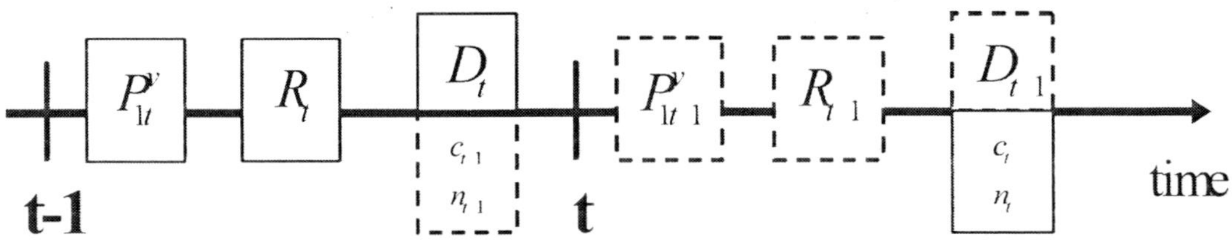

Figure 1: Timing of Relevant Decisions for Period t

2. The Economy

First, we characterize the private sector equilibrium, which includes a detailed description of the economy. Then we define the different policy equilibrium concepts considered: Markov equilibrium, Ramsey equilibrium and Exchange Rate policy equilibrium.

[5] There are mechanisms to embody a fixed exchange rate regime with some credibility, such as dollarization.

[6] See, for example, the recent literature on dollarization considering the time inconsistency problem. A small sample are Chang and Velasco (2003), Cooley and Quadrini (2001) and Mendoza (2001).

2.1 Private Sector Equilibrium

This infinite-horizon small open economy is populated by a representative household, a representative final good firm, a continuum of intermediate good firms and a monetary authority.

Figure 1 illustrates the timing of the model. Several of the decisions relevant for period t are made one period in advance. First, a fraction of the intermediate good firms--the sticky price firms indexed by $i=1$ set their nominal price for period t, P_{1t}^{y}, at the start of period t-1. Second, the monetary authority chooses the policy instrument to maximize the representative household's welfare taking P_{1t}^{y} as given. Then households choose nominal deposits D_t along with consumption c_{t-1} and labor n_{t-1}. On the demand side of the market for nominal deposits, a subset of financially constrained firms borrow their wage bill for date t. As indicated in Figure 1, date t consumption and labor decisions are made at the end of period t.

We assume that the monetary policy instrument is the nominal interest rate, R_t, that is paid at date t on nominal deposits carried from period t-1. The nominal interest rate is implemented by intervening in the market for nominal deposits. As shown below, there is a one-to-one relationship between the nominal interest rate and the inflation rate at date t, $\pi_t \equiv \frac{P_t}{P_{t-1}}$. Hence, we can think of the inflation rate as the policy instrument.

Before the monetary policy decision, the sticky price firms must form a belief about inflation in period t, denoted π_t^e, in order to set their nominal price P_{1t}^{y}. Following the literature, we commonly refer to π_t^e as private sector inflation expectations, although "beliefs" would be more accurate.

We show that real prices and allocations in a private sector equilibrium at date t are fully determined by the state of the economy $s_t = (\pi_t^e, \pi_t)$. Neither past nor future policy decisions are relevant and there is no physical state variable in the economy. By focusing on Markov perfect equilibria, we can study the monetary authority's decision as a sequence of static problems.

We do not model money directly. Implicitly, nominal deposits are as good as cash balances. This feature of the model allows us to abstract from money demand considerations and to focus on nominal frictions on the supply side of the economy.[7]

2.1.1 Households

Household preferences at date t are given by

$$\sum_{j=t}^{\infty} \beta^{j-t} u(c_j, n_j)$$

with 0<β<1. For tractability, we assume quasi-linear preferences

[7] This in the spirit of the cashless economies discussed in Woodford (2003).

$$u(c,n) = c + h(1-n)$$

where h is a strictly increasing, concave function that satisfies the usual Inada conditions.

The household's problem at date t is

$$\max_{\{c_j, n_j, D_{j+1}\}_{j=t}^{\infty}} \sum_{j=t}^{\infty} \beta^{j-t} u(c_j, n_j) \tag{1}$$

subject to

$$c_j \geq 0$$
$$0 \leq n_j \leq 1$$

and

$$P_j c_j + D_{j+1} \leq R_j D_j + W_j n_j + T_j^f \tag{2}$$

for all $j \geq t$, where D_{j+1} are nominal deposits, which pay a nominal interest rate R_j, and T_j^f are profits. Nominal deposits, D_j, are the unique asset holdings of the household.

The intertemporal Euler equation associated with the household's problem (1) at date t is

$$R_{t+1} = \frac{1}{\beta} \pi_{t+1}$$

This is the standard Fisher equation. Our timing implies that all uncertainty with respect to the monetary authority's decision at date t+1 has been resolved before the nominal deposit markets clears. Hence, next period's inflation π_{t+1} is known by the time of the household's savings decision.

Labor supply is characterized by the first order condition

$$h'(1-n_t) = w_t$$

where $w_t = \frac{W_t}{P_t}$ is the real wage.

Neither the level of deposits D_t nor the price level P_t appear in the intertemporal Euler equation and the labor supply condition. Therefore we write both equilibrium conditions in terms of the economy wide state $s = (\pi^e, \pi)$.[8] First the labor supply condition is

[8] We can do this because we restrict our analysis to Markov equilibrium.

$$h'(1-n(s)) = w(s) \tag{3}$$

As the policy choice for period t is made at period t-1, the relevant pricing equation for the date t private sector equilibrium is given by the household problem at date t-1,

$$R(s) = \frac{1}{\beta}\pi \tag{4}$$

We will drop the time subscripts for the remainder of the paper and normalize the last period's aggregate price index to 1.

2.1.2 Firms

There is a continuum $I = [0,1]$ of intermediate goods. There is a representative final good firm which combines a continuum $[0,1-\mu_x]$ of intermediate inputs $y_i(s)$ to produce the final good $y(s)$ according to

$$y(s) = \left[\int_0^{1-\mu_x} y_i(s)^\eta \, di\right]^{\frac{1}{\eta}} \tag{5}$$

with $\eta < 1$. Its profit-maximization problem is

$$\max_{c,\{y_i\}_0^{1-\mu_x}} P(s)c - \int_0^{1-\mu_x} P_i^y(s) y_i(s) di$$

subject to (5). Using the first order conditions, the demand good $y_i(s)$ is given by

$$P_i^y(s) = \left(\frac{y(s)}{y_i(s)}\right)^{1-\eta} \tag{6}$$

where $P_i^y(s) = \dfrac{P_i^y(s)}{P(s)}$.

There is a fraction α of non-tradeable intermediate goods and a fraction (1- α) of tradeable intermediate goods.

There is monopolistic competition in the non-tradeable intermediate good sector. Each good is produced by a single firm i according to a linear technology on labor,

$$y_i(s) = \theta_i n_i(s).$$

There are three types of intermediate good firms in the non-tradeable input sector. Let μ_i denote the measure of firms of type i, with $\mu_1 + \mu_2 + \mu_3 = \alpha$. We assume symmetry within each firm type.

Firms of type 1—the sticky price firms—set their nominal prices before the monetary authority's policy choice. As a consequence, their nominal price, $P_1^y(\hat{\pi})$, is a function of the private sector inflation expectations $\hat{\pi}$ but not of the actual inflation π. As all intermediate good firms, the sticky price firms take in account the demand function for its own good, $y_1(s)$. Given our specification for the demand of each good *i*, (6), profit maximization implies that the nominal price equals a constant markup over the expected marginal cost

$$P_1^y(\hat{\pi}) = \frac{1}{\eta}\frac{\hat{W}}{\theta_1}$$

where $\hat{W}$ is the expected nominal wage. Rational expectations require that $\hat{W}$ is the equilibrium nominal wage under the expectation that $\hat{\pi}$ is the actual policy choice, i.e.

$$P_1^y(\hat{\pi}) = \frac{1}{\eta}\frac{w(\hat{\pi},\pi)}{\theta_1} \tag{7}$$

where $w(\hat{\pi},\hat{\pi})\hat{\pi}$ is the nominal wage.

Firms of type 2 are flexible price setters, i.e., they set the nominal price, $P_2^y(s)$, after the monetary authority's decision. Hence it is a function of both π and π^e. We assume that firms of type 2 are financially constrained and they must borrow the nominal wage bill W_n one period in advance at the nominal interest rate $R(s)$.[9] Their optimal pricing rule is

$$P_2^y(s) = \frac{1}{\eta}R(s)\frac{w(s)}{\theta_2} \tag{8}$$

The fact that their marginal cost is augmented by $R(s)$ is reflected in the real price.

Finally, firms of type 3 are flexible price setters and financially unconstrained. Therefore we have

$$P_3^y(s) = \frac{1}{\eta}\frac{w(s)}{\theta_3} \tag{9}$$

Note that if the expectation and the actual inflation rate are the same, $\hat{\pi} = \pi$, (7) and (9) imply that prices and output are the same across sticky and non-financially constrained flexible price firms, i.e., $P_1^y(\pi,\pi) = P_3^y(\pi,\pi)$ and $y_1(s) = y_3(s)$. Moreover, if $R(\pi,\pi) = 1$, all firms' prices and production are identical. Since the production function for the final good (5) is convex, symmetry across firm types is a necessary condition for production efficiency. In other words, $R(s) > 1$ and $\hat{\pi} \neq \pi$ introduce costly price distortions.

[9] These firms provide the demand side for the household deposits. Note that the deposit demand is also determined with knowledge of the actual policy choice π.

The tradeable intermediate good sector is composed of export and import firms. There is a measure μ_x of export firms, which produce domestically and they supply exclusively to the world markets. We assume that the country's export goods are not differentiated so the export price is determined in the world markets.[10] Hence, export firms take the price as given.

The production function for export firms is

$$y_x(s) = \theta_x n_x(s) .$$

The first order conditions associated with the profit-maximization problem implies

$$p_x(s) = \frac{w(s)}{\theta_x} \tag{10}$$

In addition the law of one price equates the domestic price, in nominal terms, to the world market price for x, P_x^*,

$$P_x(s) = \varepsilon(s) P_x^*$$

where $\varepsilon(s)$ is the nominal exchange rate. In terms of real prices,

$$p_x(s) = q(s) p_x^* \tag{11}$$

where $q(s) = \frac{\varepsilon(s)P^*}{P(s)}$ is the real exchange rate and P^* is the world price for the final good. We set the last period world final good price equal to one. Then we can express the real exchange rate in terms of inflation rates

$$q(s) = \frac{\varepsilon(s)\pi^*}{\pi} \tag{12}$$

where π^* is the world rate of inflation.

Import firms do not produce domestically: they simply buy $y_m(s)$ from the world markets. Import prices are determined in the world market and taken as given by firms. Hence

$$p_m(s) = q(s) p_m^* \tag{13}$$

Imports constitute a measure μ_m of total tradeable inputs, with $\mu_x + \mu_m = 1 - \alpha$.

Because there is no trade in intertemporal assets with the rest of the world, the value of imports and exports must be equated every period,

$$\mu_m y_m(s) = \mu_x tty_x(s) \tag{14}$$

[10] This assumption suits developing economies particularly well.

where $tt = \frac{P_x^*}{P_m^*}$ are the terms of trade.

2.1.3 Market Clearing Conditions and Private Sector Equilibrium Definition

The aggregate resource constraint is

$$c(s)=\left[\sum_{i=1}^{3}\mu_i\left(\theta_i n_i(s)\right)^{\eta}+\mu_m\left(\theta_m n_m(s)\right)^{\eta}\right]^{\frac{1}{\eta}} \tag{15}$$

where (5) has been combined with each intermediate good production technology. The market clearing condition for the labor market is

$$n(s)=\sum_{i=1}^{3}\mu_i n_i(s)+\mu_x n_x(s). \tag{16}$$

Equations (3)-(16) are sufficient to solve for all real prices and allocations as function of expected and actual inflation. This confirms our conjecture that $s=(\hat{\pi},\pi)$ fully characterizes all allocations. We proceed now to define a Private Sector Equilibrium (PSE) given $\hat{\pi}$ as a collection of allocation and price functions defined over π and a sticky nominal price $P_1^y(\hat{\pi})$.

Definition 1. *Given an inflation rate expectation* $\hat{\pi}$, *a* ***Private Sector Equilibrium*** *is a number,* $P_1^y(\hat{\pi})$, *and a collection of functions,* $\{p_i^y(s), y_i(s), n_i(s)\}_{i\in I}$, $R(s)$, $w(s)$, $n(s)$, $c(s)$, $\varepsilon(s)$, $q(s)$ *and* $y(s)$, *such that*

1. The household optimal conditions, (3) and (4), are satisfied.
2. Firm maximize profits, (7)-(10) are satisfied.
3. Markets clear, (5), (6) and (12)-(16) hold.

A ***Private Sector Equilibrium*** *outcome in state* $s=(\hat{\pi},\pi)$ *is the collection of allocations and prices which occur at a PSE given* $\hat{\pi}$ *evaluated at* π.

Our definition of the PSE is sufficient to characterize the monetary authority's problem. Note that nominal prices, deposits and monetary transfers are not included in the PSE. Now we show how to characterize these variables and why they are not relevant for the monetary authority's problem.

It is straightforward to recover all nominal prices, as under our normalization, $\pi=\mathrm{P}(s)$. The nominal deposit market clearing condition is

$$D=W(s)\int_{I_2} n_i(s)di - X(D,s) \tag{17}$$

where $X(D,s)$ are monetary transfers by the monetary authority. For any level of nominal deposits D and state s, there is $X(D,s)$ that clears the nominal deposits market. Hence for any

D and $\hat{\pi}$, the monetary authority can implement its policy decision in terms of inflation by setting $X(D,s)$ correspondingly.

Finally, the household budget constraint (2) gives a law of motion for nominal deposits, $D' = R(s)D$. Since $R(s) \geq 1$, the path for nominal deposits is strictly positive given $D_0 > 0$.

2.1.4 Solving for the PSE

In our model, the PSE can be solved for analytically. We start by taking P_1^y, a number, as given. Then we solve for the PSE functions that map the actual inflation rate π into allocations and prices. Using these PSE functions, we can characterize the sticky price firms decision as function of the expected inflation rate, $P_1^y(\hat{\pi})$.

From the Fisher equation (4), the nominal interest rate and inflation are simply linked by

$$R(s) = \frac{\pi}{\beta}$$

The relative price of sticky price firm's goods is given by

$$p_1^y(s) = \frac{P_1^y(\hat{\pi})}{\pi}$$

Next we solve for relative quantities,

$$\frac{y_i(s)}{y_j(s)} = \left[\frac{p_j^y(s)}{p_i^y(s)}\right]^{\frac{1}{1-\eta}}$$

combining the demand function (6) for two given goods of type *i* and *j*.

Using the pricing formulas (7)-(13),

$$\frac{y_1(s)}{y_3(s)} = \left[\frac{1}{\eta\theta_3}\frac{w(s)}{p_i^y(s)}\right]^{\frac{1}{1-\eta}}$$

$$\frac{y_2(s)}{y_3(s)} = \left[\frac{\theta_2}{\theta_3}R(s)^{-1}\right]^{\frac{1}{1-\eta}}$$

$$\frac{y_x(s)}{y_3(s)} = \left[\frac{\theta_x}{\eta\theta_3}\right]^{\frac{1}{1-\eta}}$$

$$\frac{y_m(s)}{y_3(s)} = \frac{\mu_x}{\mu_m} tt \frac{y_x(s)}{y_3(s)}$$

where the latest equality is derived using (14). We combine these expressions with (5) to obtain

$$\frac{y(s)}{y_3(s)} = \left[\mu_3 + \mu_2\left[\frac{\theta_2}{\theta_3 R(s)}\right]^{\frac{\eta}{1-\eta}} + \mu_1\left[\frac{w(s)}{\eta\theta_3 p_i^y(s)}\right]^{\frac{\eta}{1-\eta}} + \mu_m\left(\frac{\mu_x}{\mu_m}tt\right)^{\eta}\left[\frac{\theta_x}{\eta\theta_3}\right]^{\frac{\eta}{1-\eta}}\right]^{\frac{1}{\eta}}. \tag{18}$$

Next, we use the pricing formula and demand for the intermediate good i=3,

$$\left[\frac{w(s)}{\eta\theta_3}\right]^{\frac{\eta}{1-\eta}} = \mu_3 + \mu_2\left[\frac{\theta_2}{\theta_3 R(s)}\right]^{\frac{\eta}{1-\eta}} + \mu_1\left[\frac{w(s)}{\eta\theta_3 p_i^y(s)}\right]^{\frac{\eta}{1-\eta}} + \mu_m\left(\frac{\mu_x}{\mu_m}tt\right)^{\eta}\left[\frac{\theta_x}{\eta\theta_3}\right]^{\frac{\eta}{1-\eta}}$$

and the real wage rate can be explicitly solved for

$$w(s) = \eta\left[\frac{\tilde{\mu}_3 + \tilde{\mu}_2 R(s)^{\frac{\eta}{\eta-1}} + \tilde{\mu}_m \eta^{\frac{\eta}{\eta-1}}}{1 - \mu_1 p_1^y(s)^{\frac{\eta}{\eta-1}}}\right]^{\frac{1-\eta}{\eta}} \tag{19}$$

where

$$\tilde{\mu}_i = \mu_i \theta_i^{\frac{\eta}{1-\eta}}$$

for i=1,2,3 and

$$\tilde{\mu}_m = \mu_m\left(\frac{\mu_x}{\mu_m}tt\right)^{\eta}\frac{\eta}{0_x^{1-\eta}}$$

$$\tilde{\mu}_m = \mu_m\frac{\eta}{0_x^{1-\eta}}$$

This expression is the key to solve for the PSE. With knowledge of the real wage rate $w(s)$, the rest of equilibrium allocations and prices follow. Labor $n(s)$ is given by (3). To pin down output, use (16) to derive

$$\frac{n(s)}{y_3(s)} = \frac{\mu_3}{0_3} + \frac{\mu_2}{0_2}\left[\frac{0_2}{0_3 R(s)}\right]^{\frac{1}{1-\eta}} + \frac{\mu_1}{0_1}\left[\frac{w(s)}{\eta 0_3 p_1^y(s)}\right]^{\frac{1}{1-\eta}} + \frac{\mu_x}{0_x}\left[\frac{0_x}{\eta 0_3}\right]^{\frac{1}{1-\eta}}$$

and combining the last expression with (18)

$$y(s) = \varphi(s)n(s)$$

where

$$\varphi(s)=\frac{\left[\tilde{\mu}_3+\tilde{\mu}_2 R(s)\frac{\eta}{\eta-1}+\mu_1\left[\frac{w(s)}{np_1^y(s)}\right]^{\frac{\eta}{1-\eta}}+\tilde{\mu}_m \eta^{\frac{\eta}{\eta-1}}\right]^{\frac{1}{\eta}}}{\tilde{\mu}_3+\tilde{\mu}_2 R(s)\frac{1}{\eta-1}+\frac{\mu_1}{0_1}\left[\frac{w(s)}{np_1^y(s)}\right]^{\frac{1}{1-\eta}}+\tilde{\mu}_x \eta^{\frac{1}{\eta-1}}}$$

The numerator is also equal to $\left[\frac{w(s)}{\eta}\right]^{\frac{1}{1-\eta}}$

To close the PSE, it is still needed to solve for $P_1^y(\hat{\pi})$. Given expectations $\hat{\pi}$, (7) implies that $P_1^y(\hat{\pi})$ will satisfy $p_1^y(s)=\frac{0_3}{01}p_3^y(s)$. This allows to write the real wage rate when $\pi=\hat{\pi}$ as

$$w\left(\hat{\pi},\hat{\pi}\right)=\eta\left[\tilde{\mu}_3+\tilde{\mu}_2 R(s)^{\frac{\eta}{\eta-1}}+\tilde{\mu}_1+\tilde{\mu}_m \eta^{\frac{\eta}{\eta-1}}\right]^{\frac{1-\eta}{\eta}} \tag{20}$$

and hence, using (7) again,

$$p_1^y\left(\hat{\pi}\right)=\hat{\pi}\frac{w\left(\hat{\pi},\hat{\pi}\right)}{\eta 0_1}$$

It can be easily shown that $P_1^y(\hat{\pi})$ is increasing in the expected inflation.

2.2 Policy Equilibria

We view the policy decision as an equilibrium object. We consider three different policy equilibrium concepts: the Markov equilibrium, the Ramsey equilibrium and the Exchange Rate Policy equilibrium.

In the Markov equilibrium, the monetary authority's problem is to choose the inflation rate which maximizes household welfare taking nominal prices P_1^y as given. Hence the monetary authority has no ability to manipulate the private sector inflation expectations.

The Ramsey equilibrium characterizes the optimal monetary policy with commitment. A formal definition is given below but the reader can think of the Ramsey equilibrium as the result of an alternative timing where the monetary policy is determined once and for all before sticky price are set.

Finally, the Exchange Rate Policy (ERP) equilibrium captures the possibility that the monetary authority's decision is constrained by an exchange rate policy.

2.2.1 The Markov Equilibrium

The monetary authority's problem is to choose the inflation rate that maximizes household welfare. The monetary authority takes the nominal price $P_1^y(\hat{\pi})$ as given.

The choice of the inflation rate is constrained as follows. First, the nominal interest rate is bounded below by one, i.e., $R(s) \geq 1$. This bound is implied by the arbitrage condition between nominal bonds and cash balances. The latter are not explicitly modeled here, yet we can use (4) to establish that the lower bound for inflation equals the intertemporal discount rate, $\pi \geq \beta$.

Second, the existence of a PSE outcome also imposes an upper bound, $\bar{\pi}(\hat{\pi})$, on the inflation rate. This upper bound is an increasing function of the private sector inflation expectations. As π approaches the upper bound $\bar{\pi}$, the sticky price firms have unbounded losses.[11]

Proposition 2 *For any $\hat{\pi} \geq \beta$, a PSE outcome exists for all π such that*

$$\pi < \bar{\pi}\left(\hat{\pi}\right) = \hat{\pi}\, p_1^y\left(\hat{\pi}\right) \mu_1^{\frac{\eta-1}{\eta}}$$

Proof. As long as we have a finite, strictly positive real wage rate, a PSE outcome exists. From (19), $B \geq w(s) > 0$ implies that

$$\left(1 - \mu_1 p_1^y\left(s\right)^{\frac{\eta}{\eta-1}}\right)^{\frac{\eta-1}{\eta}} > 0$$

The above restriction can be rewritten

$$p_l^y\left(s\right) > \mu_1^{\frac{1-\eta}{\eta}},$$

or in terms of π and $\hat{\pi}$,

[11] It is possible to allow firms to shut down or re-set nominal prices if profits fall below some arbitrary level. A PSE would then exist for all $\pi \geq \beta$. Whether we allow for negative profits or not does not affect our results.

$$\pi < \bar{\pi}\left(\hat{\pi}\right) = \frac{p_1^y\left(\hat{\pi}\right)}{\mu_1^{\frac{1-\eta}{\eta}}}$$

■

In Armenter and Brodenstein (2004), we show that the policy choice set can be defined without any loss of generality as

$$\beta \leq \pi \leq \bar{\pi}\left(\hat{\pi}\right) - \varepsilon$$

for an arbitrarily small $\varepsilon > 0$. First, the upper bound will never be binding. Second, we prove that the policy choice set is never empty as $\bar{\pi}\left(\hat{\pi}\right) > \beta$ for all $\hat{\pi} \geq \beta$.

Because a PSE outcome fully determines the household period welfare, we can state the monetary authority's problem as an intratemporal optimization problem

$$\max_{\beta \leq \pi < \bar{\pi}\left(\hat{\pi}\right)} u(c(s), n(s)) \tag{21}$$

where $c(s)$ and $n(s)$ belong to a PSE given $\hat{\pi}$. Let $\pi^*(\hat{\pi})$ be the best policy response function which solves (21) given any $\hat{\pi} \geq \beta$.[12]

All is set for the definition of a Markov equilibrium. The nomenclature emphasizes that equilibria based on trigger strategies are ruled out.

Definition 3 *A Markov equilibrium is a PSE given private sector expectations $\hat{\pi}$ and an inflation rate π such that the solution to (21) is*

$$\pi^*\left(\hat{\pi}\right) = \pi$$

and private sector expectations are rational

$$\hat{\pi} = \pi .$$

---

[12] Existence of $\pi^*\left(\hat{\pi}\right)$ follows from $u\left(c,n\right)$ being bounded above and the closure of the policy choice set previously discussed. However, the solution of (21) can be a correspondence. Armenter and Bodenstein (2005) carefully explores this rare possibility.

We will say that a policy π is time consistent if there exists a Markov equilibrium with $\hat{\pi} = \pi$. The definition is for an one-period economy. The corresponding definition for the infinite horizon economy is not problematic but it requires some additional formalization. We have decided then to skip it for the sake of expositional clarity.

2.2.2 The Ramsey Equilibrium

In the Ramsey equilibrium, the monetary authority pins down private sector expectations with its policy decision. The Ramsey equilibrium policy also characterizes the optimal monetary policy with commitment.

Definition 4 *A Ramsey Equilibrium is an inflation rate* π^r *and a PSE given* π^r *such that for all* π,

$$u\left(c\left(\pi^r,\pi^r\right),n\left(\pi^r,\pi^r\right)\right) \geq u\left(c\left(\pi,\pi\right),n\left(\pi,\pi\right)\right)$$

where $c(s)$ *and* $n(s)$ *are respective PSE functions.*

Not surprisingly, the optimal monetary policy with commitment turns out to be the Friedman rule. All distortions associated with price dispersion are zeroed by setting the nominal interest rate to zero, $R(s)=1$. The distortion that arises from monopoly pricing remains. However, there is nothing monetary policy can do to curtail the market power of the intermediate good firms.[13] Hence, labor remains undersupplied.

Proposition 5 *The Ramsey equilibrium features* $R(s)=1$.

Proof. Consider functions $\tilde{\varphi}(\pi) = \varphi(\pi,\pi)$ and $\tilde{w}(\pi) = w(\pi,\pi)$. Simple algebra shows that $\tilde{\varphi}$ and $\tilde{w}$ are decreasing in π, and $\tilde{\varphi}(\pi) \geq \tilde{w}(\pi)$ for all $\pi \geq \beta$. Next we show that the household welfare is increasing in φ and w. Let

$$\tilde{u}(\varphi,w) = \varphi\tilde{n}(w) + h\left(1-\tilde{n}(w)\right)$$

where $\tilde{n}(w)$ is given by (3). It is clear that $\tilde{u}$ is increasing in φ. Moreover,

$$\frac{d\tilde{u}}{dw} = \left(\varphi - w\right)\frac{d\tilde{n}}{dw}$$

so given that $\varphi > w$ and the labor supply has an upward slope, household welfare is also increasing in the wage. Hence any policy choice $\pi > \beta$ is welfare dominated by $\pi = \beta$ ■

---

[13] Dupor 03 (2003) shows that optimal monetary policy with commitment may have a random component which can alleviate the monopoly distortion. This is not the case in this economy.

Does the Friedman Rule constitute a Markov Equilibrium? Assume private sector expectations are such that $R\left(\hat{\pi},\hat{\pi}\right)=1$, i.e., sticky nominal prices are set under the belief that the Friedman Rule will be chosen by the monetary authority. Ex-post, the monetary authority can choose to inflate $\pi > \beta$ and cut the markup of the sticky price firms. However, such a move creates price distortions. The price difference between the sticky and flexible price firm goods is welcome as it reflects the improved efficiency in the sticky price firms' good production. However, there is an additional price distortion. The marginal cost of financially constrained firms are augmented by $R(s)$. This implies lower efficiency in the production of financially constrained firms. Hence, at least on the margin, whether the Friedman Rule is time consistent depends on the relative weight of each distortion which, in our model, are closely linked to each firm type.

2.2.3 The Exchange Rate Policy Equilibrium

In the exchange rate policy equilibrium (ERP), the monetary authority takes the private sector expectations as given and maximizes household welfare--as in the Markov equilibrium. However, its policy choice is exogenously constrained by the exchange rate policy.

We formalize the exchange rate policy as a set of acceptable nominal exchange rates, Σ. A fixed exchange rate regime reduces Σ to a singleton $\bar{\varepsilon}$, $\Sigma=\left\{\bar{\varepsilon}\right\}$. A soft exchange rate peg, which specifies some bands $-\delta_0/+\delta_1$, would be formalized as $\Sigma=\left[\bar{\varepsilon}-\delta_0,\bar{\varepsilon}+\delta_1\right]$. As we focus our analysis in commonly observed exchange rate regimes, we do not consider the possibility that the set Σ is history dependent.

The monetary authority's problem in a ERP is

$$\max_{\beta\leq\pi<\bar{\pi}\left(\hat{\pi}\right)} u(c(s),n(s)) \tag{22}$$

subject to

$$\varepsilon(s)\in\Sigma$$

where $c(s)$, $n(s)$ and $\varepsilon(s)$ belong to a PSE given $\hat{\pi}$.

Definition 6 *An Exchange Rate Policy Σ equilibrium is an inflation rate π and a PSE given private sector expectations $\hat{\pi}$ such that π solves (22) given $\hat{\pi}$ and private sector expectations are rational*

$$\hat{\pi}=\pi.$$

We have assumed implicitly that it is not possible to review the exchange rate policy. In other words, the policymaker is able to commit to an exchange rate regime but not to a given monetary policy.

3. Expectation Traps

In this section we show that the absence of commitment can lead to costly volatility due to self-fulfilling private sector expectations. The multiplicity of Markov equilibria is a robust property of this economy.[14]

3.1 Understanding Expectation Traps

To understand expectation traps, we first discuss the monetary authority's decision for given private sector expectations. In this economy, the costs and benefits of inflation are driven by the heterogeneous impact of inflation across firm types. Inflation reduces overall efficiency by distorting relative prices and by increasing the cost of working capital for financially constrained firms. On the other hand, unexpected inflation erodes the markup of sticky price firms thereby improving efficiency. In a Markov equilibrium, the costs and benefits from unexpected inflation are balanced.

Expectations traps arise because expected inflation changes the composition of the intermediate good sector. While the measure of each firm type is constant, inflation alters the relative output of sticky price firms and financially constrained firms.

Sector composition is the key determinant of the monetary authority's decision. When expected inflation is low, each type of firm operates at similar scale. Efficiency gains from unexpected inflation are almost zero: any cut in the markup of the sticky price firms is roughly offset by an increase in the marginal cost of the financially constrained firms. As a result, there are little net efficiency gains to outweigh the costs of price distortion. A low inflation equilibrium exists where the marginal costs of price distortion are low.

When the private sector expects high inflation, financially constrained firms operate at reduced scale because of the large costs of nominal working capital. There are considerable net efficiency gains from unexpected inflation because the sticky price sector is relatively large compared to the financially constrained sector. These large efficiency gains can exceed the higher marginal cost of price distortion. Hence, the monetary authority will find it optimal to validate the high inflation expectations.

Figure 2 displays the policy best response π^* as a function of private sector expectations $\hat{\pi}$. The 45-degree line is the set of points where actual inflation equals expected inflation, $\pi = \hat{\pi}$. This is the rational expectation locus. Crossings of the policy best response function with the 45-degree line indicate Markov equilibria. We calibrated the economy displayed in

---

[14] See Armenter and Bodenstein (2004) for an in depth exploration of expectation traps in a closed economy version of the model.

Figure 2 to match two Markov equilibria with inflation rates of 2% and 13.2%.[15] An additional feature to note is that each Markov equilibrium is locally unique.

We have argued that the changes in the composition of the intermediate good sector are behind the expectation traps. This is illustrated in Figure 3. Output for sticky price firms and financially constrained firms is plotted along the rational expectations locus, i.e., $\hat{\pi} = \pi$, for different values of inflation π. Firms' output is similar across firm types when inflation is low.[16] High inflation disproportionately reduces the production of financially constrained firms. Sticky price firm production also falls because aggregate demand is reduced by the price distortion.

The welfare implications of expectation traps dwarf the classic inflation bias analyzed by Barro and Gordon (1983). Table 1 documents this claim for several economies calibrated to match different equilibrium inflation rates. This is achieved by varying the measure of sticky price firms and financially constrained firms in the economy.

For each economy we compute the welfare implications of several experiments. First, we reduce inflation from the low inflation, π_1, to the Ramsey equilibrium, π^r. This is equivalent to correcting the classic inflation bias in an economy with a single equilibrium. Second, we evaluate the shift from the high inflation, π_2, to the low inflation equilibrium, π_1. The last two columns report the welfare change per period as given by the equivalent consumption change in percentage points evaluated at the low inflation equilibrium π_1.

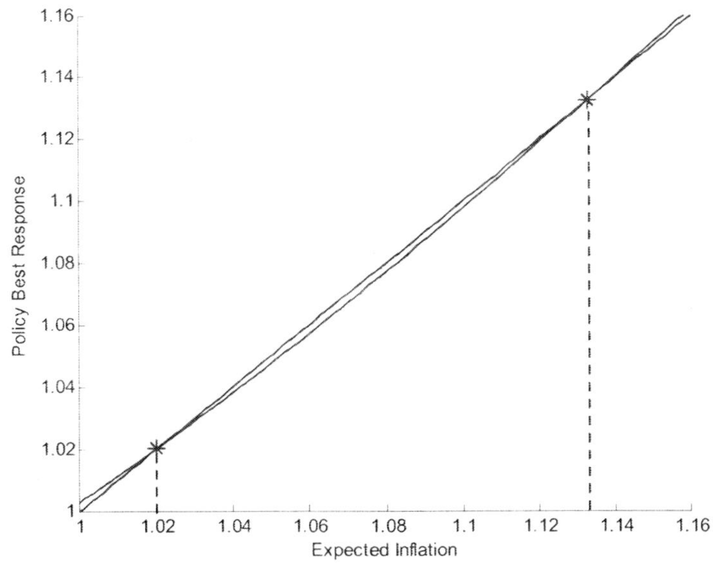

Figure 2: Expectation Traps in a Calibrated Economy

[15] In the Appendix we provide the details of our calibration.

[16] Indeed, firm production is identical when inflation is equal to β, the optimal monetary policy, as firms do not differ in productivity in this numerical illustration.

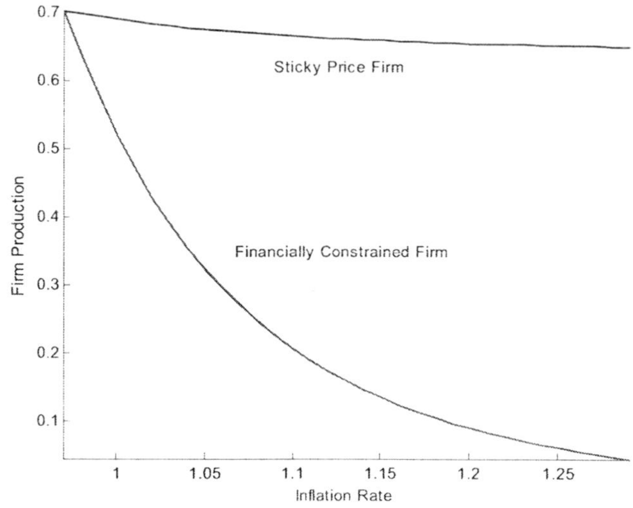

Figure 3: Intermediate Good Output for Firms i= 1, 2.

In our baseline calibration, with a low inflation of 2%, the welfare impact of an equilibrium shift is about three times the welfare gains of removing the classic inflation bias. The overall magnitude of welfare losses is significant but not large. The situation is similar for alternative calibrations.[17]

How common are expectations traps? Several papers find multiple equilibria in a variety of monetary economies. All of them focus on Markov perfect equilibria and so none of the equilibrium multiplicity results hinge on trigger strategies. Albanesi (2003) explores a cash/credit good model and show that monetary policy discretion may lead to expectation traps. King and Wolman (2004) also finds multiple equilibria in a simple new Keynesian model with two-period staggered pricing. Siu (2004) allows firms to set their degree of price stickiness and shows that, once again, equilibrium multiplicity arises. Finally, Armenter (2004) argues that the necessary conditions for the existence of expectation traps are very general.

Table 1. Welfare Implications: Several Calibrations.

Low Inflation	High Inflation	Welfare Change per period	
π_1	π_2	From π_1 to π^r	From π_2 to π_1
1.5 %	14.4 %	.11 %	.43 %
2 %	13.2 %	.12 %	.36 %
2.5 %	12.2 %	.13 %	.31 %
3 %	11.5 %	.14 %	.27 %

Welfare changes computed as percentage points of consumption at equilibrium inflation π_1. See the Appendix for calibration details.

[17] We also mentioned the possibility of expectation shifts. Rigorously speaking, this possibility is ruled out by our definition of Markov equilibrium. However, it is possible to relax the Markov restriction to allow for sunspots equilibria without allowing trigger strategies.

Armenter and Brodenstein (2004) perform a thorough characterization of expectation traps in a closed economy version. The main finding is that for all parameterizations with an equilibrium inflation rate between 2% and 2.5%, there is an additional Markov equilibrium with higher inflation. This property of the model is robust and it does not rely upon large nominal frictions.

3.2 The Case for Soft Exchange Rate Pegs

Expectation traps do not conflict with monetary policy flexibility. With respect to exchange rate policy, a soft peg with appropriately chosen bands is sufficient to rule out expectation traps, yet it allows to the monetary authority to react to real shocks.

To see this, consider an inflation cap $\bar{\pi}$ strictly below the high inflation equilibrium, $\bar{\pi} < \pi_2$, but strictly above the low inflation equilibrium rate, $\pi_1 < \bar{\pi}$. Such a cap exists because the Markov equilibria are locally unique. Assume the cap is an exogenous constraint: the monetary authority cannot validate high inflation expectations even if it would like to. Therefore the low inflation equilibrium π_l becomes the unique Markov equilibrium of the economy.[18]

Next we show how to implement a given inflation cap $\bar{\pi}$ with an exchange rate policy Σ. Combining (10) with (12), we obtain

$$\frac{w(s)\pi}{0_x} = \varepsilon(s)p^*$$

In any Markov equilibrium, $\bar{\pi} = \pi$. Using (20) and some algebra,

$$\frac{\eta}{0_x}\left[\left(\tilde{\mu}_1 + \tilde{\mu}_3 + \tilde{\mu}_m\, \eta^{\frac{\eta}{\eta-1}}\right)\pi^{\frac{\eta}{1-\eta}} + \tilde{\mu}_2\, \beta^{\frac{\eta}{1-\eta}}\right]^{\frac{1-\eta}{\eta}} = \in(s)\pi^* \tag{23}$$

where we use the normalization that $p^* = \pi^*$. The left hand side is an increasing function in inflation. Hence, there is a one-to-one relationship between inflation and the nominal exchange rate for given π^*. Thus, it is possible to implement any inflation cap $\bar{\pi}$ with the proper choice of the exchange rate policy $\Sigma = \left\{\varepsilon : \varepsilon \leq \bar{\varepsilon}\right\}$, where

---

[18] The inflation cap does not constitute a Markov equilibrium by itself because, for all $\hat{\pi} \in (\pi_1, \pi_2)$, $\pi^*\left(\hat{\pi}\right) < \hat{\pi}$, i.e., the policy best response is always below inflation expectations. This property is specific to a two Markov equilibria economy

$$\varepsilon = \frac{\eta}{\pi^{*} 0_x} \left[\left(\tilde{\mu}_1 + \tilde{\mu}_3 + \tilde{\mu}_m \eta^{\frac{\eta}{\eta-1}} \right) \bar{\pi}^{\frac{\eta}{1-\eta}} + \tilde{\mu}_2 \beta^{\frac{\eta}{1-\eta}} \right]^{\frac{1-\eta}{\eta}}$$

and $\pi_1 < \bar{\pi} < \pi_2$. Note there is a continuum of inflation caps that effectively rule out the high inflation equilibrium, so the soft exchange rate policy is not uniquely determined.

A soft exchange rate regime improves welfare even if it does not correct the classic inflation bias, i.e., it does not implement the optimal monetary policy. First, the monetary authority cannot be caught in the high inflation equilibrium. Second, there will be no volatility arising from expectation shifts.

Moreover, the exchange rate bands can be wide enough so they allow considerable monetary policy flexibility. In our calibration, the difference between the low and high equilibrium inflation rates is about ten percentage points. This leaves plenty of room for policy responses to plausible real shocks. Hence, absent any other considerations and leaving the inflation bias unchanged, the classic textbook argument a la Mundell-Fleming favors broad bands to a hard exchange rate pegs. We challenge this view in the next section.

4. PERVERSE POLICY RESPONSES

The textbook argument against fixed exchange rates builds on the classic Mundell-Fleming analysis. A fixed exchange rate regime means no independent monetary policy. The monetary authority loses its ability to react to real shocks and ends up `` importing'' the foreign monetary policy. The loss of flexibility is often seen as the downside of the gains that the commitment to a fixed exchange rate can provide.

We argue that the Mundell-Fleming argument does not hold for the case of monetary policy without commitment. We show that the policy response to certain real shocks can be perverse, i.e., worse than inaction, as shocks exacerbate the time inconsistency problem. Independent monetary policy is no guarantee for lower macroeconomic volatility.

The intuition behind a perverse policy response is quite general. A real shock can increase the welfare gains from unexpected inflation. Consequently, firms anticipate higher inflation. The monetary authority reacts, rightfully, to the real shock but also reacts, unnecessarily, to the induced change in private sector expectations. If the latter dominates, the equilibrium policy response leads to a worsening of the inflation bias and to welfare inferior allocations.

We focus on a negative terms of trade shock because of its appeal for developing economies, where the case for fixed exchange rates is often built upon time inconsistency issues.[19] A negative terms of trade shock contracts the open intermediate sector, which is characterized by perfect competition. As a result, the economy is less competitive, the

[19] We spare the reader of a re-formulation of the private sector equilibrium with uncertainty. The extension is trivial. The shock is treated as a zero-probability event, which emphasizes the positive role of stabilization policy.

distortion from monopolistic competition is larger and so is the temptation to cut markups with unexpected inflation.

To see this, we compute an `` aggregate'' markup κ by dividing the final good price by the aggregate marginal cost of production. In the Appendix, we detail the construction of the aggregate markup and show that

$$\kappa = \frac{\left[\left(\frac{\mu_1 y_1}{y} + \frac{\mu_2 y_2}{y} R^{\frac{1}{1-\eta}} + \frac{\mu_3 y_3}{y}\right)\left(\frac{1}{\eta}\right)^{\frac{1}{1-\eta}} + \frac{\mu_m y_m}{y}\right]^{1-\eta}}{\left[\left(\frac{\mu_1 y_1}{y} + \frac{\mu_2 y_2}{y} R^{\frac{1}{1-\eta}} + \frac{\mu_3 y_3}{y}\right) + \frac{\mu_m y_m}{y}\right]^{1-\eta}}$$

For simplicity we assume that all firms have identical productivity. The aggregate markup is a geometric average of the monopolistic sectors, with markup $\frac{1}{\eta} > 1$, and the perfect competitive sectors, with no markup.

In response to a negative terms of trade shock, imports contract in relative terms, i.e., $\frac{ym}{y}$ falls as the relative price of imports goes up.[20] The aggregate markup increases as the competitive sector is weighted less. In the Appendix we show that the markup is decreasing in $\frac{ym}{y}$.

The assumption that the tradeable sector is competitive is important. One possible motivation is that the country's exports are not differentiated and hence export prices p_x are set in the world markets. This particularly suits a developing economy framework.

We illustrate the perverse policy phenomenon in the calibrated version of our model. We compare a fixed and flexible exchange rate regime in the event of a unanticipated and permanent negative terms of trade shock. The fixed exchange rate regime is modeled as an Exchange Rate Policy equilibrium with $\Sigma = \left\{\bar{\varepsilon}\right\}$. For the flexible exchange rate regime, we use our concept of Markov equilibrium. Since there are usually multiple Markov equilibria, we pick the one with lowest inflation.[21]

In order to abstract from the classic inflation bias, we set the world inflation rate π^* such that the flexible and the fixed exchange rate regime deliver the same allocations in the pre-shock economy. In other words, there are no `` level'' gains in terms of inflation under a fixed

---

[20] The measure of firms μ_m is an exogenous parameter and stays constant. However, production y_m is endogenous and it adjusts to the shock.

[21] Alternatively, the reader can think of a comparison between a soft and a hard exchange rate regime. The former would be characterized by exchange rate bands chosen to rule out the high inflation equilibrium and to allow enough flexibility, as documented in the previous section.

exchange rate regime as the world inflation rate is set equal to the inflation rate π_l in the low inflation Markov equilibrium.

We model the terms of trade shock as unforeseen. This is the best scenario for active monetary policy. By adjusting inflation, the monetary authority can ease the impact of a real shock. The stabilization role ends after one period once all firms have had a chance to re-set their prices.

We also assume that the shock is permanent. We then report all welfare computations per period. Hence the assumption that the shock is permanent has no impact beyond providing us with at least one period where the shock is unanticipated and one period where the shock is anticipated by the sticky price firms.

The timing of the shock is as follows. At date $t = 0$, the economy is in the original steady state. The terms of trade deteriorate by 1% after firms of type 1 have set their sticky price for date $t = 1$ but before the monetary authority policy decision. Hence, there is a stabilization role for monetary policy. At date $t = 2$, sticky price firms are aware that the shock is permanent and they set their prices accordingly. Prices and allocations reach the new steady state at date $t = 2$.[22]

Figure 4 is titled "Equilibrium Response to a Negative Terms of Trade Shock". It contains six graphs. In each of the graphs, the x-axis is labeled "Periods" and runs from 0 to 3 in increments of 1. In the top left graph, the y-axis is labeled "Inflation" and runs form 1.015 to 1.035. A dashed horizontal line runs where inflation is 1.02. The curve in the graph is not smooth; it connects the points given at the integer time periods. At period 0, inflation has a value of 1.02. At period 1, inflation has a value of about 1.021. At periods 2 and 3, inflation has a value of 1.0325. In the top right graph, the y-axis is labeled "Shock" and runs form 0.98 to 1.005. A dashed horizontal line runs where the shock is 1. The curve in the graph is not smooth; it connects the points given at the integer time periods. At period 0, shock has a value of 1. At periods 1, 2 and 3, the shock has a value of 0.99. In the middle left graph, the y-axis is labeled "Labor" and runs from -0.0015 to 0 in increments of 0.0005. A dashed horizontal line runs where labor is 0. There are two curves in this graph; neither is smooth. The curves connect the points given at integer time periods. The first curve has a labor value of 0 at period 0. At period 1, the curve has a labor value of -0.0001. At periods 2 and 3, the curve has a labor value of -0.0011. The second curve has a labor value of 0 at period 0. At period 1, the curve has a labor value of -0.0003. At periods 2 and 3, the curve has a labor value of - 0.00025. In the middle right graph, the y-axis is labeled "Wage" and runs from -0.0008 to 0 in increments of 0.0002. A dashed horizontal line runs where wage is 0. There are two curves in this graph; neither is smooth. The curves connect the point given at integer time periods. The first curve has a wage value of 0 at period 0. At period 1, the curve has a wage value of - 0.00005. At periods 2 and 3, the curve has a wage value of -0.00079. The second curve has a wage value of 0 at period 0. At period 1, the curve has a wage value of -0.00022. At period 2 and 3, the curve has a wage value of -0.0002. In the bottom left graph, the y-axis is labeled "Output" and runs from -0.004 to 0 in increments of 0.001. A dashed horizontal line runs

[22] We need to be more precise about our terms of trade shock. Given a change in the relative price of exports and imports, there are many possible changes in the price levels. We pick the change in the price levels such that, given a constant monetary policy, the ratio of domestic to world inflation remains constant. In other words, we abstract from non-policy induced real exchange rate movements which may occur simultaneously with a terms of trade shock.

where output is 0. There are two curves in the graph; neither is smooth. The curves connect the point given at integer time periods. The first curve has an output value of 0 at period 0. At period 1, the curve has an output value of -0.002. At periods 2 and 3, the curve has an output value of -0.0035. The second curve has an output value of 0 at period 0. At periods 1, 2, and 3, the curve has an output value of -0.0022. In the bottom right graph, the y-axis is labeled "Aggregate Productivity" and runs from -0.0025 to 0 in increments of 0.0005. A dashed horizontal line runs where aggregate productivity is 0. There are two curves in the graph; neither is smooth. The curves connect the point given at integer time periods. The first curve has an aggregate productivity value of 0 at period 0. At period 1, the curve has a value of -0.0018. At periods 2 and 3, the curve has a value of -0.0022. The second curve has an aggregate productivity of 0 at period 0. At periods 1, 2, and 3, the curve has a value of -0.0018.

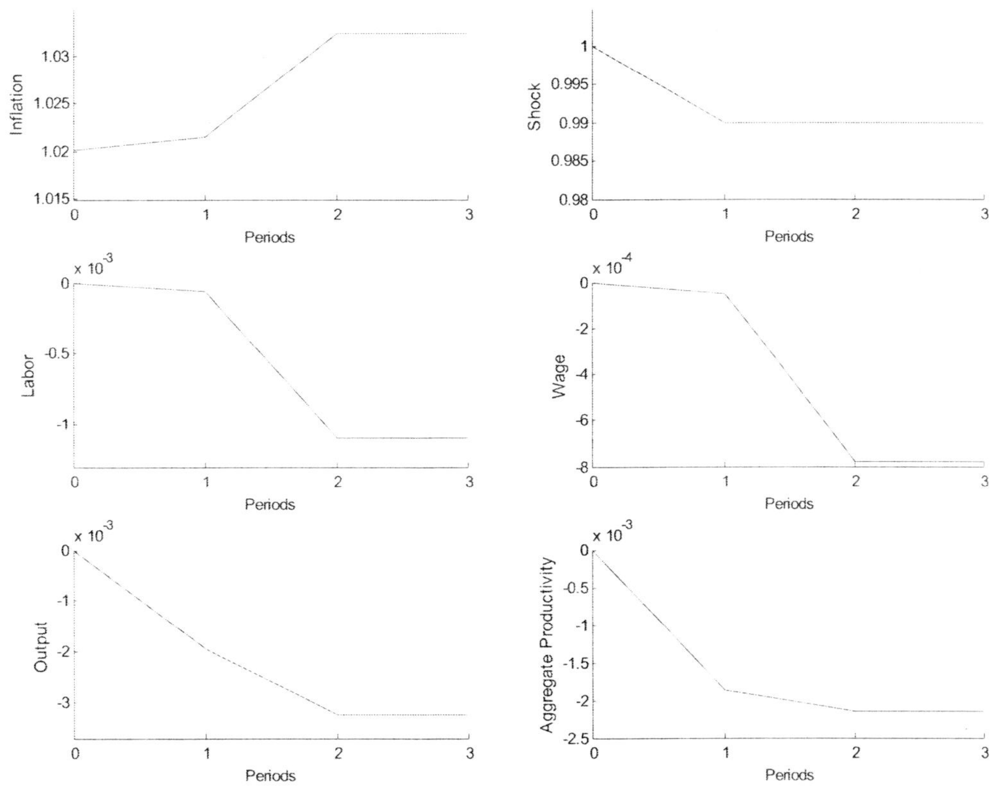

Figure 4: Equilibrium Response to a Negative Terms of Trade Shock. Solid line correspond to the low inflation Markov equilibrium. Dashed line corresponds to a fixed exchange rate regime. See text for details.

Figure 4 displays the response of selected prices and allocations. The solid line corresponds to the Markov equilibrium and the dashed line to the ERP equilibrium with $\Sigma = \left\{ \bar{\varepsilon} \right\}$. The most important graph is in the upper left corner and it displays the inflation rate. Under the fixed exchange rate inflation is constant. Under independent monetary policy, inflation increases in two steps. At date $t = 1$, there is a small inflation increase. This is the optimal response induced by the presence of nominal frictions.[23] However, at date $t=2$ inflation jumps by a large amount in the Markov equilibrium, when there is no longer a role for monetary policy to ease the real shock. From date $t=2$ onwards, high inflation only reflects higher sticky prices.[24] This response is clearly welfare reducing.

Prices and allocations tell the same story. At date $t=1$, the policy response in the Markov equilibrium keeps the wage and labor close to their steady state values despite the shock, while under the fixed exchange rate there is no smoothing. However, from date $t=2$ onwards, the impact is more pronounced under flexible exchange rate regime. Higher expected inflation brings wage, labor and output below their counterparts under the fixed exchange rate regime.

Table 2 compares the welfare properties of both exchange rate regimes. We report the per period consumption compensation, in percentage points, for a shift from the fixed exchange rate regime to the Markov equilibrium. A negative number means that households are willing to pay to keep the fixed exchange rate regime for the given period. We include several calibrations: we report the corresponding Markov equilibrium inflation rate in the pre-shock economy. In each calibration, the world inflation rate is set such that the flexible and the fixed exchange rate have the same welfare properties in the pre-shock economy.

At date $t=1$, right after the negative terms of trade shock, the Markov equilibrium dominates the fixed exchange rate. The welfare difference, though, is quite small. From date $t=2$ onwards, the fixed exchange rate equilibrium is welfare dominant. The welfare gains from a fixed exchange rate at date $t=2$ are about three times the welfare losses at date $t=1$. These are per period welfare changes. So even if the shock lasted only two periods, the fixed exchange rate would be preferred. Under the assumption of a permanent shock, we should multiply the welfare change at date $t=2$ by $\frac{1}{1-\beta}\approx 34$.

The impact of a positive terms of trade shock is not symmetric. Table 2 also reports the welfare ranking in the aftermath of a positive shock to the terms of trade. In this event, the flexible exchange rate is welfare superior both at date $t=1$ and $t=2$. However, the welfare implications under positive and negative shocks do not cancel each other. As shown in Table 2, a positive terms of trade shock brings welfare gains which are about half the welfare loss under a negative terms of trade shock. This is a direct consequence of the concavity of the policy problem.

To summarize, Table 2 clearly speaks in favor of fixed exchange rates in the event of a real shock--a scenario usually associated with the costs of losing monetary independence.

[23] This is the ex-post optimal response: the monetary authority is a benevolent policymaker. The Ramsey policy in a stochastic economy would not necessarily look alike. First, the response would be evaluated around the Friedman rule, which is the optimal level of inflation. Second, if the terms of trade shock had a positive probability of occurring, the Ramsey policy would have ex-ante considerations.

[24] Date $t=0$ and $t=3$ are, effectively, two steady states. Hence, the model implies a negative relationship between inflation and openness. Romer (1993) finds cross-country evidence of this relationship.

Table 2: Welfare Comparison: Markov equilibrium versus fixed exchange rate in the event of a terms of trade shock.

	Date $t=0$ *Inflation Rate*:		
Period	$\pi=2.0$	$\pi=2.5$	$\pi=3.0$
Date $t=0$	0	0	0
Negative Shock:			
Date $t=1$	0.00015	0.00016	0.00017
Date $t=2$	-0.0393	-0.0597	-0.0912
Positive Shock:			
Date $t=1$	0.00014	0.00016	0.00017
Date $t=2$	0.0241	0.0296	0.0348

Welfare changes reported as percentage points of consumption under non-stochastic economy. Values per period.

4.1 Other Shocks

A terms of trade shock is not the sole instance of a perverse policy response. Consider a negative shock to the financially constrained firm's sector. We have in mind an exogenous tightening of financial constraints, perhaps due to a banking crisis.

Figure 5 shows the response of selected prices and allocations to a unexpected fall in the productivity of financially constrained firms of 1%. The monetary response in date $t=1$, right after the shock, eases the impact on the wage rate and output. However, once sticky price firms adjust their prices, the resulting policy response leads to further, unnecessary inflation. Wage rate and output are significantly lower then.

Table 3: Welfare Comparison: Markov equilibrium versus fixed exchange rate in the event of a shock to financially constrained firms.

Period	*Date* $t=0$ *Inflation Rate* $\pi=2.0$
Date $t=0$	0
Negative Shock:	
Date $t=1$	0.00041
Date $t=2$	-0.0705
Positive Shock:	
Date $t=1$	0.00047
Date $t=2$	0.0388

Welfare changes reported as percentage points of consumption under non-stochastic economy. Values per period.

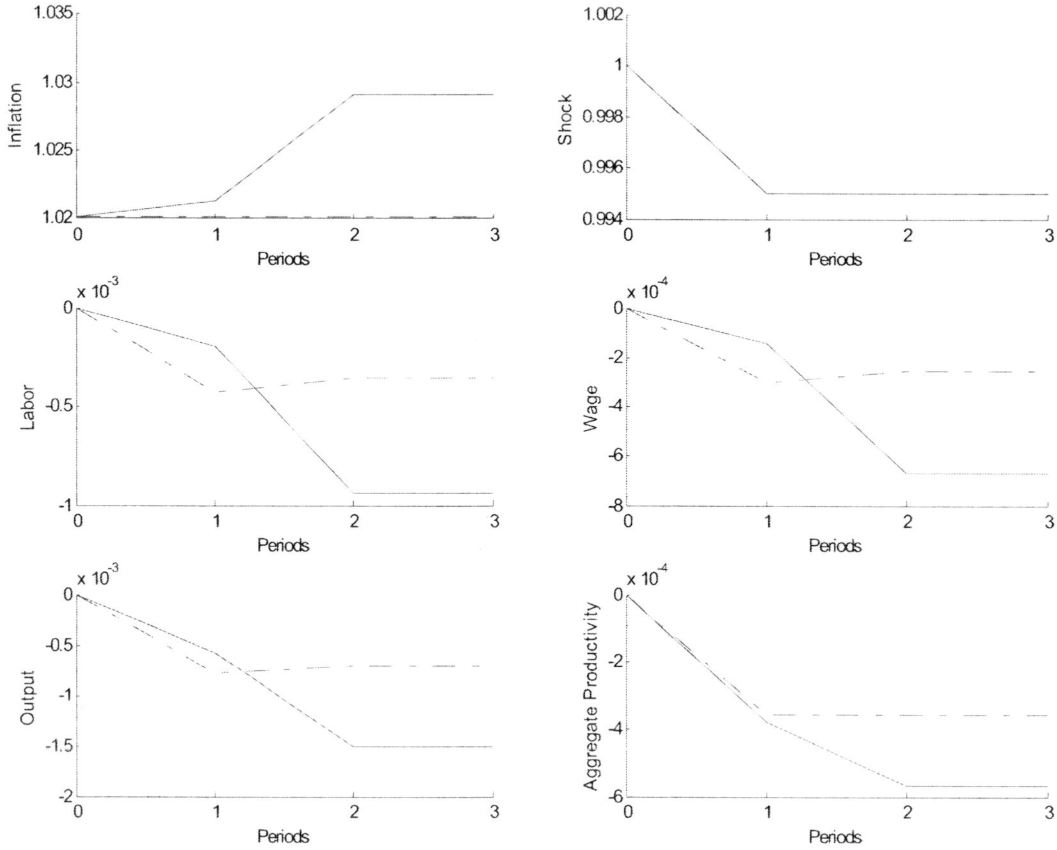

Figure 5: Equilibrium Response to a Negative Productivity Shock in Financially Constrained Firms. Solid line correspond to the low inflation Markov equilibrium. Dashed line corresponds to a fixed exchange rate regime. See text for details.

The welfare properties of the two exchange rate regimes--shown in Table 3--are not surprising. In the event of a negative shock, a fixed exchange rate shock is clearly preferred: the welfare loss associated with independent monetary policy from date $t = 2$ onwards is much larger than any welfare gains from stabilization. Due to concavity, the fixed exchange rate retains its welfare dominance even if positive and negative shocks are equiprobable.

We do not claim that a fixed exchange rate is welfare superior in the event of any shock. In some cases, stabilization is very important or the shock leaves the monetary authority's incentives unchanged. However, our robustness exercises suggest that it is the persistence of shocks that triggers the perverse policy response. Estimated real shocks typically have a half-life of over two years, which leaves no doubt that these shocks are highly persistent.

5. Conclusion

This paper contributes to the exchange rate regime debate but by no means settles it. A definitive welfare ranking of exchange rate regimes is more elusive than ever. Expectation traps and perverse policy responses increase the complexity of any welfare evaluation of exchange rate regimes--yet any such evaluation is incomplete without considering both phenomena.

The world-wide downward trend in inflation does not mean that the credibility problems are a thing of the past--and so is the case for a fixed exchange rate regime. A low inflation country may be only a shift in expectations away from high inflation. Moreover, large real volatility does not necessarily make a stronger case for a flexible exchange rate. We have to ask first what is the impact of the relevant real shocks on the time inconsistency problem and how likely is it that independent monetary policy reacts perversely.

We have abstracted from the time consistency of the exchange rate policy itself in order to highlight the credibility problems under a flexible exchange rates. Certainly, we do not think that an exchange rate regime is free of credibility problems. Trying to sustain a fixed exchange rate absent commitment can lead to self-fulfilling currency crises, as discussed in Obstfeld (1996)--although, as our paper points out, a flexible exchange rate can lead to self-fulfilling currency crises, too. Hence, a country may be left only with an extreme solution such as dollarization.

Yet, it is often the case that fixed exchange rates are brought down by fiscal rather than monetary crises. We do not view fixed exchange rates as a solution to fiscal problems. The ongoing skepticism about fixed exchange rate credibility arises very much from using the wrong tool for the wrong problem.

REFERENCES

Albanesi, S., Chari, V. and Christiano, L. J.: 2003, Expectation traps and monetary policy, *The Review of Economic Studies* 70(4), 715—742.

Armenter, R.: 2004, A general theory (and some evidence) of expectation traps in monetary policy. Working Paper, Federal Reserve Bank of New York.

Armenter, R. and Bodenstein, M.: 2004, Can the U.S. monetary policy fall (again) in an expectation trap? Working Paper, Federal Reserve Bank of New York.

Barro, R. J. and Gordon, D.: 1983, A positive theory of monetary policy in a natural rate model, *Journal of Political Economy* 91(4), 589—610.

Calvo, G. A. and Reinhart, C. M.: 2002, Fear of floating, *Quarterly Journal of Economics 117(2), 379—408.*

Chang, R. and Velasco, A.: 2000, Exchange-rate policy for developing countries, *The American Economic Review 90(2), 71—75.*

Chang, R. and Velasco, A.: 2003, Dollarization: Analytical issues, in E. Levy Yeyati and F. Sturzenegger (eds), *Dollarization, MIT Press, Cambridge, Mass. and London, pp.* 53—75.

Chari, V., Christiano, L. J. and Eichenbaum, M.: 1998, Expectation traps and discretion, *Journal of Economic Theory* 81(2), 462—492.

Clarida, R., Gali, J. and Gertler, M.: 1999, The science of monetary policy: A new Keynesian perspective, *Journal of Economic Literature* 37(4), 1661—1707.

Cooley, T. F. and Quadrini, V.: 2001, The costs of losing monetary independence: The case of Mexico, *Journal of Money, Credit and Banking* 33(2), 370—397.

Devereux, M. B. and Engel, C.: 2003, Monetary policy in the open economy revisited: Price setting and exchange rate-flexibility, *Review of Economic Studies* 70, 765—783.

Duarte, M. and Obstfeld, M.: 2005, Monetary policy in the open economy revisited: The case for exchange-rate flexibility restored. mimeo, Federal Reserva Bank of Richmond.

Dupor, B.: 2003, Optimal random monetary policy with nominal rigidity, *Journal of Economic Theory 112(1), 66—78.*

Frankel, J. A.: 1998, *No Single Currency Regime is Right for All Countries or at All Times,* number 215, Princeton University Press, Princeton. Essays in International Finance.

King, R. G. and Wolman, A. L.: 2004, Monetary discretion, pricing complementarity and dynamic multiple equilibria, *Quarterly Journal of Economics* 119(4), 1513—1553.

Mendoza, E. G.: 2001, The benefits of dollarization when stabilization policy lacks credibility and financial markets are imperfect, *Journal of Money, Credit and Banking 33(2), 440—474.*

Obstfeld, M.: 1996, Models of currency crises with self-fulfilling features, *European Economic Review 40, 1037—48.*

Obstfeld, M. and Rogo , K.: 1996, *Foundations of International Macroeconomics,* The MIT Press, Cambridge, Massachusetts.

Rogo , K. S.: 2003, Globalization and global disinflation, *Monetary Policy and Uncertainty: Adapting to a Changing Economy*, Federal Reserve Bank of Kansas City.

Romer, D.: 1993, Openness and inflation: Theory and evidence, *The Quarterly Journal of Economics 108(4), 869—903.*

Siu, H. E.: 2004, Time consistent monetary policy with endogenous price rigidity. Working Paper, University of British Columbia.

Svensson, L. E. O.: 1997, Optimal inflation targets, "conservative" central banks, and linear inflation contracts, *The American Economic Review* 87(1), 98—114.

Woodford, M.: 2003, *Interest and Prices*, Princeton University Press, Princeton.

A APPENDIX

A.1 Calibration

We start by setting the preference parameters to standard values. The inverse of β is the real interest rate in our economy: we set it equal to 3%, $\beta = .9709$, which means evaluating the model at the annual frequency.

Our choice for leisure preferences is

$$h(1-n) = \psi_0 \frac{(1-n)^{1-\psi}}{1-\psi}$$

Our parameters on the labor supply are set to match a Frisch labor elasticity of 1 and the Aristotelian proportion of leisure and work to $n = \frac{1}{2}$ in the first best.

We set the share of nontradeable goods at 60% and the share of export firms at 12%. The last of the pre-set parameters is η, which is set to replicate a 12% markup.

We calibrate the measure of firms of type 1 and 2 to match a 1.5%-3% range in the low inflation equilibrium. In every case we find a second equilibrium with inflation in the range of 11%-15%. We find that we can match these numbers with reasonable parameter values. The share of firms with sticky prices is about 12%, and the measure of financially constrained firms is just above 5%.

Our parameter choices are summarized in Table 4.

Table 4: Baseline Calibration.

Parameter	*Notation*	*Value*
Intertemporal Discount Rate	β	.9709
Leisure-Consumption	ψ_0	.5
Inverse Frisch Labor Elasticity	ψ	1
Share of Non Tradeables	α	.6
Inverse Markup	η	1.12^{-1}
Measure of Firms $i=1$	μ_1	.12
Measure of Firms $i=2$	μ_2	.0552
Measure of Firms $i=x$	μ_x	.12

A.2 THE AGGREGATE MARKUP

In order to provide some insight on the perverse policy response phenomenon, we compute an aggregate markup. From the final good firm's profit maximization problem, we write the corresponding cost minimization problem:

$$\min_{\{y_i\}^{1-\mu_x}} \int_0^{1-\mu_x} p_i^y(s)\, y_i\, di$$

subject to

$$y \leq \left[\int_0^{1-\mu_x} y_i^{\eta}\, di\right]^{\frac{1}{\eta}}$$

The first order condition is

$$p_i^y(s)^{\frac{1}{1-\eta}} \frac{yi}{y} = \lambda^{\frac{1}{1-\eta}}$$

where λ is the Lagrangian multiplier associated with the technological constraint, which equals the marginal cost of one unit of final good. The previous condition is necessary for all $y_i > 0$. Hence,

$$\left[\int_0^{1-\mu_x} p_i^y(s)^{\frac{1}{1-\eta}} \frac{y_i}{y} di\right]^{1-\eta} = \lambda$$

gives the marginal cost as a geometric weighted average of each intermediate good price.

We compute the markup in a Markov equilibrium. We substitute the pricing formula for each price to obtain:

$$\lambda = \left[\mu_1 \frac{y_1}{y}\left(\frac{w}{\eta 0_1}\right)^{\frac{1}{1-\eta}} + \mu_2 \frac{y_2}{y}\left(\frac{wR}{\eta 0_2}\right)^{\frac{1}{1-\eta}} + \mu_3 \frac{y_3}{y}\left(\frac{w}{\eta 0_3}\right)^{\frac{1}{1-\eta}} + \mu_m \frac{y_m}{y}\left(q(s)p_m^*\right)^{\frac{1}{1-\eta}}\right]^{1-\eta}$$

Absent differences in productivity, i.e., $0_1 = 1$ for all goods, this simplifies to

$$\lambda = w\left[\left(\mu_1 \frac{y_1}{y} + \mu_2 \frac{y_2}{y} R^{\frac{1}{1-\eta}} + \mu_3 \frac{y_3}{y}\right)\left(\frac{1}{\eta}\right)^{\frac{1}{1-\eta}} + \mu_x \frac{y_x}{y}\right]^{1-\eta}$$

We do not want to mix the price distortions and the markup distortion. The (social) marginal cost of producing one unit of the final good, given the current price distortions, is

$$\tilde{\lambda} = w\left[\left(\mu_1 \frac{y_1}{y} + \mu_2 \frac{y_2}{y} R^{\frac{1}{1-\eta}} + \mu_3 \frac{y_3}{y}\right) + \mu_x \frac{y_m}{y}\right]^{1-\eta}$$

Since the final good producer is competitive, λ is also the final good price. We set our aggregate markup definition as $\kappa \equiv \lambda / \tilde{\lambda}$.

To see that κ is decreasing with y_m / y, note that $\left(\frac{1}{\eta}\right)^{\frac{1}{1-\eta}} > 1$ and apply simple differential calculus.

In: International Finance and Financial Services
Editor: Kristian L. Hagen, pp. 71-98
ISBN: 1-60021-756-7

Chapter 3

ASYMMETRY IN THE INTEREST-RATE VOLATILITY TRANSMISSION MECHANISM: THE GERMAN LEADERSHIP HYPOTHESIS*

Nikiforos T. Laopodis**
Assoc. Professor of Finance, School of Business, Department of Finance. Fairfield University, North Benson Rd, Fairfield, CT 06824, USA

ABSTRACT

This paper investigates the volatility transmission mechanism within the European Monetary System (EMS) and concentrates on the German 'Leadership Hypothesis'. The empirical analysis is carried out via short-term interest rates for six European countries, namely Belgium, France, Germany, Italy, the Netherlands, and the United Kingdom, and one outside country, the United States, for the March 1972 to December 2002 period. The results essentially support the idea of a German predominance within the European Monetary System, but not in a strict sense, since Germany's short-term rates are also affected by actions from its European counterparts. When including the U.S. short-term interest rate, neither the German nor the U.S. rates surface as prevalent players in the interest-rate volatility transmission mechanism. This is explained by the fact that during Germany's post-unification era (after July 1990), the EMS and U.S. monetary policies were diverging rather than converging. This is also supported by the fact that the EMS countries (excluding the U.K.) were making serious strides to converge among themselves in preparation for the upcoming monetary union with a single currency. Another notable finding refers to the absence of asymmetric behavior within EMS after Germany's reunification, attributed to the rapid economic convergence of the EMS countries.

---

* This paper is an expanded version of my paper, titled 'European and International Asymmetry in the Volatility Transmission Mechanism: the 'German Dominance Hypothesis' revisited', which will appear in the *Journal of Economics and Business* 56(2), 2004, pp. 75-97. The usual disclaimer applies.

** E-mail address: nlaopodis@mail.fairfield.edu. Tel. (203) 254-4000 ext. 3273. Fax: (203) 254-4105

1. INTRODUCTION

The purpose of creating the European Monetary System (EMS) in March of 1979 was to alleviate the damaging effects of exchange rate volatility that surfaced since the collapse of the Bretton Woods system of fixed exchange rates in 1973. Although the original intention of the EMS was to have all member countries share the burden of adjustments to disequilibria equally, in reality the economically weaker countries frequently intervened in the foreign exchange markets to maintain their currency's pegs more often than Germany, the strongest member. As a result, Germany surfaced as the anchor in the conduct of monetary policy, thus generating asymmetric behavior within the system (that is, European asymmetry). Another type of asymmetry arises when disturbances in the monetary policies of countries outside the EMS affect the monetary policies of the EMS countries via their effects on their leader, i.e., Germany. This type is referred to as international asymmetry. Asymmetric behavior within EMS gave rise to the notion of German dominance or Leadership Hypothesis (GLH) whereby the Bundesbank independently fixes the benchmark level of interest rates against the U.S. dollar within the system, while the other member countries (or the 'periphery') stabilize the parity of their currency vis-à-vis the Deutschemark (DM). Hence, the fact that the other countries followed the Bundesbank's leadership suggests that the EMS was a *de facto* DM zone.

The evidence on both types of asymmetric behavior and the GLH, which has been presented by numerous authors, is mixed. There are several reasons for this. First, most of the empirical studies have employed techniques focusing primarily on the first moment (i.e., the conditional mean) and completely ignoring the second moment (i.e., the conditional variance) of the distribution (as in this case) of an asset's price changes. As a result, these studies did not examine whether disturbances emanating from a particular market generated meaningful information in other markets, that is, whether they determined if any simultaneous volatility spillovers among markets existed. However, it has been proven that the volatility structure of a series is more important in analyzing spillover effects. Second, these studies investigated the GLH without taking into account the dramatic changes in the EMS during the 1990s. There are several examples of such changes in the structure/nature of the EMS. First, Europe witnessed Germany's unification in July 1990. Second, evidence suggests that market fundamentals have changed since the early 1990s in view of the anticipated monetary unification of the EMS members as member countries embarked in the process of convergence based on the Maastricht Treaty criteria in 1994 [see Laopodis (1998, 2001)]. Finally, following the European Monetary Union, member countries began using the Euro as of January 1999.

However, a more important limitation of these studies is that they have employed univariate methodologies such as Granger causality tests and bivariate vector auto regressions as well as imposed restrictions on the nature of the relationships among magnitudes. Specifically, although these models are usually helpful in capturing short-term temporal causality, they do not lend themselves to policy analysis. Additionally, inferences about the extent and nature of disturbances stemming from one market and spilling over to other markets cannot be analyzed within a univariate setting because their impact surfaces as weak under the conventional vector autoregressive family of models. Rather, a multivariate framework is needed to adequately capture cross-market dynamics in the conditional variances of the respective markets. Nonetheless, despite the fact that the possible dynamic reciprocities and interactions across markets were ignored in past studies, these studies have significantly added to our understanding of the volatility transmission mechanism.

In view of the above observations, the purpose of this paper is to cast another look at the nature of the volatility transmission mechanism and re-examine the nature of the GLH, both within EMS and internationally. This task will be carried out via nominal short-term interest rates for the 1979 - 2002 period. More concretely, this paper will address the following issues. First, the nature of own and cross-market interactions will be examined. In other words, the analysis of the volatility spillover mechanism will be done within a multivariate framework which is suitable for capturing linkages and asymmetries that may exist in the volatility spillover mechanism. Hence, if these are present then negative innovations in a particular market, say in Germany, can produce higher volatility in the next market than do positive innovations of the same magnitude. The proposed model is essentially an extension of Nelson's (1991) Exponential GARCH methodology to the multivariate case. The model's advantage lies in its ability to examine all markets simultaneously and allows for own- and cross-market innovations to place an asymmetric impact on the volatility structure of a given market.

Second, the nature of disturbances (or innovations) and their impact will be investigated. This paper will look at the likelihood that the size of the innovation (i.e., quantity of the shock) and the sign of the innovation (i.e., the quality or nature of the shock) may be important ingredients in the volatility transfer mechanism across markets. Such a possibility has not been fully addressed in the empirical literature on the short-term interest rate transmission mechanism and is considered significant given evidence of asymmetric behavior in the volatility structure of a series [e.g., Koutmos and Booth (1995) and Laopodis (1998)].

Third, the paper will explicitly explore the ensuing effects of German reunification on the extent to which German short-term interest rates continue or not to carry any information about future changes in other EMS rates, and vice versa. This issue is significant in view of the economic convergence achieved by most of the EMS members in preparation for the (currently effective) monetary union. Moreover, GLH is still relevant from the perspective of the future design of the monetary policy within the European Union. Put differently, the presence of information dissemination from Germany to the rest of the European countries may parallel the linkages among the national monetary policy transmission channels. And fourth, the possibility that the true 'dominant player' may be outside the EMS, in view of the mixed results on GLH provided by the above-mentioned studies, will be explored. For this purpose, the U.S. short-term interest rates in the concurrent examination of all markets will be included. In this way, one can establish whether Germany retains its 'leadership' outside the system or it is overwhelmed by the presence of a larger, international leader.

The rest of the paper is organized as follows. Section II contains a literature review on the issue of European and international asymmetry. Section III continues with the description and the sources of the data, as well as some preliminary statistical investigation. Section IV lays out the methodological design and explains it. Section V presents the major empirical results and discusses them, whereas section VI summarizes the study and concludes with some general observations.

2. Literature Review

Since its inception in March 1979, the symmetric functioning of the European Monetary System was in doubt especially following the observation that the system was dominated by Germany's Central Bank, the Bundesbank. Consequently, the other EMS countries found themselves passively adjusting to the Bundesbank's policy actions, or giving up their monetary independence, thereby giving rise to the so-called 'European asymmetry'. Several studies have documented this behavior [e.g., Russo and Tullio (1998), Ungerer et *al.* (1990) and Griffiths and MacDonald (1994)].

European asymmetry has been diverse and has varied over the two decades of the operation of the EMS. For instance, asymmetric behavior within EMS emerged with respect to inflation determination, the distribution of intervention activity, interventions in the foreign exchange market and/or sterilization behavior, in monetary aggregates, and in interest-rate linkages (see Gros and Thygesen, 1999, pp. 168-177, for a brief description of each one of them). Regarding the first form of (the degree of) asymmetry within the system, the preponderance of the evidence points to a dominant role for Germany. For instance, Herz and Werner (1992) note that the inflation rates of the EMS countries were significantly influenced by Germany's monetary actions. France, Italy as well as Ireland found it convenient and advantageous to accept such actions as they would give them credibility in order to mitigate the costs of disinflation from implementing alternative, more restrictive monetary policies at home.

Asymmetric behavior in foreign exchange interventions has taken several shapes as Germany frequently intervened (at the margin) in the market for outside currencies such as the U.S. dollar, whereas the other EMS countries' central banks undertook intervention activities inside the EMS. Furthermore, another evidence of such disproportional behavior by the Bundesbank was the fact that it had not held significant amounts of EMS currencies and thus it would never be able to rely on its own foreign exchange reserves to support the DM within EMS. Studies reporting such behavior include Gros and Thygesen (1999) and Weber (1996).

Evidence on the asymmetry in sterilization behavior suggests that Germany embarked in the bulk of sterilization activities (between 60 and 80 percent of interventions in a quarter), while Italy and France did so only for 30 to 40 percent, respectively (see Mastropasqua et *al.*, 1988). Moreover, von Hagen's (1989) study concludes that in the short run the Bundesbank always sterilized foreign exchange interventions against the dollar, but not always EMS interventions. Regarding asymmetry in monetary aggregates, studies (using standard Granger causality tests) revealed a system of bilateral relationships in which Germany appears to have affected most of the EMS countries monetary base although there were instances of a reverse influence [e.g., Wyplosz (1989), Herz and Werner (1992)].

Finally, asymmetric behavior surfaced via the linkages of short-term interest rates since they have been regularly used as a means to conduct exchange rate policies in member countries. Evidence suggests that during pre-alignment periods, the burden of reversing exchange rate misalignments fell primarily on 'weaker' countries (such as France and Italy), and not on Germany, in an effort to ward off ruinous speculative attacks on their currencies. In this context, the studies by Fratianni and von Hagen (1990a,b), von Hagen and Fratianni (1990), Gardner and Perraudin (1993), Fujihara and Mougoué (1996), Kanas (1997), Ma and

Kanas (2000), Laopodis (2001) and Bajo-Rubio et *al.* (2001) favor a preeminent, although not a dominant, role for Germany within EMS. In particular, they find that although Germany influences some members' short-term interest rates significantly, like those of France and the Netherlands, other countries' rates reveal a much smaller impact from German interest rates. By contrast, other studies found an overpowering role for Germany in the conduct of monetary policy [e.g., Karfakis and Moschos (1990), Artus et *al.* (1991), Weber (1991), Herz and Werner (1992), Katsimbris and Miller (1993), and Gebauer et *al.* (1994)]. These authors conclude that Germany played a key role within EMS in setting the system's monetary policy, unilaterally.

International asymmetry arises when disturbances generated outside the EMS affect the EMS countries only via their effects on Germany (sometimes this is referred to as 'U.S. Dominance Hypothesis'). Additionally, the influence of the U.S. monetary policy on the EMS countries individually has not been fully contrasted with the corresponding influence from Germany's monetary policy within a multivariate framework which permits the interaction between the U.S. and Germany. There have been only a handful of studies testing international asymmetry the most notable of which are by Hassapis et *al.* (1999), Uctum (1999) and Laopodis (2004). Uctum finds support for European and international asymmetries before German reunification but not thereafter. By contrast, Hassapis et *al.* provide evidence of symmetry within EMS and U.S. dominance since the latter appears to influence the EMS rates directly and indirectly through its effects on Germany. Finally, Laopodis does not find evidence of international asymmetry within the system (when the U.S. is included only).

3. Data and Preliminary Statistical Investigation

3.1 Data Sources and Description

The sample consists of end-of-period, monthly, national short-term interest rates from March 1979 (in order to coincide with the beginning of the EMS operations) to August 2002 for Belgium, France, Germany, Italy, the Netherlands, the United Kingdom, and the United States. Data was gathered on three-month (Treasury bill) rates from sources such as the statistical tables of the Bundesbank's *Monthly Reports,* the IMF's monthly *International Financial Statistics* issues, the Federal Reserve's *FRED* online database, and the OECD's *Main Economic Indicators*, whenever necessary. The inclusion of the U.S. short-term rate in the sample allows the model to produce a true impact on all of the countries' interest rates (and not just on Germany's) given the fact that Germany has played a significant external role against these countries. Besides, the effects of the U.S. monetary policy on the EMS countries can now be compared to Germany's monetary policy conduct within a multivariate context that reflects (dynamic) monetary policy interactions among all three players.

The choice of nominal over real interest rates can be justified on the basis that the former variable can be more quickly and reliably controlled by monetary policy. It must be noted, however, that since the sample period corresponds with the years when extensive capital outflow controls were imposed by many of the countries under study there is a cause for concern about potential bias in the results. Besides, it has been argued [e.g., Chelley-Steeley,

Steeley and Pentecost (1998)] that the rate of transmission of innovations from one market to another would be less speedy under the presence of capital controls. However, as Karfakis and Moschos (1990) and Gros (1992) have pointed out, such controls were not necessarily limiting because market participants can easily circumvent them.

3.2 Unit Root Tests

Before we begin with the estimation of the model in section IV, we should check the variables for stationarity since lack thereof can make any inferences from empirical results deceptive. If each interest rate is found to be nonstationary, it would then suggest that it be differenced for conducting subsequent estimation. In this paper, we employ two approaches namely the Augmented Dickey-Fuller (1981), or ADF, and the Phillips-Perron (1988), or PP, tests for single unit roots. The ADF unit root test assumes that the error terms are uncorrelated. This test is conducted for the following regression equation:

$$\Delta r_t = \alpha_0 + \alpha_1 r_{t-1} + \alpha_2 \Sigma_i \Delta r_{t-i} + u_i \qquad (1)$$

where r_t denotes the nominal interest rate at time t and i are the number of lagged differences included to capture any autocorrelation. The latter number is selected so as the Ljung-Box portmanteau Q-statistic fails to reject the null hypothesis of no serial correlation in the residuals of equation (1). The test is a pseudo t-statistic for testing the null hypothesis that $\alpha_1 = 0$.

The PP test, which is very general and can be used in the presence of heteroscedastic and auto correlated innovations, is specified as follows:

$$ln\,(1+ r_t) = \alpha + \beta\,(t - T/2) + \delta\, ln\,(1 + r_{t-1}) + \phi_t \text{ for } t = 1, \ldots, T \qquad (2)$$

where r_t denotes the nominal interest rate at time t and (t – T/2) is the time trend (T is the number of observations). The three unit root null hypotheses to be tested are: the first hypothesis implies that the series has a drift and time trend (H_0: $\delta = 1$); the second postulates that the series has a drift but no time trend (H_0: $\beta = 0$, $\delta = 1$); and, the third one implies that the series has neither (H_0: $\alpha = \beta = 0$, $\delta = 1$). Their associated statistics are $Z(t_\delta)$, $Z(\Phi_\beta)$, and $Z(\Phi_\delta)$, respectively, and their corresponding equations are the following:

$$Z(t_\delta) = (\sigma_0/\sigma_{Tl})t_\sigma - (T^3/3^{1/2}\, 4D^{1/2}{}_{XX}\, \sigma_{Tl})\, (\sigma^2{}_{Tl} - \sigma^2{}_0) \qquad (2a)$$

$$Z(\Phi_3) = (\sigma^2{}_0/\sigma^2{}_{Tl})\Phi_3 - (1/2\sigma^2{}_{Tl})\, (\sigma^2{}_{Tl} - \sigma^2{}_0)\, [T(\delta\text{-}1) - (T^6/48D_{XX})\, (\sigma^2{}_{Tl} - \sigma^2{}_0) \qquad (2b)$$

$$Z(\Phi_2) = (\sigma^2{}_0/\sigma^2{}_{Tl})\Phi_2 - (1/3\sigma^2{}_{Tl})\, (\sigma^2{}_{Tl} - \sigma^2{}_0)\, [T(\delta\text{-}1) - (T^6/48D_{XX})\, (\sigma^2{}_{Tl} - \sigma^2{}_0) \qquad (2c)$$

where

$$\Phi_3 = \frac{T[\sigma_0^2 - (\bar{r} - \bar{r}_{t-1})]}{2\sigma^2} \tag{2d}$$

$$\Phi_2 = \frac{T\left(\sigma_0^2 - \sigma^2\right)}{3\sigma^2} \tag{2e}$$

and t_δ, σ^2 (the OLS residual variance), σ^2_0 (the variance under the particular null hypothesis) for the standard t-test for $\delta = 1$. D_{XX} is the determinant of the (X'X), where X is the T_3 matrix of explanatory variables in equation (2). Finally, σ_{Tl} is a consistent estimator of the variance of ζ and is computed as follows:

$$\sigma_{Tl}^2 = \sum_{t=1}^{T} \zeta_t^2 / T + \{2\sum_{s=1}^{l} \sum_{t=s=1}^{T} (1 - s/(l+1))\zeta_t \zeta_{t-s}\} / T \tag{2f}$$

where s and l are the lag truncation numbers and $s < l$. The estimator σ_{Tl} is consistent under general conditions because it allows for effects of serially correlated and heterogeneously distributed innovations. The three statistics are evaluated under various lags ($l = 0$ to 12).

The results from both approaches (for up to two lags) are exhibited in Panel A of Table 1. The ADF and the first PP statistics are all significant at the five percent level suggesting lack of unit root in the series. Further, the other two PP statistics rejected the random walk and the no-drift/trend structure of each series, respectively. Hence, the findings strongly imply absence of unit roots in each series so their subsequent investigation can be carried out in levels form, a finding in accordance with those by Karfakis and Moschos (1990), Katsimbris and Miller (1993) and Fujihara and Mougoué (1996).

3.3 Descriptives

In Panel B of Table 1, the descriptives are displayed along with the statistics for linear and nonlinear time-dependencies for the entire period. The means of all rates are statistically significantly different from zero, at the usual five percent level. Almost all series exhibit evidence of skewness and/or kurtosis, a finding that translates to serious departures from normality. The latter observation is corroborated from the failures of the normality test based on the Kolmogorov-Smirnov D-statistic. Finally, the series and the squared series exhibit statistically significant linear and nonlinear dependencies (for three and six lags) based on the LB(.) and LB^2(.) statistics, respectively. This finding may be due to the presence of autoregressive conditional heteroscedasticity in the series, although it does not surface as more pronounced as the linear dependencies. A usual remedy of autoregressive conditional heteroscedasticity is the modeling of the series as a GARCH-type process. Also, the rejection of normality necessitates the use of a more general density function, the generalized error distribution, in the subsequent empirical analysis. At this point, however, it is important to note that rejection of univariate normality does not preclude multivariate normality of the joint distribution of the (return) series [e.g., Koutmos and Booth (1995)].

Table 1. Preliminary Statistics on Short-Term Interest Rates

Panel A: March 1979 – August 2002		Unit-Root Tests		
Augm. Dickey-Fuller		Phillips-Perron		
Country		$Z(t_\alpha)$	$Z(\Phi_\beta)$	$Z(\Phi_\delta)$
Belgium	-6.8721*	-4.8611*	10.7779*	8.7760*
France	-4.1820*	-5.4791*	6.8447*	4.2231*
Germany	-15.6921*	-10.8181*	5.4331**	4.2292**
Italy	-16.6191*	-5.9456*	6.3310*	5.2321*
Netherlands	-5.5199*	-4.0545*	7.1228*	6.1291*
United Kingdom	5.5291*	3.5181*	10.1234*	8.3421*
United States	-4.5758*	-4.1228*	9.2125*	8.7338*

Panel B: March 1979 – August 2002					Descriptives				
	Mean	Variance	Skewness	Kurtosis	D-stat	LB(3)	LB(6)	$LB^2(3)$	$LB^2(6)$
Belgium	7.6642*	7.0231	0.5417	1.3433*	0.0942*	421.26*	455.11*	511.12*	551.17*
France	9.3441*	10.5591	0.9075*	2.2633*	0.0912*	444.16*	554.32*	522.21*	598.16*
Germany	6.4221*	5.4301	0.7731*	3.8335*	0.0932*	454.25*	532.34*	443.22*	533.25*
Italy	2.8951*	8.0017	1.4644*	2.1133*	0.0911*	322.84*	343.90*	687.11*	734.84*
Netherlands	6.6657*	5.7671	0.8943*	2.1153*	0.0942*	322.23*	323.90*	455.34*	463.39*
U.K.	9.9487*	10.0851	0.8753	-1.3221	0.0983*	543.22*	553.23*	523.32*	534.22*
U.S.		6.8221*	1.3213*	1.2327	0.0934*	544.71*	546.11*	333.12*	367.11*

Table 1. (Continued)

Panel C: March 1979 - August 2002			Correlation Matrix				
	Belgium	France	Germany	Italy	Netherlands	U.K.	U.S.
Belgium	1.0000						
France	0.9866	1.0000					
Germany	0.9671	0.9680	1.0000				
Italy	0.9779	0.9831	0.9608	1.0000			
Netherlands	0.9557	0.9533	0.9733	0.9412	1.0000		
U.K.	0.9568	0.9538	0.9490	0.9444	0.9460	1.0000	
U.S.	0.9454	0.9470	0.9432	0.9467	0.9300	0.9671	1.0000
First Subperiod: March 1979 - July 1990			**Second Subperiod: August 1991 - August 2002**				
Belgium	1.0000	**0.9885**	**0.9877**	**0.9656**	**0.9722**	**0.9511**	**0.8671**
France	0.9877	1.0000	**0.9745**	**0.9695**	**0.9640**	**0.9433**	**0.8554**
Germany	0.9710	0.9701	1.0000	**0.9499**	**0.9732**	**0.8761**	**0.8790**
Italy	0.9807	0.9903	0.9615	1.0000	**0.9144**	**0.8912**	**0.8702**
Netherlands	0.9799	0.9669	0.9798	0.9588	1.0000	**0.9000**	**0.8886**
U.K.	0.9700	0.9599	0. 9703	0.9597	0.9701	1.0000	**0.9544**
U.S.	0.9813	0.9788	0.9710	0.9713	0.9789	0.9622	1.0000

Notes: *, ** significant at 5% and 10% levels, respectively; the Augmented Dickey-Fuller test critical value: -3.431; $Z(t\alpha)$ tests the hypothesis of the series containing a unit root and a time trend; $Z(\Phi\beta)$ tests the null of unit root without a drift (critical value: 6.34); $Z(\Phi\delta)$ tests the null of no trend or drift (critical value: 4.75); D-stat is the Kolmogorov-Smirnov statistic for normality and its critical value at the 5% is $1.36/\sqrt{nobs} = 0.0825$; LB(.) and LB2(.) are the Ljung-Box statistics for linear and nonlinear dependencies, for three and six lags, respectively.

3.4 Correlations

Lastly, the correlation matrix of the interest rates for the entire period (March 1979 - August 2002) and the two sub periods, March 1979 - July 1990 and August 1991 - August 2002, are displayed in Panel C. From the entire-period results, it can be seen that the correlation coefficients for the short-term interest rates are rather large for all countries. This is especially evident for the major EMS countries, that is, Belgium, France, Germany, and the Netherlands. While for the first-period results the picture is essentially the same for the EMS and the U.S. interest rates, the second-period results (in boldface) reveal a lower degree of strength between the EMS interest rates and the U.S. interest rate. This lower degree of correlation can be explained by the fact that the EMS countries have moved away from the business cycle of the U.S. and became more synchronized in the interest rate (and exchange rate) movements among themselves, a step consistent with the realization of monetary union among them [e.g., Artis and Zhang (1999)].

4. Methodology

Let $r_{i,t}$ be the interest rate of country i (i = 1 to n) at time t (month), Ω_{t-1} the information set at time t - 1, $\mu_{i,t}$ the conditional mean, $\sigma^2_{i,t}$ the conditional variance, ν a scale parameter or degrees of freedom, $\varepsilon_{i,t}$ the innovation at time t (where $\varepsilon_{i,t} = r_{i,t} - \mu_{i,t}$), $\xi_{i,t}$ the standardized residuals (i.e., $\xi_{i,t} = \varepsilon_{i,t}/\sigma_{i,t}$), and $f(.)$ the conditional density function of $r_{i,t}$. Following the general model in Laopodis (2001), the modified Multivariate Vector-autoregressive Exponential GARCH (MVAR-EGARCH) model is expressed as follows:

$$r_{i,t}|\Omega_{t-1} \sim f(\mu_{i,t}, \sigma^2_{i,t}, \nu) \qquad (3)$$

$$r_{i,t} = \beta_{i,0} + \sum \beta_{i,j}\, r_{j,t-1} + \varepsilon_{i,t} \text{ for i,j = 1 to n} \qquad (4)$$

$$\sigma^2_{i,t} = \exp\{\, \alpha_{i,0} + \sum \alpha_{i,j}\, \phi_j(\xi_{j,t-1}) + \gamma_i \ln(\sigma^2_{i,t-1})\} \text{ for all i,j} \qquad (5)$$

$$\phi_j(\xi_{j,t-1}) = (|\xi_{j,t-1}| - E(|\xi_{j,t-1}|)) + \delta_j(\xi_{j,t-1}) \text{ for all j} \qquad (6)$$

$$\sigma_{i,j,t} = \rho_{i,j}\, \sigma_{i,t}\, \sigma_{j,t} \text{ for all i, j and } i \neq j \qquad (7)$$

Equation (4) represents a vector autoregressive process for the n series, in which the conditional mean in each return is influenced by its own past values as well as those coming from the other markets (i.e., the other countries' interest rates). News in market i becomes part of the information set in market j so it can be exploited by the home and other markets. Accordingly, coefficients $\beta_{i,j}$, for $i \neq j$, if statistically significant, reflect the extent of mean spillovers across markets, that is, the lead/lag relationships between the rates. More concretely, significant $\beta_{i,j}$ coefficients would imply that market i leads market j and thus it is possible to forecast future rates in market j from present information in market i. The intercepts of the conditional mean equations correspond to the unconditional means of the raw series.

Equation (5) describes the conditional variance of the series and follows an exponential GARCH process comprised of its own lagged standardized and cross-market innovations (shocks). This specification permits standardized shocks to affect a given market in an uneven manner, that is, it allows for asymmetric volatility spillovers. This situation is modeled through the term $\phi_j(\xi_{j,t-1})$, which is an asymmetric function of prior standardized innovations. In particular, the asymmetric impact on the volatility of market *j* is modeled by means of equation (6). Accordingly, for $-\infty < \xi_{j,t-1} \leq 0$ the slope of $\phi(.)$ is equal to $-1 + \delta_j$ whereas for $0 < \xi_{j,t-1} < \infty$ the slope becomes $1 + \delta_j$ [see Nelson (1991) for more on this]. In other words, taking the partial derivatives (∂) of equation (6) we obtain:

$$\partial \phi_j (\xi_{j,t}) / \partial \xi_{j,t} = -1 + \delta_j \text{ for } \xi_{j,t-1}<0 \quad (8a)$$

$$\partial \phi_j (\xi_{j,t}) / \partial \xi_{j,t} = 1 + \delta_j \text{ for } \xi_{j,t-1}>0 \quad (8b)$$

Asymmetry is present if δ_j is negative and statistically significant. The term $[|\xi_{j,t-1}| - E(|\xi_{j,t-1}|)]$ represents the size (or the magnitude) effect of an innovation, whereas the $\delta_j(\xi_{j,t-1})$ component reflects the matching sign (or direction) effect. Assuming a positive $\alpha_{i,j}$, the impact of $\xi_{j,t-1}$ on $\sigma^2_{i,t}$ will be positive (negative) if the magnitude of $\xi_{j,t-1}$ is greater (smaller) than its expected value $E(|\xi_{j,t-1}|)$. Similarly, the matching sign effect term, $\delta_j (\xi_{j,t-1})$, may be reinforcing or partially offsetting the magnitude effect, depending upon the sign of the coefficient and the size of the shock. For example, interest rate decreases in market *j* ($\xi_{j,t-1} < 0$) will be followed by higher volatility than interest rate increases ($\xi_{j,t-1} > 0$) if δ_j is negative and statistically significant. Furthermore, a negative (positive) $\xi_{j,t-1}$ coupled with a negative δ_j enhances (reduces) the size effect. A negative δ_j, with a positive and significant $\alpha_{i,j}$, implies that a negative shock in market *j* increases current volatility ($\sigma^2_{i,t}$) in market *i* by more than a positive shock of an equal magnitude. Such a result would reveal the asymmetric nature of the volatility spillover mechanism.

To assess the relative importance of asymmetry, the ratio of $|-1+\delta_j|/(1+\delta_j)$ must be constructed. This ratio also considers the differing impact of a market's own innovation on its current conditional variance. Volatility interactions across markets are measured by the $\alpha_{j,i}$ coefficients for j, i = 1 to 4 and $i \neq j$. Volatility persistence, in equation (5), is measured by γ_i. To gain a better understanding of the duration of volatility, the half-life (HL) of an external shock must be calculated, and is defined as $HL = \ln(0.5)/\ln(\gamma_i)$.

The conditional covariance specification (equation 7) presupposes constant correlation coefficients [as noted by Bollerslev (1990)] and, accordingly, their interpretation should be based on the fact that they measure contemporaneous relationships and not lead/lag relationships. This is equivalent to saying that the covariance is commensurate to the product of the standard deviations as described by (7). This assumption simplifies the estimation of the model and has many applications [see Bollerslev (1990)].

Finally, most studies using this model assume the normal density function. However, almost invariably, the standardized residuals obtained from ARCH-type models that assume normality seem to be leptokurtic. Such an outcome implies that the parameter estimates are not asymptotically efficient (although they are still unbiased). To deal with this problem, many researchers have employed general distributions such as Student's *t*-distribution (e.g., Akgiray,

1989) and the generalized error distribution or GED (e.g., Akgiray et *al.*, 1991). The advantage of using more general density functions is that the parameter estimates are not excessively influenced by extreme observations occurring with low probabilities (such as an unexpected event). In this paper, in view of the earlier findings about non-normality in the series, we will employ the GED the density function which is given by:

$$f(\mu_t,\sigma_t,\nu)=\nu/2[\Gamma(3/\nu)]^{1/2}\,[\Gamma\,(1/\nu)]^{-3/2}\,(1/\sigma_t)\,exp\,\{-\,[\Gamma\,(3/\nu)/\Gamma\,(1/\nu)]^{\nu/2}\,|\varepsilon_t/\sigma_t|^{\nu}\,\} \qquad (9)$$

where $\Gamma(.)$ is the gamma function and ν is a scale parameter or degrees of freedom to be estimated endogenously. For $\nu = 2$, the GED yields the normal distribution, while for $\nu = 1$, it yields the Laplace or the double exponential distribution.

Given initial values for ε_t and σ^2_t, the parameter vector can be estimated by maximizing the log-likelihood function of the multivariate EGARCH model over the sample period, which is given by:

$$L\,(\Theta|k,\,p,q) = \sum^{T}_{t=1} \log f(\mu_t,\,\sigma^2_t,\,\nu) \qquad (10)$$

where κ is the number of equations, T the number of observations, μ_t, σ^2_t, and ν are the conditional mean, conditional variance and the scale parameter (or degrees of freedom), respectively. The high nonlinearity in the arguments (Θ) of the likelihood function ℓ necessitates maximization using numerical derivatives as in the Berndt *et al.* (1974) algorithm.

5. Empirical Findings and Discussion

The empirical strategy will be as follows. First, we will begin with the investigation of the EMS countries only, that is, excluding the U.S., so we can determine Germany's status within the system. In this sense, we will determine whether European asymmetry (in the strict sense) exists if uni-directional influences from Germany's rate to the rest of the EMS rates are present. The maximum likelihood estimates of the MVAR-EGARCH model are displayed in Table 2 for the three-month interest rates for Belgium, France, the Netherlands and Germany..

Table 2. Maximum Likelihood Estimates of the MVAR-EGARCH: EMS Short-Term Interest Rates

$$r_{i,t}|\Omega_{t-1} \sim f\,(\mu_{i,t},\,\sigma^2_{i,t},\,\nu)$$

$$r_{i,t} = \beta_{i,0} + \sum \beta_{i,j}\, r_{j,t-1} + \varepsilon_{i,t} \text{ for i,j} = 1 \text{ to n}$$

$$\sigma^2_{i,t} = \exp\{\,\alpha_{i,0} + \sum \alpha_{i,j}\,\phi_j\,(\xi_{j,t-1}\,) + \gamma_i \ln(\sigma^2_{i,t-1})\} \text{ for all i,j}$$

$$\phi_j(\xi_{j,t-1}) = (|\xi_{j,t-1}| - E\,(|\xi_{j,t-1}|)) + \delta_j\,(\xi_{j,t-1}) \text{ for all j}$$

To Belgium from Netherlands, France, Germany		To Netherlands from Belgium, France, Germany		To France from Belgium, Netherlands, Germany		To Germany from Belgium, France, Netherlands	
$\beta_{1,0}$	0.0174	$\beta_{2,0}$	-0.0422	$\beta_{3,0}$	-0.0211	$\beta_{4,0}$	-0.0589*
	(0.019)		(0.037)		(0.022)		(0.027)
$\beta_{1,1}$	0.7654*	$\beta_{2,1}$	-0.1215	$\beta_{3,1}$	-0.0123	$\beta_{4,1}$	-0.0034
	(0.027)		(0.112)		(0.011)		(0.011)

To Belgium from Netherlands, France, Germany		To Netherlands from Belgium, France, Germany		To France from Belgium, Netherlands, Germany		To Germany from Belgium, France, Netherlands	
$\beta_{1,2}$	0.1147*	$\beta_{2,2}$	0.9681*	$\beta_{3,2}$	0.0422	$\beta_{4,2}$	0.0012
	(0.029)		(0.020)		(0.031)		(0.001)
$\beta_{1,3}$	0.0542*	$\beta_{2,3}$	0.0122	$\beta_{3,3}$	0.9772*	$\beta_{4,3}$	0.0111
	(0.012)		(0.011)		(0.111)		(0.011)
$\beta_{1,4}$	0.0639*	$\beta_{2,4}$	0.0623*	$\beta_{3,4}$	-0.0441*	$\beta_{4,4}$	0.9018*
	(0.021)		(0.014)		(0.021)		(0.016)
$\alpha_{1,0}$	-0.1330*	$\alpha_{2,0}$	-0.7112*	$\alpha_{3,0}$	0.5323*	$\alpha_{4,0}$	-0.3141*
	(0.031)		(0.083)		(0.072)		(0.050)
$\alpha_{1,1}$	0.1711*	$\alpha_{2,1}$	0.2311*	$\alpha_{3,1}$	0.0211	$\alpha_{4,1}$	-0.0950*
	(0.020)		(0.048)		(0.011)		(0.022)
$\alpha_{1,2}$	0.0011	$\alpha_{2,2}$	0.0111*	$\alpha_{3,2}$	0.0011	$\alpha_{4,2}$	-0.0012
	(0.001)		(0.004)		(0.005)		(0.001)
$\alpha_{1,3}$	0.2710*	$\alpha_{2,3}$	0.1223*	$\alpha_{3,3}$	0.1912*	$\alpha_{4,3}$	0.1246*
	(0.011)		(0.032)		(0.011)		(0.021)
$\alpha_{1,4}$	-0.0723*	$\alpha_{2,4}$	-0.0453*	$\alpha_{3,4}$	0.1300*	$\alpha_{4,4}$	0.2472
	(0.001)		(0.010)		(0.021)		(0.049)
γ_1	0.9410*	γ_2	0.6930*	γ_3	0.6621*	γ_4	0.8680*
	(0.027)		(0.027)		(0.022)		(0.027)
δ_1	0.6900*	δ_2	1.0670*	δ_3	-0.5620*	δ_4	1.2126*
	(0.203)		(0.043)		(0.070)		(0.210)

$\rho_{1,2}$	$\rho_{1,3}$	$\rho_{1,4}$	$\rho_{2,3}$	$\rho_{2,4}$	$\rho_{3,4}$
0.3210*	0.2160*	-0.0103	0.2070*	0.4188*	0.1657*
(0.080)	(0.070)	(0.022)	(0.073)	(0.074)	(0.063)

	Belgium	Netherlands	France	Germany
LF	-157.453			
HL	11.398	1.890	2.420	4.901
ASY			3.572	
v	1.8754* (0.021)			
R^2	0.1456	0.1519	0.1430	0.1197

Residual Diagnostics

Standardized Residual Diagnostics

	Belgium	Netherlands	France	Germany
Mean	0.0280	0.0180	0.0468	0.0135
Variance	1.0000	1.0001	1.0001	1.0001
Skewness	0.0120	0.0870	0.1000	0.9773*
Kurtosis	2.1336*	2.0330*	2.1125*	2.0721*
D-stat	0.0610	0.0570	0.0785	0.0653
LB(3)	10.440	11.452	12.1339	13.142
LB(6)	12.430	12.553	13.0458	17.229*
$LB^2(3)$	2.3231	13.555	1.23556	3.1222
$LB^2(6)$	8.3342	14.541	2.34526	3.1322

Cross-residual Diagnostics

$LB_{1,2}(3)$ 2.3231	$LB_{1,3}(3)$ 3.8422	$LB_{1,4}(3)$ 4.2323	$LB_{2,3}(3)$ 5.2421
$LB_{2,4}(3)$ 3.2221	$LB_{3,4}(3)$ 7.2234		

Notes: entire period (March 1979 - August 2002); * significant at the 5% level; asymptotic standard errors in parentheses; Belgium=1, Netherlands=2, France=3, Germany=4; D-stat 5% critical value: 0.0785; LF is the likelihood function; $\rho_{i,j}$ are the estimated correlation coefficients; $LB_{i,j}(3)$ are the Ljung-Box statistics for the cross-standardized residuals; HL is the half-life of a shock, defined as $\ln(0.5)/\ln(\gamma)$; ASY is asymmetry ratio, defined by $|-1+\delta|/(1+\delta)$; ν is the degrees of freedom parameter; R^2 is the uncentered R-square defined as $1 - (Var(\varepsilon_i)/Var(R_i))$, for i = 1 to 4.

Table 3. Maximum Likelihood Estimates of the MVAR-EGARCH: Italy, U.K. and Germany

$$r_{i,t}|\Omega_{t-1} \sim f(\mu_{i,t}, \sigma^2_{i,t}, \nu)$$

$$r_{i,t} = \beta_{i,0} + \sum \beta_{i,j}\, r_{j,t-1} + \varepsilon_{i,t} \text{ for i,j = 1 to n}$$

$$\sigma^2_{i,t} = \exp\{ \alpha_{i,0} + \sum \alpha_{i,j}\, \phi_j(\xi_{j,t-1}) + \gamma_i \ln(\sigma^2_{i,t-1})\} \text{ for all i,j}$$

$$\phi_j(\xi_{j,t-1}) = (|\xi_{j,t-1}| - E(|\xi_{j,t-1}|)) + \delta_j(\xi_{j,t-1}) \text{ for all j}$$

To Italy from the U.K. and Germany		To the U.K. from Italy and Germany		To Germany from Italy and the U.K.	
$\beta_{1,0}$	0.0122	$\beta_{2,0}$	0.2134*	$\beta_{3,0}$	0.1514*
	(0.011)		(0.011)		(0.072)
$\beta_{1,1}$	0.9618*	$\beta_{2,1}$	0.0118	$\beta_{3,1}$	-0.0222*
	(0.011)		(0.010)		(0.052)
$\beta_{1,2}$	0.0111	$\beta_{2,2}$	0.9711*	$\beta_{3,2}$	0.0122*
	(0.014)		(0.131)		(0.002)
$\beta_{1,3}$	0.0925*	$\beta_{2,3}$	0.0224*	$\beta_{3,3}$	0.9722*
	(0.021)		(0.012)		(0.012)
$\alpha_{1,0}$	1.1172*	$\alpha_{2,0}$	1.1213*	$\alpha_{3,0}$	-0.4427*
	(0.111)		(0.021)		(0.712)
$\alpha_{1,1}$	0.1132*	$\alpha_{2,1}$	0.9723*	$\alpha_{3,1}$	0.1152**
	(0.029)		(0.052)		(0.064)
$\alpha_{1,2}$	0.9412*	$\alpha_{2,2}$	0.7654*	$\alpha_{3,2}$	0.5012*
	(0.111)		(0.061)		(0.121)
$\alpha_{1,3}$	0.1814*	$\alpha_{2,3}$	0.4881*	$\alpha_{3,3}$	0.5622*
	(0.041)		(0.041)		(0.112)
γ_1	-0.2235	γ_2	0.9345*	γ_3	0.8335*
	(0.311)		(0.011)		(0.035)
δ_1	-0.2009*	δ_2	0.2541*	δ_3	0.8090*
	(0.061)		(0.111)		(0.121)
$\rho_{1,2}$	0.0552	$\rho_{1,3}$	0.1112	$\rho_{2,3}$	0.0113
	(0.111)		(0.108)		(0.101)
LF	189.150				
HL			10.237		3.806
ASY	1.500		0.594		0.105
ν	1.062* (0.012)				
Standardized Residual Diagnostics					
Mean	0.0899		0.0320		0.0918
Variance	1.0001		1.0001		1.0000
Skewness	-0.0011		-0.2243		-0.7361*
Kurtosis	3.0521*		2.6718*		3.8313*
D-stat	0.0891		0.1011		0.1014
LB(3)	5.2152		8.8178		12.219
LB(6)	10.310		10.353		13.318
$LB^2(3)$	12.421		1.4545		0.9331
$LB_{1,2}(3)$ 1.1181		$LB_{1,3}(3)$ 3.2292		$LB_{2,3}(3)$ 4.3222	
$LB^2(6)$	14.411		2.5171		2.5581

Notes: 1=Italy, 2=U.K., and 3=Germany; D-stat 5% critical value: 0.1088; entire period.

Second, the examination of Italy and the U.K. with Germany will be carried out separately in view of the fact that the first two countries were forced to end their brief membership with the Exchange Rate Mechanism in September 1992, following some severe speculative raids on their currencies. The idea is to study the nature of the volatility spillover mechanism in the absence of such non-market, non-fundamental conditions since, as Engel and Hakkio (1993) point out, these situations may contribute to extreme volatile conditions which may unduly skew the true channels of influence of information dissemination. These results are exhibited in Table 3.

Third, Table 4 presents additional evidence of European asymmetry and volatility in the short-term interest rates before and after German reunification in July 1990, in light of the substantial evidence that the post-unification period witnessed a dramatic change in the degree of economic convergence by most of the EMS members.

Fourth, as an additional test for confirming or not a change in the GLH during the 1990s we can use a dummy variable for the date of the introduction of the Euro, in January 1, 1999, within the European Union. Although the sample period is rather small (from January 1, 1999 to August 2002) amounting to 32 monthly observations, some preliminary inferences can be drawn from the results. These results are contained in Table 4 as well.

And finally, the re-examination of the GLH will be done within a wider framework, this time including the U.S. short-term interest rate. In other words, if Germany is linked to the U.S. then Germany's monetary actions will subsequently affect the other EMS countries' monetary policies indirectly. Therefore, we will see if international asymmetry exists. Consequently, Germany may not emerge as the 'true' leader within EMS especially when its policies are also affected by the other countries' policies. The findings from the investigation of international asymmetry are presented in Table 5. We now turn to the presentation and interpretation of the empirical results.

5.1. Mean and Volatility Spillovers: EMS Rates

To understand Table 2, the subscripts 1 through 4 denote Belgium, the Netherlands, France, and Germany, respectively. Upon inspection of the coefficients of each rate's conditional mean from Table 2, it is clear that two important observations can be made: first, each rate's own past values influence its current level and, second, there exist significant uni-directional influences from Germany's rate to the conditional means ($\beta_{i,4}$) of the other rates. Since only Germany affects, but is not affected by, the rates of Belgium, France and the Netherlands, it can be said that Germany emerges here as a significant player in the news-generating process, in that sense. Finally, it is interesting to note two things: first, that Germany affects France's interest rate negatively, whereas those for the other two countries positively, and second, that the only interest rate that is positively affected by lagged (past) changes in all other rates is that of Belgium's.

Table 4. Asymmetry and Persistence of Volatility of Short-Term Interest rates

Panel A: Pre- and Post-Unification Periods					
Coefficient	Belgium	France	Netherlands	Italy	U.K.
δ	0.3410	0.3610	0.0542	-0.1444	-0.0889
	(0.240)	(0.263)	(0.037)	(0.101)	(0.072)
γ	0.8412*	0.8319*	0.8101*	0.0322	0.0228
	(0.027)	(0.039)	(0.030)	(0.024)	(0.021)
Unification Dummy					
Mean	0.0146			0.0533	
	(0.010)			(0.043)	
Variance	-0.1377*			-0.8331**	
	(0.030)			(0.456)	
LogL	-216.336			227.128	
Panel B: Pre- and Post-Euro Introduction Periods					
Coefficient	Belgium	France	Netherlands	Italy	U.K.
δ	0.3133	0.3232	0.0332	-0.1323	-0.0323
	(0.232)	(0.232)	(0.027)	(0.121)	(0.022)
γ	0.8322*	0.8123*	0.8011*	0.0223	0.1003
	(0.017)	(0.011)	(0.012)	(0.014)	(0.078)
Euro Introduction Dummy					
Mean	0.1132			0.1234	
	(0.100)			(0.103)	
Variance	-0.1017*			-0.2232**	
	(0.022)			(0.066)	
LogL	-113.343			162.434	
LR_1	117.761*			37.978*	
LR_2	88.221*			63.436*	

Notes: entire period (March 1979 - August 2002); asymptotic standard errors in parentheses; *, ** denote statistical significance at the 5 and 10 percent levels, respectively; coefficients δ and γ refer to the asymmetry and persistence of volatility, respectively; the unification dummy takes the value of zero before July 1990 and one otherwise; the first unification dummy coefficients are for the Belgium, France and the Netherlands group, whereas the second two for the U.K. and Italy group; the Euro dummy takes the value of zero before January 1, 1999 and one afterwards; the LR is the Likelihood Ratio, defined as –2 (LR_u - LR_r), where u and r refer to the unrestricted and the restricted models, respectively, and is distributed as a χ^2 with one degree of freedom; LR_1 refers to Panel A and LR_2 refers to Panel B.

At this point, an important question that arises is to what extent these relationships can be exploited in order to generate excess returns (profits). In other words, are these statistically significant relationships also economically significant? To really address this question we would need to have detailed information regarding transactions costs and foreign exchange risk. However, an alternative way to answer this question is to compute the uncentered R^2 (defined as $R^2 = 1 - [Var(\varepsilon_i)/Var(R_i)]$, for i = 1 to 4. These statistics, reported in the table, are very close to each other and range from 14.5% for Belgium to 11.9% for Germany. Therefore, the percentages of variation in returns in each money market that can be explained on the basis of past information are very small. Besides, incorporating additional information on exchange rate risk and transaction costs it can be safely concluded that these money markets are weak-form efficient.

Table 5. Maximum Likelihood Estimates of the MVAR-EGARCH: All Short-Term Interest Rates

$$r_{i,t}|\Omega_{t-1} \sim f(\mu_{i,t}, \sigma^2_{i,t}, \nu)$$

$$r_{i,t} = \beta_{i,0} + \sum \beta_{i,j}\, r_{j,t-1} + \varepsilon_{i,t} \text{ for i,j = 1 to n}$$

$$\sigma^2_{i,t} = \exp\{\alpha_{i,0} + \sum \alpha_{i,j}\, \phi_j(\xi_{j,t-1}) + \gamma_i \ln(\sigma^2_{i,t-1})\} \text{ for all i,j}$$

$$\phi_j(\xi_{j,t-1}) = (|\xi_{j,t-1}| - E(|\xi_{j,t-1}|)) + \delta_j(\xi_{j,t-1}) \text{ for all j}$$

To Belgium		To France		To Germany		To Italy		To Netherlands		To U.K.		To U.S.	
$\beta_{1,0}$	-0.1434	$\beta_{2,0}$	0.2432	$\beta_{3,0}$	0.0118	$\beta_{4,0}$	0.2333	$\beta_{5,0}$	0.3434	$\beta_{6,0}$	0.3122	$\beta_{7,0}$	0.1236
	(0.110)		(0.142)		(0.010)		(0.140)		(0.192)		(0.189)		(0.110)
$\beta_{1,1}$	0.3224*	$\beta_{2,1}$	0.1332*	$\beta_{3,1}$	0.0311	$\beta_{4,1}$	0.1221	$\beta_{5,1}$	0.0551	$\beta_{6,1}$	0.1236	$\beta_{7,1}$	-0.1111
	(0.022)		(0.012)		(0.028)		(0.090)		(0.041)		(0.095)		(0.099)
$\beta_{1,2}$	0.0323*	$\beta_{2,2}$	0.8221*	$\beta_{3,2}$	0.0121	$\beta_{4,2}$	0.1067	$\beta_{5,2}$	0.0222*	$\beta_{6,2}$	0.1116	$\beta_{7,2}$	-0.0645
	(0.012)		(0.011)		(0.010)		(0.088)		(0.012)		(0.082)		(0.044)
$\beta_{1,3}$	0.0234*	$\beta_{2,3}$	0.0110*	$\beta_{3,3}$	0.6430	$\beta_{4,3}$	0.0733	$\beta_{5,3}$	0.1236*	$\beta_{6,3}$	0.0211	$\beta_{7,3}$	-0.0666
	(0.011)		(0.001)		(0.443)		(0.063)		(0.018)		(0.016)		(0.053)
$\beta_{1,4}$	0.0112	$\beta_{2,4}$	0.0113	$\beta_{3,4}$	0.7323	$\beta_{4,4}$	0.0228	$\beta_{5,4}$	0.1221*	$\beta_{6,4}$	0.0891	$\beta_{7,4}$ -	0.0555
	(0.012)		(0.011)		(0.481)		(0.019)		(0.022)		(0.072)		(0.048)
$\beta_{1,5}$	0.0213	$\beta_{2,5}$	0.0221	$\beta_{3,5}$	0.0322	$\beta_{4,5}$	0.0555	$\beta_{5,5}$	-0.1088*	$\beta_{6,5}$	0.0221	$\beta_{7,5}$	0.0436
	(0.016)		(0.012)		(0.024)		(0.042)		(0.014)		(0.018)		(0.033)
$\beta_{1,6}$	0.0445	$\beta_{2,6}$	0.0312*	$\beta_{3,6}$	0.0232	$\beta_{4,6}$	-0.0722	$\beta_{5,6}$	0.8112*	$\beta_{6,6}$	0.0211	$\beta_{7,6}$	0.0633
	(0.031)		(0.011)		(0.018)		(0.051)		(0.013)		(0.017)		(0.049)
$\beta_{1,7}$	0.0322	$\beta_{2,7}$	0.0456	$\beta_{3,7}$	0.1455	$\beta_{4,7}$	-0.1115	$\beta_{5,7}$	0.0182*	$\beta_{6,7}$	0.9411*	$\beta_{7,7}$	0.0875
	(0.027)		(0.031)		(0.132)		(0.090)		(0.010)		(0.074)		(0.071)
$\alpha_{1,0}$	-0.2311	$\alpha_{2,0}$	-0.4991	$\alpha_{3,0}$	-0.4355	$\alpha_{4,0}$ -	0.3339	$\alpha_{5,0}$	-0.2239	$\alpha_{6,0}$	0.1444	$\alpha_{7,0}$	0.1125
	(0.166)		(0.323)		(0.031)		(0.221)		(0.188)		(0.087)		(0.932)
$\alpha_{1,1}$	0.1231	$\alpha_{2,1}$	0.1388	$\alpha_{3,1}$	0.1333	$\alpha_{4,1}$	0.1234	$\alpha_{5,1}$	0.1129	$\alpha_{6,1}$	0.1346	$\alpha_{7,1}$	0.1321
	(0.106)		(0.108)		(0.103)		(0.101)		(0.088)		(0.077)		(0.079)
$\alpha_{1,2}$	0.1210	$\alpha_{2,2}$	0.0672	$\alpha_{3,2}$	0.1123	$\alpha_{4,2}$	0.1020	$\alpha_{5,2}$	0.0233	$\alpha_{6,2}$	0.0654	$\alpha_{7,2}$	0.0433
	(0.011)		(0.055)		(0.071)		(0.091)		(0.015)		(0.044)		(0.029)
$\alpha_{1,3}$	0.1112*	$\alpha_{2,3}$	0.0455**	$\alpha_{3,3}$	0.3322*	$\alpha_{4,3}$	0.0222	$\alpha_{5,3}$	0.0223	$\alpha_{6,3}$	0.0444	$\alpha_{7,3}$	0.0433
	(0.031)		(0.025)		(0.032)		(0.019)		(0.022)		(0.034)		(0.033)

Table 5. (Continued)

To Belgium		To France		To Germany		To Italy		To Netherlands		To U.K.		To U.S.	
$\alpha_{1,4}$	0.0131	$\alpha_{2,4}$	0.0655	$\alpha_{3,4}$	0.1123	$\alpha_{4,4}$	0.1007*	$\alpha_{5,4}$	0.0223	$\alpha_{6,4}$	0.0704	$\alpha_{7,4}$	0.0733
	(0.012)		(0.055)		(0.087)		(0.038)		(0.025)		(0.054)		(0.063)
$\alpha_{1,5}$	0.0553	$\alpha_{2,5}$	0.0655	$\alpha_{3,5}$	0.0543	$\alpha_{4,5}$	0.1045	$\alpha_{5,5}$	0.0864*	$\alpha_{6,5}$	0.0809	$\alpha_{7,5}$	0.0876
	(0.034)		(0.044)		(0.046)		(0.081)		(0.032)		(0.060)		(0.072)
$\alpha_{1,6}$	0.0444	$\alpha_{2,6}$	0.0644*	$\alpha_{3,6}$	0.0446	$\alpha_{4,6}$	0.1086	$\alpha_{5,6}$	0.0806	$\alpha_{6,6}$	0.0644*	$\alpha_{7,6}$	0.0722*
	(0.034)		(0.024)		(0.037)		(0.111)		(0.063)		(0.014)		(0.032)
$\alpha_{1,7}$	0.0443	$\alpha_{2,7}$	0.0332*	$\alpha_{3,7}$	0.0443	$\alpha_{4,7}$	0.0112*	$\alpha_{5,7}$	0.0222	$\alpha_{6,7}$	0.0443*	$\alpha_{7,7}$	0.0112*
	(0.032)		(0.013)		(0.034)		(0.004)		(0.016)		(0.014)		(0.006)
γ_1	0.7807*	γ_2	0.7800*	γ_3	0.6300*	γ_4	0.7611*	γ_5	0.6114*	γ_6	0.6867*	γ_7	0.6733*
	(0.022)		(0.050)		(0.050)		(0.025)		(0.031)		(0.063)		(0.044)
δ_1	-0.3444	δ_2	-0.0557	δ_3	-0.2544	δ_4	0.2337*	δ_5	0.1900*	δ_6	0.2013	δ_7	0.1321
	(0.253)		(0.051)		(0.143)		(0.013)		(0.021)		(0.132)		(0.112)

Belgium		France		Germany		Italy		Netherlands		U.K.	U.S.
$\rho_{1,2}$	0.6711*	$\rho_{1,3}$	0.6112	$\rho_{1,4}$	0.4726	$\rho_{1,5}$	0.2644	$\rho_{1,6}$	0.3443	$\rho_{1,7}$	0.2743
	(0.051)		(0.512)		(0.352)		(0.175)		(0.237)		(0.163)
$\rho_{2,3}$	0.5131	$\rho_{2,4}$	0.6678**	$\rho_{2,5}$	0.3522	$\rho_{2,6}$	0.1444	$\rho_{2,7}$	0.0834	$\rho_{3,4}$	0.4233
	(0.431)		(0.322)		(0.252)		(0.105)		(0.073)		(0.363)
$\rho_{3,5}$	0.1333	$\rho_{3,6}$	0.0522	$\rho_{3,7}$	0.2822	$\rho_{4,5}$	0.4655	$\rho_{4,6}$	0.2433	$\rho_{4,7}$	0.1339
	(0.121)		(0.039)		(0.152)		(0.373)		(0.173)		(0.138)
$\rho_{5,6}$	0.6743*	$\rho_{5,7}$	0.0823*	$\rho_{6,7}$	-0.0123						
	(0.012)		(0.062)		(0.012)						
ν	1.905*										
	(0.033)										
LF	-234.222										

	Belgium	France	Germany	Italy	Netherlands	U.K.	U.S.
HL	2.799	2.789	1.500	2.539	1.408	1.844	1.819

Table 5. (Continued)

	Belgium	France	Germany	Italy	Netherlands	U.K.	U.S.
Standardized Residual Diagnostics							
Mean	0.0200	0.0144	0.0401	0.0334	0.0311	0.0109	0.0300
Variance	1.0003	1.0001	1.0002	1.0001	1.0001	1.0002	100001
Skewness	0.0222	0.0812	0.1861*	0.9744*	0.0411	0.2337*	0.5222*
Kurtosis	1.4329**	2.3212*	0.3332	2.2222*	2.1121*	3.6333*	2.3321*
D-stat	0.0989	0.0988	0.0987	0.0972	0.0911	0.0933	0.0822
LB(3)	12.2221	12.3331	11.1555	13.3333	3.3338	3.3451	6.6660
LB(6)	13.4401	14.4552	13.0555	15.4443	5.6677	5.6788	8.7654
$LB^2(3)$	2.2171	10.2522	1.1238	2.1211	2.0883	2.3341	2.3332
$LB^2(6)$	3.3440	11.1110	2.2333	2.3331	2.5672	3.4455	3.4433

Cross-Residual Diagnostics

$LB_{1,2}(3)$ 2.1112	$LB_{1,3}(3)$ 7.2771	$LB_{1,4}(3)$ 4.5443	$LB_{1,5}(3)$ 6.6651	$LB_{1,6}(3)$ 3.0012	$LB_{1,7}(3)$ 6.5521
$LB_{2,3}(3)$ 3.3322	$LB_{2,4}(3)$ 6.2661	$LB_{2,5}(3)$ 4.4241	$LB_{2,6}(3)$ 7.1122	$LB_{2,7}(3)$ 3.1113	$LB_{3,4}(3)$ 8.7664
$LB_{3,5}(3)$ 2.1112	$LB_{3,6}(3)$ 7.2654	$LB_{3,7}(3)$ 4.3113	$LB_{4,5}(3)$ 6.7899	$LB_{4,6}(3)$ 3.2214	$LB_{4,7}(3)$ 7.66655
$LB_{5,6}(3)$ 2.1221	$LB_{5,7}(3)$ 6.5744	$LB_{6,7}(3)$ 4.3212			

Notes: 1 = Belgium, 2 = France; 3 = Germany; 4 = Italy; 5 = Netherlands; 6 = U.K.; and 7 = U.S.; see also notes in Table 2.

The message from the second-moment interdependencies or volatility interactions, however, is more informative. Specifically, Germany's conditional variance is seen to affect but is not affected by the other rates' conditional variances, some strongly and positively (i.e., France's) and some weakly and negatively (i.e., Belgium's and the Netherlands'). Moreover, the only short-term interest rate that appears to be affected by all other interest rates is that of the Netherlands. Nonetheless, the rates of France and Belgium marginally affect the German rate, which hints that Germany's monetary policy is not entirely independent of the other members' policies. Besides, the results seem to indicate that France influences all other EMS rates based on the significance of the $\alpha_{i,3}$ coefficients. This evidence is in accordance with evidence reported in Bajo-Rubio (2001) regarding a two-way causality between Germany and these countries. The overall conclusion that has emerged from this part of the analysis is that the Exchange Rate Mechanism, the essential element of the workings of the EMS, has induced a strong link between the short-term interest rates of the EMS countries and Germany. Additionally, for the case of the Netherlands this is much more evident in view of the fact that there has not been a single realignment in the Dutch guilder/mark exchange rate vis-à-vis the other EMS currencies. This finding is in disagreement with the findings of Hassapis et *al.* (1999) who, using bivariate causality tests, find that the ERM has not strengthened the links among the EMS countries and Germany.

5.2. Asymmetry and Volatility Persistence: EMS Rates

Continuing the inspection of the empirical estimates in Table 2, some additional conclusions can be inferred from these results. The first is the presence of asymmetry in the case of France (δ_3) which, coupled with the coefficient of the innovations originating from Germany ($\alpha_{3,4}$), suggests that both the size and the nature of past news are important ingredients in the volatility transmission mechanism. In other words, adverse shocks from Germany produce higher volatility on the French short-term interest rate [by 3.575 times, in particular, based on the $|-1+\delta_3|/(1+\delta_3)$ ratio, where δ_3 is -0.5620 from Table 2] than do favorable shocks of equal magnitude. This suggests that the volatility spillover mechanism is asymmetric. Note that the same shock would produce a negligible impact on Germany's and the Netherlands' rates. Specifically, 0.096 and 0.032 times since δ_4 and δ_2 are 1.2126 and 1.0670, respectively (but these results are not reported in the table). These findings seem to contradict those on asymmetric behavior in the EMS found by Katsimbris (1993) and Hassapis et *al.* (1999).

Another insight centers on the high degree of volatility persistence for Belgium (γ_1) and the low degree for France (γ_3) and the Netherlands (γ_2). These findings imply that current shocks persist in the future values (forecasts) of the conditional variance of those short-term rates. Using the half-life (HL) of a shock measure, defined as HL = $ln(0.5)/ln(\gamma_i)$, we can see that volatility persistence ranges from under 2 months to 11 months in the cases of the Dutch and the Belgian rates, respectively.

Finally, two more points worth mentioning concern the values of the pairwise correlation coefficients ($\rho_{i,j}$) for Table 2 and of the estimated scale parameter, v. Regarding the correlation coefficients, we can see that they are much lower than those of the correlation structure of the raw series in Table 1. The value of this finding rests with the fact that incorporating the series' inherent interdependencies and conditional heteroscedasticity substantially reduces the size of the coefficients so that the linkages in the monetary policies of the countries are not exaggerated. Moreover, the financial implication of this result is that the sample correlation coefficients overstate the degree of linkage among these money markets and thus understate the potential for profitable diversification in these markets. Lastly, the value of the ν parameter is close to 2, the number required for multivariate normality in the empirical distributions of the return series, and statistically significant. This provides a partial support to the assertion that departures from normality may be due to the presence of conditional heteroscedasticity in the raw series, as evidenced by their significant nonlinearities.

5.3. Residual Diagnostics: EMS Rates

As is any empirical investigation, the validity of the results hinges upon the correct specification of the model. For (G)ARCH-type models, this means that the standardized residuals follow the assumed distribution with the estimated scale parameter, ν, that they are independently and identically distributed, i.e., they are *i.i.d*, and that they have zero mean and unit(ary) variance. The suitability of the GED density function is tested on the basis of the Kolmogorov-Smirnov D-statistic, where now the null hypothesis is that the estimated standardized residuals follow the GED with the estimated scale parameter, ν. As is evident from the table, the residuals abide by all of the above requirements. Specifically, the estimated D-statistics are well below the critical value in all instances so that the assumed density function is not rejected. Furthermore, all series have a zero mean and unit variance and, most importantly, both the residual and squared residual series do not display significant linear and non-linear dependencies, as seen by the insignificant values of the LB statistics for up to six lags. As an additional test for absence or presence of nonlinearities in these series, the cross-residuals were tested via the means of the $LB_{i,j}$ statistics again. Based on these values, their insignificance attests to the earlier conclusions regarding absence of nonlinearities in the residual series. In all then, these diagnostics provide strong support for a correct model specification

5.4 Selected Country Analysis

Table 3 reports the results on Italy and the U.K. given that they had a brief encounter with the ERM. Again, Italy has subscript 1, the U.K. subscript 2, and Germany subscript 3. The basic conclusion from these findings is that Germany's short-term interest rate clearly affects Italy's and the U.K.'s conditional means and volatility structures in a positive manner. Moreover, it appears that the interest rates of both Italy and the U.K. exert a significant influence on Germany's conditional mean and variance. The extent of reciprocal influence among the three rates conditional variances surfaces equally strong, judging from the size of the estimated $\alpha_{i,j}$ coefficients. Therefore, based on this evidence, significant and reciprocal lead/lag interactions emerge among all rates' conditional variances and the volatility transmission mechanism surfaces as asymmetric only in the case of Italy. The latter result is in accordance with the findings by Weber (1991) who also found asymmetric behavior for Italy during the 1980s. Finally, the estimated scale parameter, ν, is indicating that the joint distribution of return series resembles the double exponential or the Laplace distribution since its value is around unity (a conventional *t*-test rejected the hypothesis that $\nu = 2$).

5.5 Subperiod Analysis

However, the above evidence on European asymmetry and volatility persistence does not tell us anything about any changes that might have occurred in the nature of the monetary transmission mechanism within the EMS during the 1990s. First, we must examine the nature of asymmetry and volatility persistence after Germany's reunification in July 1990. Given the substantial evidence that there was a structural change in the nature and extent of interactions among the EMS countries [e.g., Gros and Thygesen (1994) and Laopodis (1999)], the model was re-estimated with a dummy variable in both the conditional mean and the variance taking the value of zero prior to July 1990 and one afterwards. The reported results in Panel A of Table 4 only include asymmetry and volatility persistence for the sake of space preservation. Regarding asymmetric behavior, the asymmetry coefficients (δ) generally surface as insignificant suggesting absence of asymmetric behavior in the volatility transmission mechanism of all short-term interest rates. By contrast, the coefficients of the volatility persistence (γ) are significant for the interest rates of Belgium, France, and the Netherlands but insignificant for those of the U.K. and Italy. However, there was a sharp reduction in the degree of persistence in the rates of Belgium, France and the Netherlands (relative to that in Table 2), which means that the impact of a German innovation on the volatility of these three countries' interest rates was shorter in duration and weaker in intensity in the 1990s than it was in the 1980s. Finally, the reunification dummy, although not statistically significant in the conditional mean, emerged as negative and significant in the conditional variance.

In Panel B of Table 4, the results from the introduction of the Euro are exhibited. As in Panel A, we only report the persistence and volatility coefficient estimates for the sake of space preservation. As seen from the estimates, asymmetry was absent for all countries' short-term interest rates and volatility persistence was even lower (compared to the estimates in Panel A). Further, the dummy variable for the introduction of the Euro emerged as negative and significant at both the conditional mean and variance. In sum, all above results imply a reduction in the nature and extent of volatility and asymmetry in the interest rates of the EMS countries in the post-unification period. These findings are in agreement with previous findings on asymmetric behavior [see Gros and Thygesen (1992) and the references therein]. Statistically speaking, to see if there is a significant difference in the results from the previous model (the restricted, r) and the present one with the two dummies (the unrestricted, u), the Likelihood Ratio (LR) statistic, defined as $LR = -2\ (LF_u - LF_r)$, was used and calculated. The results from this test point to significance (at the usual 5% level) of the full models for the two groups of countries.

5.6. Mean and Volatility Spillovers: EMS and U.S. Rates

Finally, in Table 5 the results from all the EMS countries including the U.S. for the entire period are presented. Three important observations can be made from the table. First, there are no significant and/or pronounced mean interactions (spillovers) among Germany, Italy, the U.K. and the U.S. although some are present among Belgium, France and the Netherlands. Specifically, the last three short-term interest rates are affected by Germany's interest rate although the Dutch rate is influenced by all rates except Belgium's. Interestingly, the U.S. rate does not appear to affect any rate's conditional mean except for the U.K.'s but the U.K.'s rate seems to influence those of France and the Netherlands. Second, looking at the results for the second-moment interdependencies it is clear that neither the German nor the U.S. interest rates affect all of the other countries' conditional variances. Specifically, the German interest rate seems to influence the Belgian and the French interest rates, while the U.S. rate affects the French, Italian and the British rates. Moreover, although the conditional variance of the German interest rate is not affected by any other interest rate, except by its own, the conditional variance of the U.S. is affected by the British interest rate. Therefore, based on this evidence, there is no predominant player the regional nor the global volatility transmission mechanisms, in the strict sense of the terms. This, in turn, implies that there is no evidence of international asymmetry.

The above evidence is in sharp contrast to many studies that included the U.S. interest rate in examining the monetary policy transmission mechanism across national borders. Specifically, Artus et *al.* (1991), Katsimbris and Miller (1993), Kirchgaessner and Wolters (1993) favor unidirectional causality linkages between U.S. and several European countries' interest rates, while Hassapis et *al.*(1999) report bi-directional linkages from the to the EMS countries. Uctum (1999) finds some support for the evidence in this paper in that U.S. and European short-term interest-rate linkages during the 1990s broke down completely. Obviously, this is due to the divergence of economic policies between the EMS and the U.S. that took place after Germany's reunification, as was mentioned earlier. In fact, when Germany kept increasing interest rates in the early 1990s, in order to finance the cost of reunification and the inflationary pressures that came with that, the U.S. simultaneously engaged in interest-rate declines to fight a recession.

The third and final observation from the results in the table concerns volatility persistence and asymmetric behavior in the volatility structure of the rates. In particular, persistence in volatility is generally lower for all rates and asymmetry is not present. Figure 1 plots the conditional standard deviations for Belgium, the Netherlands, and France for the entire sample period as derived from the empirical model. As is evident from each country's interest rate's conditional standard deviation, the extent of volatility persistence for all three short-term interest rates has significantly declined since the early 1990s (after observation 160 in the graph) compared to the 1980s.

These findings are in line with similar results found by other studies. Specifically, regarding the lower degree of volatility persistence, Gros and Weber (1991) report that, during the 1990s, the relative extent of the impact of an innovation in the German interest rates, compared to that of the French or the Italian rates, declined rapidly as the former's influence remained a bit more stronger than the French's.

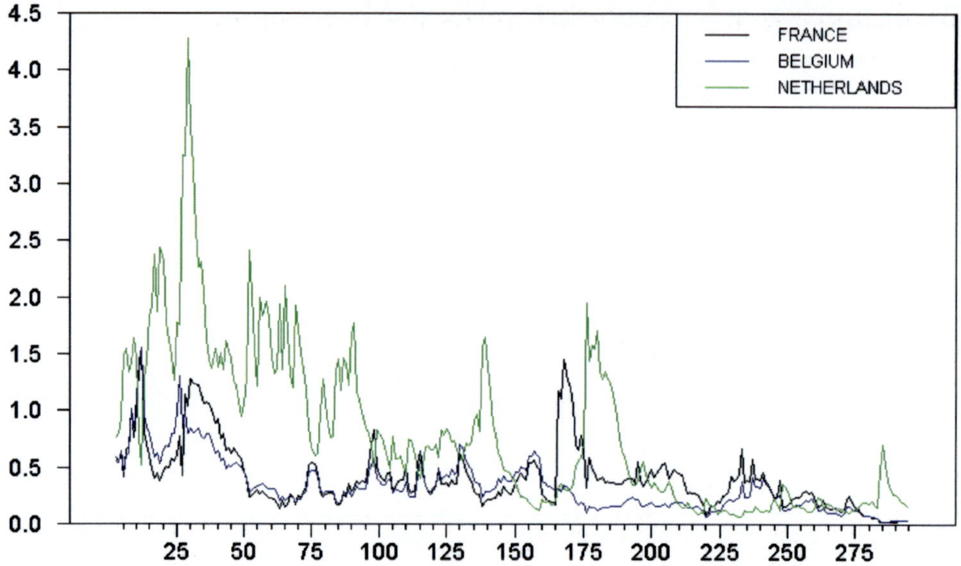

Figure 1. Conditional standard deviations.

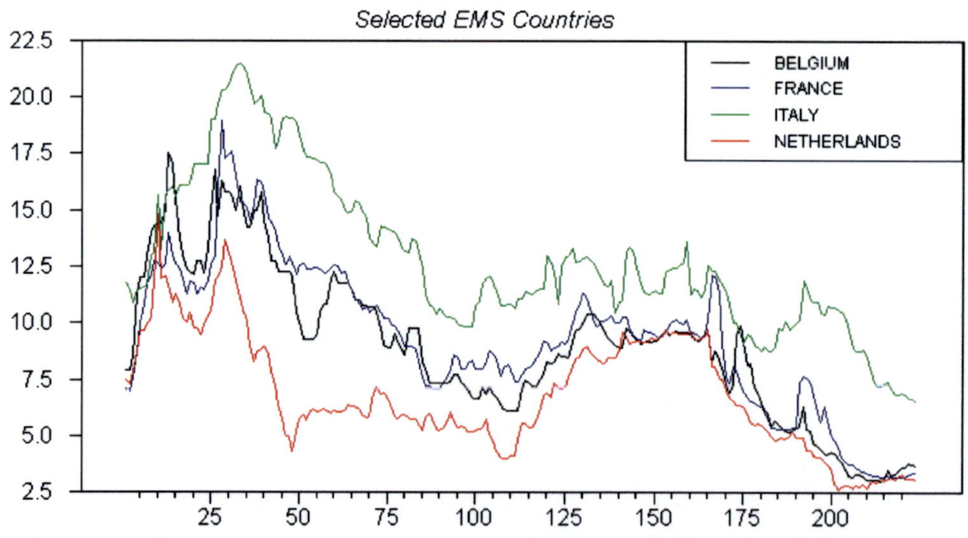

Figure 2. Short-term interest rates.

Finally, absence of asymmetric behavior is evidenced by the fact that many EMS members (especially France and Italy) had managed to bring their interest rates and inflation down sufficiently allowing them to adopt a less influential view of Germany's leadership (see Figure 2). In fact, during the 1990s there has been an increase in the degree of financial integration between France and Germany that can be attributed to the process of convergence towards the European Monetary union (see Camarero and Ordonez, 1999, p. 16). Besides, the concurrent drive for the (now in place) monetary union and the increasing degree of financial market liberalization by many European countries, in an attempt to stay on track with the single market program, further weakened the asymmetric nature of the EMS.

From a statistical point of view, correct model specification requires that the residuals have zero mean and unit variance as well as conform to first- and second-order time independencies. The results for the residuals and the cross-residuals are included at the bottom of Tables 2 through 5 (excluding Table 4). Several comments are warranted from these findings: first, the values for the skewness magnitude do not generally show any significance, while these for the kurtosis strongly validate its presence and moving closer to being normal. Second, although the normality results (from the Kolmogorov-Smirnov D-statistics) indicate a mixed picture, which may suggest that the asymptotic standard errors may be understated, the significance of most of the coefficients at more than the five percent level is usually sufficient to mitigate this concern. More importantly, the estimated Ljung-Box statistics, LB(.) and LB^2(.) for the residual series and the squared series, respectively, for three and six lags, show no evidence of either linear or nonlinear temporal dependencies in the standardized residuals. Further, the findings for the cross-product of the residuals (from the LB values again) point to absence of serial correlation, which validates the earlier assumption of constant (conditional) correlations. Taken as a whole, these diagnostics imply that the chosen model specification seems to constitute a reasonable parameterization of the variance-covariance structure of the interest rates as no remaining inter-temporal dynamics in the residual series are detected.

6. Summary and Conclusions

This paper re-examines the 'German Leadership Hypothesis', which claims that the Bundesbank's actions on monetary issues were followed by other EMS central banks, within the context of nominal short-term interest rates. The approach taken to address this hypothesis is based on the notion that German interest rates should convey valuable information to the other countries' rates, or that there exist significant multi-directional volatility spillovers from the Bundesbank's actions to the other nations' central banks. Further, to what extent does German leadership continue to exist in the presence of an outside monetary policy channel of influence, notably that of the U.S.? These questions are conveniently analyzed within a multivariate framework of the Exponential GARCH model, which is capable of capturing asymmetries of the volatility spillover mechanism.

The empirical results, in general, support the idea of a German predominance within the European Monetary System (that is, giving rise to European asymmetry), but not in an absolute (strict) sense, since Germany's short-term rates are also affected, although marginally at times, by actions from its partners. A related finding refers to the absence of asymmetric behavior within EMS after Germany's reunification due to the rapid convergence of the EMS countries with Germany's economy as they all prepared for the monetary union. In the eighties, the EMS was characterized by a high degree of asymmetry since the Bundesbank in the short-run did not consider developments in its partner countries when conducting its own monetary policy; thereafter, the asymmetric behavior of the system was gradually diminishing rendering thus the Bundesbank's policies more dependent on other countries' policies. This was due to the evolving nature of the EMS, which enabled more countries (especially France and Italy) to arrive at a German-competitor level as they were rapidly converging with Germany's economy. Another notable result is that when the U.S.

short-term interest rate is examined with the EMS rates, neither the German nor the U.S. rate surface as predominant players in the regional and international volatility transmission mechanism. This result suggests absence of international asymmetry with short-term interest rates. Finally, this is explained by the fact that during the post-unification era, the EMS and U.S. monetary policies were diverging instead of converging, although for different reasons.

A natural question to ask at this point is what might happen to the behavior of the volatility in the monetary transmission mechanism now that the Euro has been launched (for use in January 2002) in the Euroland. If the Euro assumes the (special) position that the Deutschemark enjoyed in the 1980s, then such (asymmetric) behavior in the conduct of the Euroland's monetary policy may render the European Central Bank's efforts volatile and noncredible. However, a more symmetric functioning of the system, as was found in this study to be the case since the 1990s, will enable the Central Bank to pursue policies consistent with its own, and the member countries', monetary objectives henceforth.

REFERENCES

Akgiray, V. (1989). Conditional heteroscedasticity in time series of stock returns: evidence and forecasts. *Journal of Business* 62(1), 55-80.

G.G. Booth, J.J. Hatem and C. Mustafa (1991). Conditional dependence in precious metal prices. *The Financial Review* 26, 367-386.

Artis, M. J. and W. Zhang (1999). Further evidence on the international business cycle and the ERM: is there a European business cycle?. *Oxford Economic Papers* 51, 120-132.

Artus, P., S. Avouyi-Dovi, E. Bleuse and F. Lecointe (1991). Transmission of U.S. monetary policy to Europe and asymmetry in the European Monetary System. *European Economic Review* 35, 1369-84.

Bajo-Rubio, O., S. Sosvilla-Rivero and F. Fernandez-Rodriguez (2001). Asymmetry in the EMS: New evidence based on non-linear forecasts. *European Economic Review* 45, 451-473.

Berndt, E.K., H.B. Hall, R.E. Hall and J.A. Hausman (1974). Estimation and inference in nonlinear structural models. *Annals of Economic and Social Measurement* 4, 653-666.

Bollerslev, T. (1990). Modeling the coherence in short-run nominal exchange rate: a multivariate generalized ARCH model. *The Review of Economics and Statistics* 72, 498-505.

Camarero, M. and J. Ordonez (1999). Who is ruling Europe? Empirical evidence on the German dominance hypothesis. University of Nottingham, Dept. of Economics, Discussion Paper No. DP 99/31 (October).

Chelley-Steeley, P. L. J. M. Steeley and E. J. Pentecost (1998). Exchange controls and European Stock market integration. *Applied Economics* 30, 263-267.

Dickey, D. A. and W. A. Fuller (1981). Likelihood ratio statistics for autoregressive time series with a unit root. *Econometrica* 49, 1057-1072.

Engel, C. and G. S. Hakkio (1996). The distribution of exchange rates in the EMS. *International Journal of Finance and Economics* 1, 55-67.

Fratianni M. and J. von Hagen (1990a). *The European Monetary System Ten Years After*, in C. Plosser and A. H. Meltzer, eds., Carnegie Rochester Conference Series on Public Policy 32.

(1990b). German Dominance in the EMS: the Empirical Evidence. *Open Economies Review* 1, 67-87.

Fujihara, R. and M. Mougoué (1996). International linkages between short term real interest rates. The *Quarterly Review of Economics and Finance* 36(4), Winter, 451-473.

Gardner, E. and W. Perraudin (1993). Asymmetry in the ERM: a case study of German and French interest rates before and after unification. *IMF Staff Papers* 40, 427-50.

Gebauer. W., M. Mueller, K.J.W. Schmidt, M. Thiel and A. Worms (1994). Determinants of long-term interest rates in selected countries: towards a European central bank policy design. In Johnson, C. and S. Collignon (eds.) *The Monetary Economics of Europe: Causes of the EMS crisis*. London: Pinter, pp. 189-226.

Griffiths, M. L. and D. C. MacDonald (1994). The ERM experience, in *Frameworks for Monetary Stability*, T.J.T. Baliño and C. Cottarelli (eds.) Washington: IMF.

Gros, T. (1992). Capital controls and foreign exchange market crises in the EMS. *European Economic Review* 36, December, 1533-1544. and N. Thygesen (1994). *European Monetary Integration: From the European Monetary System to European Monetary Union.* London: Logman.

Gros, T. and A. A. Weber (1991). Changing Asymmetries in the EMS - what does the high-frequency data tells us?. Manuscript, University of Siegen.

Hassapis, C., N. Pittis and K. Prodromidis (1999). Unit roots and Granger causality in the EMS interest rates: the German Dominance Hypothesis revisited. *Journal of International Money and Finance* 18, 47-73.

Herz, B. and R. Werner (1992). The EMS is a greater Deutschemark area? *European Economic Review* 36, 1413-25.

Kanas, A. (1997). The monetary exchange rate model within ERM: Cointegration tests and implications concerning the German dominance hypothesis. *Applied Financial Economics* 7, December, 587-598.

Karfakis, C. J. and D. M. Moschos (1990). Interest rate linkages within the European Monetary System: a time series analysis. *Journal of Money, Credit, and Banking* 22(3), August, 388-394.

Katsimbris, G.M. (1993). Interest rate linkages within the European monetary system: a multivariate analysis. *Journal of Multinational Financial Management* 2, 95-105. and S. M. Miller (1993). Interest rate linkages within the European Monetary System: further analysis. *Journal of Money, Credit, and Banking* 25, November, 771-779.

Kirchgaessner, G. and J. Wolters (1993). Does the DM dominate the euro market? An empirical investigation. *Review of Economics and Statistics* 75, 773-778.

Koutmos, G. and G. G. Booth (1995). Asymmetric volatility transmission in international stock markets. *Journal of International Money and Finance* 14(6), 747-762.

Laopodis, N. T. (1998). Asymmetric volatility spillovers in Deutschemark exchange rates. *Journal of Multinational Financial Management* 8, 413-430.

(1999). Asymmetries and time-varying behaviour in EMS exchange rates. *Journal of Foreign Exchange and International Finance* XIII(1), 45-56. (2001). International interest-rate transmission and the 'German dominance hypothesis' within EMS. *Open Economies Review* 12(4), October, 347-377.

(2004). International and European asymmetry in the volatility transmission mechanism: the 'German dominance hypothesis' revisited. *Journal of Economics and Business* 56(2), pp. 75-97.

Ma. Y. and A. Kanas (2000). Testing for a nonlinear relationship among fundamentals and exchange rates in the ERM. *Journal of International Money and Finance*, 19(1), February, 135-152.

Mastropasqua, C., S. Micossi and R. Rinaldi (1988). Interventions, sterilization and monetary policy in European Monetary System countries, 1979-1987, in F. Giavazzi, S. Micossi and M. Miller (eds.), *The European Monetary System*, Banca d'Italia, Centro Interuniversitario di Studi Teorici par la Politica Economica and Centre for Economic Policy Research, Cambridge University Press, Cambridge, pp. 252-81.

Nelson, D. (1991). Conditional heteroskedasticity in asset returns: a new approach. *Econometrica* 59, 347-70.

Phillips, P.C.B. and P. Perron (1988). Testing for a unit root in time series regressions. *Biometrica* 75, 335-346.

Uctum, M. (1999). European integration and asymmetry in the EMS. *Journal of International Money and Finance* 18, 769-798.

Ungerer, H. (1990). The European Monetary System: developments and perspectives, *IMF Occasional Paper* 73, November, Washington, DC.

Von Hagen, J. (1989). Monetary targeting with exchange rate constraints: the Bundesbank in the 1980s. *Federal Reserve Bank of St. Louis Review*, September/October.

Von Hagen, J. and M. Fratianni (1990). German dominance in the EMS: evidence from interest rates. *Journal of International Money and Finance* 9, 358-75.

Weber, A.A. (1991). European Economic and Monetary Union and Asymmetries and Adjustment Problems in the *European Monetary System: some empirical evidence*. European Economy 1 (special edition), Brussels: Commission of the European Communities, 187-207. (1996). Foreign exchange intervention and international policy coordination: comparing the G3 and EMS experience, in *The New Transatlantic Economy*. Centre for Economic Policy Research, London, 54-114.

Wyplosz, C. (1989). EMS puzzles. Paper presented at the Simposio de analisis economico, Barcelona, 18-20 December.

In: International Finance and Financial Services
Editor: Kristian L. Hagen, pp. 99-122

ISBN: 1-60021-756-7

Chapter 4

IRREVERSIBILITY AND COSTS OF ADJUSTMENT

F. S. Demers[1], M. Demers[1] and H. Schaller[1]
Department of Economics, Carleton University

ABSTRACT

The economic interpretation of the adjustment cost function in Q theory raises awkward questions. One common justification of adjustment costs is the disruption of production associated with the reorganization of production and the training of workers involved in installing new capital equipment. The problem with this interpretation is that reorganization and training both involve information as an input and might therefore be expected to result in decreasing marginal costs rather than increasing marginal costs.

In this chapter, we instead use the Demers (1991) model of uncertainty, irreversibility, and learning to motivate adjustment costs. In this model, irreversibility (in conjunction with the anticipation of receiving information) leads to lower investment levels than in the case of costless disposal of capital. The intuition is straightforward: errors of overinvestment are costly. In the model, irreversibility leads to an endogenous time-varying marginal adjustment cost. Thus, the "parameters" of the adjustment cost function vary over time because changes in expectations of future demand and the degree of uncertainty affect the size and likelihood of excess capital.

In our empirical work, we start by taking the Q theory as our null hypothesis; using standard assumptions, it is then possible to estimate the parameters of the adjustment cost function. If the assumptions of the Q model are correct, these parameters should be constant over time.

We use three different techniques to estimate the adjustment cost parameters. The first uses linear projections on past information to construct an estimate of the present value of the future stream of revenue from a unit of capital. The second takes advantage of market information: if the stock market is efficient, then the stock market price of a firm reflects the future revenue stream. The third avoids the construction of a present

[1] Correspondening authors: Department of Economics, Carleton University, 1125 Colonel By Drive, Ottawa ON Canada K1S 5B6, Email: fdemers@ccs.carleton.ca; mdemers@ccs.carleton.ca; schaller@ccs.carleton.ca, Tel: (613) 520-2600 ext. 3775; (613) 520-2600 ext. 3772; (613) 520-3751

value by focusing on the period-to-period arbitrage condition for the optimal choice of investment.

In order to allow the adjustment cost parameters to vary freely over time, we turn to a unique panel data set of 136 U.S. firms for which we have 36 years of data. We find that adjustment costs vary substantially over time. Furthermore, our results seem to support the irreversibility cum learning model since there is some evidence that the marginal adjustment cost parameter declines over time: as the firms in our sample mature and form a more precise estimate of the state of demand, the marginal adjustment costs due to irreversibility diminish.

Keywords: Irreversible Investments, Time-Varying Costs of Adjustment

1. Introduction

In the last decade or so, there has been a proliferation of work, both theoretical and empirical, based on the idea that investment may be at least partially irreversible. In this chapter, we present a model that emphasizes a distinctive implication of irreversibility, relative to the convex cost of adjustment-Q theory of investment, which has not been previously explored.

In Q theory, adjustment costs are assumed to be technologically determined; thus the parameters of the adjustment cost function are fixed and constant over time. The economic interpretation of the adjustment cost function in Q theory raises awkward questions. One common justification for the convexity of adjustment costs is the disruption of production associated with the reorganization of production and the training of workers involved in installing new capital equipment. The problem with this interpretation is that reorganization and training both involve information as an input and might therefore be expected to result in decreasing rather than increasing marginal costs. As Bertola and Caballero (1994) point out, "the realism of smooth adjustment costs as the source of investment dynamics is doubtful. From a microeconomic point of view, the cost of additions to an individual firm's capital stock is often linear in investment; the unit price of capital may even be decreasing in investment if lump-sum adjustment costs are present."

Furthermore, empirical studies have often found that the "adjustment cost/Tobin's Q" model did not perform satisfactorily.[2] Whereas Q theory implies that all relevant information is captured in market valuation, other variables such as cash-flow and profitability are statistically significant.[3] Estimated adjustment costs are implausibly large even in panel studies.

One way to endogenize costs of adjustment is to introduce irreversibility and uncertainty. The notion of irreversibility has been extensively applied to the investment decisions of firms. Contributions to this literature include Nickell (1977), Bernanke (1983), Demers (1985, 1991), McDonald and Siegel (1986), Bertola (1988), Pindyck (1988), Bertola and Caballero (1994), Dixit and Pindyck (1994), and Abel and Eberly (1996b).[4]

---

[2] See in particular, Abel and Blanchard (1986) and Oliner, Rudebusch, and Sichel (1995) who demonstrate that an ad hoc accelerator model performs better than a Q theoretic model.

[3] See Chirinko (1993) for a review of the evidence.

[4] See Demers, Demers, and Altug (2003), Carruth et al (2000), Caballero (1999), and Dixit and Pindyck (1994) for surveys.

In this chapter we follow Demers (1985, 1991) who combines learning with irreversibility to analyze investment behavior. Consider a risk neutral firm that is uncertain about the permanent state of demand but has prior beliefs that it updates each period by Bayes' law after receiving informative signals. Demers (1991) shows that the irreversibility of investment in conjunction with the anticipation of receiving information lead to lower investment levels than in the case of costless disposal of capital. The intuition is straightforward: errors of overinvestment are costly. In addition, irreversibility and the arrival of information lead to an endogenous time-varying marginal adjustment cost. The firm will gradually adjust its capital stock to the desired level where the desired capital stock takes on a new meaning here; it is the capital stock that the firm would choose if it knew the true state of present and future demand.

We believe that this approach embodies several realistic features of the investment decision faced by firms: the first is uncertainty, specifically in the form of imperfect knowledge of the path of future demand for the firm's product; the second is the arrival of information and learning. Uncertainty and learning, however, do not fundamentally alter the firm's problem unless it faces difficulty in disposing of capital goods. In fact, the markets for used capital goods are typically quite thin, and firms may either be unable to sell surplus capital goods or, at best, be forced to sell them at a substantial discount.

As noted above, the irreversibility model presented below has a distinctive implication that differentiates it from Q theory. In the irreversibility model presented in Section 2, the "parameters" of the adjustment cost function vary over time because changes in expectations of future demand and the degree of uncertainty affect the size and likelihood of the penalty a firm faces if it finds itself with excess capital. In our empirical work, we start by taking the Q theory as our null hypothesis; using standard assumptions, it is then possible to estimate the parameters of the adjustment cost function. If the assumptions of the Q model are correct, these parameters should be constant over time. Under the alternative model, the parameters should vary.

We use three different techniques to estimate the adjustment cost parameters. The first uses linear projections on past information to construct an estimate of the present value of the future stream of revenue from a unit of capital. The second takes advantage of market information: if the stock market is efficient, then the stock market price of a firm reflects the future revenue stream. The third avoids the construction of a present value by focusing on the period-to-period arbitrage condition for the optimal choice of investment. To the extent that our results are robust across these very different techniques, they provide relatively strong evidence.

Allowing the adjustment cost parameters to vary freely over time would be difficult with aggregate time-series data. As the time period over which adjustment costs are allowed to vary decreases, the available degrees of freedom shrink toward zero. We therefore turn to a unique panel data set of 136 U.S. firms over the period of 1951 to 1986. To give a preview of the results, we find that adjustment costs vary substantially over time. Furthermore, our results seem to support the irreversibility cum learning model since there is some evidence that the marginal adjustment cost parameter declines over time: as the firms in our sample mature and form a more precise estimate of the state of demand, the marginal adjustment costs due to irreversibility diminish.

Section 2 describes the irreversibility model. Section 3 describes a standard model of investment with convex costs of adjustment and without irreversibility. Sections 4, 5 and 6 outline the linear projection, market, and Euler approaches to estimating the marginal adjustment cost parameter. In addition, these sections present empirical results based on the respective techniques. Section 7 summarizes the main findings.

2. THE IRREVERSIBILITY MODEL

Consider a monopolistic risk neutral firm. Each period, it makes variable input and investment decisions. At time t it produces output Y_t using capital K_t (which is predetermined at t), and variable inputs L_t. The firm's production function $F(K_t, L_t)$ is twice continuously differentiable, increasing, concave, and satisfies the Inada conditions. Let p_t denote the stochastic output price. We assume a constant elasticity demand function. The inverse market demand function is given by:

$$p_t = \alpha_t (Y_t)^{-\varepsilon}, \tag{2.1}$$

where $-1/\varepsilon < -1$ is the price elasticity of demand and α_t is a stochastic parameter representing the state of demand satisfying: $\alpha_t = \bar{\alpha} + u_{\alpha t}$ where $u_{\alpha t}$ is IID.

The optimal choice of variable factors involves static optimization under certainty. We can define the short-run profit function at time t, $\Pi(K_t, \alpha_t, w_t)$, as

$$\Pi(K_t, \alpha_t, w_t) = \max_{L_t > 0} \{ p_t F(K_t, L_t) - w_t \cdot L_t) \} \tag{2.2}$$

where w_t is the variable input price. The short-run profit function Π is continuous in K_t, α_t, w_t, increasing in K_t, α_t and decreasing in w_t, and strictly concave in K_t.[5] We assume that Π is bounded for finite K_t, α_t, w_t. The firm's after-tax cash flow, R_t, is defined as:

$$R_t = (1-\tau_t)\Pi K_t, \alpha_t, w_t + \tau_t \sum_{x=1}^{T} D_{x,t-x} p_{t-x}^k I_{t-x} - (1-\gamma_t) p_t^k I_t, \tag{2.3}$$

where I_t is the firm's rate of gross investment measured in physical units, and p_t^k the non-stochastic purchase price of investment goods, τ_t is the corporate tax rate at time t, γ_t is the investment tax credit at time t as a percentage of the price of the investment good, $D_{x,t-x}$ is the depreciation allowance per dollar invested for tax purposes for capital equipment of age x

[5] The strict concavity of Π is necessary in a model of irreversible investment in order to ensure the uniqueness of the investment policy.

on the basis of the tax law effective at time t-x, and T is the life of the equipment.[6] For future reference, we define z_t as the present value of tax deductions on new investment and p_t^I as the tax-adjusted price of investment goods, where

$$z_t = \sum_{n=1}^{T} \tau_{t+n} D_{n,t} (1-i_t)^{-n} \tag{2.4}$$

where i_t is the nominal interest rate and

$$p_t^I = (1-\gamma_t - z_t) p_t^k \tag{2.5}$$

Letting δ , $0 < \delta < 1$, be the depreciation rate, the law of motion of the capital stock is:

$$K_{t+1} = (1-\delta) K_t + I_t \tag{2.6}$$

We assume that investment is completely irreversible:

$$I_t \geq 0 \tag{2.7}$$

The nonnegativity of gross investment captures the irreversibility constraint faced by the firm.[7]

Turning to the informational structure of the model the firm knows the possible states of demand but does not know with certainty which one is the true state. Let $\bar{A} \equiv \{\bar{\alpha}_1, \ldots, \bar{\alpha}_n\}$ be the set of possible states. The firm has a prior probability distribution about the true state $\bar{\alpha}$ denoted by Ψ^0, where $\Psi^0 = \left[\psi_1^0, \ldots, \psi_n^0\right]$, $\psi_i^0 > 0$, $i = 1, \ldots, n$, and $\sum_{i=1}^{n} \psi_i^0 = 1$; ψ_i^0 is the prior probability that $\bar{\alpha} = \bar{\alpha}_i, i = 1, \ldots, n$. Each period the firm observes the realization of α_t and the realization of a non-price signal b_t which is informative about $\bar{\alpha}$ and which may consist of various pieces of information such as the monetary growth rate, financial surveys, etc. We denote by H^α the set of all possible signals $h_t^\alpha \equiv (\alpha_t, b_t)$.

Letting $f_j(x_t \mid \bar{\alpha}_i), j = 1, 2$, be the density of x_t, conditional on $\bar{\alpha}_i$ being the true state, $x_t = \alpha_t, b_t$, we can define $\lambda(h_t^\alpha \mid \bar{\alpha}_i) \equiv f_1(\alpha_t \mid \bar{\alpha}_i) f_2(b_t \mid \bar{\alpha}_i)$ as the likelihood of observing h_t^α given that the true state is $\bar{\alpha}_i$. The firm revises its prior probability distribution Ψ^0 by applying Bayes' law. That is,

[6] This reflects the tax treatment in the United States. See Hayashi (1982).
[7] See Demers, Demers, and Altug (2003) for a more general model with partial irreversibility.

$$\psi_i^t = \frac{\lambda(h_t^\alpha \mid \bar{\alpha}_i)\psi_i^{t-1}}{\sum_{j=1}^{n} \lambda(h_t^\alpha \mid \bar{\alpha}_j)\psi_j^{t-1}} \qquad h_t^\alpha \in H^\alpha, \quad i = 1,\ldots,n, \quad t = 1,2,\ldots \tag{2.8}$$

$\Psi^t(h_t^\alpha) = \left[\psi_1^t(h_t^\alpha),\ldots,\psi_n^t(h_t^\alpha)\right]$ represents the firm's state of information at time t. For all $t, \Psi^t \in D(\bar{A})$ is the set of all probability distributions on $\bar{A}$. The evolution of the information state can be expressed as

$$\Psi^t(h_t^\alpha) = g\left(\Psi^{t-1}, h_t^\alpha\right), \tag{2.9}$$

where g denotes the law of motion of the information state and updating according to Bayes' law. Note that g does not have a time subscript since the revision process is time-invariant.

Let E_t denote the expectation operator using the predictive density $\Theta(h_{t+1}^\alpha \mid \Psi^t)$. Using dynamic programming, we can express the firm's problem recursively as

$$V(K_t, \Psi^t, \alpha_t, w_t, p_t^I) = \max_{I_t}\{(1-\tau_t)\Pi(K_t, \alpha_t, w_t) - p_t^I I_t + \beta E_t V(K_{t+1}, \Psi^{t+1}(h_{t+1}^\alpha), \alpha_{t+1}, w_{t+1}, p_{t+1}^I)\} \tag{2.10}$$

subject to (2.6), (2.7), (2.9), K_t, Ψ^t given and where $0 < \beta < 1$ is the discount factor. Letting V_K denote the partial derivative with respect to K_{t+1} we can write the first-order necessary and sufficient condition for the optimization problem at time t as:

$$\begin{aligned} -p_t^I + \beta E_t V_K(K_{t+1}, \Psi^{t+1}(h_{t+1}^\alpha), \alpha_{t+1}, w_{t+1}, p_{t+1}^I) &= 0 \ \text{if } I_t^* > 0 \\ &\le 0 \ \text{if } I_t^* = 0. \end{aligned} \tag{2.11}$$

Also, let:

$$\Phi_t \equiv (1-\delta)\{E_t p_{t+1}^I - E_t \min[p_{t+1}^I, \beta E_{t+1} V_K((1-\delta)K_{t+1}, g(\Psi^{t+1}, h_{t+2}^\alpha), \alpha_{t+2}, w_{t+2}, p_{t+2}^I)]\} \tag{2.12}$$

Assume that an interior solution obtains at t. After substituting for V_K and for $\beta = (1+r)^{-1}$, (2.11) can be rearranged as:

$$c_t + \Phi_t = (1-\tau_{t+1})E_t \Pi_K(K_{t+1}, \alpha_{t+1}, w_{t+1}) \tag{2.13}$$

The right-hand side of (2.13) is the marginal benefit of investing an additional unit. The left-hand side is the total cost of investing which is the sum of the Jorgensonian cost of capital, $c_t = p_t^I(r+\delta)-(1-\delta)(E_t p_{t+1}^I - p_t^I)$, and of Φ_t, a time-varying marginal risk premium when the firm invests an additional unit.[8]

Φ_t would vanish if investment were completely reversible. It can be interpreted as a "cost-of-adjustment" term which arises *endogenously*. In a model with learning, this opportunity cost of investing varies through time with the firm's state of information.[9] Our empirical tests focus on these adjustment costs. In contrast to the exogenous adjustment costs which are assumed in the standard model, the adjustment costs in the irreversibility model will vary through time since they depend on the state of information.[10] Furthermore, the marginal adjustment cost will diminish as the firm learns the true state of demand over time.

3. The Convex Cost of Adjustment Model

We now consider a standard model without irreversibility and learning but with exogenous convex adjustment costs. Let $G(I_t, K_t)$ denote the exogenous time-invariant adjustment cost function. Let subscripts on G denote derivatives with respect to its arguments. We let $G_I > 0, G_{II} > 0, G_K < 0$ and $G_{KK} > 0$. We can now define the short-run profit function, $\pi(K_t, \alpha_t, w_t)$, which incorporates costs of adjustment, as:

$$\pi(K_t,\alpha_t,w_t) \equiv \max_{L_t>0}\{p_t F(K_t,L_t) - w_t \cdot L_t - G(I_t,K_t)\} \tag{3.14}$$

---

[8] The optimality condition can be presented in an alternative manner which yields a similar interpretation. In particular, (2.11) can be expressed as:

$$\begin{aligned} & p_t^I + \beta C_K^L(K_{t+1}, p_{t+1}^I) \\ &= \beta E_{t+1}\{(1-\tau_{t+1})\Pi_K(K_{t+1}, h_{t+1}) + \beta(1-\delta)E_{t+1}V_K((1-\delta)K_{t+1}, g(\Psi^{t+1}, h_{t+2}^{\alpha}), h_{t+2}, p_{t+2}^I)\} \\ &\equiv \Xi_t + \Upsilon_t \end{aligned}$$

where $h_t \equiv (\alpha_t, w_t)$, C_K^L is the marginal call option, Ξ_t is the expected marginal value of capital if the firm neither invests nor disinvests from t+1 onward, and simply allows its capital stock to depreciate, while Υ_t represents the increase in the expected marginal value of capital due to future growth options available to the firm. The marginal call option, C_K^L is an additional cost that must be taken into account when investment is irreversible since by investing one additional unit at t, the firm loses the option to wait and invest that unit at t+1. This additional cost tends to discourage investment. It plays a role analogous to the exogenous marginal cost of adjustment term. However, it is endogenous and time-varying. See Demers, Demers, and Altug (2003).

[9] Furthermore, proceeding analogously as in Demers (1991, Proposition 4), it can be demonstrated that the anticipation of greater information increases the risk premium associated with irreversibility since the prospect of obtaining greater information depresses the expected marginal value of capital which in turn increases the likelihood of facing a binding constraint in the future. That is, the firm requires a higher premium in order to undertake an extra unit of investment that diminishes its flexibility.

[10] Alternatively, we could assume that $u_{\alpha t}$ is serially correlated without altering our results. In this case Φ would be varying through time due to both subjective uncertainty and objective risk.

Thus, marginal revenue from an additional unit of capital at time t is given by

$$\pi_K(K_t, \alpha_t, w_t) = \alpha_t(1-\varepsilon)F_K(K_t, L_t^*) - G_K(I_t, K_t). \tag{3.15}$$

where $L_t^* \equiv L^*(K_t, \alpha_t, w_t)$ is the maximized value of the variable input. We can now rewrite the optimization problem of the firm in the presence of adjustment costs as:

$$\max_{\{I_t, K_{t+1}\}_{t=1}^{\infty}} E_0 \sum_{t=1}^{\infty} \beta^{t-1}[(1-\tau_{t+1})\pi(K_t, \alpha_t, w_t) - p_t^I I_t]$$

subject to $K_{t+1} = (1-\delta)K_t + I_t,\ K_0\ given$ (3.16)

We state the first order conditions that are relevant in deriving the empirical specification. Let λ_t be the "shadow value" of a unit of capital at the beginning of t. The first order conditions with respect to capital and investment are:

$$\frac{\partial L}{\partial K_{t+1}} = \beta(1-\tau_{t+1})E_t\pi_K(K_{t+1}, \alpha_{t+1}, w_{t+1}) - E_t\lambda_{t+1} + \beta(1-\delta)E_t\lambda_{t+2} = 0 \tag{3.17}$$

$$\frac{\partial L}{\partial I_t} = -(1-\tau_t)G_I(I_t, K_t) - p_t^I + E_t\lambda_{t+1} = 0 \tag{3.18}$$

In our empirical implementation we will assume a quadratic form for costs of adjustment:

$$G(I_t, K_t) = \left(\frac{\phi}{2}\right)\left(\frac{I_t}{K_t}\right)^2 K_t \tag{3.19}$$

where $\phi > 0$ is the marginal adjustment cost parameter.

4. The Linear Projection Approach

One approach to estimating marginal adjustment costs was suggested by Abel and Blanchard (1986). The key idea is to project marginal Q on variables in the information set at time t.[11] Like the market approach discussed below, it does not require the specification of a functional form for the production technology. In addition, it can be implemented in a way which allows the econometrician to be agnostic about imperfect competition and scale economies in production.

[11] A main advantage of this approach is that we do not need to assume that the firm's stock market price necessarily represents the present value of future cash flows.

The first order condition for capital (3.17) is a difference equation which can be solved forward, subject to a terminal condition, to obtain the expected shadow value of capital at t+1:

$$E_t\lambda_{t+1} = E_t\left\{\sum_{j=1}^{\infty}\beta^j(1-\delta)^{j-1}(1-\tau_{t+j})\pi_K(K_{t+j},h_{t+j})\right\}. \tag{4.20}$$

This expression is often referred to as "marginal Q" because it represents the marginal increase in the firm's value for a unit relaxation in the capital constraint. The shadow value of capital is the present value of the revenue stream generated by a marginal unit of capital.

In this chapter, we use a slightly simplified version of the Abel and Blanchard (1986) approach.[12] In particular, we assume that the interest rate is constant so that the discount factor applied to future cash flows is $\beta = (1+r)^{-1}$ .We also let:

$$\rho \equiv \frac{(1-\delta)}{1+r} \tag{4.21}$$

The parameter ρ can be thought of as the expanded discount factor which incorporates depreciation.[13] With this notation, we can rewrite the expression for the shadow value of capital as:

$$E_t\lambda_{t+1} \equiv E_t[\lambda_{t+1}\,|\,\Omega_t] = \sum_{j=1}^{\infty}\rho^j(1-\delta)^{j-1}(1-\tau_{t+j})E[\pi_{Kt+j}\,|\,\Omega_t] \tag{4.22}$$

where Ω_t denotes the information set and where $\pi_{Kt+j} \equiv \pi_K(K_{t+j},h_{t+j})$. Expression (4.22) emphasizes the key feature of the VAR approach, namely that we project the shadow value of capital on variables in the information set, Ω_t . Since we cannot directly observe the stream of future expected marginal products of capital we estimate a VAR representation of operating profits and sales normalized by the capital stock, namely $\overline{\pi}_t$ and S_t :

$$\begin{bmatrix}\overline{\pi}_t\\ S_t\end{bmatrix} = \begin{bmatrix}a(L) & b(L)\\ c(L) & d(L)\end{bmatrix}\begin{bmatrix}\overline{\pi}_{t-1}\\ S_{t-1}\end{bmatrix} + \begin{bmatrix}v_{1t}\\ v_{2t}\end{bmatrix} \tag{4.23}$$

The equations can be stacked into a first order system:

---

[12] The approach has been successfully applied to panel data by Gilchrist and Himmelberg (1992).

[13] In the empirical work we set $\rho = 0.8$.

$$\begin{bmatrix} \bar{\pi}_t \\ \cdot \\ \bar{\pi}_{t-j+1} \\ S_t \\ \cdot \\ S_{t-j+1} \end{bmatrix} = \begin{bmatrix} a_1 & \dots & a_j & b_1 & \dots & b_j \\ 1 & & & & & \\ & & 1 & & & \\ c_1 & \dots & c_j & d_1 & \dots & d_j \\ & & & 1 & & \\ & & & & & 1 \end{bmatrix} \begin{bmatrix} \bar{\pi}_{t-1} \\ \cdot \\ \bar{\pi}_{t-j} \\ S_{t-1} \\ \cdot \\ S_{t-j} \end{bmatrix} + \begin{bmatrix} v_{1t} \\ 0 \\ \\ v_{2t} \\ 0 \\ 0 \end{bmatrix} \quad (4.24)$$

which can be rewritten in companion matrix form as:

$$Z_t = AZ_{t-1} + v_t \quad (4.25)$$

Now, let $(1-\tau_{t+1})\pi_{Kt+1} = e_1^{'}Z_{t+1}$ where e_1 is a vector whose first element is 1 and all other elements are 0. Then:

Table 1. Estimates of the Marginal Adjustment Cost Parameter Using the Linear Projection Approach

Year	φ	NT	Criterion
1954	34.8573 (2.71241)	136	0.497835
1955	25.6754 (2.26423)	136	0.353591
1956	25.3123 (1.50193)	136	0.537983
1957	17.4079 (1.50767)	136	0.403582
1958	25.6758 (2.74724)	136	0.441476
1959	23.9543 (2.31935)	136	0.594695
1960	0.8565 (2.39484)	136	0.510106
1961	25.4365 (3.20611)	136	0.591922
1962	23.4658 (2.31743)	136	0.666793
1963	20.7808 (2.00148)	136	0.579665
1964	16.3788 (1.45367)	136	0.553525
1965	13.2799 (0.966662)	136	0.594723
1966	12.6048 (0.918973)	136	0.577756
1967	11.6619 (0.927582)	136	0.421650

1968	15.5510 (0.958577)	136		0.599193
1969	14.7524 (0.997259)	136		0.501564
1970	15.2733 (1.07142)	136		0.587399
1971	15.7951 (1.27092)	136		0.515164
1972	15.1784 (1.32862)	136		0.685652
1973	12.2421 (1.08900)	136		0.666459
1974	9.25995 (0.735732)	136		0.567704
1975	10.5309 (0.800501)	136		0.422844
1976	12.9504 (0.903100)	136		0.542153
1977	10.9239 (0.849915)	136		0.575269
1978	10.1465 (0.812890)	136		0.615518
1979	8.70969 (0.861749)	136		0.584536
1980	10.1987 (0.992244)	136		0.648211
1981	12.3744 (1.39687)	136		0.672088
1982	16.7339 (1.91252)	136		0.733008
1983	36.3609 (8.31417)	136		0.804343
1984	41.0785 (18.8295)	136		0.782207
1985	19.4081 (4.19649)	136		0.767165
1954-85	11.6956 (0.216767)	4352	0.353558	59.5 [.0000]

Under the Q theory of investment, the marginal adjustment cost parameter (φ) should be constant over time. Under the irreversibility model, φ should vary over time. The F statistic tests the hypothesis that φ is constant over time. The marginal significance level for a rejection of this hypothesis is in square brackets. The linear projection approach is described in Section IV. N is the number of firms and T is the number of years, so NT is the number of observations. The estimation method is GMM. The instruments are three lags of operating income and sales (both normalized by the capital stock). Robust standard errors are presented in parentheses below the parameter estimates. The J test [Hansen (1982)] is equal to the criterion times NT.

$$P[(1-\tau_{t+j})\pi_{Kt+j} \mid Z_t] = e_1' A^j Z_t \quad (4.26)$$

This VAR allows us to form a projection, P, of the shadow value of capital at time $t+1$ on a subset, Z_t, of the variables in the information set Ω_t, namely past profitability and sales:

$$P[\lambda_{t+1} \mid Z_t] = (1-\delta)^{-1} \sum_{j=1}^{\infty} \rho^j P[(1-\tau_{t+j})\pi_{Kt+j} \mid Z_t] = e_1'(1-\delta)^{-1}\rho A(I-\rho A)^{-1} Z_t \quad (4.27)$$

By substituting this projection into (3.18), we obtain an empirically implementable version of the investment equation:

$$\frac{1}{(1-\tau_t)}\left[P[\lambda_{t+1} \mid Z_t] - p_t^I\right] = \phi \frac{I_t}{K_t} = e_t^L \quad (4.28)$$

The stochastic error term e_t^L arises when we substitute the projected value of λ_{t+1} for the true value. We use the superscript L (as a mnemonic for linear projection) to distinguish this error term from the error terms that arise in the market and Euler approaches.

We estimate the above specification separately for each year, using the cross-sectional variation in our panel data to identify ϕ. The individual firm data are constructed primarily from financial statement and share price data on the Compustat tape. Because of the desirability of a long time series for this project, we used a special version of the tape which contains much earlier data than the standard 20-year Compustat tape. The procedure for calculating each firm's capital stock and other variables is described in detail in Schaller (1990).[14] The sample of firms used in this chapter consists of all firms for which investment, the capital stock, and other required variables could be constructed for the period 1951-1985.[15]

The estimation method is GMM. This is the appropriate estimation procedure because we are estimating first-order conditions so both $P[\lambda_{t+1} \mid Z_t]$ and $\frac{I_t}{K_t}$ are endogenous. We adjust the GMM weighting matrix, and thus the standard errors, for heteroscedasticity but not serial correlation. The instruments are listed in the notes following each table.[16]

Estimates of the marginal adjustment cost parameter using the linear projection approach are presented in Table I. It is immediately apparent that the variations in the adjustment cost parameter from year to year are quite large, relative to the standard error of the estimated parameter. For example, the estimate of ϕ for 1954 is 34.9 (with a standard error of 2.7), compared with an estimate of 25.7 (with a standard error of 2.3) for 1955.

---

[14] In this chapter, a narrow measure of the capital stock is used; i.e., one which does not include inventories as part of the capital stock.

[15] The sample period for which the adjustment cost parameter can be estimated is shorter due to the need to use lagged values as instruments.

[16] Monte Carlo simulations (Tauchen (1986)) show that when longer lags are used as instruments, the point estimates concentrate around biased values and the standard errors are misleading. We therefore use short lags of each instrument.

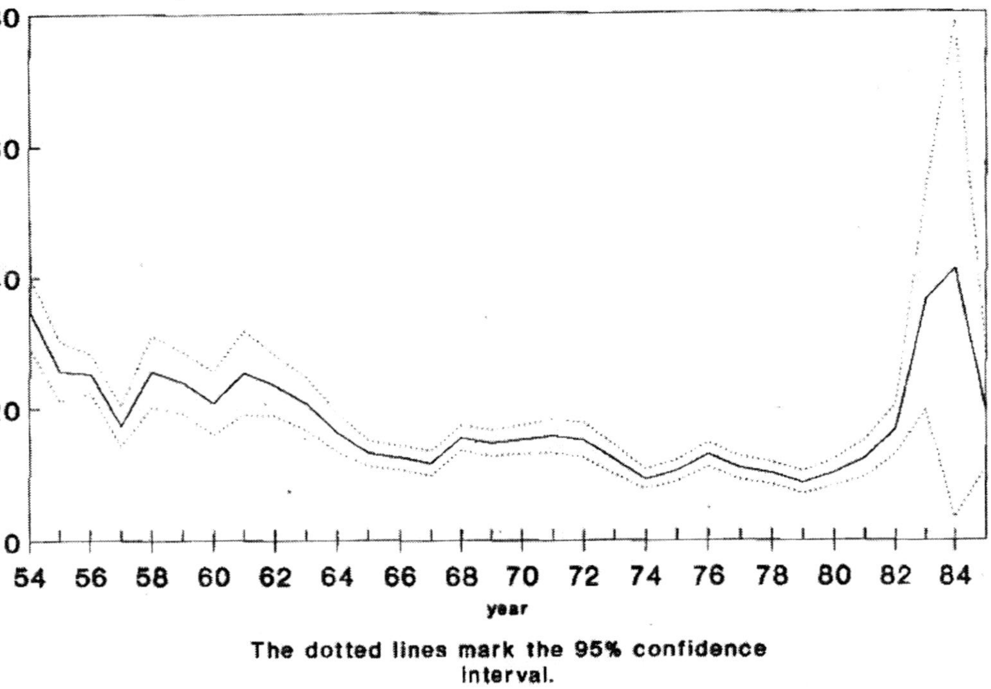

Figure 1. Estimated Marginal Adjustment Cost Parameter (Linear Projection Approach).

It is easier to see the magnitude of the fluctuations in Figure 1. Contrary to the standard cost of adjustment model of investment without irreversibility, there are substantial fluctuations in ϕ throughout the sample. Figure 1 suggests that the adjustment cost parameter displays a slightly countercyclical pattern, rising in 1958, 1961, 1974-76, and 1980-83. There is also an apparent drop in adjustment costs from the early 1950's to the early 1980's.[17] Intuitively, this is consistent with the irreversibility model. As the firm learns over time, one would expect the degree of uncertainty to decline, ceteris paribus. Thus, the marginal adjustment cost generated by the irreversibility constraint should tend to fall over time. We estimate the adjustment cost parameter using a balanced panel of firms, so the firms are older at the end of the sample than at the beginning, implying that the estimated marginal adjustment cost parameter should diminish.

The last row in Table I presents an estimate of ϕ for the full sample period and an F test for the restriction of a constant ϕ over time. The F statistic is 59.5, implying a rejection of the null hypothesis of a constant marginal adjustment cost parameter at the .0000 level.

[17] The point estimates of ϕ are very high in 1983, 1984 and 1985, but these should be treated with caution due to the large standard errors.

5. THE MARKET APPROACH

One popular way of empirically estimating marginal adjustment costs was suggested by Hayashi (1982), who showed that, under stock market efficiency, perfect competition and constant returns to scale, the unobserved shadow price of capital is equal to the value of the firm as determined by financial markets, per unit of capital. Recalling that $E_t\lambda_{t+1}$ is the firm's shadow value of an additional unit of capital and that $\beta E_t V(K_{t+1})$ is the firm's discounted expected future value as of the end of period t, we can divide the latter by the end of period t capital stock, K_{t+1} (the capital stock that will become productive starting next period) to obtain:

Table 2. Estimates of the Marginal Adjustment Cost Parameter using the Market Approach

Year	φ	NT	Criterion
1953	1.62031 (1.14820)	136	0.0714291
1954	11.8890 (2.33666)	136	0.0956132
1955	16.0949 (2.34504)	136	0.0957220
1956	11.4029 (1.63086)	136	0.0561149
1957	5.22754 (1.21631)	136	0.0626449
1958	22.6571 (3.10897)	136	0.0706061
1959	20.9623 (2.84883)	136	0.0773433
1960	17.8851 (2.99318)	136	0.108316
1961	28.9445 (3.35733)	136	0.0732486
1962	15.6330 (1.84671)	136	0.0805628
1963	20.2739 (2.54597)	136	0.0967036
1964	18.3563 (2.09570)	136	0.0997347
1965	16.5251 (2.02893)	136	0.176049
1966	9.31827 (1.20570)	136	0.143319

1967	14.6435 (1.84236)	136		0.140506
1968	17.0255 (1.87613)	136		0.156285
1969	8.47473 (1.87738)	136		0.139352
1970	10.0072 (1.41539)	136		0.216144
1971	12.9151 (2.15111)	136		0.149299
1972	13.8435 (2.34665)	136		0.124442
1973	6.36048 (1.58446)	136		0.176833
1974	- .580064 (.711570)	136		0.112116
1975	1.56381 (.849021)	136		0.120488
1976	3.42187 (.933303)	136		0.137629
1977	.351600 (.771818)	136		0.270018
1978	- .724068 (.709411)	136		0.220516
1979	.187649 (.588258)	136		0.197337
1980	1.21926 (.820654)	136		0.157647
1981	- .364777 (.626461)	136		0.198455
1982	.424847 (.773008)	136		0.220045
1983	2.95056 (.895726)	136		0.213196
1984	1.69516 (.698317)	136		0.191646
1953-84	10.8114 (0.3977)	4352	0.052118	12.1 [.0000]

Under the Q theory of investment, the marginal adjustment cost parameter (φ) should be constant over time. Under the irreversibility model, φ should vary over time. The F statistic tests the hypothesis that φ is constant over time. The marginal significance level for a rejection of this hypothesis is in square brackets. The market approach is described in Section V. N is the number of firms and T is the number of years, so NT is the number of observations. The estimation method is GMM. The instruments are two lags of q and the ratio of investment to the capital stock. Robust standard errors are presented in parentheses below the parameter estimates. The J test [Hansen (1982)] is equal to the criterion times NT.

$$E_t\lambda_{t+1} = \frac{\beta E_t V(K_{t+1})}{K_{t+1}} \tag{5.29}$$

We define "average Q", which is observable, as:

$$Q_t \equiv \left\{ \frac{\beta E_t V(K_{t+1})}{p_t^I K_{t+1}} - 1 \right\} \frac{p_t^I}{(1-\tau_t)} \tag{5.30}$$

Using the functional form assumption for adjustment costs, we can rewrite the first order condition for investment as:

$$E_t\lambda_{t+1} = p_t^I + (1-\tau_t)\phi \frac{I_t}{K_t} \tag{5.31}$$

Combining (5.31) with (5.30) and (5.29), we can write an empirically estimable investment equation:

$$Q_t - \phi \frac{I_t}{K_t} = e_t^M \tag{5.32}$$

where e_t^M is a stochastic error term. The superscript M distinguishes this error term from the error terms which arise using the other methods of estimating marginal adjustment costs.

Table 2 presents estimates of the marginal adjustment cost parameter based on the market approach.[18] Again, there is strong evidence of changes in the parameter over time. For example, the estimate of ϕ for 1968 is 17.0 (with a standard error of 1.9); for 1969, the estimate is 8.05 (with a standard error of 1.9).

Figure 2 shows the time series of the estimated marginal adjustment cost parameter. The fluctuations of the parameter are substantially larger than the 95% confidence interval. The time series pattern of the parameter estimates is distinctly different here than when we use the linear projection approach.[19]

The last row in Table II presents an estimate of ϕ for the period 1953-84 and an F test for the restriction of a constant ϕ over time. The F statistic is 12.1, implying rejection of the null hypothesis of a constant marginal adjustment cost parameter at the .0000 level.[20]

---

[18] The measure of Q includes appropriate tax adjustments to reflect the US tax system.

[19] This may be a further piece of evidence against the idea that ϕ is a well defined technological parameter.

[20] Although it is not the primary focus of their work, Hayashi and Inoue (1991) also find that the marginal adjustment cost parameter varies over time. They examine a shorter panel data set of Japanese firms over the period 1977-86.

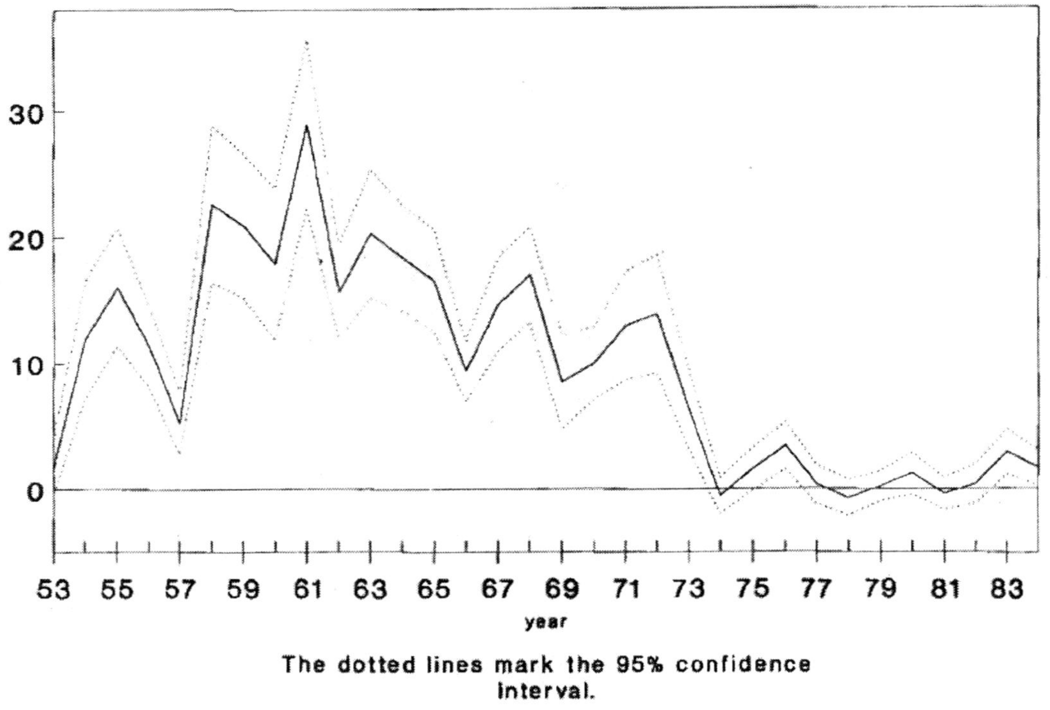

Figure 2. Estimated Marginal Adjustment Cost Parameter (Market Approach).

6. The Euler Approach

A third technique for estimating marginal adjustment costs has been suggested by several authors.[21] Economists believe that investment spending depends on the expected future stream of income generated by a new unit of capital and this is the basis for both the linear projection and market approaches. This poses both the firm and the econometrician a difficult problem: the future is unknown and hard to predict. The Euler equation approach is based on the insight that the firm's problem is recursive. As long as the firm makes the optimal tradeoff between investment today and investment tomorrow, it will choose the same time path for investment as it would if it based its decision on the whole future stream of expected marginal products of capital. The informational requirements (both for the firm and the econometrician) of predicting the next period are much less stringent than those for predicting the entire future stream of profitability.

A disadvantage of the Euler equation approach is that it requires the estimation of the marginal product of capital, which forces us to make an assumption about the functional form of the production function. We assume that the production function is Cobb-Douglas and is homogeneous of degree η, where $\eta = \alpha_K + \alpha_L$, to allow for non-constant returns to scale:

[21] See, for example, Hubbard and Kashyap (1992) and Whited (1992).

$$F(K_t, L_t) = K_t^{aK} L_t^{aK} \tag{6.33}$$

Letting F_L and F_K denote the derivatives of F with respect to L_t and K_t, the assumptions on the form of the production function imply:

$$F_K K_t + F_L L_t = \eta F \tag{6.34}$$

This allows us to express the value marginal product of capital as:

$$\begin{aligned}\alpha_t(1-\varepsilon)F_K &= \alpha_t\left[\frac{(1-\varepsilon)\eta F}{K_t} - \frac{(1-\varepsilon)F_L L_t}{K_t}\right] = \alpha_t\left[\frac{(1-\varepsilon)\eta F}{K_t} - \frac{wL_t}{K_t}\right] \\ &= \alpha_t\left[\frac{(1-\varepsilon)\eta F}{K_t} - \frac{C_t}{K_t}\right]\end{aligned} \tag{6.35}$$

where C_t is the cost of variable factors of production at time t.

In order to derive the empirical specification for the Euler equation, take the following steps. First, substitute the first-order condition for investment into the first-order condition for capital. Second, substitute in the functional forms which have been assumed. Third, rearrange the resulting expression so that the terms associated with common parameters are grouped together. Finally, replace expectations with actual future values plus an expectational error. This yields the following equation:

$$\begin{aligned}&\frac{(1-\tau_{t+1})\alpha_{t+1}Y_{t+1}}{(1-r_{t+1})K_{t+1}} - \frac{1}{(1-\varepsilon)\eta}\left[\frac{(1-\tau_{t+1})C_{t+1}}{(1-r_{t+1})K_{t+1}} + p_t^I - \frac{(1-\delta)p_{t+1}^I}{(1-r_{t+1})}\right] \\ &-\frac{\phi}{(1-\varepsilon)\eta}\left[(1-\tau_t)\left(\frac{I_t}{K_t}\right) - \frac{(1-\tau_{t+1})}{(1+r_{t+1})}\left((1-\delta)\left(\frac{I_{t+1}}{K_{t+1}}\right) + \frac{1}{2}\left(\frac{I_{t+1}}{K_{t+1}}\right)^2\right)\right] \\ &= e_t^E\end{aligned} \tag{6.36}$$

where we have let the interest rate be time-varying and where e_t^E is the expectational error.[22]

It may be helpful to provide an intuitive explanation. The Euler equation is a period-to-period arbitrage condition with the following interpretation: holding the capital stock constant in all other periods, a firm will choose its investment between two adjacent periods in order to equate the marginal costs and benefits across the periods. Under standard assumptions, the marginal costs and benefits will be determined by the firm's expectations of the price of

---

[22] As with other approaches, we estimate this specification separately for each year. Note that this means that $\alpha_t(1-\varepsilon)\eta$ can be different in each year; thus we allow for potential cyclical (or trend) changes in production technology and/or demand conditions.

investment goods and the corporate tax rate in the two adjacent periods, marginal adjustment costs, the interest rate, and the marginal product of capital.

Table 3. Estimates of the Marginal Adjustment Cost Parameter using the Euler Approach

Year	φ	NT	Criterion
1953	- 3.39551 (3.04589)	136	0.334939
1954	- 8.85833 (7.43974)	136	0.169419
1955	- 5.40516 (3.94368)	136	0.317142
1956	18.6274 (6.70821)	136	0.218089
1957	- 2.72266 (2.56725)	136	0.345026
1958	- 26.5836 (4.40803)	136	0.180165
1959	7.27334 (3.83458)	136	0.326334
1960	- 14.7608 (3.88468)	136	0.349070
1961	22.2364 (7.97736)	136	0.246288
1962	4.11370 (2.69893)	136	0.429640
1963	16.6121 (4.32435)	136	0.294984
1964	7.68578 (2.29383)	136	0.345523
1965	1.14922 (2.49375)	136	0.404600
1966	- 13.9214 (2.79131)	136	0.307325
1967	- 12.4919 (2.32686)	136	0.265223
1968	1.79368 (1.43484)	136	0.376892
1969	- 4.09808 (4.62909)	136	0.378081
1970	2.11863 (2.95719)	136	0.338673
1971	- 41.6452 (11.1214)	136	0.0908078

Table 3. (Continued)

Year	φ	NT	Criterion	
1972	- 1.61604 (4.52832)	136	0.371868	
1973	13.7151 (2.67404)	136	0.221257	
1974	.495840 (2.15071)	136	0.369927	
1975	- 5.05006 (2.90094)	136	0.343500	
1976	- 13.7927 (4.48458)	136	0.254612	
1977	- 34.6097 (15.0873)	136	0.0841305	
1978	- .619188 (3.85685)	136	0.316546	
1979	- 3.18196 (4.03470)	136	0.340973	
1980	3.62079 (3.47793)	136	0.316271	
1981	- 28.5721 (6.24456)	136	0.0862782	
1982	- 7.37474 (3.67668)	136	0.334872	
1983	- 30.5943 (13.9342)	136	0.0412270	
1984	11.3124 (6.23459)	136	0.193170	
Years	φ	NT	Criterion	F
1953-84	-9.7300 (1.8317)	4352	0.133748	18.3 [.0000]

Under the *Q* theory of investment, the marginal adjustment cost parameter (φ) should be constant over time. Under the irreversibility model, φ should vary over time. The F statistic tests the hypothesis that φ is constant over time. The marginal significance level for a rejection of this hypothesis is in square brackets. The Euler approach is described in Section VI. N is the number of firms and T is the number of years, so NT is the number of observations. The estimation method is GMM. The instruments are one-period lags of the corporate tax rate, the price of investment goods, the depreciation rate, the real interest rate, the ratio of the cost of variable inputs to the capital stock, the sales-capital ratio, the investment-capital ratio, and the square of the investment-capital ratio. Robust standard errors are presented in parentheses below the parameter estimates. The J test [Hansen (1982)] is equal to the criterion times NT.

Table 3 presents estimates of the marginal adjustment cost parameter using the Euler approach. Again there is strong evidence of changes in the parameter over time. For example, the estimate of ϕ for 1973 is 13.7 (with a standard error of 2.7); for 1974, the estimate is 0.5 (with a standard error of 2.2).

Figure 3 shows the time series of the estimated marginal adjustment cost parameter. The fluctuations of the parameter are substantially larger than the 95% confidence interval. The time series pattern of the parameter estimates is distinctly different here than when we use either the linear projection or market approaches.[23]

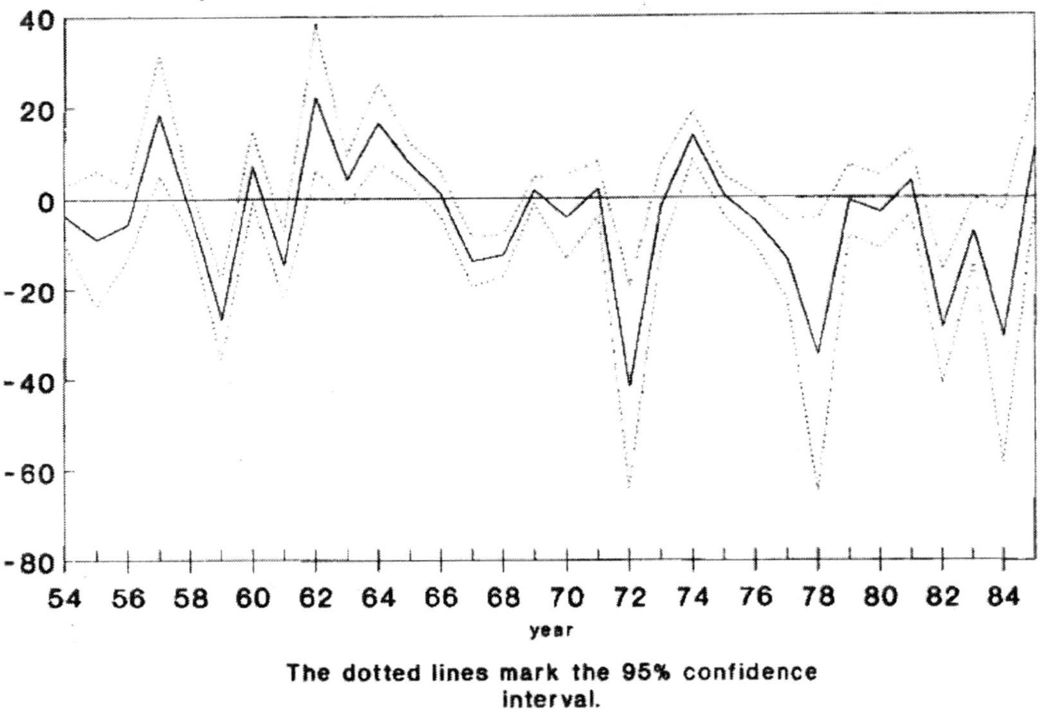

Figure 3. Estimated Marginal Adjustment Cost Parameter (Euler Approach).

The last row in Table 3 presents an estimate of ϕ for the period 1953-84 and an F test for the restriction of a constant ϕ over time. The F statistic is 18.3, implying rejection of the null hypothesis of a constant marginal adjustment cost parameter at the .0000 level.[24]

7. Conclusion

The theoretical model in Section 2 highlights a previously unexplored distinction between the convex adjustment cost-Q theory and the irreversibility models of investment. In the convex adjustment costs model, the adjustment costs associated with installing new

[23] The estimates using the Euler approach tend to be smaller in magnitude and more frequently negative. They seem to have a slightly countercyclical pattern, rising in 1957 and 1973-74.

capital are assumed to be exogenous and technologically determined. In the irreversibility model, marginal adjustment costs vary over time depending on the state of information.

In this chapter, we used a unique data set and an innovative econometric strategy to test this distinction between the Q and irreversibility models. By using a long panel data set, we take advantage of the cross-sectional dimension to estimate the marginal adjustment cost parameter for each year from the early 1950's to the mid-1980's. In order to verify the robustness of our results, we use three different techniques for estimating the marginal adjustment cost parameter. The linear projection approach constructs the expected shadow value of capital from a projection on past information. The market approach uses the stock market price of the firm to capture the expected future profitability of capital. The Euler approach focuses on the intertemporal arbitrage condition for investment and thus avoids the need to construct a proxy for the present value of future marginal products of capital. Each of these approaches has been previously used in studying other aspects of investment, but this is one of the few papers in which all of these techniques have been combined.

We find that the marginal adjustment cost parameter varies substantially over time. All three approaches lead to a rejection of the assumption of a constant marginal adjustment cost parameter at the .0000 level. This strongly suggests that the common assumption of technologically determined adjustment costs is an inadequate description of the data. The results provide new, microeconometric evidence that favors the irreversibility model. Furthermore, our results support the specific implications of the irreversibility and learning model in Section 2 since the marginal adjustment cost parameter appears to be declining over time; as the firms in our sample mature and form a more precise estimate of the state of demand, the marginal adjustment cost arising from irreversibility diminishes.

Our results are complementary to those obtained by Abel and Eberly (1996a), Eberly (1997), and Barnett and Sakellaris (1998). Using Compustat data for 1974 to 1988 and Global Vantage[25] from 1981 to 1994 respectively, Abel and Eberly (1996a) and Eberly (1997) estimate a model of investment when the firm faces fixed costs and convex adjustment costs. They estimate investment functions whose constant coefficients allow for nonlinearity. They conclude that investment responds nonlinearly to changes in Q. Using Compustat data from 1960-1987, Barnett and Sakellaris (1998) provide another empirical test of Abel and Eberly's model and find support for a nonlinear relationship between investment and Q. Whereas these studies have mainly focused on nonlinearity, our study emphasizes the time-varying nature of costs of adjustment.

If the irreversibility model is correct, the Q theory of investment is subject to the Lucas critique. An interesting question for further research would be to test this directly. Using one or more of our techniques, it would be possible to determine whether policy shocks, such as changes in monetary policy or in the corporate tax system, influence adjustment costs.

[24] Our results are consistent with those of Oliner, Rudebusch and Sichel (1995) who find evidence that the marginal adjustment cost parameter varies over time when they apply the Euler equation approach to aggregate US data.

[25] Global Vantage is an international industrial data set which includes balance sheet, flow of funds and income statement information.

8. References

Abel, Andrew B. and Olivier J. Blanchard (1986). "The Present Value of Profits and Cyclical Movements in Investments." *Econometrica* 54, 249-274.

Abel, Andrew B., and Janice Eberly (1996a). "Investment and q with Fixed Costs: An Empirical Analysis," mimeo.

Abel, Andrew B., and Janice Eberly (1996b). "Optimal Investment with Costly Reversibility," *Review of Economic Studies* 63, 581-593.

Barnett, Steven A., and Plutarchos Sakellaris (1998). "Nonlinear Response of Firm Investment to Q: Testing a Model of Convex and Non-convex Adjustment Costs," *Journal of Monetary Economics* 42(2), 261-88.

Bernanke, Ben S. (1983). "Irreversibility, Uncertainty and Cyclical Investment." *Quarterly Journal of Economics* 98, 85-106.

Bertola, Giuseppe (1988). "Dynamic Programming, Option Pricing and Irreversible Investment," MIT, mimeo.

Bertola, Giuseppe, and Ricardo Caballero (1994). "Irreversibility and Aggregate Investment", *Review of Economic Studies* 61, 223-246.

Caballero, Ricardo J. (1999). "Aggregate Investment," in John Taylor and Michael Woodford, ed., *Handbook of Macroeconomics*, Vol 1B, (North Holland: Elsevier Science), chapter 12.

Carruth, Alan, Andy Dickerson, and Andrew Henley (2000). "What Do We Know About Investment Under Uncertainty?" *Journal of Economic Surveys* 14, 119-153.

Chirinko, Robert S. (1993). "Business Fixed Investment Spending: Modeling Strategies, Empirical Results, and Policy Implications," *Journal of Economic Literature* 31, 1875-1911.

Chirinko, Robert S., and Huntley Schaller (2001). "Business Fixed Investment and Bubbles: The Japanese Case" *American Economic Review* 91, 663-80.

Demers, Fanny S., Michel Demers, and Sumru Altug (2003). "Investment Dynamics" in *Dynamic Macroeconomics* edited by S. Altug, Jagjit Chadha and Charles Nolan. Cambridge University Press, Chapter 2, 34-154.

Demers, Michel (1991). "Investment under Uncertainty, Irreversibility and the Arrival of Information Over Time", *Review of Economic Studies* 58, 333-350.

Dixit, Avinash K., and Robert S. Pindyck (1994). *Investment Under Uncertainty* (Princeton: Princeton University Press).

Eberly, Janice (1997). "International Evidence on Investment and Fundamentals," *European Economic Review* 41, 1055-1078.

Eisner, R., and R. H. Strotz (1963). "Determinants of Business Investment," in *Commission on Money and Credit, Impacts of Monetary Policy*. (Englewood Cliffs: Prentice Hall), 60-138.

Gilchrist, Simon, and Charles P. Himmelberg (1995). "Tobin's Q, Fundamental Q, and Corporate Investment: A Comparison Using Panel Data," *Journal of Monetary Economics* 36, 541-572.

Hayashi, Fumio (1982). "Tobin's Marginal q and Average q: A Neoclassical Interpretation," *Econometrica* 50, 213-224.

Hayashi, Fumio, and Tohru Inoue (1991). "The Relation Between Firm Growth and Q with Multiple Capital Goods: Theory and Evidence from Panel Data on Japanese Firms," *Econometrica* 59, 3, 731-753.

Hubbard, R. Glenn, and Anil Kashyap (1992). "Internal Net Worth and the Investment Process: An Application to U.S. Agriculture," *Journal of Political Economy* 100, 506-534.

Jorgenson, Dale W. (1963). "Capital Theory and Investment Behavior," *American Economic Review* 53, 47-56.

McDonald, Robert, and Daniel Siegel (1986). "The Value of Waiting to Invest," *Quarterly Journal of Economics* 101, 331-49.

Nickell, Stephen J. (1977). "Uncertainty and Lags in the Investment Decisions of Firms," *Review of Economic Studies* 44, 249-263.

Nickell, S.J. (1978). *The Investment Decisions of Firms*. (Cambridge: Cambridge University Press).

Oliner S.D., G.D.Rudebusch, and D. Sichel (1995). "New and Old Models of Business Investment: A Comparison of Forecasting Performance," *Journal of Money Credit and Banking* 27, 806-26.

Pindyck, Robert S. (1988). "Irreversible Investment, Capacity Choice and the Value of the Firm," *American Economic Review* 78, 969-985.

Rothschild, M. (1971). "On the Cost of Adjustment," *Quarterly Journal of Economics* 85, 605-22.

Schaller, Huntley (1990). "A Re-examination of the Q Theory of Investment Using U.S. Firm Data," *Journal of Applied Econometrics* 5, 309-325.

Tauchen, George (1986). "Statistical Properties of Generalized Method-of-Moments Estimatros of Structural Parameters Obtained from Financial Market Data," *Journal of Business & Economic Statistics* 4, 397-416.

Whited, Toni M. (1992). "Debt, Liquidity Constraints, and Corporate Investment: Evidence from Panel Data," *Journal of Finance* 47, 1425-1460.

In: International Finance and Financial Services
Editor: Kristian L. Hagen, pp. 123-141
ISBN: 1-60021-756-7

Chapter 5

EARNINGS MANAGEMENT AND INTERNAL CONTROL MECHANISMS: EVIDENCE FROM CHILEAN FIRMS*

Mauricio Jara-Bertin[1] and Félix J. López-Iturriaga[1]
[1]University of Valladolid and Austral University of Chile
[1]University of Valladolid

ABSTRACT

We analyze the impact of some internal control mechanisms -ownership structure, capital structure and growth opportunities- on earnings management in Chilean firms throughout 1991-2001. Our results are interesting due to the specific characteristics of the corporate system in Chile where investor protection is weak and banks play a prominent role. We find that ownership concentration has a non-linear relation with earnings management, consistent with both the control of directors by main shareholders and the idea of expropriation of minority shareholders by large controlling shareholders. Financial leverage and public debt gives managers incentives to accounting discretion whereas bank debt plays an active role in corporate governance as a control mechanism. Our results also show that earnings are not managed to signal growth opportunities.

Keywords: Accruals, Capital Structure, Earnings Management, Ownership Structure.

1. INTRODUCTION

The separation between corporate ownership and control is the basis of an agency problem that drives managers to pursue their own utility even at the expense of the firm's value (Jensen and Meckling, 1976; Shleifer and Vishny, 1997). This conflict of interests can also affect the quality of the accounting information because financial statements –for

1 Avenida Valle del Esgueva 6, E-47011 Valladolid, Spain, Tel. +34-983-42 30 00 (ext. 4395), Fax +34-983-42 38 99. flopez@eco.uva.es

instance, reported earnings- to some extent determine manager's compensation, the likelihood of corporate takeovers, management buyouts, debt covenants, etc. Consequently, insiders could be interested in managing earnings to distort the real performance of the firm in order to protect their own interests. For example, managers can discount future profits in the financial reports or postpone present costs to cover poor performance. Inversely, insiders can have incentives to reduce large profits in order to build reserves for the future.

Our paper aims to analyze managers' discretionary accounting decisions in Chile. More specifically, we test the influence on earnings management of a number of internal control mechanisms such as ownership structure, capital structure and the growth opportunities at the firm's disposal.

Chilean companies are especially interesting because of the big differences with the Anglo-Saxon -mainly US- area on which most of the literature has focused (Gabrielsen *et al.*, 2002). Chile has a bank-oriented corporate system in which banks play a prominent role compared to capital markets. In addition, the Chilean legal tradition differs from the Anglo-Saxon countries and the Chilean investor protection is weak. Nowadays in Chile there is much concern about the quality of accounting information and how it is related to the control mechanisms. This interest has been raised by the wave of takeovers in large firms in recent years and has led to the passing of new laws about takeovers and mergers in order to improve transparency in capital markets and corporate governance (Iglesias, 2000).

Our results point to a double effect of ownership concentration consistent with both the control of directors by main shareholders and the idea of expropriation of minority shareholders by large controlling shareholders. We also find that earnings management is positively related to financial leverage and public debt and negatively related to public debt, whereas earnings are not managed to signal the firm's growth opportunities.

This paper is divided into five sections. In section 2 we review the literature about discretionary accounting management and its relation with ownership structure, capital structure and growth opportunities. Along with this background, in the same section, we present the hypotheses to be tested. Section 3 includes the description of the sample and some methodological issues. In Section 4 we report the results of our analysis. We end with some concluding remarks and the main conclusions of the paper in section 5.

Managers' Discretionary Behavior, Earnings Management and Financial Decisions

As previously stated, the possible conflict of interests between fund providers and managers can affect managers' incentives and lead to discretionary financial decisions. A way of exercising this opportunism is the choice of accounting methods that allow managers to modify the financial statements in their own interest (Watts and Zimmerman, 1986 and 1990).

Managers have incentives to manage earnings and, therefore, to make a false impression on capital markets about the firm's and managers' performance (Healy and Wahlen, 1999). For example, insiders can use discretionary accounting criteria to increase earnings in times of poor performance. Inversely, accounting choices can reduce earnings when the firm's performance is over expectations or over the competitors' performance in order to create reserves for future and uncertain times, leading to smooth earnings. The literature has documented the opportunistic use of earnings by managers (Beneish, 2001; DeAngelo, 1988; Dechow *et al.*, 1996; Guay *et al.*, 1996; Rangan, 1998; Teoh *et al.*, 1998), especially when the managers' position depends on the reported results (Chung *et al.*, 2002; Spagnolo, 2005).

Earnings management is usually implemented through accruals (Dechow, 1994; Jones, 1991). Although accruals are aimed at improving the informational content of financial statements, there can be an opportunistic use of accruals. This is why accruals should be split into non-discretionary vs. the discretionary components. This is the core of the research into earnings management since it depends on the ability of the insiders to manage earnings. This ability can be constrained by some control mechanisms such as ownership concentration, capital structure and the growth opportunities at the firm's disposal (Azofra *et al.*, 2003).

2.1. Ownership Concentration

The influence of ownership structure (mainly, managerial ownership) on earnings management has been recently proved (Gabrielsen *et al.*, 2002; Yeo *et al.*, 2002). Due to the lack of data about managerial ownership in Chile, we focus on another ownership structure issue: the ownership concentration.

One of the characteristics of the ownership structure of Chilean companies is the high concentration -due to a concentration process throughout the 90's, and the widespread presence of economic groups (Lefort 2003; Lefort and Walker, 2000; Majluf *et al.*, 1998; Ranieri and Valenzuela, 2001). Ownership structure is pyramidal and conglomerates of firms hold a proportion of shares over the minimum needed to control firms. As a consequence, there are quite a considerable number of firms owned by the same shareholder.

Concentrated ownership is usually a mechanism to control managers' discretionary decisions (Gul, 2002; Gul *et al.*, 2002; McConnell and Servaes, 1995; Morck *et al.*, 2004; Shleifer and Vishny, 1997; Yeo *et al.*, 2002) or to protect shareholders' interests when investors' legal protection is weak. (La Porta *et al.*, 1998; Leuz *et al.*, 2003). In fact, as shown by García *et al.* (2005), the concentrated ownership in code-law countries is expected to reduce the managers' incentives to engage in income increasing strategies.

Nevertheless, concentrated ownership can raise conflicts of interests between majority and minority shareholders. In fact, in Continental Europe the conflict between large controlling shareholders and minority stockholders is more influential than the conflict between shareholders and managers (Becht and Röell, 1999; Bianco and Casavola, 1999). This means that too concentrated ownership gives incentives to large shareholders to expropriate small shareholders. As suggested by Claessens *et al.* (2000) concentrated ownership enables blockholders to use accounting information to their own advantage; for instance through income decreasing in order to diminish the other shareholders' residual claims.

Consequently, concentrated ownership could give the main shareholders incentives to monitor managers' decisions but also to expropriate minority shareholders by hiding the firm's real performance. Therefore, our first hypothesis can be formulated in two alternative ways:

HYPOTHESIS 1a: *There is a negative relation between earnings management and ownership concentration.*

HYPOTHESIS 1b: *There is a positive relation between earnings management and ownership concentration.*

Nevertheless, these hypotheses are not mutually excluding and a mixed effect or non-linear relation could be found. Consistent with previous evidence (Yeo *et al.*, 2002), the impact of ownership structure on earnings management can switch from a positive to a negative effect.

2.2. Capital Structure

The link between capital structure and accounting decisions can be due to debt covenants. Debt is positively related to earnings management in order to loosen the constraining content of debt covenants or to avoid the costs of debt covenant violations (Dechow and Skinner, 2000). From this point of view, earnings are managed to increase income in times when a firm's bad performance could prevent the commitment of debt covenants (Defond and Jiambalvo, 1994; Sweeney, 1994; Watts and Zimmerman, 1986 and 1990). In addition, earnings are likely to be managed in order to increase the results in the face of tough debt covenants. Consequently, higher earnings management could appear in the most leveraged firms and our second hypothesis could be stated as:

HYPOTHESIS 2: *There is a positive relation between financial leverage and earnings management.*

Unlike the Anglo-Saxon firms -whose main fund source are bonds traded in capital markets, Chilean firms are oriented to private debt -basically bank debt (La Porta *et al.*,1998; Lefort and Walker, 2000). Thereby, it is interesting to analyze the possible influence of the kind of creditor -private debt *vs.* public debt i.e. banks vs. capital markets, on discretionary accounting choices.

Arm's length debt implies lower incentives to manage earnings for two reasons. Firstly, banks specialize in financial intermediation and therefore can overcome moral hazards and other informational problems by more detailed debtor monitoring (Johnson, 1997; Myers, 1977). In capital markets, investors are on average less capable of screening than banks, and firms could have incentives to bias the available information. Secondly, bank debt can be more easily rolled over than public debt in case of non-payment problems (James and Smith, 2000) and fosters long term relations between firms and banks (Eber, 2001). In the long term, the accounting information becomes less relevant since interest rates and other debt covenants are based on the reputation that the firm establishes through time.

From the point of view of public debt, bond issuance can be understood as a signalling mechanism of the quality of the firm (Diamond, 1991; Hadlock and James, 2002; Yosha, 1995). Given that firms are willing to disclose beneficial information in capital markets, firms relying on public debt are more likely to manage earnings than other firms.

Consequently, we propose two complementary hypotheses concerning the impact of the ownership structure of debt:

HYPOTHESIS 3: *There should be a negative relation between earnings management and bank debt.*

HYPOTHESIS 4: *There should be a positive relation between a firm's reliance on public debt and earnings management.*

2.3. Growth Opportunities

Accruals could also be related to growth opportunities. As shown by Chan *et al.* (2001) and Lui (2004), firms with the largest accruals usually have higher valuation ratios and higher growth. In addition, firms with the highest growth opportunities are likely to have more private information about these prospects, which would exacerbate the problems of asymmetric information. Therefore, insiders try to reveal this private relevant information through financial statements in which earnings can have been managed to signal the profitable projects available to the firm (Healy and Palepu, 1993). Our last hypothesis could therefore be stated as:

HYPOTHESIS 5: *There is a positive relation between growth opportunities and earnings management.*

DATA AND METHODOLOGY

3.1. Sample and Variables

Our sample is made up of 185 Chilean industrial firms, quoted in capital markets in the 1990-2001 period. The source of the information is the *Ficha Estadística Codificada Uniforme* (FECU) of the *Superintendencia de Valores y Seguros* -Chilean Stock Exchange Commission- and provides audited financial statements -balance sheet and income statement- of the listed firms. Since all of the firms are listed, we can assert that, on average, the firms in the sample are medium-large.

The list of variables and some descriptive statistics of the sample are displayed in Table 1. The dependent variable that proxies earnings management is the absolute value of discretionary accruals (|DA|). The explanatory variables we focus on, due to their influence on discretionary accounting decisions, are the capital structure, the ownership structure, and the set of growth opportunities available to the firm.

Capital structure has been measured through the total debt-to-total assets ratio (TDTA) whereas equity ownership structure has been measured through the ownership concentration or the proportion of shares owned by the largest shareholder (OC1). As far as the ownership of debt is concerned, we have defined two complementary variables: BDTD is the ratio of banking debt-to-total debt and is aimed to measure to what extent debt financing is provided by banks, while PDTD is calculated as the ratio of public debt-to-total debt and introduces the proportion of bonds over total debt. Regarding the set of growth opportunities, it has been measured in previous research (McConnell and Servaes 1995) by Tobin's Q ratio (Q).

There are two issues which could be related to discretionary accounting decisions of managers and for which we have controlled: the size of the firm or log of total assets at book value (LNTA) and the firm performance. Given that managers compare the performance of the firm with the performance of analogous firms (Han and Manry 2000) we have introduced firm performance as the absolute value of the difference between a firm's ROA and the average ROA of the industry (ADIFROA). One could suppose that the size of the firm should affect abnormal accruals negatively –the largest firms have alternative ways to make financial statements to disclose relevant information in capital markets. On the contrary, ADIFROA is likely to have a positive relation with ABSDA because managers have incentives to smooth earnings when the performance of the firm -either in excess or very low performance- is highly abnormal.

3.2. Methodology

Our methodology can be divided into two stages. Firstly we estimate total accruals and separate the discretionary from the non-discretionary component. Secondly, we regress the discretionary or abnormal accruals against ownership structure, capital structure and growth opportunities in order to test their effect on managers' discretionary accounting decisions.

Total accruals are calculated according to Jones' model (Jones, 1991). This model is the most widely used one and is based on the idea that changes in a firm's economic condition and manager discretion results in accruals. Although there is a number of alternative models to identify earnings management (Dechow *et al.*, 1995; Dechow and Dichev, 2002; Kothari *et al.*, 2005), some authors underline that Jones' model performs better than its time-series counterparts in detecting earnings management (Bartov *et al.,* 2000). This performance is even enhanced and more consistent estimations are achieved when the suitable statistical methodology –namely, panel data- is implemented.

As it is widely known, total accruals are the difference between results and cash flow of the firm's ordinary activities. In Jones' model, non-discretionary accruals are calculated by regressing total accruals (TA) against the growth in total revenues or turnover (ΔREV) and the level of depreciable assets -gross level of property, plants and equipment, GPPE-. To avoid heterocedasticity, all the variables are scaled by total assets at book value. These two variables are supposed to be the ones closest related to accruals: GPPE controls for the portion of total accruals due to depreciation and ΔREV controls for the changes in current assets and current liabilities as a consequence of the sales.

Once we have calculated total accruals, we split them into the discretionary and the non-discretionary components. Accruals are supposed to improve the informative content of financial statements in order to correct the possible mismatch between expenses, income and cash flows. Nevertheless, accruals can be used in an opportunistic way. This is why total accruals can be divided into normal or non-discretionary accruals and abnormal or discretionary accruals. The latest can be used for managerial accounting manipulation and, therefore, we are interested in testing the effect of the control mechanisms on this abnormal component of total accruals.

Thus, we will make total accruals depend on ΔREV and GPPE as expressed in equation [1], where the subscript i identifies the individual and the subscript t identifies the time period. η_i is the term of fixed effects and $\varepsilon_{i,t}$ is the random perturbation of every observation:

$$TA_{it} = \alpha_0 + \alpha_1 \cdot (\Delta REV_{it}) + \alpha_2 \cdot (GPPE_{it}) + \eta_i + \varepsilon_{it} \qquad [1]$$

As far as the signs of α_1 and α_2 are concerned, we expect GPPE to have a negative relation with TA because a higher proportion of GPPE usually implies more depreciations and TA have been calculated subtracting depreciations from the difference between current assets and liabilities in two consecutive years. The expected sign of ΔREV is not so clear because a higher level of turnover usually increases both current assets –receivables- and current liabilities -suppliers-, so we cannot know which of them increases more.

The estimated values of TA in equation [1] are considered the normal accruals given the sales of the firm and the depreciation of the assets. Consequently, the errors of the regression are supposed to be the abnormal or discretionary accruals (DA) in the sense that they are not motivated by either sales or the depreciation of assets and could arise due to discretionary decisions of managers. Therefore, DA is defined as follows in equation (2) where a_i is the estimated coefficient of α_i:

$$|DA_{it}| = TA_{it} - (\alpha_0 + \alpha_1 \times (\Delta REV_{it}) + \alpha_2 \times (GPPE_{it})) \qquad [2]$$

Discretionary accruals are supposed to be a proxy of the ability of managers to opportunistically modify earnings. We should not forget that earnings management does not necessarily mean income increasing accruals but rather earnings smoothing, so that DA can be both positive and negative. A negative value of DA must not be understood as the managers not having managed earnings but as having reduced income -perhaps in order to transfer earnings to the future-.

Then, as the second stage of our work, we try to find out the effect of the control mechanisms -capital structure, ownership structure and the set of growth opportunities- on earnings management. As usual in the literature on earnings management (Dechow, 1994; Dechow and Skinner, 2000), the lagged value of the dependent variable (DA_{it-1}) is introduced as an explanatory variable since earnings management tends to smooth earnings, so it is likely to be conditioned by accounting decisions in previous years. Consequently, the model to be tested includes the control variables and can be expressed as follows[2]:

$$|DA|_{it} = \alpha + \beta_1 |DA|_{it-1} + \beta_2 OC1_{it} + \beta_3 TDTA_{it} + \beta_4 Q_{it} + \beta_5 LNTA_{it} + \beta_6 ADIFROA_{it} + \eta_i + \eta_t + e_{it} \qquad [3]$$

The empirical analysis is implemented by two different procedures both based on the econometrics of panel data because this methodology is the most suitable when data combines information from different firms over several years. Our sample is an unbalanced panel with 1,583 observations from 181 firms over 12 years. Panel data methodology allows the so-called unobservable constant heterogeneity -the control of fixed effects- to be controlled and provides more efficient estimators than the usual cross-section models (Arellano, 2003; Baltagi, 1995).

Jones' model, as stated in equation [1], is estimated by the within groups method since TA is supposed to be exogenous. On the contrary, equation [3] poses a problem of endogeneity due to the introduction of lagged dependent variables among the set of explanatory variables. If this is the case, the estimation of the model must be done through the Generalized Method of Moments (GMM). The GMM estimation in first differences (Arellano and Bond, 1991) eliminates any bias caused by the fixed and specific effects and allows the

2 ηi stands for the individual effect, ηt stands for the time effect and eit is the stochastic error. The individual effect can include several specific effects which are supposed to be specific to the firm and constant through time. The time effect includes macroeconomic effects such as interest rates, inflation, etc., that affect all the companies in the same period in a cross sectional way. Finally, the term of stochastic error captures the possible misspecification of measurement in the independent variables as well as any other omitted independent variable.

use of lagged independent variables in order to avoid the simultaneity bias (Arellano and Bover, 1990; Bond, 2002). However, the estimation in first differences also has some drawbacks (Alonso-Borrego and Arellano, 1999) which can be solved with the so-called system estimator (Arellano and Bond, 1998), an extended GMM method (Blundell y Bond, 2000; Blundell *et al.*, 2000; Bond, 2002). Additionally, the system estimator does not need so strong assumptions as other methods.

The consistency of the GMM estimations relies on the validity of the variables used as instruments and on the autocorrelation of the residuals. This is why we present some specification tests of the model (Arellano and Bond, 1991 and 1998). The validity of the instruments is tested through the Hansen test of over-identification of restrictions which assesses the joint validity of the selected instruments, while errors may keep first but not second order serial correlation.

RESULTS

4.1. Descriptive Statistics

As far as the main descriptive statistics are concerned, Table 1 shows the standard deviation, mean, minimum and maximum values of the main variables and Table 2 shows Pearson's correlations.

Unlike Anglo-Saxon countries, where corporate ownership is usually widely spread, the ownership of Chilean firms is highly concentrated. As reported in Table I, the average stake of the main shareholder is around 45% of total equity, far above the percentage of ownership owned by the main shareholders in the Anglo-Saxon countries (La Porta *et al.*, 1998). Dewatripont and Tirole (1994) suggest that firms with concentrated ownership tend to borrow from banks in countries where takeovers are ineffective and the banking system is well developed. In Chile the enforcement of the laws is lower and prevents the efficient development of capital markets. In turn, firms are prone to borrow from banks rather than from capital markets. In fact, as shown in Table 1, almost half of total debt (41.2%) has been borrowed from banks.

In contrast, Chilean firms use public debt much less than their Anglo-Saxon counterparts. As shown in Table 1, the average ratio of public debt to total debt is 9.6%, far under the levels reported by Anglo-Saxon countries where capital markets are the principal way of raising funds.

This very preliminary descriptive analysis is complemented with a means comparison test. We have split the whole sample into three subsamples according to |DA| with the same number of firms in each one. Table 3 shows the mean value of the variables for the two extreme groups. Although it is not conclusive evidence, these results give us some clues to interpret forthcoming results. Firms with the highest discretionary accruals have the most concentrated ownership and the least growth opportunities. In addition, discretionary accruals seem to be positively related to financial leverage and to the use of public debt. Consequently, means comparison lends some partial support to capital structure, ownership structure and growth opportunities as factors potentially driving earnings management. Nevertheless, a more explanatory analysis is required.

Table 1. Descriptive statistics

Variable	Observations	Mean	Std. dev.	Minimum	Maximum
TA	1583	0.01	0.18	-0.925	0.99
ΔREV	1583	0.026	0.183	-0.971	0.991
GPPE	1583	0.636	0.557	-0.33	2.409
DA	1583	0.01	0.224	-0.7	0.389
OC1	1583	0.451	0.253	0.0005	1
TDTA	1583	0.249	0.187	0	0.908
BDTD	1583	0.412	0.345	0	1
PDTD	1583	0.096	0.206	0	0.999
Q	1583	1.196	0.699	0.25	4.976
ADIFROA	1583	0.0611	0.0616	0.00009	0.524
LNTA	1583	17.393	1.901	11.727	22.058

Mean, minimum and maximum values and the standard deviation of the main variables.

TA	=	Total accruals
ΔREV	=	Difference in revenue respect year t-1
GPPE	=	Gross plant, property and equipment scaled to total assets at the start of the period.
DA	=	Discretionary accruals of Jones' model
OC1	=	Proportion of shares owned by the largest shareholder
TDTA	=	Total debt to total assets ratio
BDTD	=	Bank debt to total debt ratio
PDTD	=	Public debt to total debt ratio
Q	=	Tobin's q
LNTA	=	Log of total assets
ADIFROA	=	Absolute value of the difference between the ROA of firm and the average ROA of its industry.

Table 2. Pearson's correlations

Variable	OC1	TDTA	BDTD	PDTD	Q	ADIFROA	LNTA
OC1	1.000						
TDTA	0.145	1.000					
BDTD	-0.004	0.312	1.000				
PDTD	0.012	0.130	-0.278	1.000			
Q	-0.002	0.001	-0.126	0.139	1.000		
ADIFROA	0.078	-0.032	-0.054	-0.105	0.122	1.000	
LNTA	-0.054	0.080	-0.016	0.300	0.023	-0.136	1.000

OC1	=	Proportion of shares owned by the largest shareholder
TDTA	=	Total debt to total assets ratio
BDTD	=	Bank debt to total debt ratio
PDTD	=	Public debt to total debt ratio
Q	=	Tobin's q
LNTA	=	Log of total assets
ADIFROA	=	Absolute value of the difference between the ROA of firm and the average ROA of its industry.

Table 3 Means comparison tests

Variable	Low accruals	High accruals	p-value
OC1	0.406	0.463	0.000
TDTA	0.216	0.275	0.000
BDTD	0.410	0.419	0.659
LTBD	0.36	0.35	0.787
PDTD	0.08	0.10	0.102
Q	1.264	1.084	0.000
ADIFROA	0.058	0.062	0.300
LNTA	17.431	17.391	0.731

The sample was split into three groups depending on the absolute value of discretionary accruals (|DA|). The third column shows the p-value to test the null hypothesis of no-differences.

OC1	=	Proportion of shares owned by the largest shareholder
TDTA	=	Total debt to total assets ratio
BDTD	=	Bank debt to total debt ratio
PDTD	=	Public debt to total debt ratio
Q	=	Tobin's q
LNTA	=	Log of total assets
ADIFROA	=	Absolute value of the difference between the ROA of firm and the average ROA of its industry.

Table 4 Estimation of Jones' model

Variables	
Intercept	0.267***
	(25.76)
GPPE	-0.407***
	(-26.18)
ΔREV	0.084***
	(3.52)
Adj-R^2	0.348
F-statistics	372.87***

Estimated coefficients and (t-statistics) of equation [1]. *** means significant at 99%, ** at 95% and * at 90%.

TA	=	Total accruals (Dependent variable)
ΔREV	=	Difference in revenue respect year t-1
GPPE	=	Gross plant, property and equipment scaled to total assets at the start of the period.

4.2. Explanatory Analysis

The results of the estimation of the first stage -Jones' model- are reported in Table 4. Both GPPE and ΔREV are highly significant, the signs are consistent with the expected ones and both the adjusted-R^2 coefficient and the F-statistics are high enough. Nevertheless, that regression is just the first step in our analysis because we are interested in abnormal accruals and how they can be affected by the control mechanisms. This is why the residuals of equation [1] have been taken as discretionary accruals and have been regressed against the set of explanatory variables according to equation [3] -Tables 5 and 6-.

Firstly, all the estimations show a consistently positive and quite significant relation between $|DA_t|$ and $|DA_{t-1}|$ -Tables 5 and 6-. This positive relation is a key issue and supports the idea of earnings smoothing: after a period of income increasing management, earnings must be managed downwards; on the other hand, managers have the ability to increase earnings when earnings have been reduced in order to transfer them into the future.

Table 5 Regression results for the absolute value of abnormal accruals

Variables	(1)	(2)	(3)	(4)	(5)	(6)	(7)
Intercept	0.286***	0.356***	0.315***	0.264***	0.290***	0.274***	0.460***
	(12.82)	(12.7)	(10.2)	(12.02)	(10.45)	(9.79)	(13.38)
$\lvert DA_{t-1}\rvert$	0.029***	0.024***	0.018***	0.029***	0.032***	0.040***	0.025***
	(6.48)	(5.14)	(4.09)	(5.93)	(7.47)	(8.81)	(4.45)
OC1	-0.031***	-0.407***					-0.437***
	(-3.11)	(-8.77)					(-7.61)
$OC1^2$		0.356***					0.387***
		(8.19)					(7.27)
TDTA			0.104***				0.141***
			(7.62)				(7.49)
BDTD				-0.011**			-0.034***
				(-2.16)			(-5.15)
PDTD					0.020*		
					(1.7)		
Q						-0.012***	-0.014***
						(-9.43)	(-8.79)
ADIFROA	0.046**	0.042	0.062**	0.057***	0.040**	(0.128***	0.114***
	(2.16)	(1.48)	(2.4)	(2.62)	(2.12)	(5.98)	(3.28)
LNTA	-0.005***	-0.005***	-0.010***	-0.006***	-0.007***	-0.006***	-0.011***
	(-4.1)	(-3.08)	(-5.03)	(-4.25)	(-4.23)	(-3.43)	(-5.08)
Auto (1)	-5.88***	-5.89***	-5.77***	-5.85***	-5.93***	-5.82***	-5.89***
Auto (2)	1.28	1.00	0.73	1.05	1.32	1.49	1.33
Hansen test	132.47	132.12	130.09	130.3	132.9	129.38	128.78

Estimated coefficients and (z-statistics) of equation [3]. Statistical significance: *** at the level of 1%, ** to 5% and * to 10% registered together with every estimated coefficient.

Dependent variable:

$\lvert DA\rvert$	=	Absolute value of the discretionary accruals of Jones' model

Independent variable:

$\lvert DA_{t-1}\rvert$	=	
OC1	=	Proportion of shares owned by the largest shareholder
TDTA	=	Total debt to total assets ratio
BDTD	=	Bank debt to total debt ratio
PDTD	=	Public debt to total debt ratio
Q	=	Tobin's q
LNTA	=	Log of total assets
ADIFROA	=	Absolute value of the difference between the ROA of firm and the average ROA of its industry.

Statistical tests:

Auto (1): Test that average autocovariance in residuals of order 1 is 0

Auto (2): Test that average autocovariance in residuals of order 2 is 0

Hansen test: Test of over-identified restrictions, test with a chi-square distribution

Table 6 Robustness analysis for the absolute value of abnormal accruals

Variables	(1)	(2)	(3)
Intercept	0.618***	0.980***	0.384***
	(16.72)	(27.17)	(6.54)
$\|DA_{t-1}\|$	0.016**	0.025***	0.029***
	(1.96)	(3.08)	(4.6)
OC1			-0.357***
			(-6.79)
$OC1^2$			0.134***
			(3.45)
TDTE	0.002***	0.004***	0.001***
	(8.34)	(19.91)	(3.48)
BDTD	-0.043***	-0.051***	-0.065***
	(-5.92)	(-8.83)	(-9.84)
MTB	-0.002	-0.001	0.003
	(-0.98)	(-0.73)	(1.33)
ROA	-0.275***	-0.260***	-0.328***
	(-10.45)	(-9.56)	(-8.48)
LNS	-0.004**	0.002	-0.003
	(-2.06)	(1.00)	(-1.36)
OC2	-1.184***		
	(-18.05)		
$OC2^2$	0.900***		
	(18.28)		
OC5		-2.296***	
		(-21.43)	
$OC5^2$		1.558***	
		(21.49)	
Industry effect	No	No	Yes
Auto (1)	-6.05***	-5.76***	-5.75***
Auto (2)	0.92	0.47	0.95
Hansen test	126.33	130.27	118.86

Estimated coefficients and (z-statistics) of equation [3]. Statistical significance: *** at the level of 1%, ** to 5% and * to 10% registered together with every estimated coefficient.

Dependent variable:

$\|DA\|$	=	Absolute value of the discretionary accruals of Jones' model

Independent variable:

$\|DA_{t-1}\|$	=	
OC1	=	Proportion of shares owned by the largest shareholder
TDTE	=	Total debt to total equity ratio
BDTD	=	Bank debt to total debt ratio
MTB	=	Market to book ratio
LNS	=	Log of total sales
LNTA	=	Log of total assets
ROA	=	ROA of the firm
OC2		Proportion of shares owned by two largest shareholders
OC5		Proportion of shares owned by five largest shareholders

Statistical tests:

Auto (1): Test that average autocovariance in residuals of order 1 is 0

Auto (2): Test that average autocovariance in residuals of order 2 is 0

Hansen test: Test of over-identified restrictions, test with a chi-square distribution

Concerning hypothesis 1, Columns (1), (2) and (7) in Table 5 report a negative and significant relation between ownership concentration (OC1) and the absolute value of abnormal accruals (|DA|), consistent with hypothesis 1a. Notwithstanding, our results reveal a different and complementary effect when we introduce a non-linear specification of ownership concentration through $OC1^2$. As shown in columns (2) and (7) in Table 5, earnings management is U-shaped with respect to ownership concentration: whereas more concentrated ownership initially implies less discretionary accruals -as stated in hypothesis 1a-, there is a threshold[3] and thereinafter the relation turns out to be positive -consistent with hypothesis 1b-. This mixed evidence means a two-sided effect: an initial convergence or disciplinary effect and the subsequent expropriation of minority shareholders by large controlling shareholders by reducing the residual claim over profits. This evidence is consistent with the view of the severe conflicts between controlling shareholders and minority shareholders in non-Anglo Saxon countries with concentrated corporate ownership.

As far as the effect of capital structure is concerned, columns (3) and (7) in Table 5 show a positive relation between leverage (TDTA) and the absolute value of discretionary accruals (|DA|). These results corroborate our second hypothesis and stress the incentives of managers to report higher earnings when debt burden is heavier and the firm could become financially constrained. Similarly, managers may be willing to postpone earnings or recognize bad results quickly when the firm's debt is not too high and firm creditors are less concerned with the results of the firm.

Having analyzed the broad relation between debt and accounting discretion, we are interested in studying the ownership structure of the debt as a possible mechanism to monitor managers. This is why our third hypothesis focuses on the effect of bank debt on abnormal accruals. As we hypothesized, columns (4) and (7) in Table 5 point to a negative impact of bank debt on the absolute value of discretionary accruals, which means that borrowing from banks reduces managers' accounting discretion. This result lends support to the idea of banks as efficient control mechanisms in countries when firms are not under the scrutiny of capital markets. Inversely, public debt (PDTD) has a positive impact on the absolute value of discretionary accruals (|DA|) as shown in column (5) in table 5. Hence, managers seem to have incentives to modify financial statements by earnings management when credit conditions depend heavily on the financial reports.

Our last hypothesis has to do with growth opportunities. Contrary to hypothesis 5, the estimated coefficient of Q in columns (6) and (7) in Table 5 is negative. This lack of support of the influence of growth opportunities on earnings management could be explained by the characteristics of Chilean capital markets. Chile is a bank-oriented system rather than a market oriented one, so capital markets could not be efficient enough and stock prices do not fully reflect all the company prospects.

Finally, some comments about the role played by the control variables LNTA and ADIFROA are pertinent, although these variables are not the core of the paper. Firm size has a consistent, negative and significant influence on discretionary accruals (|DA|). According to previous research (Dechow and Dichev, 2002; Doyle *et al.*, 2005), this result makes sense because small firms have lower quality accruals due to weak internal controls. Additionally, large firms can afford some alternative ways of disclosing information in capital markets on top of financial statements, so managers do not have such great incentives to manage

[3] This critical level can be estimated around 25%.

earnings. Firm performance as related to the performance of the industry (ADIFROA) has a positive and consistent influence on discretionary accounting decisions. This could mean that earnings are managed in order to follow the average performance of the industry (Fairfield *et al.*, 2003; Sloan, 1996).

4.3. Sensitivity Analysis

In order to test the robustness of our results we have run some additional regressions whose results are reported in Table 6. Firstly, we have replace OC1 by alternative measures of ownership concentration such as OC2 and OC5 -proportion of shares owned by the two and five largest shareholders- as shown in columns (1) and (2) of table 6. Results are unaffected and the non-linear relation between ownership concentration and abnormal accruals also holds.

Regarding the measure of capital structure, we have replaced TDTA with the total debt-to-total equity ratio (TDTE). This new variable does not modify our results -columns (1) to (4) in Table 6- and the positive effect of debt on discretionary accounting decisions is confirmed.

Another sensitivity analysis concerns the way we measure growth opportunities. Instead of Tobin's *q*, we have used the equity market-to-book ratio (MTB) according to McConnell and Servaes (1995) and Lasfer (1995). The estimated coefficients of this variable are consistent with those previously obtained for Tobin's *q* and do not lend any support to hypothesis 5. The explanation of the lack of empirical support for this hypothesis can also be connected with the efficiency of Chilean capital markets and the possibility that stock prices do not fully account for the growth opportunities.

As regards the control variables, we have also replaced ADIFROA with just ROA. The results in Table 6 show that the performance of the firm is negatively related to discretionary accruals. The underlying intuition is that the worse the performance of the firm, the more incentives managers have to manipulate earnings. When the size of the firm is measured through turnover instead of total assets, this variable no longer has a significant effect, which could be explained by the use of the growth in sales as an explanatory variable in equation [1].

Finally, we have controlled, for the industry effect due to the differences among industries in legal regulation, the specialization of Chilean economy for some industries, the growth of each sector, etc. (Alvarez and Fuentes, 2004). Consequently, we have introduced a set of dummy variables to take into account eight industries[4]. Although the coefficients of the dummy variables are not displayed for the sake of simplicity -column (3) in Table 6-, the results of the most relevant remain unaffected.

---

[4] We have introduced the following industries: farming, forestry and fishing; mining; manufacturing; electricity, gas and water; construction; trade; transportation and communication and other services.

CONCLUSION

In recent years there has been great concern among both academia and practitioners about corporate government and, more generally, about the role played by capital markets to improve firms' performance and best practices. Although most of the research has focused on Western European or Anglo-Saxon countries, the literature gradually takes into account other emergent geographical areas with very different investor protection and institutional design. Chile is one of these countries where policy makers have engaged in deep legal reforms in order to achieve better protection of investors‘ rights and the disclosure of more reliable information in capital markets. Earnings management and accruals are some of these corporate practices under scrutiny. Although accruals are aimed to improve the informational content of financial statements, they can be used to disclose opportunistic information about managers' performance and, therefore, to convey false signals to capital markets.

Our paper has centered on the analysis of the ability of some corporate governance mechanisms to control the discretionary use of accounting decisions by the managers of Chilean firms. The analyzed mechanisms are the firm's capital structure, the firm's equity and debt ownership structure and, to a lesser extent, the growth opportunities within the firm's reach. So, the contribution of our paper is twofold: it provides new evidence about earnings management from a non-European or USA country with an institutional setting where capital markets and financial intermediaries play a different role and it includes the analysis of the ownership structure of debt.

Our results show that leverage is positively related to earnings management. The underlying intuition is the incentives of managers to manage financial statements in order to reduce interest rates, to get better debt covenants and to loosen financial constraints.

As regards the impact of ownership concentration, we find a non-linear effect: initially ownership concentration reduces earnings management up to a point where the relation becomes positive. From our point of view, this result is motivated by the conflicts of interest between large controlling shareholders and minority shareholders. The ownership structure of debt is also relevant. Chile has a bank-oriented financial system and banks have a prominent role as financial intermediaries. In this sense, banks act as monitoring institutions to overcome the informational deficiencies of capital markets. Banks have a more detailed knowledge of borrowers and, consequently, bank debt is negatively related to abnormal accruals and to earnings management. Likewise, we have found that public debt is positively related to accounting discretion given the incentives of managers to make a good impression in capital markets and to provide information in their own interests. Our final result has to do with the firm's growth opportunities and does not support the use of accruals as a signaling mechanism.

There are several directions for future research. For instance, the role of Chilean boards of directors and the audit committee in earnings management could shed some light. The equity ownership structure deserves particular attention conditional on the characteristics of the main shareholders. More specifically, a comparison between the impact of institutional investors on earnings management between Chile and common law countries could be quite interesting.

References

Alonso-Borrego, C. and M. Arellano (1999), 'Symmetrically normalized instrumental variable estimation using panel data', *Journal of Business & Economic Statistics*, vol. 17, pp. 36-49.

Alvarez, R. and R. Fuentes (2004), *'Patrones de especialización y crecimiento sectorial en Chile'*, Working paper (Central Bank of Chile).

Arellano, M. 2003. *Panel data econometrics*. Oxford University Press, Oxford.

Arellano, M. and O. Bover (1990), 'La econometría de datos de panel', *Investigaciones Económicas*, Vol.14, No. 1, pp. 3-45.

Arellano, M. and S. Bond (1991), 'Some tests of specification for panel data: Monte Carlo evidence and an application to employment equation', *Review of Economic Studies*, Vol. 58, pp. 277-297.

Arellano, M. and S. Bond (1998), Dynamic panel data estimation using DPD98 for Gauss: A guide for users: 1-27. Azofra, V., L. Castillo and M. Delgado (2003), 'Ownership concentration, debt financing and the investment opportunity set as determinants of accounting discretion: empirical evidence from Spain', *Spanish Journal of Finance and Accounting*, Vol. 115, pp. 215-255.

Baltagi, B (1995), *'Econometric Analysis of Panel Data'*. New York, NY: John Wiley and Sons.

Barber, B. and J. Lyon (1996), 'Detecting abnormal operating performance: The empirical power and specification of test statistics', *Journal of Financial Economics*, Vol. 41, pp. 359–399.

Bartov, E., F. Gul and J. Tsui (2000), 'Discretionary-accruals models and audit qualifications', *Journal of Accounting and Economics*, Vol. 30, pp. 421-452

Becht, M. and A. Röell (1999), 'Blockholdings in Europe: An international comparison', *European Economic Review*, Vol. 43, pp. 1049-1056.

Beneish, M (2001), 'Earnings Management: A Perspective', *Managerial Finance*, Vol. 27, pp. 3-17.

Bianco, M. and P. Casavola (1999), 'Italian corporate governance: Effects on financial structure and firm performance', *European Economic Review*, Vol. 43, pp. 1057-1069

Blundell, R.W. and S.R. Bond (2000), 'GMM estimation with persistent panel data: an application to production functions', *Econometric Reviews*, Vol. 19, pp. 321–340.

Blundell, R.W.; S.R. Bond and F. Windmeijer (2000), 'Estimation in dynamic panel data models: improving on the performance of the standard GMM estimator, In: Baltagi, B. (Ed.), Nonstationary Panels, Panel Cointegration, and Dynamic Panels', *Advances in Econometrics*, Vol. 15, pp. 53–91.

Bond, S. (2002), *'Dynamic panel data models: A guide to micro data methods and practice'*, Working Paper (The Institute for fiscal Studies).

Chan, K., Chan, L., N. Jegadeesh, and J. Lakonishok (2001), *'Earnings quality and stock returns'* Working paper (University of Illinois at Urbana-Champaign).

Chung, R., M. Firth., and J.B. Kim (2002), 'Institutional monitoring and opportunistic earnings management'. *Journal of Corporate Finance*, Vol. 8, pp. 29-48.

Claessens, S., S. Djankov, and L. Klapper (2000), 'The role and functioning of business groups in east Asia and Chile'. *ABANTE*, Vol. 3, No. 1, pp. 91-107.

DeAngelo, L (1988), 'Managerial competition, information costs, and corporate governance: the use of accounting performance measures in proxy contests', *Journal of Accounting and Economics*, Vol. 10, pp. 3 –36.

Dechow, P. (1994), 'Accounting earnings and cash flows as measures of firm performance. The role of accounting accruals', *Journal of Accounting and Economics*, Vol. 18, pp. 3-42.

Dechow, P. and D. Skinner (2000), 'Earnings management: Reconciling the views of accounting academics, practitioners, and regulators', *Accounting Horizons* (June), pp. 235-250.

Dechow, P. and I. Dichev (2002), 'The quality of accruals and earnings'. *The Accounting Review*, Vol. 77, pp. 35-59.

Dechow, P.; R. Sloan, and A. Sweeney (1995), 'Detecting earnings management'. *The Accounting Review*, Vol. 70, No. 2, pp. 193-225.

Dechow, P.; R. Sloan, and A. Sweeney (1996), 'Causes and consequences of earnings manipulations: An analysis of firms subject to enforcement actions by the SEC'. *Contemporary Accounting Research*, Vol. 13, pp. 1-36.

DeFond, M. and J. Jiambalvo (1994), 'Debt covenant violation and manipulation of accruals', *Journal of Accounting and Economics*, Vol. 17, pp. 145-176.

Dewatripont, M. and J. Tirole (1994), 'A theory of debt and equity: Diversity of securities and manager-shareholder congruence', *Quarterly Journal of Economics*, Vol. 109, No. 4, pp. 1027-1054.

Diamond, D. (1984), 'Financial Intermediation and Delegated Monitoring', *Review of Economic Studies*, Vol. 51, pp. 393-414.

Doyle, J., W. Ge, and S. McVay (2005), '*Determinants of weaknesses in internal control over financial reporting*'. Working paper (University of Utah, University of Michigan, and New York University).

Eber, N. (2001), 'Les relations bancaires de long terme. Une revue de la literatura', *Revue d'Économie Politique*, Vol. 111, No. 2, pp. 195-246.

Fairfield, P., S. Whisenant, and T. Yohn (2003), 'The Differential Persistence of Accruals and Cash Flows for Future Operating Income versus Future Return on Assets', *Review of Accounting Studies*, Vol. 8, Nos. 2-3, pp. 221-243.

Gabrielsen, G., J. Gramlich, and T. Plenborg (2002), 'Managerial ownership, information content of earnings, and discretionary accruals in a non-US setting'. *Journal of Business Finance & Accounting*, Vol. 29, Nos. 7-8, pp. 967-988.

García Lara, J.M., B. García Osma, and A. Mora (2005), 'The effect of earnings management on the asymmetric timeliness of earnings', *Journal of Business Finance & Accounting*, Vol. 32, Nos. 3-4, pp. 691-726.

Guay, W., S.P. Kothari, and R. L. Watts (1996), 'A market-based evaluation of discretionary-accrual models', *Journal of Accounting Research*, Vol. 34, pp. 83-105.

Gul, F. (2002), '*Law, Enforcement and Corporate Debt Policies Around the World*', Working paper (Hong Kong, PRC).

Gul, F., Tsui, J., X. Su, and M. Rong (2002), '*Legal protection, enforceability and test of the debt hypothesis: An international study*', Working paper (Hong Kong, PRC).

Hadlock, C. and C.M. James (2002), 'Do banks provide financial slack?', Journal of Finance, Vol. 57, No. 3, pp. 1383-1419.

Han, B. and D. Manry (2000), 'The Implications of Dispersion in Analysts' Earnings Forecasts for Future ROE and Future Returns', *Journal of Business Finance & Accounting*, Vol. 27, Nos. 1-2, pp. 99-126.

Healy, P. and J. M. Wahlen (1999), 'A review of the earnings management literature and its implication for standard setting', *Accounting Horizons*, Vol. 13, No. 4, pp. 365-383.

Healy, P. and K. Palepu. (1993), 'The effect of firms′ financial disclosure strategies on stockprices', *Accounting Horizons*, Vol. 7, No. 1, pp. 11.

Iglesias, A. (2000), 'Pension reform and corporate governance: Impact in Chile', *ABANTE*, Vol. 3, No. 1, pp. 109-141.

James, C. and D. C. Smith (2000), 'Are banks still special? New evidence on their role in the corporate capital-raising process', *Journal of Applied Corporate Finance*, Vol. 13, No. 1, pp. 52-63.

Jensen, M. C. and W. H. Meckling (1976), 'Theory of the firm: Managerial behavior, agency costs and ownership structure', *Journal of Financial Economics*, Vol. 3, pp. 305-360.

Johnson, S. A. (1997), 'An empirical analysis of the determinants of corporate debt ownership structure', *Journal of Financial and Quantitative Analysis*, Vol. 32, No. 1, pp. 47-69.

Jones, J. (1991), 'Earnings management during import relief investigations', *Journal of Accounting Research*, Vol. 29, No. 2, pp. 193-228.

Kothari, S.P., A. Leone, and C. E. Wasley (2005), 'Performance matched discretionary accrual measures', *Journal of Accounting and Economics*, Vol. 39, pp. 163–197

La Porta, R., Lopez-de-Silanes, F., A. Shleifer, and R. Vishny (1998), 'Law and finance', *Journal of Political Economy*, Vol. 106, pp. 1113-1155.

Lasfer, M.A. (1995), 'Agency costs, taxes and debt: the UK evidence', *European Financial Management*, Vol. 1, No. 3, pp. 265-285.

Lefort, F. (2003), 'Gobierno corporativo: ¿Qué es? ¿Cómo andamos por casa?', *Cuadernos de Economía*, Vol. 120, pp. 207-237.

Lefort, F. and E. Walker (2000), 'Ownership and capital structure of Chilean conglomerates: facts and hypotheses for governance', *ABANTE*, Vol. 3, No. 1, pp. 3-27.

Leuz, C., D. Nanda, and P. D. Wysocki (2003), 'Earnings management and investor protection: an international comparison', *Journal of Financial Economics*, Vol. 69, pp. 505-527.

Lui, D. (2004), *'When Accruals Meet Growth: Do Analysts' Forecasts Fully Reflect the Future Earnings Implications of Accruals and Growth*?', Working Paper Series (London Business School).

Lyon, J., B. Barber, and C. Tsui (1999), 'Improved methods for tests of long-run abnormal stock returns'. *Journal of Finance*, Vol. 54, pp. 165–201.

Majluf, N., Abarca, N., D. Rodríguez, and L. A. Fuentes (1998), 'Governance and ownership structure in Chilean economic groups', *ABANTE*, Vol. 1, No. 1, pp. 111-139.

McConnell, J. and H. Servaes (1995), 'Equity ownership and two faces of debt', *Journal of Financial Economics*, Vol. 39, pp. 131-157.

Morck, R., Percy, M., T. Gloria., and B. Yeung (2004), '*The Rise and Fall of the Widely Held Firm - A History of Corporate Ownership in Canada*', Working Papers (National Bureau of Economic Research).

Myers, S. C. (1977), 'Determinants of corporate borrowing', *Journal of Financial Economics*, Vol. 5, pp. 147-175.

Rangan, S. (1998), 'Earnings management and the performance of seasoned equity offerings', *Journal of Financial Economics*, Vol. 50, pp. 101– 122.

Ranieri, R. and P. Valenzuela (2001), *'El valor de las estructuras de propiedad en eldesempeño de las empresas Chilenas'*, Working paper (Pontificia Universidad Catolica).

Shleifer, A. and R. W. Vishny (1997), 'A survey of corporate governance', *Journal of Finance*, Vol. 52, No. 2, pp. 737-783.

Sloan, R. G. (1996), 'Do stock prices fully reflect information in accruals and cash flows about future earnings', *The Accounting Review*, Vol. 71, pp. 289-315.

Spagnolo, G. (2005), 'Managerial incentives and collusive behavior', *European Economic Review*, Vol. 49, No. 6, pp. 1501-1523.

Sweeney, A. (1994), 'Debt covenant violation and managers' responses', *Journal of Accounting and Economics*, Vol. 17, pp. 281-308.

Teoh, S. H., I. Welch, and T.J. Wong (1998a), 'Earnings management and the underperformance of seasoned equity offerings'. *Journal of Financial Economics*, Vol. 50, pp. 63– 99.

Watts, R. L., and J. L. Zimmerman (1986), *Positive accounting theory*, Prentice Hall (Englewood Cliffs).

Watts, R. L., and J. L. Zimmerman (1990), 'Positive accounting theory: A ten year perspective', *The Accounting Review*, Vol. 53, pp. 175-195.

Yeo, G., Tan, P., K. Ho and S. Chen (2002), 'Corporate ownership structure and the informativeness of earnings', *Journal of Business Finance & Accounting*, Vol. 29, Nos. 7-8, pp. 1023-1046.

Yosha, O. (1995), 'Information Disclosure Costs and the Choice of Financing sources', *Journal of Financial Intermediation*, Vol. 4, No. 1, pp. 3-20.

In: International Finance and Financial Services
Editor: Kristian L. Hagen, pp. 143-155
ISBN: 1-60021-756-7

Chapter 6

INTERNATIONAL FISCAL COMPETITION, TRANSFER PRICING AND MULTINATIONAL FIRMS' STRATEGIES

Isabelle Soubaya
CERESUR
Faculty of Law and Economics
University of la Reunion, 15, Av. René Cassin, B.P. 7151
97715 Saint Denis Messag Cedex 9
France

ABSTRACT

Globalisation, commonly defined as the increasing market integration, also involves the expansion of multinational enterprises and foreign direct investment (FDI), mostly by such enterprises. This investment is influenced by the comparative tax regimes of host countries. This contribution involves consideration of two types of taxation effect. The first is the effect on the FDI decisions of multinational enterprises of international variations in taxation rates and rules. The second is their effect on intra-firm trade and pricing policy once an MNE establishes a foreign subsidiary. The first aspect involves international fiscal competition and the second entails transfer pricing. Indeed, manipulation of this transfer price is often used to minimise a multinational enterprise fiscal burden. It is argued that fiscal competition is desirable because it maintains welfare in host countries by acting as a disincentive for transfer pricing manipulation.

1. INTRODUCTION

It is widely agreed that three vectors drive globalisation: international trade, foreign direct investment (FDI), and capital movements (portfolio investments). Expansion of multinational enterprises (MNEs) contributes to the globalisation process because they are involved in these three flows. Concentrating on FDI decisions by MNEs, the objective of this chapter is to point out the relative importance of taxation, even after the internationalisation decision is taken by an enterprise.

FDI and location decisions of enterprises depend on different determinants. Some studies present low tax levels in host countries as an important incentive for FDI and location of subsidiaries by MNEs. One of issues arising here is whether countries compete for FDI by undercutting tax levels in other nations, thus engaging in the so-called "race to the bottom" in tax rates. In other words, do countries engage in fiscal competition in order to attract foreign enterprises?

When a firm decides to internationalise, two possibilities are offered: duplicating its whole production process or cross-border relocation of some of its activities. This second possibility means that MNE segments its production process and relocates their production facilities according to the comparative advantage of the countries, establishing for instance some part of their production in low cost developing countries. Taxation is also likely to influence these two phenomena.

Lastly, the international segmentation of the MNE's production process obviously calls for intra-firm trade between these segments. Indeed, affiliates established in different countries need to be supplied. So, international exchange occurs between those affiliated units. This trade is different from arm's length trade as it occurs within a MNE and "out" of the market. This characteristic is important as it allows the MNE to manipulate the price of this trade, called *transfer pricing* in the literature. Several reasons entice the MNE to manipulate its transfer pricing. One of these is tax differentials between countries. MNEs use these variations to transfer profits from high tax countries to low ones. Because low tax rates attract multinational activities, would potential host countries be inclined to set taxes at low levels to attract such activities?

In this chapter, the major determinants of MNEs' location, with a particular attention to the influence of taxation, are outlined first. It is observed that tax variation results in a globalisation-induced change, namely increased geographical segmentation of the firm's production process. In a second section, we pose the question of whether, in the global context, fiscal competition is likely to be reinforced by MNEs' strategies involving transfer pricing.

2. Tax Policy and Foreign Direct Investment

Many theories attempt to explain the determinants of FDI. A unified theory does not exist. However, one could make the following assumptions in considering decisions by enterprises about relocating their economic activities internationally. The investor differentiates between the different potential host countries according to several factors, in particular their political and economic stability, their quality of infrastructure, their availability and skills of labour, the proximity to markets, their markets size, their potential market power, their similarity in language and culture, their fiscal burden, and so on.

As a consequence, the investment decision does not depend on only one factor but rather results from a global evaluation of all these factors. The analysis of the effects of these determinants is interesting for understanding the strategies of MNEs. Indeed, some determinants such as the tax rate or the fiscal regime, may not influence the decision of a business to relocate its economic activities as much as the differential in factor cost or market size but fiscal factors are an influence. So, MNEs make a trade-off between the tax differential and other factors such as infrastructure quality or labour availability. In the following, focus is solely on the impact of tax levels on location decisions.

One of the globalisation-induced changes is the segmentation of production process. The relocation of units, traditionally called affiliates, is made considering the panel of incentives provided by each potential host country. In other words, MNEs segment their production process and relocate their production facilities according to the comparative advantage of the potential host countries, placing for instance some of their production units in low cost developing countries. One may think that fiscal consideration is not very important at this stage but some studies highlight the importance of tax rates in the segmentation of the production process. More precisely, some studies argue that there is a significant impact of taxation on FDI whereas others conclude that the effect is not significant. Consider these different studies.

The first set argues that taxation is one of the main determinants in location decisions by enterprises. Empirical evidence on the effect of corporate taxes on location decision is provided by the following studies.

Tiebout (1956) was the first to present location decisions by enterprises as being influenced by a combination of consideration of taxes and public goods at the alternative available locations. He found that countries offering high quality of public goods can charge high corporate taxes and still be favoured locations for MNEs.

Lastly, Grubert et al. (1998) analysed the reasons why US MNEs established affiliates in Puerto Rico. They conclude that taxation is such that MNEs are motivated to relocate some of their affiliates there because they can benefit from a favourable fiscal treatment. They can minimise their fiscal burden in moving profits in favour of affiliates settled in Puerto Rico.

Devereux et al. (1998) found that the average effective tax rate is a quantitatively significant factor in the choice of location. They showed that a negative correlation exists between the average effective tax rate and the location probability. For example, in UK, a one-percentage point increase of the first implies a reverse variation, equivalent in quantity, in the second term.

Bénassy-Quéré et al. (2000) tested the impact of corporate tax discrepancies on FDI among nine OECD countries. These authors identify a negative impact of corporate tax rate on bilateral FDI flows.

Markusen et al. (2001) showed that the choice between producing abroad and exporting is determined by the proximity-concentration trade-off[1]. When producing abroad is preferred, taxation and other cost-related factors are important and significant determinants.

De Mooij et al. (2001) completed a meta-analysis based on 25 studies published between 1984 and 2001. They found a negative correlation between the tax rate and FDI inflows.

Bretin et al. (2001) found that MNEs are sensitive to tax levels in host countries but tax rates in origin country do not matter.

Lastly, Nunnenkamp (2002) argued that the nature and importance of FDI determinants have changed over time with non-traditional determinants increasing as influences. Thus, traditional factors such as market size have decreased in importance to be replaced by non-

[1] In line with Brainard (1997), these authors pointed out that when proximity reasons are prevalent, firm would choose to produce abroad whereas exporting is preferred when concentration is necessary.

traditional ones. Among the latter, Nunnenkamp includes cost differences between locations, infrastructure quality and taxation.

A second set of studies, essentially derived from the new economic geography models, argues that taxation does not play a significant role in location decisions by enterprises. Indeed, agglomeration effects dominate and erase the influence of potential tax differentials (Mayer et al., 1999, Jayet et al., 1999). In these models, a race to the bottom in corporate tax rates does not take place even though capital is becoming increasingly mobile in globalisation context. Ludema et al. (1998) integrate the possibility of taxation impact even in the presence of agglomeration effects but do not succeed in showing that FDI inflow is driven by a decrease in tax rates. Ottaviano et al. (2002) find that effects of agglomeration are higher in terms of capital returns than effects of a decrease in taxation in terms of returns due to FDI inflows.

But, the fiscal issue can be viewed differently. This debate is not based solely on the effect of tax rates but also on the way host countries behave to influence location decisions by business enterprises, namely by varying the fiscal schemes. Indeed, the taxation of profits includes several stages. Profits are usually taxed at the statutory legal tax rate in the host country. However, some host countries vary fiscal schemes for FDI according to their objectives.

- If they want to avoid fiscal evasion, they may choose a *credit system* in which investors pay taxes at the rate in their origin country. This is particularly useful for countries that want to avoid transfer of profits if foreign tax rate is lower than home tax rate.
- At the opposite extreme, is an *exemption system*. Investors are enticed to locate their business activities in low tax countries in which they will be taxed.

Hines (1995) showed that MNEs from countries with a credit system are less sensitive to tax differentials than MNEs from countries with an exemption system.

Thus, it appears that the tax influence is not clearly determined. But, in spite of this controversial effect, a study made by Ernst and Young International[2], in 1995, of 85 MNEs, found that 80% of respondents stated taxation as the main factor influencing their international activities. So, in the following, it is assumed that taxation does influence the location decisions of businesses. Furthermore, there will be an investigation of whether countries compete to attract economic activities and MNEs using tax variations as an incentive.

In the following, tax competition is defined as the lowering of tax rates. In investigating *whether fiscal competition does exist*, it questions *whether the observed tax variations are proof of fiscal competition*.

Let us see if tax competition is reflected in a decrease of tax rates. Table 1 shows a clear downward trend in corporate tax rates. In 2001, statutory corporate tax rates in OECD countries were centred around 35%. This may be due to the increasing integration in goods and capital markets. This seems to confirm the existence of tax competition.

---

[2] This study consisted in the interview of 25 MNEs having activities in 8 countries, of whom Canada, United States, United Kingdom and Japan, and of 50 American enterprises and 10 Japanese ones.

Table 1. Statutory tax rates[3] from 1986 to 2001 for particular years

	1986	1991	1995	1998	2001	Percentage variation (1986-2001)
Austria	50	30	34	34	34	-32%
Belgium	45	39	39	39	39	-13%
Denmark	50	38	34	34	30	-40%
Finland	33	23	25	28	29	-12%
France	45	42	33.3	41.6	36.4	-19%
Germany	56	50/36	45/30	45/25	25	-55%
Greece	49	46	35/40	35/40	35	-29%
Ireland	50	43	40	32	20	-60%
Italia	36	36	36	37	36	0%
Luxembourg	40	33	33	30	30	-25%
Netherlands	42	35	35	35	35	-17%
Portugal	42/47	36	36	34	32	-32%
Spain	35	35	35	35	35	0%
Sweden	52	30	28	28	28	-46%
United Kingdom	35	34	33	31	30	-14%
Mean EU	44.3	36.7	35.1	34.9	32	-28%
Australia	41	39	33	36	34	-17%
United States	46	34	35	35	35	-24%
Japan	50	50	47.5	46.4	46.4	-7%

Source: OECD and author's calculations.

Note: The rate is the one of central government; mean for European Union is non-weighted. For Australia, it is 1993's tax rate instead of that for 1991's. For Portugal, tax rate of 47% has been taken into account in the variation calculation.

That MNEs take advantage of tax differentials does not mean, however, that countries undertake fiscal competition. Nevertheless, as FDI inflows are an important contributor to economic growth, many countries adopt incentives to attract investors. Typical incentives are, for instance, an exemption or a reduction in corporate tax. Devereux et al. (2002) notice that countries are particularly interested in attracting MNEs as their investment are likely to bring higher profits for the countries.

Moreover, the deep integration of the market for goods and services and the capital market reinforces gradually the fear of tax competition. As a result, companies attach more and more importance to the tax aspects in their locational choices and, in reaction, the governments compete with one another by altering the taxation incentives.

Another point of view is that these tax differentials do not necessarily result from tax competition between countries: they can be used, for instance, to compensate the lack of

[3] These rates do not take into account the fiscal burden difference between countries: they do include the average local tax and the temporary overtaxes but not the income tax.

attractiveness of concerned country or can be justified by a differential in supply conditions such as infrastructure quality of labour. Bénassy-Quéré et al. (2003) argue that globalisation (defined as increasing international economic integration) has led to growing pressure on tax policies. These authors showed that "although tax differentials do matter for FDI flows, this should not lead to "race to the bottom", because market potential and public investment also matter". A MNE may decide to relocate in a high tax country if its infrastructure is of good quality and labour presents high skill. In this situation, countries with the largest markets may attract FDI even if they impose high tax rates. However, small countries do have incentives to cut taxes because they are relatively more sensitive to tax-base relocation.

Moreover, if tax is seen as a distortion, competition that reduces tax variations, is useful as it reduces a distortion. However, the drawback of tax competition is that human capital and physical capital are mobile factors. Consequently, the source of fiscal revenue is shifted from these mobile factors to immobile factors such as non-skilled labour. Thus, MNEs attentive to their workers' fiscal burden would be less inclined to relocate in countries where tax competition is based on immobile factors.

To conclude, it appears that the question of whether fiscal competition is encouraged by growing globalisation has not received a clear-cut answer. Taxation is a determinant but two other elements moderate this influence. First, it seems that countries are motivated to compete and to diminish their tax rates to attract FDI. However, large countries can afford to set high taxes as they can provide compensation in terms of high levels of public goods. Second, as Bénassy-Quéré et al. (2003) noticed, the influence of tax differentials is not symmetric. Thus, if host countries report higher taxes than at home, it is clearly a disincentive but relatively lower taxes do not necessarily FDI attract.

All these studies point out that taxation is important in the international location decision businesses of firms but this influence does not stop there. As we mentioned in the introduction of this chapter, taxation is likely to still have an influence once the internationalisation decision is undertaken. The debate in this chapter is about the influence of taxation on multinational enterprise's business strategy. This influence can also be important once an international affiliate is established. Therefore, it is necessary to discuss the transfer pricing issue. On this subject, a study by Fontagné et al. (1999) showed that Ireland, often pointed out as attracting FDI because of its favourable tax system, reports high unit value for its exports. This can be considered as an example of relocation for tax motives and be a sign of the use of transfer pricing. This pricing manipulation can influence the volume as well as the direction of intra-firm trade. In the next section the different reasons and consequences of this manipulation are discussed.

3. Intra-Firm Trade and the Use of Taxation

As OECD (1995) underlined, the increasing importance of networks implies that MNEs must work more efficiently across borders. Consequently, intra-firm trade, i.e. trade between a parent company and its affiliates, grows in volume and scope.

Table 2 indicates the share of intra-firm trade (cross-border) as a percentage of total trade is rising significantly.

Table 2. Share of intra-firm trade in total trade (in %)

	Exports		Imports	
	1994	1999	1994	1999
United States	32.8	36.3	43.7	39.4
Japan	16.6	30.8	14.7	23.6
France	34*	40.6	18*	35.8

Note: * In 1994, intra-firm flows represent 34% of French exports and 18% of French imports.
Source: CPCI Report (2002) for France, UNCTAD (2002)

But, this growing relative importance of intra-firm trade gave rise to a specific issue: transfer pricing manipulation. Indeed, as this trade occurs within multinational group, it is "out" of the market and thus, probably, at a different prices than market prices. Contrary to national enterprises, MNEs have the ability to manipulate this price, fiscal evasion being their motive. Operating in different environments, these firms face different tax regimes. This international dimension induces MNEs to manipulate their transfer prices to transfer profits and reduce their tax burden. This response affects the welfare of those involved in each economy and the fiscal revenues of governments affected by intra-firm operations.

The survey by Ernst and Young (1999) provides a useful example of the importance of transfer pricing as an issue. This study involved interviews of 600 financial departments of MNEs located in 19 countries[4] and 124 affiliates of large multinational groups in Canada, Europe, United States and Mexico. Sixty-one per cent of interviewed MNEs considered transfer pricing as the most important element in their international fiscal problem. Among the affiliates, 97% answer similarly. This survey shows thus that transfer pricing is entirely integrated into the strategies of MNEs. Let us examine this price and its influence.

In the present section, we want to discuss how taxation is a major influence on intra-firm trade. MNEs integrate tax differentials into their business strategies and will choose transfer prices that allow them to artificially transfer revenues. This influences both the volume of intra-firm trade but also its price. The influence of taxation on the choice of this price is discussed. In this context, countries that would attract FDI might encourage fiscal competition.

Recall the different reasons why MNEs manipulate their transfer price. MNEs modify the price of their intra-firm operations because of some advantages. First, this behaviour is the way of avoiding various restrictions imposed either by the host country's FDI, or by the home country's FDI (Kim, 1999). These restrictions are of several types. The main reason why MNEs manipulate transfer prices is to avoid fiscal barriers related to tariffs and also reduce taxes on profits. Indeed, even marginal manipulation of transfer prices can have a substantial consequence on the amount of profits declared by an affiliate.

Manipulation of transfer price makes it possible for the MNE to transfer before-tax-profits from a country (with a high tax level) to another (with a low tax level) and thus to maximise its global after-tax-profit. As intra-firm trade represents almost 40% of international trade, this strategy allows the MNE obtain significantly higher income.

[4] These countries are Argentina, Australia, Brazil, Canada, Denmark, Finland, France, Germany, Italy, Japan, Korea, Mexico, Netherlands, Norway, Spain, Sweden, Switzerland, United Kingdom, and the United States.

The MNE may also want to manipulate its transfer price if there are tariff barriers in the host country. Its aim is to minimise the effect of these barriers, setting for instance a transfer price as low as possible if the tariff is high. This strategy has the consequence of artificially diminishing the foreign affiliate's value of imports, which consequently pay a lower level of custom duty than otherwise. But this low transfer price has the other effect of increasing the tax on profit. Indeed, imports can be counted as a cost for affiliates. If its cost decreases, its profit increases and so its fiscal burden increases. In sum, in order to maximise its profit, MNEs make a trade-off between tariffs and taxes.

Manipulation of transfer price may also allow the MNE to modify its affiliate's value added, between interests and dividends so as to reduce its taxability and thus to minimise its fiscal payments in the host country.

The second type of incentive includes risks of change and risks linked to financial management that bring MNE to "adapt" their price policy according to risks prevailing in each country. These motives are linked to wage claims, the volatility of exchange rates, and the financial problems of the affiliate.

Tariff barriers, or corporate taxation, do influence intra-firm trade. The choice of an appropriate transfer price allows the MNE to artificially transfer profits from parent company to its affiliate (or vice versa), according to the taxation level in each country. In adopting such strategy, the MNE can minimise its total tax burden.

All these factors provide incentives to manipulate transfer prices. But let us now analyse how MNEs can benefit from transfer pricing designed to transfer profits to take advantage of differing tax regimes.

We start from a model of two countries (*H, F*) and one multinational enterprise (composed of a parent company in *H* and an affiliate in *F*). Following Horst (1971) and Kant (1989), we assume a tax differential between the two countries and show how that influences the transfer price.

We assume a horizontal integration situation[5], and add a tax on profits in each country. So, MNE' s profit function can be written as:

$$\Pi = (1-t_H)\pi_H + (1-t_F)\pi_F \tag{1}$$

with π_H and π_F respectively profit of parent company and profit of the foreign affiliate, and t_F and t_H are respectively tax rates in affiliate's country and the one in parent company's country.

Assume that a fraction $f \in [0,1]$ of the affiliate' s profits is repatriated to the parent company. This part is thus taxed, not at the rate t_F but at the rate t_H and so the effective tax rate in the affiliate's country, noted t_e , is then:

$$t_e = t_F + f(t_H - t_F) \tag{2}$$

[5] In this situation, the affiliate does not produce anything, and behaves like a distribution affiliate having the only role to resell final goods produced by the parent company. The other case is vertical integration and consists in a division of the production process between two countries depending on its comparative advantage. The parent company produces an intermediate for its affiliate that uses it for final goods production.

The net profit function, derived from equation (1), is thus:

$$\Pi = (1-t_H)\pi_H + (1-t_e)\pi_F \tag{3}$$

The objective of MNE is to maximise this function. To do that, it chooses a transfer price, p, which allows it to reach this maximum[6].

Results are the following[7]:

$$\frac{\partial \Pi}{\partial p} \rangle 0 \quad if \quad t_H < t_F \tag{4}$$

$$\frac{\partial \Pi}{\partial p} \langle 0 \quad if \quad t_H > t_F \tag{5}$$

Notice that this result does not change if it is assumed that there is no profit repatriation. Indeed, if $f = 0, t_e = t_F$, the profit function can be written by taking into account this equality.

Two interpretations of this result are possible:

- When taxation level in affiliate' s country is higher that the one in parent company' s country ($t_F > t_H$), affiliate' s profit is taxed relatively at a higher rate. The MNE thus chooses to artificially transfer profit from affiliate to the parent company. For that, it must reduce the affiliate' s profit and consequently increase its total cost. Hence, it increases its transfer price. In the same way, the MNE will have to increase parent company' s profit, i.e. to increase its total revenue and thus increase p.
- When ($t_F < t_H$), the reverse situation occurs; the MNE must transfer profit from the parent company to the affiliate and, for that, must reduce its transfer price[8].

If we add a custom duty to this tax differential, MNE will make a comparison between tax differential and the tariff. We must keep in mind that in a globalized world, tariffs decreasing over time (due to WTO), this action levy tends to disappear for governments. But tax differentials remain a great incentive to transfer profits.

---

[6] Parent company's profit can be written as the sum of the sales revenues on the domestic market, the exports revenues and the production costs. The affiliate has revenue from the sales on local market and must pay for production and for imports. Furthermore, producing anything, its only function is to resell parent company production. So, total profit is the sum of both profits.

$$Max\ \Pi(Q_H, Q_F) = (1-t_H)\left[RT_H(Y_H) + pX - CT_H(Q_H)\right] + (1-t_e)\left[RT_F(X) - (CT_F(X) + pX)\right]$$

[7] See Soubaya (2002) for more details.

[8] Eden (2001) remarks that this manipulation of transfer price, for reducing the MNE's tax burden, conduces to artificially modify the intra-firm exports and imports values.

Does it mean that this behaviour of MNEs encourages governments to modify their fiscal policy and to compete with one another?

Let us see how this can be represented. This is done in Figure 1. It assumes a division of the enterprise' s production process with one segment settled in country H (where there is the parent company) and a second segment settled in country F (where there is the affiliate). Two cases are considered.

We review two cases: in the first one, there is a tax differential; in the second one, the tax differential decreases because tax rate in H decreases. We assume in other words that there is a fiscal competition.

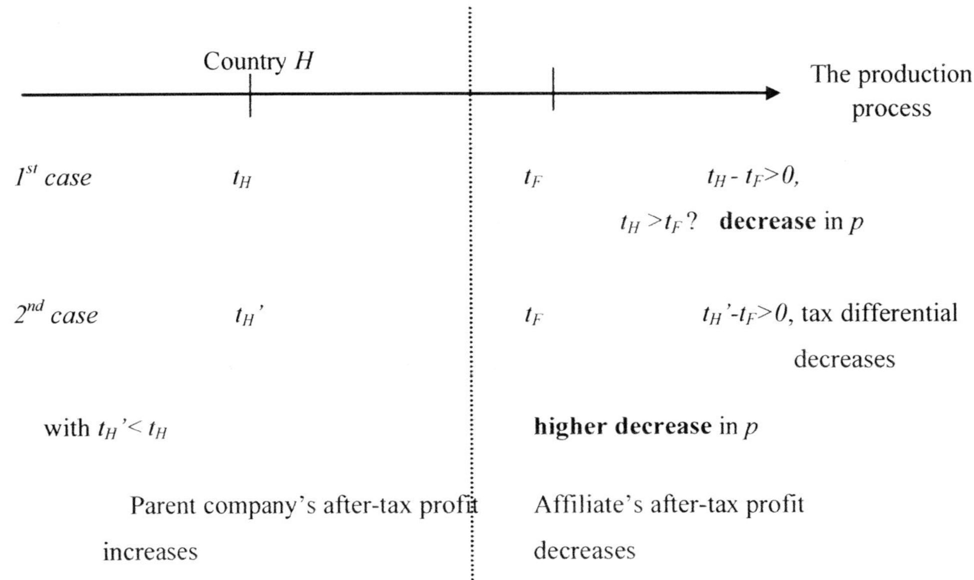

Figure 1. MNEs, fiscal policy and fiscal competition: an illustration

In the first case, tax rate in country F is lower than in country H. So, in the second country, profit is relatively more taxed. One possibility for MNE is to transfer profit from H to F, which means a decrease of the transfer price. Moreover, another consequence of this lower tax rate in country F is that it will attract FDI and foreign MNEs. When analysing their relative low attractiveness in terms of FDI, country H will be incited to diminish their tax rate.

In the second case, we assume that in order to attract FDI, country H set a tax rate lower than in the first case. This implies that parent company' s profit will increase relatively to the first case. As tax rate decreases in this country, MNE will have to transfer relatively less profit to country F that still has a lower tax rate. Transfer price is then lower and then implies that affiliate in country F will have a lower profit.

So this example helps us to support the hypothesis that fiscal competition has a non-symmetric influence.

- When a tax differential decreases between nations (because the higher tax rate decreases), MNEs have less incentive to transfer profits and to set a transfer pricing artificially different from market price; and

- On the other hand, when tax differentials increase because host countries decrease their tax rates, MNEs are more inclined to transfer profits and to set a higher transfer price.

The findings of Bénassy-Quéré et al. (2003) accord with these results because they conclude that "while narrow tax differentials do not much discourage inward FDI, large tax discrepancies produce proportionally more important FDI outflows".

4. Conclusion

In this chapter, I wanted to point out the importance of taxation on MNE' s business strategies, namely on their location decisions, on their decisions about cross-border relocation, and finally in their choice of transfer prices. In the first matter, profit-shifting opportunities drive FDI flows and bring MNEs to locate in countries with low tax rates. Hence, fiscal competition is encouraged to attract foreign activities.

Secondly, MNEs segment their production processes internationally. This is determined *inter alia* by the type of incentives put in place in host countries. One of these is taxation incentives; credit schemes having no impact on location whereas exemption schemes clearly attract FDI.

Finally, in the third type of decision, an MNE has to choose adequate transfer pricing to maximise its global (international) profits. This means that this firm has to take advantage of tax differentials to minimise its fiscal burden. Although fiscal competition is encouraged by this, it has asymmetrical effects depending on the direction of the variations. Indeed, high tax encourages transfer of profits whereas the decrease in this discrepancy does not favour manipulation of transfer prices. So one may conclude that fiscal competition is useful for host countries' welfare as it is a disincentive for transfer pricing manipulation. But, this type of competition means also a loss in fiscal revenues. Hence, countries will have to make a trade-off.

Acknowledgements

Isabelle Soubaya would like to thank Serge Svizzero for his comments on the first draft of this paper and Clem Tisdell for his remarks at the First French-Australian Workshop on "Business and Globalisation: Economic and Managerial Issues". The usual caveat applies.

References

Bénassy-Quéré A., Fontagné, L., and Lahrèche-Révil, A. (2000). Foreign Direct Investment and the Prospects for Tax Co-ordination in Europe. *Centre D'Etudes Prospectives et D'Informations Internationales, CEPII Working Paper No. 2000-06*, 1-49.

Bénassy-Quéré A., Fontagné, L., and Lahrèche-Révil, A. (2003). Tax Competition and Foreign Direct Investment. *Centre D'Etudes Prospectives et D'Informations Internationales, CEPII Working Paper No. 2003-17*, 1-40.

Brainard, S. L. (1997). An Empirical Assessment of the Proximity-Concentration Trade-off Between Multinational Sales and Trade. *The American Economic Review*, *87*(4), 520-544.

Bretin, E., and Guimbert, S. (2001). Tax Competition for Firms: To Cure or to Care? Conference *"Corporate and Capital Income Taxation in the European Union: the EU Commission Report on Companies' Taxation and Beyond"*, Fucam, December.

CPCI Report (2002). L' industrie française en 2001-2002. *Commission Permanente de Concertation pour l' Industrie,* Ministère de l' Économie, des Finances et de l' Industrie.

De Mooij, R., and Ederveen, S. (2001). Taxation and Foreign Direct Investment: A Synthesis of Empirical Research. *CPB (Netherlands Bureau for Economic Policy Analysis) Discussion Paper*, *003,* 1-52.

Devereux, M., and Griffith, R. (1998). Taxes and the Location of Production: Evidence from a Panel of US Multinationals. *Journal of Public Economics, 68*(3), 335-367.

Devereux, M. P., Griffith, R., and Klemm, A. (2002). Corporate Income Tax Reforms and International Tax Competition. *Economic Policy, 17*(35).

Eden, L. (2001). Transfer Pricing, Intrafirm Trade and the BLS International Price Program. *U.S. Bureau of Labor Statistics Working Paper No. 334*, 1-61.

Ernst and Young (1999). *Transfer Pricing: 1999 Global Survey.* Ernst and Young International.

Fontagné, L. and Freudenberg, M. (1999). Marché Unique et Développement des Échanges. *Économie et Statistique, 326-327*, 71-95.

Grubert, H., and Slemrod, J. (1998). The Effects of Taxes on Investment and Income Shifting to Puerto Rico. *The Review of Economics and Statistics, 80*(3), 365-373.

Hines, J. R. (1995). Taxes, Technology Transfer, and the RandD Activities of Multinational Firms. In M. Feldstein, J. R. Hines, and R. G. Hubbard (Eds.), *The Effects of Taxation on Multinational Corporations*, Chicago: University of Chicago Press.

Horst, T. (1971). The Theory of the Multinational Firm: Optimal Behavior under Different Tariff and Tax Rates. *Journal of Political Economy*, *79*(5), 1059-1072.

Jayet, H., Bénard R., and Rajaonarison D. (1999). L'environnement Souhaité par les Entreprises. *Economie et Statistique, 326-327(6/7)*, 177-188.

Kant, C. (1989). Perverse Intra-Firm Trade. *Southern Economic Journal*, 56(1), 233-235.

Kim, S. H. (1999). International Transfer Pricing. In R. Z. Aliber, and R. W. Click (Eds.), *Readings in International Business: A Decision Approach*, Oxford.

Ludema, R. D. and Wooton, I. (1998). Economic Geography and the Fiscal Effects of Regional Integration. *Centre for Economic Policy Research* (*CEPR) Discussion Paper No. 1822.*

Markusen, J. R. and Maskus, K. E. (2001). General Equilibrium Approaches to the Multinational Firm: A Review of Theory and Evidence. *National Bureau of Economic Research* (*NBER) Working Paper No. 8334,* 1-53.

Mayer T. and Mucchielli, J-L. (1999). La Localisation à L'étranger des Entreprises Multinationales: Une Approche d'économie Géographique Hiérarchisée Appliquée aux Entreprises Japonaises en Europe. *Économie et Statistique*, *326-327*, 159-167.

Nunnenkamp P. (2002). Determinants of FDI in Developing Countries: Has Globalization Changed the Rules of the Game? Kiel Institute for World Economics, Germany, July.

OECD (1995). *Principes Applicables en Matière de Prix de Transfert à L'intention des Entreprises Multinationales et des Administrations Fiscales*, Paris, OECD.

Ottaviano, G., and Van Ypersele, T. (2002). Market Access and Tax Competition, miméo, University of Bologna.

Soubaya, I. (2002). *Commerce Intra-firme et Investissements Directs: Aspects Théoriques et Application aux Multinationales Françaises.* PhD thesis, University of Paris I - Panthéon Sorbonne, December.

Tiebout, C. M. (1956). A Pure Theory of Local Expenditures. *Journal of Political Economy* *64*(5), 416-424.

UNCTAD (2002). *World Investment Report 1998*. United Nations, New York.

In: International Finance and Financial Services
Editor: Kristian L. Hagen, pp. 157-189 ISBN: 1-60021-756-7

Chapter 7

THE WORLD COMPETITION AGENCY AS A NECESSARY INTERNATIONAL INSTITUTION

Denis Borges Barbosa
Pontifícia Universidade Católica do Rio de Janeiro
Rio de Janeiro RJ 20040-001 20040=030, Brazil

ABSTRACT

The breeding of an international apparatus to deal with the crucial aspect of world competition policy, as it is anticipated to be finally discussed on the Cancun Ministerial Meeting of the WTO in September 2003. Should this matter be restricted to the WTO context? Is the WTO the proper venue, especially when analyzing the theme from the standpoint of Brazil and other developing countries? There should be any international institution dealing with the matter, or, for instance, an unattended system of bilateral treaties would do? Given the complexity of international, domestic, regional and Third World-specific interests, the criteria of fairness and rationality seem to advise the setting up of an international institution, entirely dedicated to competition matters. It would seem that, if such assumptions are correct, a non-trade entity should be built upon the joint experience of both pre-WTO and post Doha competition collaboration. We are not certainly proposing an international institution that should chase and prosecute the international public interest on an autonomous and cavalier fashion. On the contrary, the reality of multilateral negotiation and complex national and regional policies indicate that only a prudent entity, acting in the same, ad hoc, case-by-case basis as the international judicial courts have been hitherto acting, could be of any practical import.

THE ISSUE

As the Brazilian saying goes, "those who impose and dispose and don't get what they chose, or are fools or have no Art". The breeding of an international apparatus to deal with the crucial aspect of world competition policy, as it is anticipated to be finally discussed on the Cancun Ministerial Meeting of the WTO in September 2003, shall be a very fine display of such wisecrack, or else the central market economies have certainly lost all their long honored art.

The previous Ministerial meeting at Doha, in 2001, issued a declaration with a specific mandate as to competition policy:

1. .Recognizing the case for a multilateral framework to enhance the contribution of competition policy to international trade and development, and the need for enhanced technical assistance and capacity-building in this area as referred to in paragraph 24, we agree that negotiations will take place after the Fifth Session of the Ministerial Conference on the basis of a decision to be taken, by explicit consensus, at that Session on modalities of negotiations.
2. We recognize the needs of developing and least-developed countries for enhanced support for technical assistance and capacity building in this area, including policy analysis and development so that they may better evaluate the implications of closer multilateral cooperation for their development policies and objectives, and human and institutional development. To this end, we shall work in cooperation with other relevant intergovernmental organizations, including UNCTAD, and through appropriate regional and bilateral channels, to provide strengthened and adequately resourced assistance to respond to these needs.
3. In the period until the Fifth Session, further work in the Working Group on the Interaction between Trade and Competition Policy will focus on the clarification of: core principles, including transparency, non-discrimination and procedural fairness, and provisions on hardcore cartels; modalities for voluntary cooperation; and support for progressive reinforcement of competition institutions in developing countries through capacity building. Full account shall be taken of the needs of developing and least-developed country participants and appropriate flexibility provided to address them.

Such instructions to Cancún seem to bring into attention not only a substantive theme but also an institutional one. Should this matter be restricted to the WTO context? Is the WTO the proper venue, especially when analyzing the theme from the standpoint of Brazil and other developing countries? There should be any international institution dealing with the matter, or, for instance, an unattended system of bilateral treaties would do?

We shall undertake to answer such questions in this study. However, it would seem adequate to express an initial discomfort as to the effective result the current exercise might impact as to "needs of developing and least-developed country participants and appropriate flexibility provided to address them":

"Although developing countries have a great interest in pursuing an active domestic competition policy, this can and should be done independently of the WTO. Given the mercantilist basis of multilateral trade negotiations, the WTO is less likely to be a powerful instrument to encourage adoption of welfare-enhancing competition rules than it is as a forum for the abolition of border measures. Priority should therefore be given to pursuit of the traditional market access focus of the WTO—further reduction in direct barriers to trade in goods and services." [1]

WHY COMPETITION SHOULD BE REGULATED ON AN INTERNATIONAL LEVEL?

The answer is axiomatic: because competition happens, or should happen, at such level. Phenomena like cross border mergers and cartels proliferate, and welfare-reducing factors would seem to result from it more acutely than within any singular jurisdiction[2]. But there is another good reason: competition regulation and policy (or, better, *policy*, and regulation) are perhaps a good antidote to the various problems caused precisely by trade policies as generated at the WTO context.

Competition laws are directed to optimize the (hopefully beneficial) results of free market economies, by preventing that scarce resources are lost through the shenanigans of economic agents powerful enough to distort the market access and regular working, to their private purposes. The prestidigitation of the free hand of market (and so goes the ideology) works optimally when the private interest meet at a *public* space, which is so always kept. Some considerations on the fairness of the procedure are sometimes required.

But such public interests defy the private ones that are instrumental to it. Corporate executives pay lip service to competition and free market, but (as a decision of the Brazilian Antitrust Authority says) cherish the opportunity to be free from the market constrictions[3].

The emergence of multinational corporations (or, in the official UN parlance, *transnational corporations)* in the global markets have emphasized also in the international scene the dual goal of such economic actors: fight for a market free for all, but work hard lest such liberty threatens its own private objectives. Therefore, it is advisable to follow our discussion assessing this specific issue - the relationship between the transnational corporation and the host country.

Obviously, the international competition issue does not affect only transnational corporations[4]; purely domestic actors may act in such a way to cause impact on a cross border fashion (*hard core* cartels are an obvious example).

Our basic contention in this study is that competition is not only, nor essentially, a trade subject. Even though the theme was brought from the start in the pre-1947 GATT discussions

---

1 Bernard Hoekman and Peter Holmes, Competition Policy, Developing Countries and the WTO, World Bank Paper, April 1999.

2 Hoekman and Holmes, op. cit.

3 becoming in the last few years a very important actor in the Brazilian economy. As CADE has expressed it: "There is no space for delusion. From a private perspective, that one of the operating economic agent in the market, the competition is a source of annoyance and pressure. The dream of all company is to become monopolist and to conquer a calm life; it would not be rational if it was not in this way. The engine of the capitalism is the innovation, what is nothing more than the stubbornness in leading to the somewhat new, exclusive market, that's to say, to have its monopoly, even for a short time. It is exactly the persistence of if becoming monopolist - to gain economic profit or over normal - what supports the competitive dynamics. (Ato de Concentração 83/96. Voto da Conselheira Lúcia Helena Salgado)

4 Defined for our present purposes as a business entity with active establishments in different national jurisdictions and using this diversity as a significant business mechanism.

and a trade matter[5], it would seem that the various interests at play, and especially de interests of developing countries, would be better served by an autonomous international institution, and not by WTO.

The International Practices having Local Effect

Granted that transnational corporation behavior (or, as the case may be, domestic corporations cooperating cross borders) may have disruptive effects on the competition, it is interesting to check how that international competition issues affect national competition systems. Just as an index of such problem, we shall take as examples (in no way exhaustive ones) the American and Brazilian practices[6].

United States Practice

The American Antitrust Law, at least on a first inspection, seems quite condescending as to competition restraining practice conducted abroad. Only those practices that may have a *direct, substantial and reasonably foreseeable* effect on the competitive patterns of the domestic, import or export markets of the United States require special care[7]. Under the applicable criteria, therefore, the first step to check the impact of U.S. Antitrust Law on non competitive practices abroad is to see whether there is any effect whatsoever on such markets[8].

5 "Support for international disciplines in the area of competition law was originally stimulated by US perceptions that international cartels and the absence or non-enforcement of national competition law impeded the ability of US firms to contest markets. The US has been arguing for many years that Japanese corporate groups (Keiretsu) undermine market access for foreign suppliers by buying predominantly from each other and retaining close vertical linkages between manufacturers, wholesalers and retailers. In the 1940s at the time of the negotiations to establish an International Trade Organization (ITO), the US supported inclusion of a chapter dealing with restrictive business practices, reflecting its opposition to German cartels and Japanese zaibatsu". Hoekman and Holmes, op. cit.

6 National competition authorities are relatively rare specimens even today. In Latin America, only Argentina, Brazil, Chile, Colombia, Costa Rica, Jamaica, Mexico, Panama, Peru and Venezuela have such agencies.

7 Sherman Act, Section 7, as amended by the Foreign Trade Antitrust Improvement Act of 1982, 15 U.S.C. § 6a. (1982). See Eurim-Pharm GmbH v. Pfizer Inc., F. Supp. 1102, 1105 (S.D.N.Y. 1984). According to the DOJ International Antitrust Guideline (1995), "Under the Sherman Act and the FTC Act, there are two principal tests for subject matter jurisdiction in foreign commerce cases. With respect to foreign import commerce, the Supreme Court has recently stated in Hartford Fire Insurance Co. v. California that "the Sherman Act applies to foreign conduct that was meant to produce and did in fact produce some substantial effect in the United States." There has been no such authoritative ruling on the scope of the FTC Act, but both Acts apply to commerce "with foreign nations" and the Commission has held that terms used by both Acts should be construed together. Second, with respect to foreign commerce other than imports, the Foreign Trade Antitrust Improvements Act of 1982 ("FTAIA") applies to foreign conduct that has a direct, substantial, and reasonably foreseeable effect on U.S. commerce".

8 Incidentally, a similar pattern results from EC case law: see Gencor Ltd v. Commission of the European Communities and Federal Republic of Germany, Case T-102/96, 25 March 1999, para. 90, 1999 [E.C.R.] ___(available under http://europa.eu.int/...).

If the two first steps were complied with, it would be the case of ascertaining whether the restriction is *unreasonable*, that is to say, whether the non competitive effect is balanced by other relevant considerations[9].

Irrespective of the existence of any U.S. Governmental initiative against the action in analysis, either through FTC or the Department of Justice, American Law harbors the *private antitrust actions*, which may be initiated by any interested parties, among which industrial consumers of the restricted products. Frequently those actions result in large treble indemnifications[10].

However, if such extraterritorial action is liable to affect, for instance, the export markets of the U.S. transnationals shall be taken into account[11]. The case law has thus considered that the acts of companies in the exterior that affect the American importations or exportations improperly, including the agreements between companies that may diminish the American sales potential in other countries. Thus, an English industry, with a good American clientele, entering into an alliance itself with another society of the same country to regulate the market of an African nation, to where also they export in competition with United States firms, is subject to U.S. Antitrust laws.

This very intruding procedure may obviously cause international sensibility, especially in connection with jurisdictional clashes between other national agencies. Some rules on comity were developed[12], but there is the feeling that foreign laws being compatible, no actual conflict should occur[13]. Recently, however, the International Competition Policy Advisory Committee (ICPAC) of the DOJ has recommended that to minimize the possibility for conflicts arising from U.S. extraterritorial enforcement and to increase the possibility of meaningful of the perceived problem, the Antitrust Division should review the ability of the foreign authority in addressing the claim[14].

---

9 Hunt v. Mobil Oil Corp., 550 F. 2d 68 (2d Cir.), cert. denied, 434 U.S. 984 (1977); Timberlaine Lumber Co. v. Bank of America NT & SA, 549 F.2d. 597, 606-07 (9th. Cir. 1977); Interamerican Refinery Corp. v. Texaco Maracaibo, Inc., 307 F. Supp. 1291 (D.Del. 1970).

10 Van Cise, Lifland, e Sorkin, Understanding the Antitrust Laws, 9th. Ed., p. 199.

11 Reynolds, Sicilian e Wellman, The Extraterritorial Application of the U.S. Antitrust Laws to Criminal Conspiracies, p.155: .the application of U.S. antitrust law to conduct that occurs outside the United States but has no impact in the United States is firmly established

12 DOJ Guidelines (1995): "3.2 Comity In enforcing the antitrust laws, the Agencies consider international comity. Comity itself reflects the broad concept of respect among co-equal sovereign nations and plays a role in determining "the recognition which one nation allows within its territory to the legislative, executive or judicial acts of another nation." Thus, in determining whether to assert jurisdiction to investigate or bring an action, or to seek particular remedies in a given case, each Agency takes into account whether significant interests of any foreign sovereign would be affected". Relevant U.S case law in connection with antitrust comity include necessarily Hartford Fire Ins. Co. v. California, 509 U.S. 764 (1993). Other prior cases: 39 See, e.g., Mannington Mills, Inc. v. Congoleum Corp., 595 F.2d 1287 (3rd Cir. 1979); Timberlane Lumber Co. v. Bank of America Nat'l Trust & Sav. Ass'n, 549 F.2d 597 (9th Cir. 1976). But see, e.g., Laker Airways Ltd. v. Sabena, Belgian World Airlines, 731 F.2d 909 (D.C. Cir. 1984); In re Uranium Antitrust Litigation, 617 F.2d 1248 (7th Cir. 1980); In re Ocean Shipping Antitrust Litigation, 500 F. Supp. 1235 (S.D.N.Y. 1980)Timberlane Lumber Co. v. Bank of America Nat'l Trust & Sav. Ass'n, 549 F.2d 597 (9th Cir. 1976). Cf. Restatement (Third) of Foreign Relations Law of the United States § 403 (1987)

13 DOJ Guidelines, (1995): "There may be no actual conflict between the antitrust enforcement interests of the United States and the laws or policies of a foreign sovereign. This is increasingly true as more countries adopt antitrust or competition laws that are compatible with those of the United States"

14 The issue gets more and touchier with the concept of positive comity. As notes Edward Swaine, Against Principled Antitrust, Social Science Research Network Electronic Paper Collection, http://ssrn.com/abstract_id=383781. "Traditional or "negative" comity, put generally, requests that an antitrust authority consider the other party's interests in deciding whether to initiate an investigation or

Brazil

Brazil has participated in the recent WTO discussions on Competition Policy, and is generally favorable to such exercise[15]; other Latin American countries are not on a similar disposition[16]. The Brazilian position expresses a concern with hard core cartels and the great operations of concentrations of international companies, as well as a due appreciation for an enhanced cooperation among agencies, with extensive exchange of experiences. In the discussions of 2000 and 2001, the Brazilian government it did not present any written manifestation, being consigned only its verbal commentaries concerning the cooperation[17].

The Brazilian Antitrust Law (Federal Law nr. 8.137 of December 27, 1990), in Art. 4, I a) and II, holds a series of competition-voiding practices to be a crime against the Economic Order or an abuse of economic power, either by dominating the market or by eliminating partially or on the whole the competition, through any accord, convention, agreement or alliance purporting to achieve the regional control of the market by a firm or group of firms.

Also here it shall be applicable the *rule of reason* standard, to take into account, for instance, the eventual broadening of the local market or the technology development resulting from the act under analysis[18].

At the administrative court level (Ministry of Justice and CADE, the Antitrust Authority) it must be also considered the Law 8.884 of June 11, 1994 that in its Art. 20 § 2 deems

- To be in a *dominant position* the firm that holds more than twenty percent of a given market;
- To be an *abuse of a dominant position* any agreement with a competitor to establish prices, assign market shares, prevent the access of new firms, regulate markets and so on.

This statute does not require any evidence of willful intent by the firms concerned, punishing both the unwilling causation of anti-competitive effects and the willing but frustrated actions directed to the same purpose.

On another aspect of the matter, it should be considered the provisions of the Law 8.884, at its Art. 54[19], whereby all agreements entered into by competitors or other persons, which may result in dominance as to any relevant market must be registered with CADE[20].

---

proceeding, in determining an investigation's scope, and in determining remedies. Positive comity, the newer and less frequently employed of the two notions, involves honoring the request of an antitrust authority for the investigation of anticompetitive activities occurring within the requested party's territory that affect the requesting authority's important interests".

15 Communication from Brazil to the Working Group on the Interaction between Trade and Competition Policy, WT/WGTCP/W/100.

16 As remarks Carlos Correa, Competition Law and Development Policies, p. 378, developing countries position in Singapore Conference, however, was flexible with regard to the study of competition issues, but negative in terms of any possible future negotiation.

17 As noticed by the most thorough Brazilian study on this matter, by Maria Cecília Andrade, A Política Da Concorrência E A Organização Mundial Do Comércio, Boletín Latinoamericano de Competencia, N° 14 Abril 2002, found at http://europa.eu.int/comm/competition/international/others/

18 Sodré Filho e Lionel Zaclis, Comentários à Legislação Antitruste, Atlas, 1992, p. 33.

19 Law 4.137/62, in its art. 75 already included a similar requirement, but most rarely implemented in practice.

20 The request for registration is mandatory whenever economic concentration, by means of a consolidation of business organizations and any one of the participating firms holds a yearly income higher than four

Registration shall be granted if and only if the agreement satisfies all of the following requirements:

1. Has as its purpose the increase of productivity, or the enhancement of product and service quality; and
2. The resulting benefits are shared evenhandedly among all its parties, the consumers or final users; and
3. The effect is not a complete elimination of a substantial portion of the relevant market; and
4. The restraint of trade is strictly limited to the amount necessary to fulfill the agreement's otherwise acceptable purposes.

Even in those cases when *all* four conditions cannot be satisfied, the registration may be granted if *three* of them are satisfied, provided that no harm might issue to the consumers and provided furthermore that it advances an outstanding objective concerning the national economy or the general well being. To ensure the issuance of registration, the firms affected must establish a performance commitment with CADE, including quality and quantity targets (Law 8.884/94, Art. 58).

Article 2nd. of Law n. 8,884/94 admits its extraterritorial application to the practices occurring in all or part of the domestic territory or that in it they produce or they can produce effects[21]. As there is a clear perspective that this type of application of the law can come to cause constraints or international conflicts of jurisdiction, actions of international cooperation have been fomented in this organism, for example, the agreements celebrated for the CADE with Argentina in 1996, U.S.A. and Portugal in 1999[22].

The international jurisdiction of CADE is however limited[23]. When considering, for instance, the 400M real threshold, an *effective impact* could be taken into account:

> It is not any effect in the market that compels the examination for the CADE. Many operations occur all year, involving global companies who act in the international market. They are potential competitors or by way of exportation. It is possible that these operations affect the Brazilian market in terms of prices, quality and amount of commodities. However, the antitrust authority can do nothing to repair, to restrict or to eliminate such effect, through the measures foreseen in articles 54 § 9°, 58, 63, 69 and following ones of same Law 8.884/94. In thesis, the only pertinent sanctions, with direct external effect in the international

---

hundred million reais or a market share equal to or higher than 20%. But any other case of agreements entered into by competitors or other parties, the effect of which is to cause a restraint of trade or the domination of markets is likewise subject to the registration requirement.

21 Article 2nd provides both for jurisdiction based in effects and in economic presence in the territory. The first time the Brazilian agency asserted its international reach was in the 60's (consult in the case of the financing of Mineração Rio do Norte S.A. e Alcan Bermuda Ltd.); under the new Law 8.884, the first case was the Kolynos/Colgate one, where the merger of the two firms abroad had its effects in Brazil thoroughly scrutinized. See José Gabriel Assis de Almeida, A Atuação Do Cade No Brasil Frente Ao Processo De Globalização, Boletín Latinoamericano de Competencia, N° 7, p. 75, July 1999, found at http://europa.eu.int/comm/competition /international/other and José Carlos de Magalhães, "As Leis da Concorrência e a Globalização - A Competência Extraterritorial do CADE", in Estudos-Documentos do Conselho Superior de Assuntos Jurídicos -CONJUR, da Federação das Indústrias do Estado de São Paulo, novembro, 2000

22 See at http://www.cade.gov.br

23 José Carlos de Magalhães, op. cit..

movement of goods and services would be the restrictions to the importations (prohibition, quota and tariff of importation) applicable in the domain of the commercial defense, outside the scope of the Law of the CADE. Therefore, the requirement of the invoicing only applies when the operation to involve commercial subsidiary plants or installed in Brazil (physical unit coordinated by an enterprise action), and the carried through legal transaction in the exterior makes use on such assets, or the production or commercialization of products or services of resultant them. [24]

In a recent case, however, CADE acted to prevent the local effects of a merger carried out entirely outside the Brazilian jurisdiction, but having serious impacts in the internal telecom market[25].

THE MULTINATIONAL CORPORATION AND THE REGULATORY ISSUE

The question here under scrutiny in this section is the role of transnational corporations facing the competition and other policies of singular Governments. Arguments have been developed that such entities are prone to entertain alliances with some Governments that could be detrimental to their own home Government[26], or to other countries; those *runaway corporations*, as the argument goes, play with such duplicity to prevent compliance with competition and other policies.

Our contention here is that transnational corporations should not be allowed to run from any *international* public interest; the eventual lack of effective power of any international regulation would not be an unprecedented case in the international context, and has already found some imperfect but none the less effective solutions.

---

24 Antonio Fonseca, Aquisição De Ativo Industrial Situado No Exterior - Exame dos efeitos à luz da Lei nº 8.884/94, Boletín Latinoamericano de Competencia, N° 15, Octobre, 2002, found at http://europa.eu.int/comm /competition/international/other

25 As reports Maria Cecília Andrade, op. cit., footnote 102: "By October, 1999 the MCI and the Sprint had notified the CADE on its project of concentration that also had been considered simultaneously by FTC and the European Commission. However, in Brazil, when the privatization of the sector of the telecommunications occurred, the MCI acquired the EMBRATEL, and a composed trust for the SPRINT, National Grid and France Telecom acquired the Intelig (a mirror company). The EMBRATEL and the Intelig were, therefore, competitors in the market of national and international long-distance calls. This act of concentration raised serious problems in relation to the Brazilian telecommunications market, as it was a typical case of crossed participation, a time that the SPRINT withheld 25% of participation of the Intelig, which was competing with EMBRATEL, which in turn was controlled for the MCI. The operation was suspended in Brazil through one Administrative Preventive Order (Decision LHS n. 03/2000, B.C. 08012.005846/99-12), the companies had been forbidden to change any types of information between officers and the SPRINT had its suspended right to vote in the decisions of the Intelig. As consequence, in Brazil, the SPRINT was obliged to sell its shares in Intelig, in order to prevent the closing of the telecom market. The same transaction was suspended by the European Commission (MCI WorldCom/Sprint, JO C 14, 19.01.2000)".

26 This chapter is largely borrowing from our study "Investment and Trade", a partial submission to obtain the degree of Master of Laws, Columbia Law School, 1983.

The Laudatory Era

In the quarter of century subsequent to the Second World War, there was a powerful trend of opinion as to the potential benefits of private foreign investment in developing economies not unfriendly to the transnational enterprises. The arguments then advanced can be thus summarized:

> "Dynamic international firms transferred by their investments not only urgently needed capital, but technology, know how and managerial skills, stimulated local habits, of saving and investment and provided training at different levels. For export oriented industries, the cooperation with foreign investors guaranteed an easier access to markets in the developed countries.
>
> Development economists advised that balance-of payments and taxation issues should be given more serious consideration, advocated increased utilization of domestic human and physical resources, and also pointed out reasons for closer association between local entrepreneurs and investors in order to receive the maximum gain from foreign investment on the development of the Third World countries. But the warnings that were expressed about possible distortions to the economies concerned were generally disregarded:"[27]

Some economic analysts of that time concluded that the private foreign investment was not flowing more steadily to the poorer countries because, in first place, of the characteristic weaknesses of such countries such as the defective economic infrastructure, the faulty political institutions or the unskilled and unwilling labor-force.

In second place, as the analysts pointed out, was the lack of "investment climate", the uncertainty as to the Government policies regarding the foreign investors. Compensatory inducements were to be devised to make for the weak points and some special legislation should be drafted to assure the continuing willingness of the host country to be friendly. In some cases, as happened in Brazil after 1964, a special treaty had to be signed to guarantee the private investors of their absolute protection[28].

Those changes were to be made instantly, if the development goals were to be achieved. The Under Secretary of State of the United States, George Ball, said in an address in 1964 to the United Nations Conference on Trade and Development:

> "Nations must make their choices of national policy with full awareness of inescapable economic facts. Nations that elect to pursue policies that tend to eliminate the private sector or discriminate against outside investment should be aware that they are denying themselves a source of capital that could otherwise greatly speed their own economic development...
>
> Private capital admittedly cannot be more than one element in an interrelated approach to development. Yet, with regard to this question as to so many others, the developing countries have it within their own hands to determine how fast they will move in achieving growth. The World Bank, particularly, urged LDC's to accept private foreign investment and to give the investors the incentives required to render the country attractive "Developing countries should preserve the greatest possible stability in their laws and regulations affecting foreign investment...

27 Juhua Kuusi, "The host Country and the Transnational Corporation", Saxon House, 1975, p. 37-39.

28 Agreement signed on Feb. 6. 1965. between Brazil and the U.S.

Developed countries should strengthen their investment incentive schemes wherever possible... Developing countries should structure their tax systems so as to encourage profit reinvestment by foreign companies... [29]

The Theme of Free and Unregulated Market

The controversy on the value of the foreign investment, for the host country and for the international trade, particularly that effected through the multinational corporations, was however never settled. The advantages of analysis stressing the needs for unregulated exchange of goods and resources:

"The principal arguments of the antagonists in this conflict waged on the political and ideological level are fairly evident. The proponents of the MNE as a medium for international trade and investment stress those same considerations which underlie the policy and theoretical justifications for relatively free world trade and investment. The cardinal justification and goal remain the same as those for the relatively "unregulated" laissez-faire market within a *national* economy - namely, maximization of efficiency, or maximizing the value of the world's production through profit-oriented investment and production decisions of private (that is, non-governmental) actors on the world scene. This goal embraces varied business activities the world's mineral resources would be most efficiently exploited, manufacturing industry would be located wherever marginal returns upon investment (in view of varying labor costs, markets, transportation factors and so on) were highest, and so on." [30]

However, the main problem with this approach is the inherent conflict between international unregulated flows and national economic goals, including the *competition* ones. The chairman of the Union Carbide Corporation in 1975 recognized that flow in the free trade reasoning:

"Multinationals have been extraordinarily successful in meeting the needs of the consumers of the world but, in the process, have failed to articulate their contributions to nation state economies.[31]"

If the problem is one of simply articulating the benefit, or one of finding benefits, is not always clear. The gap between the transnational corporate planning and national interests, especially their competition standards, is conspicuous both in home and host countries; but it is comparatively wider in relation to those countries where the nationally controlled enterprises themselves have not achieved a transnational status, as it happens in most Third World nations.

29 "Partners in Development", Pearson Commission Report, 1968

30 Steiner and Vagts, "Transnational Legal Problems", 2nd Ed. p. 1188.

31 The New York Times, March 11, 1975, p. 35

The Treason of the Giants

In the nations acting predominantly as home countries, notably in the U.S., the main grievances against multinationals are centered in the word "shift" - they shift labor consumption, they shift capital, technology and so forth; as George Meany (then President of AFL-CIO) told the U.S. Senate Finance Committee in May, 1971, they are "runaway corporations".

In the European countries, where a reasonable number of locally controlled corporations are also transnationals, the feeling, for an extensive period, was that American multinationals were liable to align with U.S. foreign policy to the detriment of host countries economic interests, as the Russian pipeline incident appeared to demonstrate. The competition distortions brought by the sheer size of the U.S. multinationals in the local market are also felt as relevant.

Certainly the European standpoint was vindicated by the United States itself. The reactions to the perilous nature of the transnational corporation, in face to host Governments, are particularly evidenced by the enactment in 1988 of the "Exon-Florio Provision"[32]. The President is empowered under this rule to prevent foreign direct investments in the U.S. on grounds of national security. This is a very broad concept in such law:

> "it should be interpreted without limitation to particular industries. The Report further advises that the relevant factors include, but are not limited to domestic production needed for projected defense requirements; industrial capacity and capability to meet national defense requirements; the availability of human resources, products, technology, materials and other supplies and services; and the control of the foreign ownership of domestic industries as it affects the ability of the United States to meet its internal security requirements". [33]

Some LDC countries, understandably, were at least as sensitive to such risks as the United States themselves. As an American legal writer puts it:

> "In the less developed countries, the tensions are sharper. As we have noted, the attacks upon the MNEs form part of a broader antagonism towards foreign investment in general, as well as towards their sources in Western capitalism and forms of industrialization. Thus the MNE becomes, almost inevitably, the evident and stark symbol of exploitation, domination, and imperialism - themes captured in the developing literature about dependencia that has issued from nationalistic and Marxist-oriented thinkers of Latin America". [34]

But equally relevant, if no more, is the economic impact of the multinationals on the internal market and competition standards of the host LDC country:

> "... [T]he large MNE entering a foreign country will frequently secure a monopolistic or oligopolistic position on the local market - almost inevitably a function of the enormous financial and technological resources that it commands and of the skills which it has developed, but sometimes the result of a grant by the foreign government. Thus the MNE at once expands, structures and confines the development of the local economy. It introduces,

32 Included in the Omnibus Trade and Competition Act of 1988 (Sec. 5021, Pub.L. nº 100-418, 102 Atat. 1107, 1425-26.

33 Barry K. Robinson, Practical Comments on the Exon Florio Provisions and Proposed Regulations, in The Commerce Department Speaks 1990, vol. I, p. 184.

but may by this very token permit no further introduction. Thus the normal constraints, even within traditional market theory, of competition in products and prices may not be present." [35]

After the ITT episode in Chile in the early 70's, the most vocal third world critics seemed to be vindicated in their analysis. The turmoil resulting from the issue and its discussion in the U.S. Congress probably prompted Henry Kissinger's address to the U.N. Assembly in September 1, 1975, a most spirited support of the multinational's performance and a quite uncommon engagement from the U.S. Government on the issue. After listing the positive aspects of the multinational corporation's activities in the international production system, the then Secretary of State stressed what the U.S. considered to be the basic arrangements the multinationals and the governments should endeavor to achieve[36]:

"Specifically, the United States believes that: Transnational enterprises are obliged to obey local law and refrain from unlawful intervention in the domestic affairs of host countries. Their activities should take account of public policy and national development priorities. They should respect local customs. They should employ qualified local personnel or qualify local people through training.

Host governments in turn must treat transnational enterprises equitably, without discrimination among them and in accordance with international law. Host governments should make explicit their development priorities and the standards which transnational enterprises are expected to meet and maintain them with reasonable consistency.

Governments and enterprises must both respect the contractual obligation that they freely undertake. Contracts should be negotiated openly, fairly and with full knowledge of their implications. Greater assurance that contracts will be honored will improve the international commercial environment, increase the flow of investment and expand economic transactions. Destructive and politically explosive investment disputes, which spoil the climate for large commitments and investment, will occur less frequently."

Kissinger's statement apparently reflected the growing awareness of the problems caused on the long run by the lack of bargaining ability (if not bargaining power) by the local governments. Some international and private institutions were employed at times to enhance the governments' ability to negotiate favorable terms with the incoming capital in such a way as to assure the continued equitable sharing of benefits between the parties, which seemed to be a wise manner to prevent future political repudiation of the agreements[37].

The underlying rationale of those undertakings is that the option to confrontation is sharing, and a conscientious bargain improves long term Government-multi national relationship. Those new partnerships, however, notwithstanding their increased potential for peaceful internationalization of the economic production, are from time to time object of attack in the U.S.:

"Thus the MNE is caught in a peculiar bind. The more that it is associated politically and economically with policies of an autonomous and internal character, the more suspiciously and hostilely it will be viewed by the foreign country. On the other hand, the more it is perceived as pursuing policies of a foreign or international character, the more suspiciously

34 Steiner and Vagts, supra, p. 1184.
35 Idem, p. 1185.
36 The New York Times, September 2, 1975.
37 For instance, the New York-based UN Center for Transnational Corporations.

and hostilely it will be viewed within the United States. And indeed, precisely that phenomenon has developed in recent years (...) Particularly if the MNE becomes more "un-American" through increasing the proportion of foreign operations, foreign management and foreign stockholdings, policymakers in the United States are apt to take an increasingly skeptical view of it." [38]

This distrust was expressed in a particularly poignant tone by C. Fred Bergsten in his statement to the U.S. Senate Sub-Committee on International Economic Policy in July 30, 1980:

"In essence a bargaining process is created; both sides probe for maximum advantage until a deal acceptable to both is struck, and the result may frequently be an alliance, if an uneasy one, in some cases, between the firms and the governments of the host countries, with possible detriment - and this is the policy point - with possible detriment to the economic interests of the home countries, notably the United States."

In fact, Bergsten's position is not only that Government control over transnationals is wrong, but that the transnationals themselves are trade distorting even if free from State intervention:

"As C. Fred Bergsten, former assistant for international economic affairs in the Nixon administration, has written, a foreign economy which emphasizes investment weakens the forces of free trade in the United States.

We have already discussed the increase in protectionist sentiment among labor, due in large part to foreign direct investment by American corporations. But of equal, or even greater, importance is that the corporations themselves lose much of their interest in free trade. They gain access to foreign markets through investment rather than through the lowering of trade barriers. Moreover, foreign direct investment also decreases the incentives of host governments to lower trade barriers. On the contrary, they have an incentive to raise trade barriers and thereby encourage corporations to establish production facilities within their borders." [39]

The multinationals defy the trade barriers by leaping over the borders and using beyond the protectionist wall the factors of production transferred from the home country. The protectionist countries thereby begin to enjoy some of the advantages of the free trade without paying some of its prices; the principle of optimum allocation of resources begin to be interpreted from a microeconomic standpoint (that of the multinationals).

All that is anathema for the classical economic theory and consequently, liable to attract all the contempt reserved for perverted acts against the economic nature.

Goods are Free to go, but should Capital be so?

Perhaps even more relevant is the lack, in which it relates to the investment policy, of a widely accepted dogmatic principle concerning the freedom of movement of factors of

38 Steiner and Vagts, supra, p. 1187-1189.

39 R. Cherton, "U.S. Power and the Multinational Corporation", Basic Books, 1976, p. 204-206.

production. No "optimum allocation" or "competitive advantage" theory was developed specifically to the investment issue that had achieved the popularity of the Ricardo doctrine.

Even by the late 70's, there was no consensus, even among the OECD members, on the desirability of a entirely free flow of capital, and the IMF rules, much to the contrary, allows expressly for national restrictions (Art. VI.3) of capital transfers[40]. However, the benefits of the comparative advantage are not bestowed at same time upon all the people, in all the places. As noticed by Wynne Godley, comparative advantages strengthen the strong nations and keep the weaks weak [41]

Governments rarely have the power to convince their constituency of the ultimate advantage of limiting itself to the banana crop, when the price of the fruit in relation to the imported TV-set has been steadily falling in the last decades. If the prospective TV-set buyers are in sufficient number to justify the assembly of the imported components in a locally made wooden cabinet, such Government shall be seriously tempted to relinquish its country's competitive advantage by inflating tariffs and offering tax holydays to the possible assembler.

Behrman, a former Assistant Secretary for Domestic and International Business in the Kennedy Administration offered exactly this perspective of the problem as it appeared thirty years ago, in one article published in 1972[42].

The international institutions then in existence, said Behrman, were rooted in an economic concept of the role of international trade and capital movement in which there are no place for the international investment. The notion was that only the products, and not the factors of production, were to move across borders; no basic comprehensive theory of the multinational corporation, as such, was thereto developed[43].

A new heuristic notion, therefore, would have to be developed - that concept of an "international production", meaning production by a company, which however established in one country, is owned and controlled by a person in another country. The old concept of international trade assumed that the goods exchanged were derived from indigenous resources, natural or manufactured; the new notion encompasses partially the previous one, but goes further, to include movement of goods and capitals.

This approach is required because, says Behrman, the assumption that free trade and capital movement would necessarily lead to the best allocation of resources for all countries involved in trade has not corroborated in practice:

> "Nations as disparate as those in the lesser developed countries, that are seeking new technical knowledge and production capacity, and Western Europe and Japan, that are seeking only the most advanced technology, are increasingly unwilling to accept as "equitable" the distribution of economic activity and benefits produced by free trade. Efforts to reduce trade

---

40 The status of International Law regarding restrictions on foreign investment is reviewed in our book Direito de Acesso do Capital Estrangeiro, Lumen Juris, 1996.

41 Fortune, March 21, 1983, p. 80. The Cambridge Group, leaded by Godley, however, after noticing that went on proposing a system whereby the third world would revert to raw product exporting, in an economic version of the "let us bomb them to stone age".

42 "Sharing International Production Through the Multinational Enterprise and Sectorial Integration", 4 Law & Pol'y Int'l Bus. 1.

43 The lack of theoretical basis for the analysis of Foreign Direct Investment subsists, twenty years after Behrman. See Edwards, Sebastian, "Capital Flows, Foreign Direct Investment, and Debt-Equity Swaps in Developing Countries" (Apr 27, 2000). NBER Working Paper No. W3497. http://ssrn.com/abstract=226689 . See also the last chapter our book Direito de Acesso do Capital Estrangeiro, supra, where I mentioned some of the then current theories on FDI.

> barriers are hardly likely to generate progress toward the international integration of industrial or agricultural activity, even within regional groupings, until means are developed for sharing the benefits of increased production among all nations".[44]

The implied reasoning is that, irrespective of the tenets of the economic theory, the national expectations in the practical and political sense are not fulfilled by a "best allocation" argument = governments are supposed to act in favor of the nations:

> "This best allocation concept is only a mythical creation perpetrated on governments by economists, for there is no procedure for making decisions that will produce the most efficient allocation of world resources. Free market allocation relies on a pattern of demand that is based on inadequate or erroneous "Knowledge" of the nature and kinds of products available and an income distribution that does not necessarily reflect the ‘ "contributions" of the factors of production. Even if there were such a procedure, efficient allocation is not the primary objective of government policy".[45]

The policy content of the rational Government action, says the author, has been prevailing over the abstract Ricardian dogma of the comparative advantage. That results, at least in part, from the tangible and ubiquitous presence of the multinational corporation as an economic unit, the main purpose of which is to submit the macroeconomic and political conditions of the world trade to its own benefits:

> "While governments accept the concept of specialization, they do not accept the kind of specialization that would be determined by the "free market" or by the decisions of multinational enterprises. Instead, governments hosting industry and enterprise wish to make an independent determination based on their own national interests and, no doubt will rely heavily on the advice of their national industries.

This view is the result of a feeling among many governments that the free market does not produce "equity" solutions for their particular problems and that multinational enterprises do not make "economically ‘rational’ decisions regarding the use of world resources".[46]

The natural consequence of this approach is the engaging of the multinational, itself, in the achievement of the Government’s economic targets:

> "The best approach, then, is for nation-states first to adopt goals that serve their national interests, such as higher employment, higher production, and lower personal taxes, and then to achieve those goals by employing the efficiency of multinational enterprises. The nature of multinational corporations gives them certain advantages in solving problems encountered in lesser developed countries, particularly in the area of technology transfer".[47]

---

44 J. N. Behrman, supra, p. 4
45 Behrman, supra, p. 18.
46 Behrman, supra, p. 14.
47 Behrman, supra, p. 4.

As the "international production", already in 1981, was equivalent to the "international trade", and represented one sixth of the Gross World Product48, the alliance seems to be inevitable: the alleged distortion in the ideal allocation of resources had become the rule and the bargaining process had to go on.

By the early 80´s, the effects of foreign government manipulation of the inflows of capital were being denounced by its U.S. critics in a very peculiar conjunctural situation. As stated the Secretary of Commerce Malcom Balbridge to the U.S. Senate Committee of Finance in July 9th, 1981:

> "The traditional U.S. policy of neither encouraging nor discouraging U.S. international investment has become the subject of increasing controversy in recent years, especially in relation to large increases in foreign investment in the United States since the mid-1970s.
>
> These investments have included the acquisition of significant U.S. corporations - some in quite sensitive U.S. industrial sectors - as well as the attempted takeover of numerous other U.S. businesses. Several bills have been introduced in recent sessions of Congress that would place additional requirements on potential foreign investors, temporarily restrict specific types of inward investment, and even significantly change the environment for such investment.
>
> In addition, increasing instances of restrictions – such as performance requirements - relating to outward investment pose new challenges to the U.S. international economic position.
>
> The cumulative effect of these developments suggests that a major reassessment of U.S. international investment policy may soon become appropriate."

The Assimilation of Investment into the Trade Context

Investment Issues under GATT 1947

The issue of national policies favoring or influencing international investment through policy measures was brought into consideration within the GATT ambiance since a relatively early stage. Both at the international and at the national level, there were significant legal instruments to deal with the eventual trade distortions caused by policies, subsidies and other investment measures; however, there was until the 70's an objective limit to the usage of such devices: the subsidy must be somewhat trade-related.

The general subsidization of investment, even if it caused effects on trade, was not ordinarily held to be covered by the legal instruments in force in the trade area. On the other hand, the national investment policies, not being direct, conspicuous restrictions on flows of trade, would arguably be also exempt from the trade-related national and international measures already in force. That situation changed with the GATT Code on subsidies of 1979.

The alleged instrument for bringing investing issues into the GATT environment was the Article III of the General Agreement on Tariffs and Trade (1947). This provision dealt with

48 Prepared statement of C. Fred Bergsten, to the U.S. Senate Sub-Committee on International Economic Policy,
p. 13.

"National Treatment on Internal Taxation and Regulation". The thrust of the provision is that a member-state cannot use taxation and some specified kinds of regulative legislation to afford protection to domestic production. Aside from tax levies, the Article covers Government requirements (either legal or otherwise) "affecting the internal sale, offering for sale, purchase, transportation, distribution or use of products and internal quantitative regulation requiring the mixture, processing or use of products in specified amounts or proportions".

The Proposal of a GATT Investment

Authors had for a long time suggested that a more formal mechanism should be included in the GATT structure. The implementation of this idea, initially suggested by Goldberg and Kindleberger in 1970 [49], was held to be difficult to initiate, not to mention achieve it in due time, as there was the need of extensive negotiations for an Investment GATT.

By the early 80's, the U.S. Government was working to set the basis for a future concerted action of the main trading countries to achieve such target[50]:

> With decisive support from the U.S., OECD started in 1976, on the basis of its Investment understandings, a survey and analysis of the performance requirements of its member countries. The OECD mechanisms were to be used especially in the national treatment area.

In the GATT, besides the filing a claim against Canada, the U.S. Government is trying to find the opportunity to use the Art. III against value added - local content rules. This was the only case eventually brought under GATT, dealing on investment issues.

In the IMF (IBRD) area the United States was requesting a major study on the issue by the IFC, following an initial review on investment incentives made by a joint Committee whose membership included also LDCs.

The 40 Friendship, Commerce and Navigation treaties signed by the U.S. provided legal basis to the U.S. Government to complain against discriminatory treatment of various kinds.

New Bilateral Investment Treaties were being negotiated with various countries.

Fontheim and Gadbaw[51], rekindling the idea, also suggested primarily a multilateral approach. The U.S. action in OECD, World Bank, GATT and other international fora, said the authors, have shown that the conflict of interests even with the OECD countries would probably prevent the start of any meaningful negotiation towards an Investment GATT at that time (early 80's). In order to obviate those problems, they recommend reinforcing the internal

---

49 Goldberg, P.M. and Kindleberger, C.P., "Toward a GATT for Investments: a proposal for supervision of the international corporation", 2 Law & Poly Int'l Bus. 295. The authors envisaged the creation of a body of international law indented to control the multinationals, not to control the host countries. As it was mentioned before, the investment issue was in the ample pre-1947 GATT discussions, but was not included in the vastly smaller GATT 1947.

50 Statement of Feb. 23, 1982 to the House Committee on Foreign Affairs of Elinor G. Constable, Deputy Assistant Secretary for International Finance and Development.

51 Fontheim, C.G.B and Gadbaw, R.M. "Trade Related Performance requirements under the GATT System and U.S. Law", 14 L. & POL'Y INT'L BUS. 129 (1982)

U.S. legislation, basically through a strengthening of section 301 (what was eventually questioned under the WTO system).

The usage of the Generalized System of Preferences as a pressure tool against the LDCs (a menace reinvigorate recently) is also suggested; but most countries using the performance requirements are medium level economies, some of them not entitled to the GSP benefits anyway.

Fortheim and Gadbaw also suggested the utilization of the U.S. firepower within international financial institutions to countervail performance requirements at the level of the financing decision making process, the conditioning of OPIC investment insurance mechanism to that objective and, finally, the broadening of the private right of action in order to allow private parties to require "mirror" action against foreign government requirements.

Eventually, many of those hints were used, section 301 and its enhancements fully employed; on the other hand, the only case where an investment issue was brought to the GATT multilateral dispute-settlement device (the Canada case), the results were felt as being less than adequate.

The TRIMs Agreement

With the Uruguay Round, the theme of investment was at last included in the negotiating agenda. The 1994 package included the TRIMs Agreement, which applies to investment-inducing or manipulating measures by governments, but only to those measures that affect trade in goods. The very important GATS Agreement, which covers other very important aspects of international investment, was an essential part of the same package[52].

The subject of investment was introduced in the thematic agenda of the Uruguay Round by the developing countries, as an attempt of continuation of the unfinished quarrels occurring during the Code of Conduct for the Transfer of Technology, negotiated for almost one decade in the scope of the UNCTAD, Geneva (see below, our section on TRIPs).

The result of the discussions in the Uruguay Round ended by achieving an inverse result: what came to be regulated was the use, on the part of the developing countries, of mechanisms of alliance with the multinational investment, in detriment with the native countries from where the capital flowed. The TRIMS covers, in fact, the commerce of physical goods, as well as the regulation of certain practical and legislative measures of incentive or restriction to the investment, concerning the expansion of exportations or substitution of importation - in particular the so called *performance requirements*.

The TRIMs determines that certain investment measures can have trade-restrictive and distorting effects, and extends to such actions the provisions of GATT Article III (national treatment) or Article XI (quantitative restrictions). Examples of measures offensive to GATT, as indicates the Annex's Illustrative List, include local content or trade balancing requirements.

---

52 See Avila, Urrutia e Mier, Regulacíon del Comercio Internacional tras la Ronda Uruguay, Tecno, Madri, 1994, p. 205; See also the various articles on the Uruguay round included in 29 The International Lawyer vol. 2 (summer 1995). See also our book on Market Access.

The Measures rejected are the following

> "the purchase or use by an enterprise of products of domestic origin or from any domestic source, whether specified in terms of particular products, in terms of volume or value of products, or in terms of a proportion of volume or value of its local production; or that an enterprise's purchases or use of imported products be limited to an amount related to the volume or value of local products that it exports. (...) the importation by an enterprise of products used in or related to its local production, generally or to an amount related to the volume or value of local production that it exports; the importation by an enterprise of products used in or related to its local production by restricting its access to foreign exchange to an amount related to the foreign exchange inflows attributable to the enterprise; or the exportation or sale for export by an enterprise of products, whether specified in terms of particular products, in terms of volume or value of products, or in terms of a proportion of volume or value of its local production".

The Agreement contains transitional arrangements allowing Members to maintain notified TRIMs for a limited time following the entry into force of the WTO (two years in the case of developed country Members, five years for developing country Members, and seven years for least-developed country Members). The Agreement also establishes a Committee on TRIMs to monitor the operation and implementation of these commitments.

The GATS Agreement

The extension of the GATS Agreement to investment issues results from the initial provision that defines the scope of application of the Agreement, which if extends to the supply of services by a supplier of a country member, with commercial presence in one another country member, including therein the maintenance of an establishment or a subsidiary legal entity. Thus, the GATS, in this specific form of rendering of services, one of its four possible modalities, is a clear norm of international investment.

The GATS includes provisions on notification, transparency, MFN, national treatment, access to markets, subsidies, as well as prohibits restrictions in exchange transactions not only in current transactions as capital ones. It envisages the accomplishment of successive rounds of negotiations, as the carried since 1946 in the scope of the GATT for physical goods, in which if it would implant a regimen gradually more liberal of exchanges between the national economies. The coverage of the investment issue will be thus increasing and inexorable.

There we have a complex treaty with a considerable ratio of blank norms - which shall be prescriptive only in function of posterior consensus. Divided in four parts, some annexes and one list of national concessions, its essence is in Part III, that they will count to the provisions related to the access to the markets and national treatment,

The antitrust scope of the GATS is separately established. Article VIII requires certain limited undertakings with respect to the abuse of a dominant position by monopoly suppliers of services, and Article IX imposes a duty to consult and afford sympathetic consideration to other complaints regarding anticompetitive conduct in services.

The TRIPs Agreement

The attempt to establish internationally accepted basis for the competition review of technology and intellectual property issues precedes the TRIPs Agreement. It could be identified, certainly, with the UNCTAD exercises, starting in 1975[53], for the establishment of a code of behavior for technology transfer.

The nodal point of this code was the set of practices deemed to be restrictive, and, as consequence, to be rejected in such transactions; however, exactly this point encountered an insuperable dissent between the developed and developing countries. The first point of divergence was - on which grounds such practices should be rejected? While the industrialized nations only accepted to base the repudiation of the restrictive practices in the injury to the competition, the non industrialized countries understood that the same practices should also be forbidden, even without affecting the internal competition, if they were liable to disturb the flow of technology for their productive sector.

For the first thesis, the problem of rejection of practices would be restricted to the traditional questions of the antitrust right. The second attitude took also into consideration the social interest of the pertinent technology.

The other important discordance was in the treatment of the power of control of the corporations. Traditionally, there is no purpose to set a prohibition on practices developed in the relations between companies in the same economic group: as where there is no competition, an injury to the competition will not occur.

Restrictive clauses enclosed in a contract of technology celebrated between subsidiary and parent company, therefore, could not be forbidden by the norms of protection to the existing competition, while control did exist. Evidently, the developing countries rejected, in theory, the predominance of such private sovereignty on its public sovereignty[54].

The third point of conflict was the *rule of reason* concept, as an exculpatory of illegal practices. For the developing countries, the rule of reason standard would have to be surveyed in relation to the national public interest in concrete, taking itself in account the peculiarities of the national market of the receiving country. But, according to representative of the developed countries, in a case of international transfer of technology, the parameters would have to be considered with base in a public in abstract, and the necessity or not of a restrictive disposal would have evaluated to the light of the principles of a usual international business law.

In other words, the harmony of the practice to the deduced economic objectives of the international interchange of the developed countries of market economy would be the standard of what is reasonable. Such impasse led to the shipwreck of the exercises of the Code of Conduct, after many years of quarrel.

TRIPs Included a Specific Provision on the Theme:

Article 40

53 The course of this negotiation was simultaneous, even though not similarly successful, to the United Nations Conference on Restrictive Business Practices, the result of which was adopted as an annex to its Resolution of 22 April 1980.

54 However it seemed that, in the whole world, only the Brazilian law (Law 6,404/76, Art. 117) considered abuse of the control power and orientation everything that stamps the national interest, or harms the national economy

- Members agree that some licensing practices or conditions pertaining to intellectual property rights which restrain competition may have adverse effects on trade and may impede the transfer and dissemination of technology.
- Nothing in this Agreement shall prevent Members from specifying in their legislation licensing practices or conditions that may in particular cases constitute an abuse of intellectual property rights having an adverse effect on competition in the relevant market. As provided above, a Member may adopt, consistently with the other provisions of this Agreement, appropriate measures to prevent or control such practices, which may include for example exclusive grant back conditions, conditions preventing challenges to validity and coercive package licensing, in the light of the relevant laws and regulations of that Member. (…)

The rule is completed by the requirement of consultations between the members in the case of application of the repression of such practices. The provision declares that there was a consensus between the countries that some practices incident to the licensing of Intellectual Property rights, when liable to restrict the competition - may *also* affect adversely the commerce, thus bringing to the scope of WTO. Moreover, such contractual provisions or practices can hinder the transference and dissemination of technology. As result of such consensus between the members, it becomes acceptable that the national legislation restrains such practical and rejects such clauses.

It is noted that the TRIPs provision does not solve the basic problems raised in the UNCTAD exercises. Says J.H. Reichmann [55]:

> (…) article 40 of the TRIPs Agreement reiterates the legitimacy of controlling anticompetitive practices in contractual licenses affecting intellectual property rights generally.[56] However, article 40 (1) acknowledges the lack of consensus in the area [57] by conceding that states agree only "that some licensing practices or pertaining to intellectual property rights... restrain competition" and "may have adverse effects on trade and may impede the transfer and dissemination of technology. " [58] (…) Evidently, this provision attempts to address the kinds of abuse sounding in antitrust principles that developed counties normally recognize, [59] *without necessarily impeding the developing counties from proceeding on other grounds* either under the formulation of article 8 or under broader principles inherent in the objectives set out in article 7 and in the public interest exception set out in article 8(1). [60] „

55 The International Lawyer, Summer 1995, Volume 29, Number 2

56 [Original footnote] See TRIPS Agreement, supra note 4, art. 40 and title do Part II, Section 8 ("Control of Anti-Competitive Practices in Contractual License")

57 [Original footnote] See supra notes 63-73 and accompanying text; Matsushita, supra note 197, at 92-93; Spencer Weber Waller & Noel J. Byrne, Changing View of Intellectual property and Competition Law in the European Community and the United States of America, 20 Brook J. Int'l L. 1 (1993); see also Reichman, Competition Law, Intellectual Property Rights and Trade, supra note 3, at 87-94 ("Pressures on the Doctrine of Misuse").

58 [Original footnote] See TRIPS Agreement, supra note 4, art. 40 (I).

59 [Original footnote] See supra notes 64, 72-73 and accompanying text.

60 [Original footnote] See TRIPS Agreement, supra note 4 arts. 7, 8(1); supra text accompanying notes 65-71 77-80;

As Professor Reichman notes, as a more general measure, TRIPs also provides for the adequate balance between competition and Intellectual Property interests:

Article 8 Principles - (…) 2. Appropriate measures, provided that they are consistent with the provisions of this Agreement, may be needed to prevent the abuse of intellectual property rights by right holders or the resort to practices which unreasonably restrain trade or adversely affect the international transfer of technology.

This TRIPs experience is, so this author believes, a very important precedent for the negotiation of competition themes within WTO[61]. For, as it is remarked in the legal literature, Intellectual property rights are essential, but not sufficient, conditions for competition. Both the excessiveness of scope and misuse need to be balanced by way of the regulation of competition. Even considering that some balance is inherent to TRIPS art. 8, it could be certainly helped by the establishment of some further discipline on private party conduct and competition in the WTO[62].

The Emergence of a Specific Competition Issue within the WTO

A secondary issue within the investment context was raised in WTO, as the need of a competition mechanism to supplement the investment issue. It was a *Singapore issue*, that is, a working group set up by the 1996 Singapore Ministerial Conference has been studying it. Despite any misgivings as to the role of WTO in regard competition, the theme is already there [63]

The Step seemed Inevitable to some authors [64]

Following the growing process of globalisation and regional integration, and the removal of several governmental trade barriers between States conducted by the architecture of principles wisely launched within the framework of the World Trade Organisation the international harmonization of competition rules seems inevitable. Markets are truly global and most conflicts arising from these transactions transcend national borders.

The world economy has changed in a remarkably short period of time. State-managed economies have collapsed following the degradation of communist governments; new

61 Not all writers would agree. Swaine remarks (op. cit) "First, however unsophisticated many countries were with respect to intellectual property, and however ideologically divisive those issues may potentially be, TRIPS profited considerably from the drafters' ability to incorporate norms and members from the World Intellectual Property Organization (WIPO). See Leebron, supra note 118, at 19-20. Antitrust has no such precedent. Second, an indispensable issue for cross-issue trades – the trust of the parties – may have been partly exhausted in the aftermath of TRIPS, as developing countries came to recognize the potential costs of recognizing intellectual property rights and to doubt the market access commitments by the developed countries. This is reflected in the emphasis on implementation issues at Doha.

62 Cottier and Maitinger, The TRIPs Agreement without a Competition Agreement?, found at www.feem.it/NR/rdonlyres/364E97CC-2C8D-42E2-BE36-D87542C3A67C/ 299/6599.pdf , visited 17/8/2003

63 John J .Jackson, Afterword: The Linkage Problem – Comments on Five Texts, 96 AM. J. INT'L L. 118, 124 (2002): "In short, as to competition policy being dealt with by the WTO Agreements, there is already a substantial position for the WTO (those who resist are too late!)".

64 Danielle S. Borgholm, The Interaction between Trade and Competition Policies: Towards the Process of Trade Liberalisation and Global Competition Rules, Boletín Latinoamericano de Competencia, N° 16, Mayo 2003. found at http://europa.eu.int/comm/competition/international/others.

economic blocks have been formed, legal monopolies have been reduced or even eliminated, joint ventures and mergers are not restricted by national boundaries and domestics markets have been increasingly open to foreign trade and investment, exposing the world to the principles of free market access.

The forces of economic liberalisation and the spread of democracy across nation aggregated with the speed and scope of technology diffusion, in the area of globalisation, shaped the new business environment, where giant corporations are clearly global and where the state clout is in retreat. State-authority has been compelled to adjust its political role, as well as the societies in which it exerts control under the weight of an integrated and worldwide growing corporation reality that owes allegiance to no state.

The Doha Mandate Expressed by its Paragraph 25 is so Explained[65]:

In the period up to the 2003 Ministerial Conference, the declaration instructs the working group to focus on clarifying:

- core principles including transparency, non-discrimination and procedural Fairness, and provisions on "hardcore" cartels (i.e. cartels that are formally set up)
- ways of handling voluntary cooperation on competition policy among WTO member governments
- support for progressive reinforcement of competition institutions in developing countries through capacity building

The declaration says the work must take full account of developmental needs. It includes technical cooperation and capacity building, on such topics as policy analysis and development, so that developing countries are better placed to evaluate the implications of closer multilateral cooperation for various developmental objectives. Cooperation with other organizations such as the UN Conference on Trade and Development (UNCTAD) is also included.

The WTO Basic Document for the Cancun Ministerial Broadens the Issue:

> "A multilateral framework would provide important benefits for all Members, and would ensure that the gains from liberalisation were not undermined by anti-competitive behaviour of private actors. Developing countries that lacked the necessary legislation and/or enforcement powers were among the most vulnerable to the effects of anti-competitive activities, notably international cartels.
>
> A multilateral framework on competition policy would establish a coherent set of principles for sound competition policy among all Members, without imposing a harmonized approach, and would promote a more transparent and predictable climate to encourage foreign trade and investment. It would also contribute to the building of institutional capacity in developing countries, and would assist Members lacking a competition law in drafting an appropriate law and establishing an enforcement authority.
>
> Cooperation in the context of a multilateral framework offered the prospect of shortening the time frames that developing countries would need to build and embed competition laws

65 The Doha Declaration explained, found at http://www.wto.int/english/tratop_e/dda_e/dohaexplained_e.htm . visited in August 15. 2003

> and policies that would support their development goals; a key consideration in this regard was the more supportive environment it would provide for better-targeted assistance and capacity building. Finally, an agreement would encourage beneficial cooperation among Members which was important given the increasing prevalence of cross-border anti-competitive activities. [66]

The Doha mandate is not to be understood as requiring a uniform national system, or creating an international competition authority. As states the report of the Competition group, what was proposed was "a set of principles that would embody common values and promote cooperative approaches to competition law enforcement that were in the interest of all Members, while respecting the extensive differences that prevailed in economic and legal circumstances and cultures".

Those principles, at the initial stage, would be mostly of a procedural nature: national reviewing authorities should observe the standards of transparency, non-discrimination (in fact, the GATT age-old rules of national treatment and most-favored nation - MFN) and procedural fairness[67]. But the mandate target one specific illicit practice, which could be rejected in any jurisdiction.

The chosen example is the formally established cartels[68], identified as being "the most unambiguously harmful kind of competition law violation and imposed heavy costs on the economies of countries, particularly developing countries, that lacked effective tools to deal with them. Such cartels are to be condemned as they raise the prices and restricted the supply of essential goods and services, which made such goods and services unavailable to some users and unnecessarily expensive for others. Further, cartels reduced participating enterprises' incentive for cost control and propensity to innovate, and could also have the effect of impeding the transfer of technology to developing countries"[69].

Beyond such universally rejected practice[70], other already multilaterally established principles could provide as an initial content of a multilateral framework[71].

---

66 Doc. WT/WGTCP/7 17 July 2003

67 According to the proposal of the International Competition Network, the procedures "should not discriminate in the application of competition laws and regulations on the basis of nationality," and merger reviews "should be transparent with respect to the policies, practices, and procedures involved in the review, the identity of the decision-maker(s), the substantive standard of review, and the bases of any adverse enforcement decisions on the merits," and that the merger review should respect various terms designed to ensure procedural fairness. ICN, Merger Notification and Procedures Subgroup, Guiding Principles for Merger Notification and Review arts. 2-4 (adopted Sept. 29, 2002), http://www.internationalcompetitionnetwork.org/ICN%20NP%20Working %20Group %20%20Guiding%20Principles.pdf.

68 According to the OECD document CCNM/GF/COMP/TR(2003), a "hard core cartel" is an anticompetitive agreement, anticompetitive concerted practice, or anticompetitive arrangement by competitors to fix prices, make rigged bids (collusive tenders), establish output restrictions or quotas, or share or divide markets by allocating customers, suppliers, territories, or lines of commerce; b) the hard core cartel category does not include agreements, concerted practices, or arrangements that (i) are reasonably related to the lawful realisation of cost-reducing or output-enhancing efficiencies, (ii) are excluded directly or indirectly from the coverage of a Member country's own laws, or (iii) are authorised in accordance with those laws.

69 Doc. WT/WGTCP/7 17 July 2003, § 41.

70 Some developing countries have expressed their views that such cartels are beasts nurturing particularly in developed countries.

71 For instance, the UNCTAD, The set of multilaterally agreed equitable principles and rules for the control of restrictive business practices, adopted by the United Nations Conference on Restrictive Business Practices as an annex to its Resolution of 22 April 1980), in which negotiation this author had the opportunity to discuss participate at UNCTAD in 1979.

The Doha model is the progressive interagency cooperation as advanced initially by the U.S., but built as a multilateral and not bilateral construction. It is suggested that once such framework is operating, the overall WTO apparatus shall apply, including the dispute settlement system[72]. One important aspect of the current state of the discussion is the possible institution of a peer review system, whereby another national authority could be brought to examine the same competitive matter[73].

A TRADE-BASED OR A COMPETITION-BASED MECHANISM?

The question here is the proper grounds for an international legal environment for competition matters. Should it be constructed as an item of the international trade agenda? Or should it be considered as an internationally relevant issue on its own merits?

The danger of a *trade* approach is address only on a partial and imperfect fashion the competitive issue. Critics distinguish four distinct problems to be dealt by any international action on competition policy:

a) The fact that transnational anti-competitive activity outside control of any single nation has been growing exponentially;
b) The emergence of enforcement conflicts, not hitherto solved by comity or cooperation;
c) The market access problems resulting from non-competitive environments in target countries (non-existent or poorly enforced competition laws are argued to hinder access for exporters by allowing domestic firms to foreclose or greatly increase the cost of entry[74]) and
d) Unnecessary costs of compliance with multiple national regimes[75].

The trade approach would, apparently, stress problem c), on the detriment of the other three, and in defiance of some of the original purposes of the competition policies. As Hoeckman and Holmes say:

> Summing up, efforts to put competition-related issues on the WTO agenda are largely driven by classic producer interests in major OECD countries, with governments pursuing a

72 See Claus-Dieter Ehlermann and Lothar Ehring, WTO Dispute Settlement and Competition Law (European University Institute Florence, Policy Paper 02/12 (2002)).

73 Doc. WT/WGTCP/7 17 July 2003 §§ 91 to 95. *

74 Hoeckman and Holmes, on the other hand, note that "other high-income countries argue that the main issue from a WTO market access perspective is not competition law and policy but the use of traditional instruments of contingent protection such as antidumping to restrict access to markets. This is the position of Japan and other Asian WTO members, most vocally Hong Kong. Smaller countries, especially developing ones, have also been concerned about possible anticompetitive behavior by large (dominant) multinationals".

75 Tarullo, Daniel K., Competition Policy for Global Markets, Journal of International Economic Law, Vol. 2, No. 3, Pp. 445-455, September 1999. Personally, I have no illusion that this analysis would express a general consensus. Klein has insisted that there is no worldwide consensus on the legal and economic principles that sound antitrust enforcement demands, and that a trade-focused forum like the WTO is not the right place to develop such a consensus. See KLEIN, JOEL I. A Reality Check on an Antitrust Rules

> traditional "export promotion" objective. The primary concern is not welfare or efficiency—the major focus of many national antitrust regimes. Hence a basic tension exists that leads to the following question: how might an international agreement on competition policy that is geared towards dealing with market access pressures and will be driven by a desire to defend national producer interests help to enhance welfare?
>
> (...)The pursuit of a market access agenda may result in outcomes that are detrimental from a welfare point of view (the latter possibility is a major reason some competition authorities are leery of putting antitrust on the WTO agenda, see e.g., Marsden (1997)). For the WTO dynamic to "work" one must start from the presumption that competition law and policy in developing countries has been or will be captured by domestic producer lobbies, and therefore does not focus on welfare maximization. If so, and this may indeed be the case in some cases, there would be a rationale for pursuing international competition disciplines in the WTO.76

Choosing the grounds here is not necessarily a matter of content, but purpose. If the intention is of raising competition is fulfilling the traditional roles that competition regulation are given domestically, then the welfare enhancement pattern should be adopted. It is granted that trade enhancement also has welfare effects, albeit indirect ones.

The question here, therefore, seems to be one of political and not logical choice. Historical drive and opportunity may have induced to use the *negotiating* context of WTO and its trade related ambiance as, for instance, the most efficacious manner to deal with the claims and requests of any Third World mumbling crowd. It has actually shown to be quite efficient in the Intellectual Property field, where WIPO was (by the early 80´s) ceasing to be a solid OECD battleground[77].

But it is also possible that the trade approach reveals a specific trade thrust of the main trading parties. Some authors state that the main interest of the EU and US is to use competition policy disciplines as an export-promoting device and to reduce the scope for conflict in the approval of mergers between large firms; that they are less interested in subjecting the behavior of their firms in foreign markets to international disciplines that will benefit foreign consumers. They remark that market access is also of interest to small countries, but these may be concerned as well with being able to invoke assistance in disciplining anticompetitive behavior of firms located in foreign jurisdictions[78].

---

in the World Trade Organization, and a practical Way Forward on International Antitrust, in OECD Proceedings, Exploring the Ways Forward, Paris, 1999, pp. 37-45, at 42.

76 Hoeckman and Holmes, op. cit.

77 A negotiating field is, on the other hand, a give and take opportunity. Hoeckman and Holmes stress: "The fact that the competition agenda is being driven by market access considerations does not mean this is the only factor that could enter into play. Pressure for modifications in anti-dumping law and for commitments by OECD competition authorities to provide assistance to developing country competition authorities are examples of the type of quid pro quo that could be sought. Realism suggests, however, that the primary focus should be on the design of appropriate national policies. Developing countries should use the opportunities offered by the WTO to implement a pro-active, broad-based competition policy stance as this is in their own interest, while seeking all the leverage they can to increase the contestability of world markets.

78 Hoekman e Holmes, op. cit., p. 5.

If we take, as we should and Hoeckman and Holmes do, the standpoint of the developing countries, the trade approach, as an isolate aspect in a global commercial negotiation, may not be advisable. Carlos Correa [79] has indicated:

> "under certain conditions, a competitive protectionism may be more beneficial to a nation than rivalry with foreign firms, since in the former case the industry and consumers benefit from competition, while in the latter a whole local industry may be wiped out by foreign competition. In other words, neither liberalization means more competition, nor State regulation and promotion of domestic industrialization necessarily means lack of competition. The relationship between competition policies and development are likely to depend on the peculiar circumstances of an economy and, particularly, on market size and the available industrial endowments".

The trade approach may be also nonfunctional when applied to competition problems. Swaine [80] notes that trade law generally addresses governmental measures, while antitrust law addresses private conduct, even though it is necessary to take account of state enterprises and regulatory barriers to competition. Up to now, international competition rules as have developed are principally intergovernmental in character.

All those four aspects considered - there is one more not mentioned before. Our long chapter on the transnational corporations was intended to point out that, according to some analysts not clearly suspect of a Third World bias, such ungainly beasts have their own interests, which may or not be assimilated to their home (if they have any) or host Government purposes.

It also indicates that they may establish alliances with Governments, which may be detrimental to their home or third party countries. We see no reason to exclude *competition* policies from those standards that could be bargained.

The notion advanced here is that there could be an *international* public interest in assuring that the economic power of transnational corporations or other actors in the international area should be subject to general standards of public welfare and optimization of economic resources. That interest should not necessarily identify to the coordinated interest of the various national policies.

WHAT KIND OF INSTITUTIONAL CHARTER WOULD IT HAVE

Given the complexity of international, domestic, regional and Third World-specific interests, the criteria of fairness and rationality seem to advise the setting up of an international institution, entirely dedicated to competition matters. This is a current trend in International Law. As states the foreword of the fall 1999 edition of the Columbia International Affairs Journal

79 CORREA, Carlos M. Competition Law and Development Policies, in Roger ZÄCH, Towards WTO Competition Rules. Key Issues and Comments on the WTO Report (1998) on Trade and Competition, Kluwer Law International, The Hague, 1999, pp. 361-393, at. 370

80 Edward Swaine, op. cit;

> Truth and reconciliation commissions and ad hoc tribunals seem to represent a renewed faith in institutions and progress toward a place where normative international law must depend on more than the moral suasion of a select few. Even those skeptical of the inclusive concept of world governance must recognize the increased cooperation between states and among peoples brought about by formal and informal institutions. The increased influence of nonstate actors such as corporations and nongovernmental organizations requires a consideration of their role in the process of building such institutions. What remains to be seen is whether the creation of these new institutions works to unite the world or further divide it along political lines.

However legalist may appear such approach, economic and political reasons could be also brought in support of such proposal:

> "even economically inefficient international institutions can be winning political solutions for national politicians, because international institutions allocate property rights in international markets, increase the efficiency of these markets, and thus increase the amount of wealth available for domestic redistribution. In short, reelection-seeking national politicians can increase the supply of wealth available for transfer to domestic constituents—and thereby increase their own electoral support—by regulating international markets, even if these regulatory rules are inefficient (as compared to other possible regulatory rules). [81]

The Roles of the Institution

That specific interest could certainly be served by the congregate action of the main countries experienced in antitrust regulation, by regional or setorialized entities. But if a specifically international competition standpoint should be created, a world competition agency would appear as a reasonable solution. Its functions could certainly encompass the adjucatory, researching and (as some authors indicate as a domestic authority function) institutional advocacy roles of the international governance system.

It would seem that, if such assumptions are correct, a non-trade entity should be built upon the joint experience of both pre-WTO and post Doha competition collaboration. We are not certainly proposing an international institution that should chase and prosecute such international public interest on an autonomous and cavalier fashion. On the contrary, the reality of multilateral negotiation and complex national and regional policies indicate that only a prudent entity, acting in the same, *ad hoc*, case-by-case basis as the international judicial courts have been hitherto acting, could be of any practical import.

International Judiciary Courts do not profit from a large body of statutory law, or from centuries of precedential case law. They create their grounds with segments and figments of legal material as inputs, and their diverse and rich legal training as processing machinery. The deliberations of any international competition agency should be likewise, not too far from their domestic counterparts on antitrust matters:

> Most of the conflicts among OECD countries concern vertical restrictions, and there is no agreement if and when these are detrimental. The Chicago School of economists would hold

81 John E. Richards, Toward a Positive Theory of International Institutions: Regulating International Aviation Markets. International Organization 53, 1, Winter 1999, pp. 1-37

that vertical restraints can almost never be harmful. Others argue that vertical restraints can exacerbate other market imperfections especially with asymmetric information. US courts therefore use a rule of reason approach, as the costs and benefits must be assessed on a case-by-case basis[82].

No Code, No Harmonization

Therefore, such international institution would not presuppose any harmonization of substantive law. Given the current absence of a consensus, we (echoing once more Hoecke and Holmes) "are doubtful about any substantive international régime forcing the acceptance of one set of rules rather than another. And, as pointed out by many scholars, even if identical language were to be adopted in different jurisdictions, interpretations and decisions could easily differ depending on the weights put on various factors by national authorities".

We also do not advance particularly initiatives like the Draft Antitrust Code generated by antitrust scholars in the early 1990s – known as the Munich Code[83]. Swaine notes that the submissions by WTO members to the post Doha exercises reveal very different sentiments on the appropriate norms depending (among other things) on their trade patterns, and "we should not be surprised if a net importer favors antitrust enforcement in excess of the optimum while a net exporter prefers less enforcement. Though this suggests that national-level regulation will veer between excess and laxity, and that net gains might be obtained from international cooperation, it will equally be hard to reconcile the two perspectives in any international forum. The result might explain past failures at multilateralism and continuing features of the regulatory landscape.

Serious doubt could also be raised as to the quality of any substantive body of law related to the agency's scope. The United States have signified its fear that even the current substantive WTO negotiations might result in the "lowest common denominator."[84] A final remark is here is that the US are certainly not willing to create a predominant international régime of any kind; its present goal is to reinforce and sophisticate the bilateral cooperation already in course, through a improved "multilateral" mechanism full of wind and devoid of teeth [85].

---

82 Hoeckman and Holmes, op. cit.

83 Draft International Antitrust Code as a GATT MTO-Plurilateral Trade Agreement (International Antitrust Code Working Group Proposed Draft 1993), published and released July 10, 1993, 64 Antitrust & Trade Reg. Rep. (BNA) No. 1628 (Aug. 19, 1993) (Special Supp.) . See Daniel J. Gifford, The Draft International Antitrust Code Proposed at Munich: Good Intentions Gone Awry, 6 MINN. J. GLOBAL TRADE 1 (1996).

84 Joel I. Klein, A Note of Caution with Respect to a WTO Agenda on Competition Policy, Remarks to the Royal Institute of International Affairs (Nov. 18, 1996), http://www.usdoj.gov/atr/public/speeches/jikspch.htm

85 The United States have advanced the idea that bilateral agreements would be more efficient way of building and international experience in competition matters. See the DOJ's International Antitrust Guidelines (1995): "Formal written bilateral arrangements exist between the United States and the Federal Republic of Germany, Australia, and Canada.46 International antitrust cooperation can also occur through mutual legal assistance treaties ("MLATs"), which are treaties of general application pursuant to which the United States and a foreign country agree to assist one another in criminal law enforcement matters. MLATs currently are in force with over one dozen countries, and many more are in the process of ratification or negotiation. However, only the MLAT with Canada has been used to date to obtain assistance in antitrust investigations.47 The Agencies also hold regular consultations with the antitrust officials of Canada, the European Commission, and Japan, and have close, informal ties with the antitrust

And if there was no Institution at all?

In fact, the discussion may be already dispensing with any international institutional apparatus entirely. As a recent study [86] explains:

> Central to the internationalization of competition law has been the emergence of transnational networks of competition officials and experts. These networks have operated in three main areas: co-ordination on enforcement; technical assistance; and moves to develop overarching competition principles at the level of the WTO. The debate over the nature of internationalization of competition norms has fallen into three phases: early failures mainly due to the lack of any network; politicization of competition policy within a UN context followed by the emergence of a network primarily focused on the OECD. The current phase concerns coordination and the attempt to develop a competition law regime at the WTO level. This process is spearheaded by the European Union, with the United States of America favouring bilateral agreements on enforcement and technical assistance only. The way the debate has changed over the past ten years and how the two main protagonists have modified their positions, is indicative of the influence and importance of networks which, while they may give rise to formal agreements, can operate through soft power and persuasion. What emerges from the analysis is the centrality of these networks to this important aspect of contemporary international governance. They supplement rather than replace more traditional forms of internationalism and, while they may fundamentally regard themselves as technocratic, deriving legitimacy from outputs, current pressures on international policy making require them to attend to the process aspects associated with legitimacy of democratic regimes.

The "power by technocratic consensus", however tempting could it be, seems to be actually undemocratic. Real legitimacy does not flow from efficacy, but participation, albeit imperfect, imprecise and unsatisfactory; the tenets of efficient economy do no translate into the realm of national and international politics. Our inquiry did evaluate the need for a new international institution beyond any intentions of practicing a pilfered power[87].

---

authorities of many other countries. Since 1990, the Agencies have cooperated closely with countries in the process of establishing competition agencies, assisted by funding provided by the Agency for International Development. On November 2, 1994, President Clinton signed into law the International Antitrust Enforcement Assistance Act of 1994, 48 which authorizes the Agencies to enter into antitrust mutual assistance agreements in accordance with the legislation". As to the EC position, see Competition Policy in the New Trade Order: strengthening International Cooperation Rules, European Commission, and p. 7. The net of bilateral treaties established by the U.S. and the EC may be found at http://europa.eu.int/ comm/competition/interna/bilateral.htm and http://www.usdoj.gov/atr/public /international /int_arrangements.htm .

86 Imelda Maher, Competition Law in the International Domain: Networks as a New Form of Governance, Journal of Law and Society, Vol. 29, pp. 111-136, 2002

87 As a former technocrat of the Brazilian Federal government, this author certainly sympathize with the idea of a cleaner, more efficient administrative process, as compared to the customary sheer inaction resulting international unresolved issues; but our goal here is to weight the need for an active, democratically running, and fair institution to accomplish the same targets.

REFERENCES

Agreement between the European Communities and the Government of the United States of America on the application of positive comity principles in the enforcement of their competition laws, in http://europa.eu.int/comm/dg04/interna/en/dftusa.htm

Andrade, Maria Cecília, A Política Da Concorrência E A Organização Mundial Do Comércio, Boletín Latinoamericano de Competencia, N° 14 Abril 2002, found at http://europa.eu.int/comm/competition/international/others/

Araújo, José Tavares de; Tineo, Luís. Harmonization of competition policies among Mercosur countries, *The Antitrust Bulletin*, vol. XLIII, n.° 1/Spring 1998, pp. 45-70.

Assis de Almeida, José Gabriel, A Atuação Do Cade No Brasil Frente Ao Processo De Globalização, *Boletín Latinoamericano de Competencia*, N° 7, p. 75, July 1999, found at http://europa.eu.int/comm/competition/international/other

Barbosa, Denis Borges , Do capital Estrangeiro, Universidade de Campinas, 1993.

Barbosa, Denis Borges, *Direito de Acesso do Capital Estrangeiro*, (Direito do Desenvolvimento Industrial, vol. 1). Ed. Lumen Juris, 1996.

Barbosa, Denis Borges, *Incentives and Trade*, a partial submission to obtain the degree of Master of Laws, Columbia Law School, 1983

Barbosa, Denis Borges, Licitações, *Subsídios e Patentes*, Lumen Juris, 1997 (Direito do Desenvolvimento Industrial, vol. 2).

Borgholm, Danielle S., The Interaction Between Trade And Competition Policies: Towards The Process Of Trade Liberalisation And Global Competition Rules, *Boletín Latinoamericano de Competencia*, N° 16 , Maio 2003, found at http://europa.eu.int/comm/competition/international/other

Brittan, Sir Leon. The need for a multilateral Framework of Competition Rules, in OECD Proceedings, *Trade and Competition Policies*. Exploring the Ways Forward, Paris, 1999

Carl, Mogens Peter, *Toward basic rules on trade-related competition policy*, 2001, in http://europa.eu.int/comm/trade/speeches_articles/sp_mpc01.htm

CASELLA e Araminta de Azevedo MERCADANTE *Guerra Mundial ou Integração Mundial pelo Comércio? A OMC e o Brasil*, Ed. Ltr, São Paulo, 1998, pp. 800-809.

Celli Junior, Umberto, Regras De Concorrência No Direito Internacional Moderno, *Livraria Do Advogado Editora*, Porto Alegre 1999

Cocuzza, Claudio; MONTINI, Massimiliano. International Antitrust Co-operation in a Global Economy, *European Competition Law Review*, March 1998, issue 3, pp. 156-163.

Comissão Européia. Competition Policy in the New Trade Order: Strengthening International Cooperation and Rules . Report of the Group of Experts, European Commission, Brussels, July/1995, in htpp://europa.eu.int/comm/dg04/interna/en/strengh.pdf

Comissão Européia. Projeto de Comunicação da Comissão ao Conselho e ao Parlamento Europeu. Abordagem da União Européia em relação ao Millennium Round, Bruxelas, 1999.

Comissão Européia. *Seattle Conference preparation . EC Approach to Trade and Competition*, European Commission, May 1999, in http://europa.eu.int/comm/trade/2000_round/seacomp.htm

Comissão Européia. *Trade and Competition (discussion paper), European Commission, DG-Competition*, 1999, in http://europa.eu.int/comm/dg04/interna/en/wto_discussion_paper.pdf

Connur, John. International Convergence of Antitrust Laws and Enforcement, *Antitrust Law & Economics Review*, vol. 28, n°s 1 e 2, 1997, pp. 17-30 e 13-26.

Conselho Administrativo De Defesa Econômica. *Relatório Anual do CADE*, Brasília,1998/1999.

Correa, Carlos M. Competition Law and Development Policies, in Roger ZÄCH, *Towards WTO Competition Rules. Key Issues and Comments on the WTO Report (1998) on Trade and Competition*, Kluwer Law International, The Hague, 1999, pp. 361-393.

Cottier, Thomas and Meitinger, Ingo, "The TRIPs Agreement Without a Competition Agreement?" (Jan 03, 2000). Fondazione Eni Enrico Mattei Working Paper No. 65-99. http://ssrn.com/abstract=200622

Final Report of the International Competition Policy Advisory Committee (February, 2000) Executive Summary, Chapters 5 & 6 available at www.usdoj.gov/atr/icpac

Fonseca, Antonio, Aquisição De Ativo Industrial Situado No Exterior - Exame dos efeitos à luz da Lei n° 8.884/94, *Boletín Latinoamericano de Competencia*, N° 15 , Octobre, 2002, found at http://europa.eu.int/comm/competition/international/other

Fox, Eleanor M, "Toward World Antitrust and Market Access", *American Journal of International Law*, Jan. 1997 Vol 91 No 1

Government of the United States of America and the Government of the Federative Republic of Brazil regarding cooperation between their competition authorities in the enforcement of their competition laws, in http://www.ftc.gov/os/1999/9910/VrazilUStreaty.htm

Guzman, Andrew T. Guzman, Global Governance and the WTO, U.C. *Berkeley Public Law Research Paper* No. 89 (Aug. 2002), http://papers.ssrn.com/sol3/delivery.cfm/SSRN_ID321365_code020815630.pdf?abstractid=321365;

Guzman, Andrew T. Is International Antitrust Possible?, 73 *N.Y.U. L. REV.* 1501 (1998)

Hoeckman, B, "Competition Policy and the Global Trading System" *The World Economy* Vol 20 (July 1997) pp 383-406.

Hoekman, Bernard; Holmes, Peter, Competition Policy, *Developing Countries and the WTO*, in http://papers.ssrn.com/

Imelda Maher, Competition Law in the International Domain: Networks as a New Form of Governance, *Journal of Law and Society*, Vol. 29, pp. 111-136, 2002

Janow, Merit E., "Competition Policy" available in The Next Trade Round, J. Bhagwati, ed. University of Michigan Press (1999)

Janow, Merit E., "Public and Private Restraints that Limit Access to Markets", in Market Access After the Uruguay Round (OECD 1996) pp.101-121.

Jenny, Frédéric. Globalization, Competition and Trade Policy: Issues and Challenges, in Roger ZÄCH, *Towards WTO Competition Rules.*

Key Issues and Comments on the WTO Report (1998) on Trade and Competition, Kluwer Law International, The Hague, 1999, pp. 3-41.

Khor, Martin. Comment on the WTO Draft Ministerial Declaration

Klein, Joel I. Time for a Global Competition Initiative? Address to the EC Merger Control 10th Anniversary Conference, Brussels, Belgium, September 14th, 2000. Available at http://www.usdoj.gov/atr/public/speeches/6486.htm, visited on 18th July 2002.

Klein, Joel I., A Reality Check on a Antitrust Rules in the World Trade Organization, and a pratical Way Forward on International Antitrust, in OECD Proceedings, *Exploring the Ways Forward*, Paris, 1999, pp. 37-45.

Klein, Joel I., "A Note of Caution with Respect to a WTO Agenda on Competition Policy", Address to Royal Institute of International Affairs, London. November 18, 1996.

Lamy, Pascal *Post-Seattle: what next?*, 2000 in http:europa.eu.int/comm/tradespeeches_articles/spla11_en.htm

Lamy, Pascal. *What are the options after Seattle?*, 2000 in http:europa.eu.int/comm/trade/speeches_articles/spla09_en.htm

Magalhães, José Carlos de, "As Leis da Concorrência e a Globalização - A Competência Extraterritorial do CADE", in Estudos-Documentos do Conselho Superior de Assuntos Jurídicos -CONJUR, da Federação das Indústrias do Estado de São Paulo, novembro, 2000.

Miert, Karel Van. Globalization of Competition: the need for global governance, *1998*, in Trade and Competition Policies. Exploring the Ways Forward, Paris, 1999, pp. 7-23

Monti, Mario, *Antitrust in the US and Europe: a History of convergence*, General Counsel Roundtable . American Bar Association, Washington, USA, 2001.

Oliveira, Gesner, *Concorrência . Panorama no Brasil e no Mundo*, Editora Saraiva, São Paulo, 2001.

Organization for Economic Cooperation and Development. *CLP Report on Positive Comity*, [DAFFE/CLP(99)19]

Organization for Economic Cooperation and Development. *Report on Notification of Transnational Mergers*, [DAFFE/CLP(99)2/FINAL]

Organization for Economic Cooperation and Development. *Summary by the Secretaria*t, in OECD Proceedings,

Organization for Economic Cooperation and Development. The Role of .Special and Differential Treatment. at the Trade, Competition and Development Interface, [COM/TD/DAFFE/CLP(2001)21/FINAL]

Petersmann, Ernst-Ulrich (1999) .Legal, Economic and Political Objectives of National and International Competition Policies: Constitutional Functions of WTO "Linking Principles" for Trade and Competition, in Symposium: Competing Competition Laws: DO We Need a Global Standard? Panel Three: Is Reconciliation Possible? 34 *New England Law Review* 145-162, at 162.

Petersmann, Ernst-Ulrich. Competition-oriented Reforms of the WTO World Trade System . Proposals and Policy Options, in Roger ZÄCH, *Towards WTO Competition Rules. Key Issues and Comments on the WTO Report (1998) on Trade and Competition*, Kluwer Law International, The Hague, 1999, pp. 43-71.

Swaine, Edward, Against Principled Antitrust, Social Science Research Network Electronic Paper Collection, http://ssrn.com/abstract_id=383781

Tarullo, Daniel K. (2000) .Norms and Institutions in Global Competition Policy., 94 *American Journal of International Law* 478-504, p. 479

Tarullo, Daniel K., Competition Policy for Global Markets, *Journal of International Economic Law,* Vol. 2, No. 3, Pp. 445-455, September 1999

Wood, Diane P., "The Internationalization of Antitrust Law: Options for the Future", Address to DePaul Law Review Symposium (February 3, 1995)

In: International Finance and Financial Services
Editor: Kristian L. Hagen, pp. 191-207
ISBN: 1-60021-756-7

Chapter 8

The Development of the Single European Market for Financial Services and its Effects on Slovenia

Silva Deželan and Marko Košak

Introduction

Over the last two decades, the development of the European financial market has been influenced by the advances in information technology and finance theory, retreat of state financing, capital flow liberalization, institutionalized savings management, and population maturation. It has also been stimulated by the introduction of the euro as a common currency, and the implementation of a single market.[1]

One of the EU's key priorities since the beginning of the 1990s, when the idea of a single market was formalized, was to ensure the conditions for the single market for financial services. Efforts to build the single financial market received greater emphasis in the Financial Services Action Plan (FSAP) created in 1999. The importance of the single financial market for the EU's development and the fulfillment of goals specified in the Lisbon declaration are both reflected in the Sapir report. This report explicitly recommends that market financing should be stimulated in the EU in order to increase investment levels in both research and development, and education.

In the concluding part of the Sapir report, the role of the single market is also promoted through growth stimulation policies. It has long been proclaimed in financial literature that the financial market development is important for economic growth. We present a review of the relevant literature in section two of this chapter. Section three brings an overview of the achieved integration level of the European financial market, and the most important barriers to its implementation. In section four, we briefly compare the development of the Slovenian and European financial markets. Section five concludes by summarizing the most important findings.

---

[1] Perée and Riess (2004).

FINANCIAL SECTOR AND ECONOMIC GROWTH: BANK VS. ARM'S LENGTH FINANCING

A developed financial sector presents an important platform for balanced and sustainable economic growth. An underdeveloped and vulnerable financial sector can quickly endanger the goal fulfillment and stability of macroeconomic policy. This was evident in transition economies where the success of the banking system reform was proven to be necessary for both fiscal and monetary stability (Feldman and Wagner, 2002).

There is a vast amount of literature in regards to a developed financial system's positive influence on economic growth, both theoretically[2] and empirically,[3] originating with Schumpeter. By summarizing Levine (1997) financial systems induce trade, provide for risk diversification, accumulate and hedge risk, allocate and mobilize savings, and allow for corporate governance and control. Consequently, financial systems positively influence capital accumulation as well as growth productivity. Eschenbach (2004) points out a developed financial sector stimulates growth in early stages of economic development while, in later stages, the causality runs in the opposite direction. Numerous studies also demonstrate that the causality may go both ways.

With respect to the prevailing financial source for the corporate sector, economies may be divided into two groups: bank-based, or market-based. In bank-based systems, financing is relationship-based. On the other hand, we have market-based or arm's length financing. The question arises of whether the type of financial system holds importance regarding economic growth. Empirical studies show that no financing structure is dominant, and that economic policies should not be aimed at favoring one system or the other. Rather, the conditions for the efficient provision of financial services such as efficient investor protection, and transparent and high quality accounting standards should be implemented. (Perée and Riess, 2004).

In the financial systems of European countries, which have traditionally been more bank-based, the problem of financing small companies arises. These companies may have high-growth potential but the information asymmetry in their case is so large that it makes the estimation of their risk impossible. Hence, banks typically avoid financing such companies. The scarce or absent financing of both innovations and innovative firms is also emphasized in the Sapir report as one reason for the slow growth seen in EU countries. Endogenous growth theories demonstrate that the crucial element for innovation development and the resulting economic growth is that innovators keep at least part of the income from their innovations (Aghion and Howitt, 1998). The latter is very important for venture capital funds that invest in innovative companies. A favorable tax system and appropriate exit routes for venture

---

[2] See Eschenbach (2004), for example, for a chronological review of studies on the relationship between the development of the financial sector and economic growth.

[3] Many of these studies confirm the premise that financial intermediaries induce economic development via their influence on the growth of total factor productivity. Beck et al. (2000) found a statistically significant positive correlation between the level of development of financial intermediaries and the growth of GDP per capital and total factor productivity. Similarly, Levine and Zervos (1998) empirically confirmed there is a significant impact of stock market liquidity on the contemporaneous and future growth of GDP, productivity and physical capital. Further, Rajan and Zingales (1998) showed that developed financial markets positively affect the growth of corporate sectors that depend on outside sources of financing. This means that developed financial systems represent a comparative advantage in those industries that depend on external financing.

capitalists, in particular through the secondary market, are crucial for the development of venture capital. Implementing the conditions for the market financing of innovations

EU financial market development has been marked by the following trends over the last decade: the decreasing importance of traditional banking at the expense of institutionalized savings, the rapid growth of capital markets, the emergence of numerous financial innovations, and the increasing internationalization of European stock markets despite a strong and remaining home-bias. The latter is reflected in the growing number of cross-border transactions and parallel firm listings. Other trends include mergers and strategic alliances of European stock exchanges, an increasing need for the consolidation of the clearing and settlement systems of the exchanges and the increasing volatility or prices of financial assets in general.[4] A fully integrated or single financial services and capital market in the EU is supposed to bring significant and multiple benefits, the most important being the better allocation of capital in the European economy, the more efficient allocation of European savings and, in the last stage, the strengthening of the European economy to make it more attractive to domestic and foreign investment.

A single and integrated financial system would benefit both the citizens of member-countries and their corporations. The former would be better off primarily due to the higher real returns on their investments in capital markets, lower costs of transactions and portfolio management and more investment opportunities that allow for better risk allocation.[5] Small and medium-sized firms could choose among several financing instruments and their access to venture capital would improve. Large companies would benefit mostly through the lower cost of capital (see Table 7.1), which is relatively high in the EU compared to the USA.

Table 8.1. Selected Macroeconomic Effects of EU Financial Market Integration

Expected effect	Size of the effect
EU-wide real GDP level	+1.1%
due to reduced cost of equity finance	+0.5 p. p.*
due to lower cost of bond finance and the increased share of bond finance in total debt finance	+0.3 p. p.
due to lower cost of bank financing	+0.3 p. p.
GDP per capita	+ 600 EUR (*in current prices*)
Total business investment	+ 6%
Private consumption	+ 0.8%
Total employment	+ 0.5%

* p. p. = percentage points.

Source: London Economics, 2002.

Financial integration should also induce competition and innovation, which should further stimulate new financial instrument development, and decrease transaction costs. The

4 Many issues with respect to the clearing and settlement of cross-border transactions remain unsolved. Should there be one central European clearing house or multiple companies? Should they be vertically or horizontally integrated etc? Within the EU there are currently 26 different settlement systems (Lamfalussy et al., 2001 and Hartmann et al., 2003).

5 Heinemann and Joop (2002) estimate that in this way around EUR 5 billion could be saved by investment funds alone, while the interest rates on mortgage loans are supposed to drop significantly as well (from 0.8 to 2.6 percent of borrowed funds).

result of financial integration should have significant macroeconomic effects: a better allocation of savings resulting in a higher GDP level and eventually growth. The size of the macroeconomic effects of financial integration is presented in Table 7.1, the summarized results of a study by London Economics (2002).

Implementation of the Single EU Market for Financial Services by Segments

In this section we look at the most important trends that have been observed in different segments of the European financial sector, while emphasizing the principal problems seen in the course of implementing the single market for financial services.

Banks and the Money Market

Formally, the program for creating the single European banking market was included in the Maastricht Treaty of 1992, and is based on the decentralization and allocation of regulation to the monetary authorities of member-countries. In combination with the liberalization of capital flows and inducements from the banking directives, this should ensure the development of competition among banking service providers in the EU (Dermine, 2002). With harmonization, the level of banking sector integration in the EU is high, although some price measures of integration still show significant differences between market segments (Baele et al., 2004). Interest rate analysis for corporate loans show a higher level of market segmentation for short-term loans than for medium- and long-term loans. A certain convergence of interest rates can be observed at rates on mortgage loans, while the market for consumer loans is still very fragmented. Cross-border financial flows in the retail-banking segment remain limited, and the home-bias effect is evident. This effectively means that small non-financial companies and households are primarily limited to their domestic local banks.[6] Implementation of the single market for banking services in the Euro area would require the removal of all entry barriers in some local markets. Some empirical studies have revealed that the latter is almost never achievable in real life (see i.e. Petersen and Rajan, 2002; Berger et al., 2001; Degryse and Ongena, 2002). In spite of all of this, many existing entry barriers in the banking business have been reduced or completely eliminated (see Hartmann et al., 2003). This has led to a decrease of costs and increased consolidation, which is also shown in the falling total number of banks (see Table 7.2).[7]

As expected, the effects of the single currency and start-up of the single market have initially been reflected in the money market. Two conditions had to be satisfied for the introduction of the euro to be accompanied by the common monetary policy of the European Central Bank (ECB): (1) the existence of a common short-term interest rate regulated by the central bank for the overall euro area; and (2) a functioning payment system for large

[6] Similar results can be found in Hartman et al. (2003). They find a relatively fast convergence of short-term interest rates after the euro was introduced. Cabral et al. (2002) on the other hand report a certain convergence of lending interest rates on corporate and consumer loans, but they argue that it is primarily a result of the monetary convergence at the macro level and not of the integration of the market for banking services.

[7] In spite of the increasing number of mergers that included at least one bank from the EU area until 1999 when it stabilised (Hartmann et al., 2003), empirical studies show that these mergers were primarily directed at the expropriation of economies of scale and to a lesser degree economies of integration (Buch and DeLong, 2002).

transactions in the whole Euro area, i.e. the TARGET payment system. Only in this case will bank deposits within the EMU become nearly perfect substitutes, and all differences in geographically dispersed market segment interest rates can be arbitraged away. An analysis of three-month interest rates in the period between 1995-2003 confirmed that interbank interest rates converged almost immediately after the euro was introduced in the beginning of 1999 (Hartmann et al., 2003). Similarly, other studies have demonstrated that the integration of the inter-bank money market is almost complete for unsecured claims and interest rate swaps, while the integration of the repo market is much worse (see e.g. Baele et al., 2004). Data on the increasing volume of cross-border transactions in the inter-bank money market of the Euro zone provide a similar picture of integration. The share of these in all cross-border transactions has increased by 10 percentage points due to introduction of the euro (Gaspar et al., 2003). In particular, transactions with unsecured claims have expanded while the repo market remains less developed and less integrated.[8]

Table 8.2. Total Number of Monetary Financial Institutions In The Euro Area

	1999	2000	2001	2002	2003
Credit institutions	7897	7521	7218	6906	6593
Money market funds	1525	1651	1631	1620	1654
Central banks and other institutions	20	21	19	18	22
All monetary financial institutions	9442	9193	8868	8544	8269

Source: Baele et al., 2004.

According to the experts, banks' non-harmonized regulations remain one of the most critical areas in the implementation of the single market for banking services and money. Therefore, a considerable amount of the EU's attention has been devoted to the elimination of regulatory obstacles. The banking sector and money market of a particular country falls under the supervision of both *banking regulators* and *market competition authorities* (Carletti and Hartmann, 2003). Non-cooperation and differences in relative power are also responsible for the relatively slow implementation of the single banking market. National regulators typically claim that their power stems from the second banking directive and the danger that fierce competition might endanger the stability of the banking sector, which has also been suggested by the theory.[9]

Securities Market

A securities market is financially integrated when there are no geographical or other obstacles preventing investors from allocating their savings in the most favorable assets. The benefit of such a market for corporations is primarily the lower cost of capital used to finance

8 According to the data, the share of trading in national markets is still higher for repo markets (just above 40 percent) than for the inter-bank market for unsecured deposits (about 30 percent). In addition, more than half of the trading in the repo market is still hedged with exclusively domestic financial instruments (Hartmann et al., 2003).

9 Nevertheless, Carletti and Hartmann (2003) argue that recent literature does not fully support the hypothesis that increased competition in banking can put the stability in danger. Therefore, they claim it is significant that banking supervisors be as important as the competition authorities and that neither of the two is dominant. The authority of both institutions should be clearly defined and banking supervision should not dominate.

investments that are supposed to contribute to faster economic growth. In a fully integrated market, investors can efficiently diversify risk at lower transaction costs. Introduction of the euro gave an important push to integration. The market became more homogenous and this expanded the set of potential investors, which finally led to increased competition. The data on the value of corporate bonds issued in the Eurozone in the period between 1990-2002 shows that the volume of issued bonds increased significantly after the introduction of the euro in 1999. In addition, fees on the new issues have decreased (Santos and Tsatsaronis, 2002), while the differences in bond returns seem no longer to be related to the location of the issue (Baele et al., 2004). Despite the elimination of currency risk, the increased homogeneity of issued government bonds and their improved convertibility, the EU member treasuries have decided to specialize in certain market segments in order to increase liquidity and lower the cost of borrowing.[10] As a result, there is no homogenous yield curve for the Eurozone, which would be national market based. This issue remains an important obstacle to full financial integration and arbitrage. A slow improvement of the integration in the Eurozone government bond market can also be seen in the data presented in Table 7.3. It shows that the share of issued bonds in GDP was shrinking in the period between 1995-2001, but the percentage of bonds bought by non-residents was growing. The increase in the non-residents' share was more significant after introduction of the euro.

Table 8.3. Investors in Government Bonds Issued in the Euro Area (As a % Of GDP)

	1995	1996	1997	1998	1999	2000	2001
Domestic	58.3	58.9	56.9	53.3	49.7	46.0	45.0
Non-residents	15.9	16.5	17.9	19.8	22.3	23.6	24.1
Total	74.2	75.5	74.9	73.1	72.0	69.5	69.1

Source: ECB, 2003.

The European *stock market* is facing many obstacles that keep it further away from integration. Advances in integration are reflected in the following: the transfer from the country to sectoral diversification of an institutionally managed portfolio, the increased ownership of stocks by households and institutional investors,[11] the growing share of stock ownership by non-residents, the heightened sensitivity of stock returns to the so-called European shocks,[12] the more 'European' portfolio structure of investment companies, the rapid growth of market capitalization of European stock exchanges (in the mid-1990s it represented about 25 percent of GDP and had almost doubled by the end of 2003) and in the increased number of cross-border transactions with securities (Hartmann et al., 2003). An important barrier to the implementation of a fully integrated European securities market is the large number of physically separated stock exchanges, whose clearing and settlement systems for cross-border transactions remain fragmented, which in turn increases investor transaction

[10] The premiums and discounts on the 10-year German government bonds, for example move within the range of 10 to 30 basis points, which indicates that market segmentation limits the price convergence (Hartmann et al., 2003).

[11] The share of stocks among the financial assets of these two investor groups in the EU doubled in the period between year 1995 and 1999 (Baele et al., 2004). It should be added, that equity capital represents only 31% of the capital of companies in EU-15 (Financial Integration Monitor 2004), where the differences in the sources of financing among European companies remain huge.

[12] See for example Baele et al. (2004) for the review of relevant literature.

costs. The large number of (small) stock exchanges also leads to the fragmentation of liquidity, and from this perspective, the strategic alliances and consolidation of traditional European stock exchanges is both meaningful and necessary. In addition to consolidation, so-called parallel markets have emerged. They represent a separate segment of existing exchanges where the stocks of specific sectors, such as high-tech companies, are traded. The advantage of these parallel markets lies in the cheaper and simplified trading for a limited number of specific stocks.

Despite the boom of these new European exchanges in the 1990s (at some point there were about 20 such markets in Europe), their experience shows that the development of market financing for high-growth companies in Europe will not be simple (Ferray and Groslambert, 2004). The markets that emerged are unfortunately too fragmented, meaning they cannot reach the critical mass required for their liquidity.

The aforementioned processes witnessed in European stock exchanges bring additional problems related to the regulation and supervision of newly established institutions. The clearing and settlement of cross-border transactions also remains problematic as each country maintains its own legal structure, regulation, and a specific platform for transaction settlement.[13]

Institutional Investors

The growth of institutional investors such as pension funds, insurance companies and investment companies has been one of the most important characteristics of financial markets in the last few decades. EU implementation, and population maturation are further stimulating pension fund growth of pension funds, investment funds and life-insurance companies. In the rest of this section we will briefly present the integration level achieved by these institutions.

European pension funds: Each member-state independently determines what share of pension expenditures will be covered within the social security system and what will be the contribution of the funded pension plans (2nd pillar).[14] The Pension Funds Directive of 2003 (IOPR, 2003/41/EC) as the first directive for pensions sets the basic rules for the operations of a pension fund that ensure additional pension income on an investment principle. Their assets already represent about 29 percent of the EU-15 GDP (Bešter, 2004). Economies of scale will probably encourage some pension insurance providers to offer their services across the borders of their country of origin. This should contribute to the implementation of the single market while simultaneously positively affecting the mobility of labor within the EU. So far, the integration of European pension funds is primarily shown in the increasing share of foreign stocks in their portfolios. The latter has grown significantly since the introduction of the euro. Nevertheless, foreign securities remain relatively more important for the pension

---

13 As a result, a lot of effort has recently been put into finding the solutions for the problems of financial integration at the highest EU level. As part of these efforts, the so-called Lamfalussy group prepared a report on the reform of the securities market regulation in the EU in 2001, the FSAP was prepared and the so-called Giovannini group was formed in 1996 to advise the European Commission on the preparation of capital markets for phase 3 of the EMU. Currently, it is critically evaluating the clearing and settlement of international transactions within the EU. The success of these initiatives is discussed by Bishop (2003), for example.

14 Due to unfavourable demographic movements and budgetary restrictions the combination of one and the other is necessary for a sustainable pension system in the long-term. Although existing pension systems are based on the principle of safe and prudent conduct of business and the protection of rights of the beneficiaries, countries implement these principles in different ways. In addition, the supervision of pension providers is also not unified.

funds of smaller EU countries while the funds from the larger countries primarily invest at home.

Insurance companies: The legal obstacles to retail insurance market integration were minimized, although not completely removed, with the passing of the third insurance directive concerning life and non-life insurance in July 1994. These directives enable insurance companies to operate in the entire EU area on the basis of a single license obtained in one member-country. Despite the increase in collected premiums, in the past decade integration of the insurance market has not followed these growth rates, which has also been reflected in the structure of insurance companies' financial assets. The proportion of foreign shares in the total amount of shares held in EU insurance companies' portfolios remained under 50%, but has significantly increased especially in small EU member-countries. For example in Belgium shares grew from 8% to 72%, with small capital markets in the 1992-2000 period (Baele et al., 2004). Another important integration indicator is the foreign insurance company penetration rate in the domestic markets of EU member-countries. According to the available data, insurance companies have been entering other markets via mergers and acquisitions in target markets and only rarely by opening up their branches and agencies. It is interesting that non-life insurance companies have more often decided on the cross-border expansion of their operations than other types of insurance companies. The number and market share of predominantly foreign-owned insurance companies have substantially increased in the last few years. According to statistical data for 1999, the market share of foreign-owned life insurance companies[15] amounted to 21% and the market share of non-life insurance companies to approximately 25% (Beckmann et al., 2002). Beside natural entry barriers that prevent the establishment of the single insurance market, there are also many formal barriers that result from the different national taxation systems, different accounting standards, different regulations and supervision standards and the diverse marketing channels used in various markets. Since the obstacles to establishment of the single insurance market are especially pronounced in the segment of the life insurance, many more initiatives are expected in the future for to reduce entrance barriers.[16]

Investment funds: Passed in 1985, the UCITS directive has in many respects stimulated the marketing of investment funds within and especially between EU member-countries.[17] The total asset value of investment funds in the Euro area increased by 184% in the period between 1995-2000, while the proportion of assets in GDP grew from 23% to 52% in the same period. Especially pronounced was the growth proportion of shares held among investment funds' assets in the same period, increasing from 15% to 40%. The proportion of foreign shares among all shares held in investment funds' portfolios increased from about 40% in 1995 to 70% in 2003 (Baele et al., 2004). The international diversification of European investment funds' assets has improved, and the number of investment funds investing abroad has increased. Despite the impressive growth rates, the investment funds

---

[15] As foreign-owned insurance companies are considered companies that have more than a 50% foreign ownership stake.

[16] Among the most important issues included in new directives, currently being prepared at different levels in the EU, are the Solvency II project, supervision of reinsurance companies, the implementation of guarantee schemes, electronic marketing of insurance products, equality of both genders and accounting (Gorišek, 2004).

[17] UCITS funds are investment funds established in any EU member-country in accordance with the directive 85/611/EEC and which possess a single licence from the moment of their foundation. UCIT stands for 'Undertakings for Collective Investment in Transferable Securities'.

market in the EU is not 'European' in the literal meaning. Within the EU, national markets are still dominated by domestic investment management companies.[18] The national fragmentation of investment funds has many negative consequences: investors have limited choice, the existing funds are too small to be able to exploit economies of scale effectively (the average European fund is five times smaller than the average American fund), and the weak competitiveness results in higher operating costs that are finally borne by investors (Heinemann, 2004). The obstacles that still need to be removed in the investment funds industry are administrative and 'natural'; the most important of these is the diverse and discriminatory taxation of investment funds in different countries (Price Waterhouse Coopers, 2001).

In order to achieve the complete implementation of the single European financial market, many open issues still need resolution, such as the following examples: a Europe-wide single license for the issuers of securities and their organized markets, the unification of disclosure rules, regulation of the OTC market, the establishment of efficient regulation of the financial services and capital markets, etc. Despite numerous obstacles such as slow implementation of the new legislation framework in the EU, differences in legal systems, and differences in taxation and culture, we are already witnessing the realization of several important initiatives for establishing the single financial market at the EU level.[19]

THE SLOVENIAN FINANCIAL MARKET AND THE SINGLE EUROPEAN MARKET FOR FINANCIAL SERVICES

Banks

The Slovenian banking system has been characterized by significant structural changes since 1991. The changes have been reflected in the declining number of banks, which has dropped from 31 in 1995 to 19 in 2004. Simultaneously, the market concentration increased and reached its highest levels in 2001 and 2002, whereas after 2002 concentration rates have been gradually falling due to the faster market share growth of banks with an Austrian majority ownership (Bank of Slovenia, 2004). The total assets of Slovenian banks amounted to close to 90% of GDP at the end of 2003, much less than the average assets in Euro area countries, as the latter was 260% of GDP at the end of 2002. This comparison indicates there is still significant growth potential for the Slovenian banking sector in the future, although

---

[18] Heinemann (2002) reports that there are only three EU-15 member countries from which investment funds' shares are sold in two-thirds of other member countries at least, whereas in no member-country are more than six investment funds from other countries available. Among foreign funds available to investors in EU member-countries, the largest number of funds is registered in Luxembourg, Dublin or other 'tax haven' countries. This type of funds is tailor-made funds for investors from those member-countries where such investments have an unfavourable tax status. There are estimations that the market share of foreign-owned funds, measured by total assets, does not exceed 13% in Germany and 5% in France, Italy and Spain, whereas in Sweden their market share is below 1% (Heinemann, 2004).

[19] At least two initiatives deserve special mention, first the establishment of the Forum of European Securities Commissions (FESCO) in 1997, which tries to develop standards supplementing European directives and, second, the European Commission Action Plan for Financial Services from 1999 which serves as a programme for realization of the optimal single financial market.

banks currently already represent 72% of the total assets of the entire financial sector and are the most important financial intermediaries in the country.

While in other transition countries mergers and acquisitions by foreign banks have represented the main driving power for change in the banking sector, foreign banks have been entering the Slovenian banking market almost exclusively through the establishment of subsidiaries. Among the few inter-bank mergers that have taken place in Slovenian banking, small banks were the only targets. Significant changes in the ownership structure happened in 2001 and 2002 when foreign investors bought stakes in some important Slovenian banks (SKB banka, Banka Koper, Krekova banka), which increased the market share of foreign-owned banks to about one-quarter of the market, also taking into account the market shares of three other foreign-owned banks (BA-CA, Hypo Alpe Adria Bank, Volksbank-ljudska banka) and one foreign branch (Tomaž and Košak, 2004). Hence, the real impact of foreign banks in the Slovenian banking market was not detected before 2000, when it became evident that Slovenia was going to become a member of the EU.

Similarly as in other EU countries, we can expect that the introduction of the euro, presumably in 2007, will provide the next important spur for further Slovenian banking integration into the single EU market for financial services. In the meantime, we can expect the dual nature of integration processes, despite the formal openness of Slovenia's banking sector, to competition from other EU countries, as supported by the EU banking directives. The dual nature of integration processes, also observed in other EU member-countries, is reflected in the fact that the highest degree of integration was achieved in wholesale banking markets, whereas the degree of integration in retail markets remained weak (Noyer, 2001).

There are at least two sets of evidence about the intensified adjustment of Slovenian banks to the operating conditions in the EU single market for financial services. First, the decreasing interest rates in Slovenia, and closing interest rate gap[20] between EU and Slovenian markets (ECB Convergence Report, 2004). Second, the intensified credit activity in foreign currencies after 2001, and especially in 2003 and 2004. So the data for the first half of 2004 show that 88.6% of new loans were denominated in foreign currencies, while at the same time borrowings from abroad were reduced (Bank of Slovenia, 2004).

Some indications of Slovenian future banking adaptations to the developments in the EU single market for financial services may be inferred from a comparison of financial statements and adaptation procedures in the banking sectors of comparable EU member-countries. Such a comparison shows (Jašovič and Košak, 2004) that the proportion of securities and proportion of bank deposits among bank assets will be reduced. The former amounted to 34% in Slovenia and only 21% on the EU average in 2003, whereas the latter came to 81.4% in Slovenia and 62.6% on the EU average. With regards to the asset structure, a significant increase in credit activity is expected, which will be reflected in increased borrowings from abroad and disinvestments in both the government's and the Bank of Slovenia's securities.

---

[20] The short-term interest rate differential is calculated as a difference between three-month inter-bank interest rate in Slovenia and the three-month Euribor interest rate. For Slovenia, inter-bank bid rates (SMOM) are included in the comparison until 15 July 2003, after that date interbank offer rates are used (SITIBOR).

Institutional Investors

Slovenian institutional investors have recently experienced extremely high growth rates. There have been several driving factors stimulating rapid growth rates: pension scheme reform, falling interest rates on bank deposits, and growing returns in Slovenian capital markets. Despite the intense development of Slovenian institutional investors (the situation is similar to other new EU member-countries), they still remain behind the majority of EU-15 countries.

Insurance Companies

At the end of 2003 there were 12 insurance and 2 reinsurance companies operating in the Slovenian insurance market.[21] Compared to banks, the insurance companies were almost ten times smaller at the end of 2003 when measured by their total assets. With Slovenia's accession to the EU, Slovenian insurance companies became part of European insurance market, meaning they should be able to trade their insurance products in EU member-countries. On the other hand, the Slovenian insurance market has also opened up to insurance companies from other EU countries.[22] Slovenia's insurance legislation is completely harmonized with the EU legislative framework. The other characteristics of the Slovenian insurance market are as follows (Kaluža, 2004; Štiblar, 2004b):

- The premium volume to GDP ratio (insurance penetration rate) was about 5% at the end of 2001 and represented about 57% of the EU-15 average in 2002, whereas premium volume per capita (insurance density) achieved only 28.5% of the EU-15 average.
- A small share of life insurance in total premium volumes: this share was 33.7% (or one percent of GDP) in 2002, while in the EU-15 it was 62.7% or 5.4% of GDP.
- Good coverage of the insurance market, which has even improved with the new products offered.
- The predominant orientation of customers to local insurance suppliers.
- The unconsolidated ownership of insurance companies, where domestic ownership prevails.[23]

The most important disadvantage of Slovenian insurance companies is their low productivity, as reflected in some quantitative indicators. Accordingly, Slovenian insurance companies reached only 25% of average productivity in the EU-15, when measured by the premium volume to insurance agent ratio, whereas the average number of employees in the insurance sector exceeded the EU average by 93% (Štiblar, 2004). Insurance companies' financial assets have been growing at high rates in the last few years. The share of insurance companies' assets in GDP reached 7.8% in 2003, which is still substantially less than in the

---

21 Besides the abovementioned insurance companies, there were other participants operating in the insurance market: four pension companies, Nuclear Pool (slov. Jedrski pool), the Slovenian Export Corporation, the Slovenian Insurance Association – Restitution fund and The Capital Fund which manages the First pension fund of the Republic of Slovenia.

22 From the day of Slovenia's accession to the EU until July 2004 the Insurance Supervision Agency approved the entrance of 45 foreign insurance companies (Bank of Slovenia, 2004).

23 At year-end 2003 foreigners owned 20.9% of the equity in Slovenian insurance companies.

EU, where this share was 52.6% of GDP at the end of 2001 (Bank of Slovenia, 2004). The development prospects of Slovenia's insurance industry can be seen through insurance company integration within financial groups, an immediate improvement in productivity, and their orientation to those foreign markets where they can use their comparative advantages.

Pension Funds

Four pension companies,[24] 3 insurance companies and 6 mutual pension funds[25] currently offer supplementary pension insurance. Market concentration has been reduced in recent years, although it is still significant in the case of mutual investment funds since the share of the largest fund exceeded 77% of total assets at the end of 2003. Since the Act on Pension and Disability Insurance (ZPIZ-1) was passed by parliament in 2000, all pension insurance suppliers have experienced rapid growth rates. Despite the fast pension fund growth, their total asset volume did not even reach one percent of GDP at the end of 2003, while the share of their counterparts in EU-15 countries approached 30 percent.[26]

The Slovenian legislation on supplementary pension insurance is in many respects completely harmonized with the European pension directive IORP. There are only a few areas that remain open such as: the definition and calculation of guaranteed returns, the asset structure,[27] the capital adequacy of insurance suppliers, the notification of customers (claimants), and the appropriate asset valuation (Bešter, 2004). With the implementation of collective supplementary pension insurance schemes for public servants in 2004, the share of supplementary pension insurance beneficiaries has increased to 48% of the active population. Taking into account the size of the Slovenian market and given the need for efficiency improvements, we can expect the further consolidation of pension insurance providers and increased involvement of banks (through their ownership stakes) in the pension insurance industry in the future.

Investment Funds

At year-end 2003 in Slovenia there were 20 management companies (DZU) operating, 18 authorized investment companies, a further 8 investment companies (ID), 18 special mutual funds, and 2 mutual funds.[28] By the end of September 2004, the number of mutual funds had increased to 30 and the number of investment companies (ID) to 10. The number of investors deciding to invest in mutual funds jumped from 5,481 at the end of 1998 to 58,781 at the end of September 2004 (www.vzajemci.com, October 2004). So we can conclude that mutual fund investments have become an ever more important form of long-term savings. This is also reflected in the increasing savings inflow into mutual funds in the last three years, and

---

[24] According to the Slovenian legislation pension companies are organized as corporations.

[25] One of the insurance companies has already transferred its customers to a pension company, another is expected to do the same in the near future (Bank of Slovenia, 2004)

[26] Pension companies increased the volume of their operations and improved their performance in 2003, but they still operated at a loss (SIT 14 billion).

[27] The share of government bonds was between 49% (mutual pension funds) and 73% (insurance companies), whereas equity holdings only represented a small portion of their assets at the end of 2003 (Bank of Slovenia, Financial stability report for 2003).

[28] Data as reported in the Annual Report of the Agency for Securities Markets (ATVP) for 2003. In the mutual funds market the concentration is high. The largest fund had a market share of 31% (at the beginning of October 2004), while the two largest funds, operated by the same DZU, represented 45% of the entire market. The market share of the largest investment management company (DZU) amounted to 22% at the end of March 2004.

rapid mutual fund asset growth. Investors have been attracted by growing returns in the Ljubljana Stock Exchange, falling bank deposit interest rates, and very likely by the announced taxation of interest income. Consequently, time deposits (in domestic and foreign currencies) increased by 3.4% in first three months of this year, while mutual funds assets grew by 40% (Bank of Slovenia, 2004).

Despite the high growth rates recorded in the last few years, total investment fund assets amounted to just SIT 440 billion or 7.6% of GDP at the end of April 2004, eight times less than the share of bank deposits in GDP at the same time. The share of mutual funds in the total assets of investment funds amounted to only 32.5% at the end of April 2004, although the transformation of some IDs in mutual funds will significantly contribute to the further growth of mutual funds.

The degree of integration of Slovenian mutual funds with the European market is also reflected in the structure of their assets. The assets are dominated by domestic long-term securities (81.4%), while foreign long-term securities represented a mere 7.2% of total assets at the end of 2003.[29] The share of foreign assets was largest in equity funds, which had 15% of foreign shares at the end of March 2004. These figures reflect the abolition of the 10% investment limit for non-domestic securities brought about by the ZISDU-1 act in 2002. Slovenia's accession to the EU has made it easier for foreign fund managers to start their operations in Slovenia, which should result in lower market concentration rates in the future. Access to foreign markets should also be easier for domestic investment management companies (DZU). The opening up of the Slovenian market has enabled Slovenian investors to better diversify their assets and risks and, at the same time, they can also enjoy the greater diversity of investment funds, still not known in the domestic market (money market mutual funds, real estate funds, index funds etc.).

Capital Market

The Ljubljana Stock Exchange is still young and its development has been influenced by the privatization process and the banking-oriented culture of Slovenian companies. The most important problem of the Slovenian capital market is the underdeveloped primary market, reflected in the small number of public offers for new shares. There were only 23 public offers for new shares in the period between 1994-2004 (the last one was in 2000), and among them 13 public offers or 75% of all collected funds were from the banking sector (Bank of Slovenia, 2004). Somewhat more developed is the primary market for debt securities, where the government and financial institutions have an absolutely dominant position. The limited supply of investment opportunities (securities) in the domestic market has forced institutional and individual investors towards foreign investments.[30]

As is evident from Table 7.4, the Slovenian secondary capital market has irreversibly developed in the last decade in terms of its increasing market capitalization and growing turnover. The market capitalization of shares represented about 30% of GDP in May 2004, together with bonds at 46% of GDP, which is close to the proportion reached solely by equity

---

[29] Short-term securities represented 5.4% of the total assets of mutual funds at year-end 2003, while the share of bank deposits was only 2.1% (ATVP Annual Report, 2003). The asset structure of mixed and equity funds is dominated by domestic shares: at the end of 2004 the proportion of shares was 52% in mixed funds and 57% in equity funds.

[30] The organized market for financial derivatives has not developed yet, although some instruments, e.g. forward contracts, are actually in use in the OTC market (Veselinovič, 2004).

market capitalization in EU-15 countries. The market capitalization growth in the organized market can be attributed to the stable growth of equity prices, lower interest rates, and growing investments of mutual funds stemming from record high inflows of savings in these funds in the last two years.[31] In terms of turnover, the picture of the organized market is completely different as turnover has permanently decreased. The latter indicates the worsening liquidity of the secondary market, which can also be read from the data on the marketability of shares and bonds in Table 7.4.

One indicator of Slovenia's poor integration into the European capital market is the weak connection of stock exchange indexes and small proportion of foreign investors among those who invest in Slovenian equities. In addition, this characteristic is naturally related to the low turnover of foreign-owned securities in the domestic organized market in the last few years. The share of non-residents in the ownership structure of Slovenian companies amounted to 5.91% at the end of December 2003 and declined with respect to the end of 2002.

Table 8.4. Basic Data on the Organized Market in the 1998-2003 Period

	1998	1999	2000	2001	2002	2003
The number of securities	173	237	267	270	265	254
- all equity type securities	122	180	197	193	172	162
- shares of PID companies	30	46	44	37	29	18
- bonds	51	56	68	76	92	92
Market capitalization (SIT bill)	628	795	967	1.218	1.930	2.215
Share of market capitalization in GDP (in%)	19,3	21,9	24,0	26,8	36,3	43,1
Share of turnover in GDP (in %)	5,7	7,3	6,7	7,7	9,0	6,0
Marketability of shares (without PID)	0,28	0,30	0,21	0,28	0,23	0,11
Marketability of bonds	0,15	0,16	0,22	0,14	0,16	0,15

Note: The data refer to the end of a year, except for turnover data which refer to the entire year.
Sources: ATVP (2004) and Bank of Slovenia (2004).

Mergers and acquisitions conducted by foreign companies represent a serious threat to the Ljubljana Stock Exchange in the future since merged and/or acquired companies are usually delisted. The second threat is the withdrawal of investment limits for institutional investors, which consequently decide on the international diversification of their assets. The strategies for the long-term development of small stock exchanges, such as the Ljubljana Stock Exchange, should take the following activities into account (Claessens et al., 2004): rationalization of operations, regional co-operation or at least the development of common regionally oriented trading systems that would reduce costs and improve market liquidity, and finally, mergers or acquisitions.[32] The existence of the Ljubljana Stock Exchange will depend in the long run on pension, investment, and joint venture fund development, since the presence of institutional investors has proven to be essential for the development of small stock exchanges.

---

[31] Partly taken from Bank of Slovenia (2004).

[32] Small stock exchanges have no comparative advantages when servicing big companies but they can service small and medium-sized companies which cannot access large stock exchanges. Since these companies are important for the stimulation of economic growth and need additional capital for their own development, the elimination of local stock exchanges could have devastating consequences for national economies (Claessens et al., 2004).

Conclusion

In the article the remaining obstacles pertaining to the establishment of financial services for a single European market are analyzed. These obstacles are vanishing and EU financial markets are becoming more integrated. The establishments of the single European market and the dwindling barriers between banking and financial markets have contributed to intensified competition in the entire financial market and the improved competitiveness of specific market segments. This enhanced competitiveness should lead to higher economic growth.

Slovenia's accession to the EU also triggered the intensified integration of its financial market with the single European market for financial services. The key future events prompting the full integration of Slovenia's financial market will be entrance to the EMU and the adoption of the euro. At this stage of integration, Slovenian investors are already enjoying a greater number of financial services suppliers, especially an increased number of foreign mutual funds. Currently, the banking sector is still the most important segment of the Slovenian financial system, although we can expect the relative importance of the banking industry to be diminy and adjustished in relative terms in the future. The ongoing integration processes and resulting intensified competition in the financial sector will force Slovenian providers of financial services to further improve their efficienc their portfolio of services in line with those offered by financial institutions from other parts of the EU. Ultimately, it is customers who should benefit the most.

References

Agencija za trg vrednostnih papirjev 2004. "Letno poročilo o stanju na trgu vrednostnih papirjev za leto 2003."

Agencija za zavarovalni nadzor RS 2004. "Letno poročilo za leto 2003."

Aghion, P., and Howitt, P. 1998. *Endogenous Growth Theory.* MIT Press.

Baele, L., Fernando, A., Hördahl, P., Krylova, E., and Monnet, C. 2004. "Measuring Financial Integration in the Euro Area." *ECB Occasional Paper Series* No. 14.

Bank of Slovenia 2004. "Financial stability report for 2003."

Beck, T., Levine, R., and Loayza, N. 2000. "Finance and the Sources of Growth." *Journal of Financial Economics* 58 (1/2): 261-300.

Beckmann, R., Eppendorfer, C., and Neimke, M. 2002. *Financial Integration within the European Union: Towards A Single Market for Insurance*. Ruhr-University Bochum.

Berger, A., Klapper L., and Udell, G. 2001. "The Ability of Banks to Lend to Informationally Opaque Small Business" *Journal of Banking and Finance* 25 (12): 2127-2167.

Bešter, H. 2004. "Pokojninska direktiva – prvi korak k evropskemu pokojninskemu trgu." *11. dnevi slovenskega zavarovalništva: zbornik člankov*:189-204.

Bishop, G. 2003. "The Role and Development of EU Capital Markets." *EIB Papers* 8 (2): 57-74.

Boot, A.W.A. 1999. "European lessons on consolidation in banking." *Journal of Banking and Finance* 23 (2-4): 609-613.

Cabral, I., Dierick, F., and Vesala, J. 2002. "Banking integration in the euro area." *ECB Occasional Paper* No. 6.

Claessens, S., Lee, R., and Zechner, J. 2003. *The Future Of Stock Exchanges In European Union Accession.* Corporation of London.

Davis, P. E. 2003. "Institutional Investors, Market Efficiency, and Financial Stability." *EIB Papers* 8 (2): 77-103.

Degryse, H., and Ongena, S. 2002. "Distance, lending relationships, and competition." *Manuscript, Tilburg University.*

Dermine, J. 2003. "European banking: past, present and future." In V. Gaspar, P. Hartmann and O. Sleijpen (eds.): *The Transformation of the European Financial System.* Proceedings of the 2nd ECB Central Banking Conference, ECB Frankfurt.

Eschenbach, F. 2004. "Finance and Growth: A Survey of the Theoretical and Empirical Literature." *Tinbergen Institute Discussion Paper* No. 2004-039/2.

European Central Bank 2004. "Convergence Report 2004."

European Central Bank 2003. "The Integration of Europe's Financial Markets." *Monthly Bulletin*: 53-66.

European Commission 2004. "Financial Integration Monitor." Staff Working Document.

Feldman, R. A., and Wagner, N. 2002. "The Financial Sector, Macroeconomic Policy and Performance." *EIB Papers* 7 (2): 13-30.

Ferray, M., and Groslambert, B. 2004. "European Stock Market Financing For High-Growth Companies: An Analysis of the European New Markets Experience." EVCA Research Paper.

Giannetti, M., Guiso, L., Jappelli, T., Padula, M., and Pagano, M. 2002. "Financial Market Integration, Corporate Financing and Economic Growth." European Commission DG ECFIN Economic Paper No 179.

Gorišek, J. 2004. "Članstvo Slovenije v Evropski uniji in zavarovalni nadzor." *Bančni vestnik* 53 (7-8): 29-37.

Hartmann, P., Maddaloni, A., and Manganelli, S. 2003. "The Euro Financial System: Structure, Integration And Policy Incentives." ECB Working Paper No. 230.

Heinemann, F. 2002. "The Benefits Of Creating A Real EU Market For Investment Funds." ZEW Mannheim.

Jašovič, B., and Košak, T. 2004. "Trendna gibanja v strukturi bančnega sektorja Slovenije." *Bančni vestnik* 53 (6): 11-20.

Kaluža, M. 2004. "Slovenske zavarovalnice na razpotju." *Bančni vestnik* 53 (7-8): 2-3.

Lamfalussy, A., Herkstroter, C., Rojo, L.A., Ryden, B., Spaventa, L., Walter, N., and Wicks, N. 2001. "Final Report of the Committee of Wise Men on the Regulation of European Securities Markets." Report to the European Commission.

Levine, R., and Zervos, S. 1998. "Stock Markets, Banks and Economic Growth." *American Economic Review* 88 (3): 537-558.

Levine, R. 1997. "Financial Development and Economic Growth: Views and Agenda." *Journal of Economic Literature* 35 (2): 688-726.

London Economics, PriceWaterhouseCoopers and Oxford Economic Forecasting 2002. "Quantification of the Macro-Economic Impact of Integration of EU Financial Markets: The Final Report to the European Commission." London Economics.

Noyer, C. 2001. "Banking in the euro area." Speech delivered by C. Noyer, Vice-President of the European Central Bank, at the 30th Anniversary of the Association of Foreign Banks' Representatives, Frankfurt, 8 November 2001.

Perée, E., and Riess, A. 2003. "The Transformation of Finance in Europe: Introduction and Overview." *EIB Papers* 8 (2): 11-34.

Petersen, M., and Rajan, R. 2002. "Does distance still matter? The information revolution and small business lending." *Journal of Finance* 57 (6): 2533-2570.

PriceWaterhouseCoopers 2001. "Discriminatory Tax Barriers in the Single European Investment Funds Market." FEFSI Discussion Paper.

Rajan, R.G., and Zingales, L. 1998. "Financial Dependance and Growth." *American Economic Review* 88 (3): 559-586.

Rajan, R.G., and Zingales, L. 2003. "Financial Systems, Industrial Structure and Growth." *Oxford Review of Economic Policy* 17 (4): 467-482.

Sapir, A., Aghion, P., Bertola, G., Hellwig, M., Pisani-Ferry, J., Rosati, D., Vinals, J., and Wallace, H. 2003. "An Agenda for a Growing Europe: Making the EU Economic System Deliver." Report of an Independent High-Level Study Group to the European Commission (the Sapir Report). European Commission.

Štiblar, F. 2004b. "Ekonometrična analiza zavarovalništva novih članic EU." *Bančni vestnik* 53 (7-8): 17-27.

Štiblar, F. 2004a. "Zavarovalništvo Slovenije ob priključitvi EU." *Bančni vestnik* 53 (5): 71-79.

Tomaž, A., and Košak, M. 2004. "Konkurenčnost bančnega sektorja ob vključitvi v EU." *Bančni vestnik* 53 (5): 61-69.

Veselinovič, D. 2004. "Slovenski finančni trg in EU." *Bančni vestnik* 53 (5): 81-87.

Vzajemci.com, *http://www.vzajemci.com*, 30.9.2004.

In: International Finance and Financial Services
Editor: Kristian L. Hagen, pp. 209-225
ISBN: 1-60021-756-7

Chapter 9

PROGRESSING TOWARDS LEGITIMACY: FINANCIAL SERVICES SECTOR POLICYMAKING IN THE EU AFTER LAMFALUSSY

***Heather McKeen-Edwards*[1] *and Ian Roberge*[2]**
Department of Political Science,
McMaster University [1] and Glendon College, York University [2], Canada

ABSTRACT

The European Union (EU) is often perceived as lacking legitimacy. Yet, this understanding of EU policymaking is more and more contested through discussion of input and output legitimacy. The paper speaks to this issue by focusing specifically on integration in the financial services sector, particularly the securities industry, and by assessing how the policy process facilitates or impedes the legitimacy of policymaking in this field. By analyzing the Lamfalussy regulatory process, we argue that the EU has made important strides in ensuring both output and input legitimacy although there remain gaps in its approach. The legislative agenda of the Financial Services Action Plan was adopted on time and the regulatory process favours consultation with market actors. However, complete implementation of measures across the Union remains a problem as is the inability of end-users and consumers to fully access the policy process.

INTRODUCTION

The European Union (EU) is often assumed to lack legitimacy. The structure of the European Central Bank is often pinpointed as an important part of the problem. Yet, recent scholarly work suggests the opposite – the European Union, when fairly compared with the practices of states, is actually largely democratically legitimate (Moravcsik 2004; Schmidt 2004). One of the useful distinctions that have been made to address these questions is between output and input legitimacy (Scharpf 1999). The former relates to government *for* the people and focuses on the results of governmental action. The latter refers to government *by* the people and speaks to the openness of the policy process. Arguably, both output and input legitimacy are necessary to ensure democracy. In the EU, it is clear that the European level is more and more intrusive in almost all areas of public policy. The EU has made real progress in furthering integration especially in regards to the economy (output legitimacy), but has been less successful in responding to citizen's welfare concerns. EU institutions also appear to make increasing attempt to consult and include all relevant actors in the policymaking process (input legitimacy), yet there are many challenges for private and social actors when it comes to having voice and influence in Brussels.

A useful way by which to determine if the EU is democratic, accountable and legitimate is to study its actions in specific policy fields. The paper undertakes this process of appraisal by focusing on policymaking in the financial services sector. This sector is apt for analysis for at least two reasons. First, it is generally agreed that in order for the EU to benefit fully from the creation of the euro and to facilitate the integration of the continent's economies as a whole, it needs to have a fully integrated financial services sector marketplace. As such, the integration of financial markets has become a priority for EU decision-makers who see it as essential in furthering economic developments. Second, the financial services policy field is a good test case because policymaking in this sector at the state level also poses inherent issues of democracy and legitimacy. The field is technical in nature and the policy network is usually composed of large, often influential, private corporate sector actors rendering it difficult for non-experts and citizens more generally to participate in the policy process. If the EU can be shown to have a certain level of legitimacy in this field, than it can be said to be more legitimate than often assumed.

How does the policy process facilitate or impede the legitimacy of policymaking in the financial services sector? By focusing on the Lamfalussy regulatory process,[1] we argue that the EU has made important strides in ensuring the legitimacy of policies for finance industries, acknowledging that there remain some gaps in its approach. Financial services sector policymaking, especially in the securities industry which is the core focus of our analysis, has partly achieved output and input legitimacy. More remains to be done, however, for the people of Europe to benefit from the integration process and for them to have real input in the way policies in this field are elaborated.

The paper is divided in three parts. First, the concept of legitimacy is further discussed. Second, the policy process in the financial services sector is duly analyzed, after we provide a short summary of integration in this sector. Particular attention is paid to the consultation practices used in policymaking. Finally, we will return to discussing what this shift in the policymaking process has meant for the legitimacy of the policy sector.

1 The Lamfalussy process is a four-stage policymaking process that the EU implemented in 2001 to increase the speed and effectiveness of their policy (outlined in the Financial Services Action Plan [FSAP]) in the securities sector.

1. Input and Output Legitimacy

Questions about the legitimacy of EU policy processes and outputs are not new. As more policymaking authority has been transferred up to this level, these questions have only grown. While the EU has historically developed in a piecemeal fashion, it would now appear that the Union must focus on minimizing its democratic deficit and enhancing its legitimacy with EU citizens. One potential source of EU policy legitimacy emerges from the belief that there is some indirect legitimacy conferred through its composition of democratically legitimate actors. As interstate bargaining is at the basis of at least broad level European governance, it is essential that the national governments involved in the arena be democratically accountable to their constituencies (and parliaments) (Horeth 1999: 251). However, the potential of indirect legitimacy has been challenged. On a philosophical level, Majone (1999) argues that democratic institutions cannot transfer their legitimacy to non-majoritarian ones even though they may transfer policymaking responsibility. Others argue that there are indications that some of the practices which emerge in this relationship actually negatively impact legitimacy, including the practices of blame shifting, displacing national legitimacy problems to the European level without the appropriate shift in resources and the 'cartelization' of the relationship between state and Union by the bureaucratic elites (Lord and Beetham 2001: 444). Therefore, EU bodies must pursue strategies to ensure their own legitimacy. Lord and Beetham (2001) go so far as to argue that the EU cannot be seen as legitimate unless it directly develops the three dimensions of legitimacy: performance, democracy and identity.

One way to conceptualize the direct legitimation strategies that the EU undertakes is to look at the importance placed on input and output legitimacy. The three dimensions of legitimacy just mentioned map with input and output legitimacy in that the first is output legitimacy and the second and third are more measures of input legitimacy. In general, claims of legitimate policymaking in the EU are often inherently – whether acknowledged or implicit – based on notions of output legitimacy. Output legitimacy involves focusing on the legitimacy of policy based on whether the outcome is *for* the people. Horeth states 'The underlying assumption here is that the legitimacy of a political system depends on its capacity to achieve the citizens' goals and solve their problems' (1999: 251).

Although output legitimacy has traditionally been seen as sufficient, there has been a growing recognition of its inadequacy (Majone 2000; Skogstad 2003). As this has occurred more attention has been paid to the potential for input legitimacy of EU policymaking. At its core input legitimation relies 'on the rhetoric of 'participation' and of "consensus"' (Scharpf 1999: 7). Unlike output legitimacy's focus on policy outcomes, the focus here is on the policy process – or government *by* the people. The importance of determining who is included in 'the people' has led some, particularly Scharpf (1999), to conclude that the EU cannot achieve input legitimacy in its current form because it lacks a thick European collective identity or demos. Although a 'demos' is not necessarily an 'ethnos', its members must still recognize each other as members of the same political community in order to acceptably use the majority principle of democracy (Horeth 1999). In essence, in order to achieve government *by the people,* it is argued that one needs to identify who the self-recognized 'people' are, something more easily done at the state than at a supra-national level.

Acknowledging that the lack of European identity is important, in this paper we sidestep the matter by taking a broader understanding of what can be included in input oriented legitimacy. Conventionally, utilization of this concept has been focused on the legitimacy achieved through traditional democratic institutions like elections or even direct forms of democratic decision-making of citizens (Michalowitz 2004). However, drawing from Skogstad (2003), we understand input legitimacy to include all strategies that the European bodies undertake to democratize the procedures which create policies. In this understanding the assessment of appropriateness under input legitimation is the 'conformity of decision-making procedures with democratic norms of public participation and control' as distinguished from output legitimation strategies which rely instead on the perceived merit of policy outputs as the measure of appropriateness (Skogstad 2003: 324-5).

There are a number of different but overlapping legitimating strategies that the EU can take to enhance its claims of input legitimacy. Some of these strategies include: the use of the co-decision procedure with the European Parliament, initiating reforms to EU decision-making which seek to increase transparency and reduce discretion, the use of network forms of governance to increase the participation of private actors, including non-governmental organizations (NGOs), in the policymaking process, and enabling citizens jointly to define and share a view of the common good through the utilization of 'deliberative democracy' mechanisms (Skogstad 2003: 324). In the case of the policy process in financial services governance, one can look particularly at the first three strategies as potential sources of increased input legitimacy. The introduction of co-decision procedures in financial services sector policymaking can be clearly understood as increasing input legitimacy as it formally includes the only directly elected EU body, the European Parliament, in the process of policy creation. Second, the potential of increased transparency in the decision-making process is less consistent. This includes the potential to overcome a 'democratic deficit by being more transparent, providing more opportunities for public participation, giving reasons for their decisions, and exercising less technical or administrative discretion' (Skogstad 2003: 325). The third strategy, the inclusion of private and non-governmental actors into policy networks, is of particular interest. As we will see, European institutions have made a real attempt to include at least financial services actors in the structure of governance.

Whether consultation with outside actors has the potential to increase input legitimacy is contested. Not all scholars agree on the usefulness of direct consultation in enhancing input legitimacy. Michalowitz argues that the inclusion of 'civil society' does not necessarily improve legitimacy. She highlights the key problem as:

> '...the paradox that lobbying actors are generally perceived as rationalist, self interest-guided actors who may contribute to democratic decision making by inserting special interest views, but who do not strive for a common good themselves. For a European civil society that is able to contribute to the input legitimacy of the European political system however, actors are needed whose principal aim is to serve the common good by engaging in decision making' (Michalowitz 2004: 147).

Furthermore, it has been argued that EU bodies do not necessarily encourage previously uninvolved citizens to become active but may actually further reinforce the involvement of those 'citizens and groups who benefit from their intellectual and financial resources to try to influence EU politics and policies' (Magnette 2003: 156). Magnette acknowledges though that this trend does not necessarily mean that the system is undemocratic because (1) widespread active citizenship is rare in most Western countries and (2) 'all citizens benefit from the mobilisation and vigilance of the more active citizens among them' (2003: 250-1).

Those arguments aside, there are a number of scholars that underscore that input legitimacy is enhanced by the inclusion of non-state actors' consultation and/or participation in policymaking (Héritier 1999; Lord and Beetham 2001; Lord 2001; Skogstad, 2003). Schmidt (2004) argues that one does not really see 'government *by* the people' as occurring through political participation in the EU but 'government *with* the people', which is achieved through consultation with organized interests. Government *with* the people can also be seen as enhancing both input and output legitimacy (by potentially improving the overall quality of emerging regulation). For example, Bowen asserts that business interest representation can act as a source of both input and output legitimacy at the sectoral level, though it functions more as part of output legitimacy at the systemic level (2003: 8).

Even if there is acceptance of consultation as part of input legitimacy, there is still some debate around the actual role that these actors and processes play. Some like Héritier (1999) assert that participation can act as a substitute to more traditional forms of government-based legitimacy. Others like Lord and Beetham (2001) argue that the innovative input legitimation strategies of the EU are constrained to a complementary role. For them, the development of a representative political system is still necessary because the minimum legitimacy requirements for states also apply to the Union directly. Despite the limits on the potential impact of this type of strategy, it is still worth examining as an attempt by EU institutions to be more inclusive.

Finally, as our analysis focuses largely on interactions that occur within a committee structure it is also important to briefly reflect on the role committee governance has on these legitimacy questions. The use of committees in the European policymaking process is not a new phenomenon and their impact on EU legitimacy has received specific attention from a number of different scholars (Rhinard 2002; Dehousse 2003; Egeberg, Schaefer and Trondal 2003). There appears to be agreement that the use of these committees raises important concerns around the areas of input legitimacy, particularly transparency and access. Schmidt (2004) argues that input legitimacy problems are exacerbated by the committee system. She highlights the inherent problems with assuming that 'governance "with *some* of the people" and possibly not "for *all* of the people" is meant to make up for the lack of government "by and of the people"' (Schmidt 2004: 985-6). In addition, Dehousse aptly highlights the paradox of committees, 'initially conceived as control devices, "comitology" committees are now increasingly perceived as transnational bureaucratic networks, which themselves need to be controlled' (2003: 810). As such, many elements and potential contributions of a comitology system remain contested. Joerges and Neyer (1999), however, find that the comitology system does present the potential for a certain degree of 'deliberative democracy'. Although Rhinard finds that the committee structure leads to the preference of system effectiveness over democratic legitimacy, he also acknowledges that as small, insulated groups these committees are highly suitable institutional mechanisms to pursue consensual and depoliticized decision-making allowing for extensive, ongoing consultation in an intimate atmosphere among actors from multiple levels of government and society (2002: 187).

2. Policymaking in the Financial Services Sector

2.1. The Policy Process

The integration of the financial services sector is often held up as one of the key successes of the European Union. Policy and regulation in this sector has a substantial history beginning in 1977 with the First Banking Directive. Yet by the 1990s the process seemed paralyzed by interstate conflict (Josselin 1997). In a *Euromoney* article, Shirreff reported at the time, 'After nearly a decade of fanfare, the single European market for financial services is a ghost of what it should be' (1999). It was not until late in the century that a new round of integration was kick-started by a combination of political and economic factors, including the adoption of the euro in 1999 and the increasing willingness of markets to operate cross-continent as indicated by the creation of Euronext, a pan-European exchange, in 2000. These developments were matched on the political side when the European Commission presented the Financial Services Action Plan (FSAP). The Action Plan was aimed at the integration of the continent's securities markets and was ambitiously composed of 42 directives to be adopted in a period of five years. Despite the initial doubts, the FSAP is considered by most to be a success (European Commission 2005), in large part due to its efficiency. The legislative agenda of the FSAP at the European level has been completed within the agreed timeframe with 39 directives adopted.[2]

The efficiency of the FSAP was gained in large part through the introduction of a multistage regulatory process. The comitology apparatus emerged when the Committee of Wise Men, as created and called by the European Commission, came together to propose ways by which to implement the FSAP. The Committee's final report in 2001 concluded that the previously existing policy process was often too slow in the adoption of legislation, that legislative texts tend to be ambiguous, that there are delays in the transposition process, that important issues were often left out of the legislation, that directives were difficult to update and that communication across regulators was still problematic (2001). As such, the Committee, chaired by Baron Lamfalussy, suggested a shift in policymaking to a four level comitology-based approach.

At the first level, the Council and Parliament agree upon broad directives, also referred to as essential measures, through the co-decision procedure. These directives are intended to set out the basis for regulation with most of the technical detail left to Level II legislation. After this, these directives are passed to the second level where European Commission and the European Securities Committee (ESC) set out the modalities of the Directive. The content of this second level of legislation is framed as technical or non-essential measures. However, it is at this level that much of the detail of the broad directives is elaborated.[3] At the third level, the Committee of European Securities Regulators (CESR), formerly the Forum of European Securities Commissions (FESCO), is to provide advice to the ESC and the Commission on

2 Schaub, among others, point out that although the legislative part of the FSAP is complete, implementation and enforcement has not yet been undertaken partly diminishing the perceived success of the Action Plan (2005).

3 Significant regulatory decisions are still made at level II, even though they are presented as technical. For the first Level II measures (Market Abuse adopted in October 2003) it has been shown that Level II also involved policy decisions (European Parliamentary Financial Services Forum 2003). Avgerinos (2002) notes the distinction between where actual essential rule-making ends and implementation begins can be problematic making the distinction between political and technical ambiguous.

the elaboration of Level II regulations. CESR is also to facilitate consistent (day-to-day) implementation of Community law at the national level. Level III rules do not have any legally binding force, instead relying on softer measures and voluntary convergence. Finally, in the fourth level, national regulatory authorities implement the directive. It is the role of the Commission to ensure states' compliance with the legislation at this level.[4]

The ESC is thus created as part of this process. It is a committee of governmental actors from each member state operating within the European Commission. Primarily active in the second level of the comitology process, the ESC acts in both advisory and regulatory capacities. Its advisory functions revolve around advising the Commission on policy issues and potential Level 1 developments. The regulatory function of this committee is 'to assist the Commission when it takes decisions on implementing measures under Article 202 of the EC Treaty' (European Commission 2005c). In essence this is the committee responsible for creating and implementing Level 2 regulation, which is still legally binding.

Also created to take an advisory and coordinating role in the Lamfalussy process was CESR. Created in 1997 the original forum, FESCO, was to informally encourage collaboration between the EU's different financial services sector regulators. The creation of CESR enhanced the activities of this group, making it a formal and integral part of the drafting of securities regulation at the European level. In particular, the European Commission requests formal advice from CESR on the potential structure of Level II legislation. Through this role, the advice of CESR is not only taken into account but in many cases seems to generally frame what the European Commission proposes to the ESC for Level II measures. The Secretary General of FESCO noted very early in the FSAP venture that 'FESCO is the necessary engine that links the broad directives adopted at the European level to the daily harmonized applications of such legislation at the domestic level' (Demarigny 2001: 134).[5] CESR has been capable of establishing itself as a credible source of European authority for national regulators and market actors. For instance, Howard Davies, the Chairman of the Financial Services Authority, the British financial services sector regulator, stated, 'I am not sure that the directives, in practice, have been as spare as Lamfalussy envisaged. But what has certainly worked is the new regulatory network. CESR, as it is modestly known, has begun to be an effective deliverer of what we might call secondary legislation' (2003). In its coordinating role, CESR continues in its FESCO role of providing a forum for national regulators to discuss and potentially harmonize the national implementation of EU securities law. Most of our discussion about input legitimacy focuses on the work of this committee

The European Commission has started assessing the FSAP and the Lamfalussy process. It issued a Green Paper in the spring of 2005 on the future steps to be taken to further integration and a White Paper is forthcoming. It is expected that the White Paper will not propose a second version of the FSAP, focusing instead on left-over business from the first Action Plan with only a few minor new measures. Regulatory fatigue is said to have set in preventing another ambitious Plan as put forth at the turn of the millennium.

4 Because many of the measures of the FSAP are not yet implemented nationally, we will not focus on this level of decision-making. At Level IV, national governments must implement EU policies so the issue of legitimacy can be argued to be brought back to the traditional arena of the state.

5 Authors' translation.

2.2. Output Legitimacy

The Lamfalussy process was created in large part to help increase the output legitimacy of policies in the FSAP. [6] It sought to achieve this by increasing the efficiency and effectiveness of financial services policymaking by replacing a system that was perceived as ill-equipped to deal with the needs of a rapidly changing marketplace. In its 2001 Report, the Committee of Wise Men made the strong point that 'the European Union has no divine right to the benefits of an integrated financial market. It has to capture those benefits by building an integrated European market... If it does not succeed, economic growth, employment and prosperity will be lower, and competitive advantage will be lost to those outside the European Union' (2001: 8).

The Lamfalussy process has been seen as an effective way to increase efficiency. The EU has already extended its use, largely unaltered, to include the fields of banking and insurance. This indicates 'that there is overall agreement among political actors concerned with financial markets that the process is a viable instrument through which decision-making can be made more efficient' (Inter-Institutional Monitoring Group 2004: 37). In addition, the policy process is intended to increase the effectiveness of legislation by shifting much of the detail of directives to Level II. This is intended to allow for the easier altering of the details of regulation as the market evolves without having to renegotiate a new broad directive. Such an approach allows for flexibility while maintaining the overall broad substantive basis of the directive. Finally, the addition of more avenues for private consultation and participation can also be important for increasing output efficiency. Information obtained from individuals or groups that are affected by the legislation can be used to improve the design of policy and, therefore, their effectiveness.

However, there are still concerns which emerge within this process. For example, while the involved actors seem generally pleased with its efficiency over previous directive negotiations, recent consultations have indicated that market actors' concerns have shifted towards the quality of legislation rather than the speed of its adoption. (Inter-Institutional Monitoring Group 2003: 11) Therefore, care must be given to ensure that effectiveness is maintained and not simply efficiency.

2.3. Input Legitimacy

As argued in the theoretical section, there are three key institutional features which seek to enhance participation and representation of the public in the process: co-decision, transparency, and network governance. The first important attempt to achieve input legitimacy is the use of co-decision at Level I of the Lamfalussy process. Formalizing a potential veto point for the European Parliament, the EU's only directly elected body, the process does move slightly closer to ensuring input legitimacy through representation. Furthermore, recent reviews of the Lamfalussy process have highlighted that the creation of

---

6 Effectiveness, as to the extent to which there actually is financial services sector integration, is hard to measure. Suffice to say for our purpose that integration in the financial services sector is uneven. The securities industry, for instance, tends to be more integrated than banking, money markets as well as the government and corporate bond markets are particularly integrated (Freixas *et al.* 2004).

directives at Level I has not been marked by a conflictual relationship. The Inter-Institutional Monitoring Group (2004) found that there has been a significant improvement in co-operation between the Council, Commission and Parliament since the introduction of the new policy process. It highlights,

> 'conscious efforts have been undertaken between the Secretariat of the Economic and Monetary Affairs Committee (ECON) of the European Parliament and DG Internal Market on the Commission side to work closely together and pick up emerging difficulties well in advance. The Group was informed that a positive new experience has been holding monthly meetings between the two services – thereby concretising the "systematic contacts on informal basis" suggested in the original report of the Wise Men' (Inter-Institutional Monitoring Group 2004: 11).

The role of Parliament in creation of Level II legislation is more circumscribed. However, Parliament is informed of the ongoing policy process and it does issue opinions on proposed measures at this level. As the ESC's mandate states, 'The Commission will inform the European Parliament on a regular basis of the ESC's proceedings acting under its regulatory capacity. It will send it at the same time and on the same terms as to the members of the ESC, the agendas for Committee meetings, the results of any votes and the summary records of meetings, as well as the list of the authorities to whom the representatives of the Member States belong' (Commission of the European Communities 2001: 4). Specific to the Lamfalussy process is that the European Parliament receives more than just the ESC approved draft measures for review but is kept informed by the Commission of the drafts that the ESC considers (Inter-Institutional Monitoring Group 2003: 10). After the completion of a final draft regulation at this level the Parliament has one month to examine it. If the Parliament determines that the measures exceed the scope of the Level II mandate it issues a resolution stating this fact. However, this is not a formal veto or call-back mechanism. Therefore, the level of accountability that the ESC has towards the Parliament is somewhat curtailed.[7]

A second input legitimization strategy is the increase of transparency. Since the introduction of the Lamfalussy process it is generally agreed among market participants and regulators that the transparency of the regulatory process has improved and this is an important feature of the process's success (Inter-Institutional Monitoring Group 2004; European Commission 2005b). The information made available, particularly via the internet, is quite extensive. In the case of the ESC, agendas and summaries of committee meetings are made available on the Europa website. In addition, they have begun to publish written explanations of those places where the secondary legislation adopted and CESR's advice differs. CESR also publishes consultation papers, some committee minutes and feedback papers on consultations on its website. In addition, it has formalized and made available its procedures for public consultation. The use of feedback statements and explanations of policy decisions also help to lower perceptions of an opaque and secretive decision-making process. Nonetheless there are still areas where transparency has not been achieved. For example, the Commission argues that transparency could be increased if CESR were to adopt a more transparent set of procedures for elaborating their advice and opinions (European

---

7 In practice, however, the process which has developed does appear to maintain the more collaborative nature of Level I. There has been no resolution of this type issued by the Parliament to date.

Commission 2004: 9). There is, therefore, still room to increase the transparency and potentially the input legitimacy of the process.

The final input legitimization strategy within the Lamfalussy process is the inclusion of private actors and civil society. To address this we will look at the role of participation in the consultation mechanisms used in the Lamfalussy process. There are a number of access points with EU institutions promising consultation pre, during and post the implementation of a directive. The Inter-Institutional Monitoring Group's Second Report found that 'consultation has reached an appropriate level for all parties so that it is ensured that the views of market participants can be taken into account properly in the legislative and regulatory process' (2003: 5). It also finds that consultation activities at Level I are more extensive and systematic following the introduction of the Lamfalussy process, indicating more access points for private input and response to directives and regulations. The actual representativeness, however, is skewed heavily toward input from business actors over other potential stakeholders.

Providing a number of key points for participation at level II, CESR is also an important feature of input legitimacy primarily because it only forwards its advice to the European Commission after having consulted with the market. There are essentially three formal participatory mechanisms used by CESR in consultation - consultation papers, expert and market committees and open hearings.

Respondent	Total # Responses	Average # Responses per Consultation	Percentage of Total Responses
European Industry/Business Associations (Financial Sector)	716	15.57	42.62%
Corporations	593	12.89	35.30%
European Industry/Business Associations (Non-financial)	118	2.57	7.02%
Governmental Actors (Non-European)	96 (29)	2 (1)	5.80% (1.72%)
Foreign and International Associations	94	2	5.60%
Individuals	30	0.7	1.79%
Investor/Shareholder Groups	12	0.3	0.71%
Consumer Groups	13	0.3	0.77%
Other Civil Society	8	0.2	0.48%
Total	*1680*	*36.53*	*100%*

Figure 1. Breakdown of CESR Consultation Responses.

The first, consultation papers, is the key mechanism used by CESR to consult with the public. To assess this mechanism each consultation was reviewed and respondents were divided into categories covering a range of business, governmental and other civil society actors. Overall, response rates have been solid with 1680 responses to 46 consultations held between October 2002 and 10 June 2005. However, the lack of civil society participation in this mechanism is clearly apparent even through a simple cursory review of the consultation responses. There are no responses from outside of business or governmental actors in twenty of the forty-six consultations. Out of all the responses received by CESR for all of its on-line consultation, only 63 were from individuals, consumer organizations, investor groups, organized labour, and any other group that is not a corporation or business association. That equates to less than four per cent of all responses to CESR's online consultations. This is compared to forty-two per cent of all responses coming from financial services sector industry associations within Europe. Another thirty-five percent of the respondents to the consultations were corporations.[8] The dominance of business groups in the consultation process is made apparent in Figure 1.

A second access point for participation is sitting on one of the market consultation committees created by CESR. CESR generally creates a market consultation committee of relevant players for each area of regulation it is working on. Members of these committees are drawn from a variety of market participants (including consumers and end-users) that spread across the member states. The role of these participants is to provide technical advice during the drafting of proposals and they are not to represent national or firm-specific interests. Currently there are seven active market consultation committees. The make-up of these committees demonstrates clearly once again that there are only a handful of non-corporate or business actors involved in these committees.[9] CESR also established the overarching, permanent *Market Participants Consultative Panel* whose work focuses more broadly on the working priorities of the institution and assessment of developments in the market. This panel was established in June 2002 at the urging of the European Parliament (European Commission 2004). Its undertakes a number of different roles: to assist in the definition of priorities and work program, to provide commentary on how CESR carries out its work, and in particular how it puts into practice its *Public Statement of Consultation Practices*, to alert CESR to regulatory inconsistencies and suggest areas for further work to improve supervisory co-ordination, and finally to inform CESR on major developments and to identify new elements in financial markets (CESR 2005). The Panel meets three times a year. Individuals from shareholders groups are represented in two of the fifteen places, including the President of Euroshareholders (a main European level shareholders association).

A final method of consulting with industry and end-users used by both the ESC and CESR is holding open hearings around proposals in coordination with the internet consultations. The Commission has held a small number of such hearings, while CESR has held 23 open hearings since January 2003. The lack of information about these meetings renders assessment based on representation difficult.

Interestingly, the EU bodies, particularly the Commission, have taken note of the lack of consumer and SME participation. To remedy this, in 2004 the Commission set up an independent expert forum – FIN-USE – to respond to financial services regulation proposals in the general Lamfalussy process from the perspective of users and consumers. The panel of 10 Commission appointed experts has a mandate 'to strengthen the role of consumers and small businesses in the on-going evolution of the EU financial services sector' (FIN-USE

8 Similar statistics were compiled for the Committee of European Banking Supervisors (CEBS) and the Committee of European Insurance and Occupational Pension Supervisors (CEIOPS). These organizations were created more recently, in 2003, and therefore have produced fewer consultation documents. However, from the limited number of consultations the results appear similar to CESR.

9 Looking at EU committees on a broader scale we can find further confirmation of this trend toward business. Mahoney argues: 'Far from fostering balanced dialogue, the committee system reinforces the bias of the interest group community. Business remains the dominant force, making up approximately 72% of the groups (trade, business and professional) holding a committee position' (2004: 450). She notes a number of resource-based reasons for this, including the financial resources to maintain a Brussels-based office and staff to undertake a broader range of activities.

2004). The forum is to respond to Commission initiatives which involve consumers and small businesses and the larger financial services industry as well as to identify and promote issues that affect these actors. In its first request, FIN-USE was asked to provide opinions on the Reports of four Expert Groups which reviewed the integration of financial services markets in Europe as the FSAP mandate came to an end. FIN-USE argued that on the whole reports largely ignore concrete user concerns. It also disagreed with the overall implications of the reports which imply that protecting user interests is best accomplished by competition, reducing barriers created by national protective legislation, encouraging supplier home country regulation and prioritizing self-regulatory tools. In responding to this, FIN-USE put forward ten general recommendations for further developments in financial services regulation that take into account user concerns and protection. They also provided a number of specific recommendations to each report (FIN-USE 2004). Therefore, FIN-USE could become a potentially important avenue particularly for consumers and other societal interests to assess the regulatory process of financial services, although this is not guaranteed.

3. Discussion

It thus appears that the European Commission has made a real effort to improve input legitimacy in financial services sector policymaking. Despite these efforts, there remain some concerns in regards to popular participation. Certainly, there is more room for input in this policy field than exists in other areas of policymaking, especially if compared to monetary policy. As stated in the introduction, financial services sector policymaking at the national level also poses issues of legitimacy and democracy. The steps, therefore, taken by the EU are significant. Yet, as financial services sector integration starts to move away from the securities fields more towards banking, an area that affects directly a broader segments of society, EU institutions will need to find ways to better incorporate end-users and consumers in decision-making.

There are a number of potential reasons that likely affect the current lack of participation from actors outside of the corporate sector in the regulation of financial services. One partial explanation for the general lack of engagement with a broader spectrum of society in this sector is the disconnection of the working of financial services from the popular discourse more generally. Finance is often a highly technical area which encourages a reliance on expert regulation and discourages an active non-business civil society from forming. Given the attention drawn because of the many corporate scandals in the previous few years and the stated importance of these initiatives to the overall integration of European by officials publicly this argument seems too simplistic. The world of financial markets has been thrust more into the general popular consciousness, creating opportunities for a wide-ranging civil society to emerge.

The reliance on technical language in the consultation process, particularly in the calls for response, would seem to encourage fewer non-industry responses. In many ways, the structural foundation for access exists but the discursive institutions within it may be minimizing its effectiveness. For example and as stated earlier, CESR is generally transparent in that it posts most of its documentation on its website. However, simply sifting through the document requires a certain technical expertise which may not be possessed by many of societal actors. In addition, over 30 of the 48 internet consultations by CESR were framed as technical discussions or as calls for evidence. One can assume that this is not a conscious attempt to close the discussion and exclude non-business dialogue with CESR given their stated consultation policy. However, CESR's proposals are largely reflections of the mandates passed down from the Commission, who in turn are attempting to technically flesh out broad directives passed through the Council and Parliament at Level I for the ESC. In essence, the very language of the comitology process works to discursively confine this level to a language of technical elements and the implementation techniques, although the decisions made often may have much broader effects. The Inter-Institutional Monitoring Group's most recent review of the Lamfalussy process has highlighted this problem. They note, 'Where texts are highly technical, non-specialists with limited language skills are effectively shut out of the process" (2004: 24). In addition to language issues posed by the large scale use of technical jargon, consultations with consumers and SMEs are also hampered by the common practice of providing consultation documents through CESR only in English, placing the onus on national regulatory agencies to provide translation in many places.

Third, on a material level the lack of participation of social actors in financial services sector policymaking likely relates to the differences in available resources between business and non-business actors. Non-business groups often have fewer financial and administrative resources available to participate in different consultations.

The emphasis on speed and efficient implementation has also lead to rather tight deadlines on some consultations, adding to the stress on resources. Even for business, the speed of CESR's consultations has posed some problems. There are a number of market actors who have indicated that short consultation and examination deadlines have limited the quality of interaction (Deutsche Bank 2005). In addition to this stress, non-business groups often need to keep an eye on a much larger scope of initiatives in a number of different sectors and directorates, stretching scarce resources even further. This does not hold as true for many of the business actors involved as they are often more specific in nature. This also does not hold as true for investor groups, who are more visibly active in the financial services consultative practice discussed above. On a systemic level, this structural disadvantage is well recognized in the academic literature on interest representation at the EU level (Mazey and Richardson 1999; Schmitter 2000; Greenwood 1997).

Even though there is a structure in place for open consultation with society in the Lamfalussy process, this has not directly translated into broad participation. Looking at groups that are actually involved, there is a noticeable lack of participation from consumers, labour and other social groups and a plethora of interaction from business interests. This is problematic when one considers the broader implications that financial services regulation has on economic features like the cost of capital, as well as the more direct elements of retail finance.

4. Conclusion

Returning to the original question – the extent to which the policy process facilitates or impedes the legitimacy of policymaking in the financial services sector – it is clear that the policy process in financial services does achieve a certain amount of both output and input legitimacy. The legislative agenda of the Financial Services Action Plan was implemented on time and the regulatory process favours consultation with market actors. However, complete implementation of measures across the Union remains a problem (impeding the possibility for the EU to fully profit from financial services sector integration) as is the inability of end-users and consumers to fully access the policy process.

It is obviously impossible to generalize the conducted analysis to the whole of policymaking in the EU. However, the findings obtained in the financial services sector suggest a real effort by the institutions of the Union to not only appear legitimate through output legitimacy, but to respond to critics and improve input legitimacy. Experimenting with new policy processes is obviously easier in technical fields that have active policy networks, as is the case in finance. However, such policy fields are also highly at risk of being exclusionary. In the case of finance, achieving inclusion is particularly important due to its central role for furthering economic integration and for the health of the general health of the economy. Broadly speaking, the banking sector is much more open to political debate than the securities field. Until the EU undertakes real integration in banking, groups representing larger social interest may simply be less interested in participating in policymaking. Nonetheless, if the EU is to increase its overall legitimacy, it is necessary for it to work towards ensuring inclusion across all policy fields. Our analysis suggests that in finance the EU is at least making progress towards that end. Since more generally financial policy is seen as among the policy fields that are most resistant to input legitimacy this progress is an especially significant challenge to those who see the EU as incapable of legitimizing itself.

References

Avgerinos, Yannis V. (2002) 'Essential and Non-essential Measures: Delegation of Powers in EU Securities Regulations' *European Law Journal*, 8(2): 269-89.

Commission of the European Communities (2001) *Commission Decision of 6 June 2001 establishing the European Securities Committee* (COM (2001) 1493 final), Brussels, 6 June.

Committee of European Securities Regulators (2001) *Public Statement on Consultation Practices,* [Online], Available from: <http://www.cesr-eu.org> [15 September 2005].

Committee of European Securities Regulators (2004) *The Role of CESR at Level 3 Under the Lamfalussy Process*, Consultation Paper, 28 October 2004, [Online], Available from: <http://www.cesr-eu.org> [15 September 2005].

Committee of the Wise Men (2001) *Final Report of the Committee of the Wise Men on the Regulation of European Securities Markets*, Brussels, [Online], Available from: http://www.europa.eu.int/comm/internal_market/securities/docs/lamfalussy/wisemen/ final-report-wise-men_en.pdf [19 October 2005]

Davies, Howard (2003) 'The Future Shape of European Regulation of the Capital Markets – An Introduction from the FSA', *Financial Services Authority Conference* London, [Online], Available from: <http://www.fsa.gov.uk/ pubs/speeches/sp117.html> [15 August 2005].

Demarigny, Fabrice (2001) 'Le Forum of European Securities Regulators: Une réponse au besoins de regulation du marché unique des services financiers', *Revue d'économie financière*, 60 : 125-134.

Dehousse, Renaud (2003) 'Comitology: who watches the watchmen?', *Journal of European Public Policy*, 10(5): 798–813.

Deutsche Bank (2005) *Response to Green Paper on Financial Services Policy (2005-2010)*, [Online], Available from: <http://www.dbresearch.com/PROD/ DBR_INTERNET_DEPROD/PROD0000000000190099.pdf> [1 August 2005].

Egeberg, Morten, Schaefer, Gunther F. and Trondal, Jarle (2003) 'The Many Faces of EU Committee Governance', *West European Politics*, 26(3): 19–40.

European Commission (2004) *Commission Staff Working Document - The Application of the Lamfalussy Process to EU Securities Markets Legislation: A preliminary assessment by the Commission services*, SEC(2004) 1459, Brussels, 15.11.2004 [Online], Available from: <http://europa.eu.int/comm/ internal_market/securities/docs/lamfalussy/sec-2004-1459_en.pdf> [15 Sept-ember 2005].

European Commission (2005) *Green Paper on Financial Services Sector Policy* (2005-2010), [Online], Available from: <http://europa.eu.int/comm/ internal_market/ finances/actionplan/index_en.htm.> [1 August 2005]

European Commission (2005b) *Lamfalussy Review - Summary of responses to the consultation organised by the European Commission,* [Online], Available from: <http://europa.eu.int/comm/internal_market/securities/docs/lamfalussy/ review_synopsis_en.pdf> [15 October 2005]

European Commission (2005c) *Summary Record of the 29th Meeting of the European Securities Committee / Members* (ESC/14/2005), March 21st.

European Parliamentary Financial Services Forum (2003) *The Lamfalussy Process: does it work and what are the consequences of extension?,* Briefing Paper prepared, 2 December 2003 [Online], Available from: <http://www.epfsf.org/meetings/2003/ briefings/briefing_2dec2003.htm>, [1 August 2005]

FIN-USE. (2004) *Financial Services, Consumers and Small Businesses - A User Perspective on the Reports on Banking, Asset Management, Securities and Insurance of the Post FSAP Stocktaking Groups*. Brussels, 4 October (final), [Online], Available from: <http://europa.eu.int/ comm/internal_market/fin-use_forum/documents/index_en.htm.> [15 September 2005].

Freixas, Xavier, Philipp Hartmann and Colin Mayer (2004) 'The Assessment: European Financial Integration', *Oxford Review of Economic Policy*, 20(4): 475-489.

Greenwood, Justin (1997) *Representing Interest in the European Union*, London: Macmillan Press Ltd.

Héritier, Adrienne (1999) 'Elements of democratic legitimation in Europe: an alternative perspective', *Journal of European Public Policy,* 6(2): 269–82.

Horeth, Marcus (1999) 'No Way Out for the Beast? The Unsolved Legitimacy Problem of European Governance', *Journal of European Public Policy,* 6: 249-268.

Inter-Institutional Monitoring Group (2003) *Second Interim Report Monitoring the Lamfalussy Process,* Brussels, 10 December 2003 [Online] Available from: < http:// www.europa.eu.int/ comm/internal_market/ securities/docs/ monitoring/second-report/2003-12-monitoring_en.pdf> [15 October 2005]

Inter-Institutional Monitoring Group (2004) *Third Report Monitoring the Lamfalussy Process*, [Online], Available from: <http://europa.eu.int/comm/ internalmarket/securities/ docs/monitoring/third-report/2004-11-monitoring_en.pdf> [1 September 2005].

Joerges, Christian and Jürgen Neyer (1997) 'From intergovernmental bargaining to deliberative political processes: the constitutionalization of comitology', *European Law Journal*, 3: 273–99.

Josselin, Daphne (1997) *Money Politics in the New Europe: Britain, France and the Single Financial Market*, New York: St-Martin's Press.

Lord, Christopher (2001) 'Assessing democracy in a contested polity', *Journal of Common Market Studies,* 39(4): 641–661.

Lord, Christopher and Beetham, David (2001) 'Legitimizing the EU: is there a ''postparliamentary basis'' for its legitimation?', *Journal of Common Market Studies,* 39(3): 443–62.

Magnette, Paul (2003) 'European Governance and Civic Participation: Beyond Elitist Citizenship?', *Political Studies,* 51: 144–160.

Mahoney, Christine (2004) 'The Power of Institutions: The State and Interest Group Activity in the European Union', *European Union Politics*, 5(4): 441-466.

Majone, Giandomenico (1999) 'The regulatory state and its legitimacy problems', *West European Politics,* 22(1): 1–13.

Majone, Giandomenico (2000) 'The credibility crisis of Community regulation', *Journal of Common Market Studies,* 38(2): 273–302.

Mazey, Sonia, and Richardson, Jeremy (1993) *Lobbying in the European Community*, Oxford: Oxford University Press.

Michalowitz, Irina (2004) 'Analysing Structured Paths of Lobbying Behaviour: Why Discussing the Involvement of "Civil Society" Does not Solve the EU's Democratic Deficit', *European Integration,* 26(2): 145–170.

Moravcsik, Andrew (2004) 'Is there a Democratic Deficit in World Politics? A Framework for Analysis', *Government and Opposition*, 36(2): 336-363.

Rhinard, Mark (2002) 'The Democratic Legitimacy of the European Union Committee System', *Governance: An International Journal of Policy, Administration and Institutions*, 15(2): 185-210.

Scharpf, Fritz (1999) *Governing in Europe, Effective and Democratic?*, Oxford: Oxford University Press.

Schaub, Alexander (2005) 'The Lamfalussy Process Four Years On', *Journal of Financial Regulation and Compliance*, 13(2): 110-120.

Schmidt, Vivien A. (2004) 'The European Union: Democratic Legitimacy in a Regional State?', *Journal of Common Market Studies*, 42(5): 975-997.

Schmitter, Philippe C. (2000) *How to Democratize the European Union... And Why Bother?*, New York and Oxford: Rowman and Littelfield.

Shirreff, David (1999) 'Disgrace at the Heart of Europe', *Euromoney*, 366: 75.

Skogstad, Grace (2003) 'Legitimacy and/or policy effectiveness?: network governance and GMO regulation in the European Union', *Journal of European Public Policy,* 10(3): 321–338.

In: International Finance and Financial Services
Editor: Kristian L. Hagen, pp. 227-243 ISBN: 1-60021-756-7

Chapter 10

IT Service Delivery: Cost and Core Competency in Financial Services

Alea M. Fairchild

Introduction

IT outsourcing (ITO) received mainstream acceptance in the 1980s and the term still is used to describe, in regards to technology, "a contractual relationship with a specialized outside service provider for work traditionally done in-house" (Corbett and Associates, 2002). Although it is now recognized in industry that IT outsourcing relationships actually are more related to strategic partnerships than to sub-contracting activities, the term reflects the fact that the work was seen as moving "outside" the company, or "outsourced".

Business process outsourcing, or BPO, is a term coined in the mid-1990s to suggest something more specific. BPO implies a more comprehensive – or business process oriented – approach to outsourcing. Instead of outsourcing along traditional functional lines, the scope of the services outsourced cuts across the organization in a more horizontal way. BPO contracts are widely seen as being more inclusive, covering a great deal of process redesign work, redeployment and retraining of the people doing the work, and almost always include the information technology that enables and supports the business process. The goal of outsourcing models such as BPO is to provide opportunity for generating innovation, speed to market and shareholder value. But BPO is slow to take hold in financial services, for reasons involving trust, complexity, and risk in service delivery.

The current focus of IT in financial services is to increase innovation via decreasing costs, particularly on IT spending. Optimization of IT cost, using various methods of cost allocation, is one way that banks believe they can be more innovative and flexible in their portfolio of market offerings. Part of the optimization process is creating a cost mechanism that allows charge-back and service level agreement (SLA) relationships to IT usage. This may be done through an outsourcing relationship. In examining the economic benefits and tradeoffs for financial service institutions deciding for a closer, more integrated relationship with an external IT service provider, we examine whether the goal of opportunities for innovation is the case in the longer term, i.e. if the choice of IT infrastructure, as in hardware, applications and networks, is a factor in the innovation.

This paper first examines economic theory on the financial services industry issues of cost, innovation, relationships and trust, and risk. It then examines four recent case studies from late 2002 to describe the economics drivers for outsourcing and the thoughts on innovation from interviews conducted for this research. The paper concludes with an analysis of the cases, contribution to contracting research and future directions for this research.

Overview of Industry Rationale for IT Outsourcing

Organizational Economics

Agency theory and transaction cost economics are key aspects of organizational economics that provide theoretical perspectives on how firms can reduce costs and maximize shareholder value through the creation of their capital structure, including their use of technology. Beath and Straub (1989) employed an agency model to illustrate why information services may be managed in different ways: either by their users, by the different functions of the firm, or by centralization in an independent department.

Transaction cost economics examines the comparative costs of planning, adapting, and monitoring transaction activities under alternative governance structures. Lacity and Hirschheim (1993) employed a transaction cost framework, along with a political perspective, to interpret outsourcing decisions. They found that outsourcing decisions were, to a certain extent, based on cost considerations, and that managers were concerned with the threat of opportunism when evaluating a proposition from a supplier.

The theory of transaction cost economics, along with resource-based theory, provides an argument that ownership of infrastructure is increasingly important for firms with strategies that require support for innovation or rapid responsiveness to change, such as financial services. The determination of whether to make or buy resources, according to Williamson (1983, 1985), depends on the efficiency of the market for the needed resource (Duncan, 1995). The transaction cost view of outsourcing information technology would indicate that the longer a firm has been dependent on the market for its resources, the less flexibility its IT resources are likely to demonstrate. We discuss this in the case studies within this paper.

Besides cost and innovation, another economic factor in the outsourcing decision is the decision-maker's assumption about IT skills and abilities. This issue is explained in terms of the concept of core competencies (Prahalad and Hamel 1990, Stalk *et al.* 1992), as recent high-profile outsourcing cases in banking have given this rationale for their decision (e.g. Deutsche Bank). Proponents of this view argue that their firms are not in the technology business, and thus managing this effort in-house requires a diversification of skills that may distract from the firm's central goals (Duncan, 1995). In this view, the financial services firm is better off turning to a vendor whose purpose is IT service, and thus whose core competencies will be in IT development and management. Because vendors work with a variety of customers, they develop greater expertise with a wider variety of technologies. They also become more familiar with recurring problems and their solutions. Hence these service providers can offer a level of efficiency sufficiently greater than an in-house provider and will make the market costs of the service comparable to or better than could be achieved internally. (Duncan, 1995).

Infrastructural Motivations

Financial services spending on IT outsourcing is set to grow by 27 percent in Europe to GBP 7.7 billion by 2005, according to analysts Datamonitor (2003). Outsourcing IT by banks is more likely to be sought for a mix of cost reduction, service improvement and control of contextual determinants of transaction costs. Motivations and management decision basis for the banks to arrange IT outsourcing are mainly categorized into: 1) operating cost reduction, 2) predictable cost forecasting, 3) efficient capital allocation, 4) flexible business expansion, 5) professional resource assurance, and 6) availability of large-scale outsourcers.

The new wave of outsourcing arrangements is transforming the institutions' IT infrastructure and, in some cases, the applications and related business processes. From the perspective of traditional IT cost, the expectation is a reduction of expenses. As shareholder profits in financial services have been under severe pressure for quite some time, reducing cost is a pressing issue in the securities and investments space. In the post-dot-com world, financial service institutions (FSIs) increasingly use return on investment (ROI) models to increase the likelihood that projects achieve targeted returns. FSIs also base outsourcing decisions on qualitative factors, including information security requirements, operational risk considerations and process control. Evidence presented in Lacity-Hirschheim (1993), Datamonitor (1994), McFarland and Noland (1995), Alexander and Young (1996), O'Heney (1996) and Lacity *et al.* (1996), among others, supports Williamson's (1975) market transaction cost arguments for outsourcing and suggests several reasons for firms to outsource IT intensive processes (see Table 1).

Table 1. Reasons for Expansion of Outsourcing

Incentives to Outsource	Characteristics
Coping with Market Volatility	Companies abandon diversification to focus on core capabilities.
	Reduce cost structures by turning fixed into variable costs.
Lack of Skills	Improve access to more skilled staff.
Improve Budget Allocation	Exposure of otherwise difficult to control functions to market discipline.

Source: Lacity et al. (1996); Lacity and Hirschheim (1993); Wood and Batiz-Lazo (1997)

Outsourcing, where it occurs, tends to concentrate on standardized operations. Again in terms of the work of Williamson (1975), standardized processes, such as a help desk in an insurance company, lend themselves to straightforward outsourcing contracts with low transaction cost. Alpar and Saharia (1995) concur in that information systems functions that are stable and routine are the best outsourcing candidates.

Banks have traditionally viewed IT as a fixed cost, but with a high degree of complexity for cost/usage analysis. In addition to standardizing platforms in pursuing perceived economies of scope to achieve greater cost efficiency, some banks discovered competitive advantage is more clearly defined in terms of capabilities than range of products and markets (Teece, 1980). As costs become more complex and strategic, their control and strategic implications are more difficult to handle and make an outsourcing relationship difficult to measure from the perspective of strategic outcomes. Therefore the clarity of definition of tactical, straightforward costs of volume activities lends them to an outsourcing action, as shown in Figure 1.

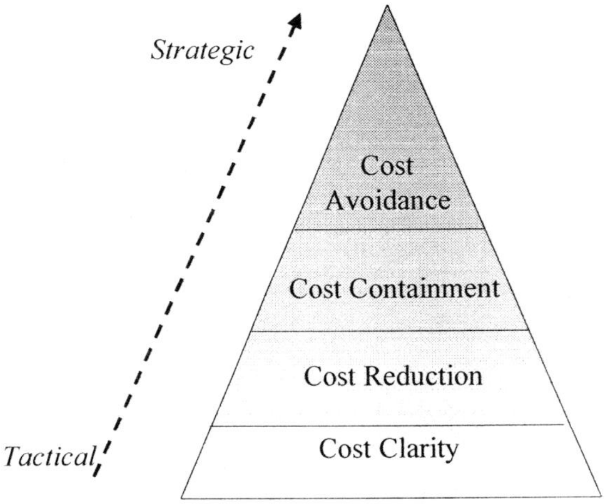

Figure 1. Tactical to strategic view of IT cost approach in banking (Saxton, 2003).

Core Competency and Innovation in FSI

An important driver of IT outsourcing is opportunity cost. This may be based on a reflection of what the core competency of a bank is and a determination of whether the bank of an IT service provider operates the technology infrastructure more effectively.

Banks themselves state that their core competency is integrated relationship management (IRM). IRM applications supporting the organization provide banks the ability to access a wide range of customer information, with the objective of improved account management, enhanced customer service and greater productivity in cross-selling other financial products and services. As the competition from non-bank financial services organizations (e.g. E*Trade, Charles Schwab) intensifies, a strategic IRM framework is a critical success factor for organizations. Such an IRM framework needs to leverage the potential of both traditional (branch, ATM) and newer channels (call centers, web, voice response). A comprehensive business perspective and technical framework are essential to the execution of such an IRM strategy. Organizations such as Wells Fargo, Charles Schwab, and Fidelity Investments view IRM as their core competency. These organizations have a comprehensive IRM strategy and an execution model that relies of continuous improvements to deliver superior customer service and maintain sustained strategic advantage over their competition.

In order to implement IRM, organizations have to transform their IT architecture from a point-to-point interface model to an architecture where consistent business rules and relationship strategies can be deployed across all channels of delivery.

Traditional innovation literature would suggest that organizations innovate by getting new and/or improved products to market, with innovation measured by market share of the product. However, in a service, the product is the *process*. Thus, innovation in banking lies more in process and organizational changes than in new product development in a traditional sense. Given the mix of content and infrastructure for providing a banking service, marketing, business units, IT, and a complex web of IT suppliers and consultants drive the innovation processes in banking (Frei *et al.*, 1998). Metrics for measuring a service can include market share, customer satisfaction and increased revenue growth.

Financial services performance improvements that drive innovation will arise in the integration of front- and back-office functions; i.e., in integrating business processes. Roach (1993) points out that the consolidation of back-office operations is due in large part to scale economies due to IT investments, but that these investments are becoming increasingly difficult to find.

Trust and Risk

In outsourcing relationships, specific investments have to be made by both parties that tie them together and specific arrangements are needed to safeguard the long-term perspective of the relationship because the transaction parties, given a chance, are naturally prone to opportunistic behavior (Van der Meer-Kooistra and Vosselman, 2000). If hierarchy were not an option, then transaction cost theory would recommend that special (contractual) arrangements are needed to make outsourcing relationships "safe" despite the asset specificity. In transaction cost theory, the characteristics of the transaction itself (degree and type of asset specificity, transaction frequency, and length of transaction period), the transaction environment (uncertainty about future contingencies, extent of risks and nature of institutional environment) and the characteristics of the transaction parties (risk attitude, experience, reputation, bargaining power) need to be considered when choosing between alternative governance options (see Van der Meer-Kooistra and Vosselman, 2000).

Transaction cost theory, however, does not consider the possibility of using trust as a means to reduce the risk of opportunistic behavior. Williamson (1993) acknowledges that the "social embeddedness" (Granovetter, 1985) of transactions has an influence on the contracting parties' behavior and can reduce their propensity towards opportunism, but he treats social embeddedness largely as an institutional-environmental factor and thereby denies trust the status of a means to reduce the risk of opportunistic behavior in inter-firm relationships its own right. Van der Meer-Kooistra and Vosselman (2000) combine transaction cost theory and trust in their conceptual model and distinguish between market-based, bureaucracy-based and trust-based patterns as three ideal types of management control patterns in inter-firm relationships. Either a bureaucracy-based or a trust-based pattern of inter-firm governance can govern outsourcing relationships. We discuss this further in the case studies in this paper.

The differences between ITO and BPO are defined in Figures 2. ITO activities are generally tactical in the sense that they are standardized and are volume oriented. BPO activities, in contrast, are generally strategic and involve core competencies with value-generating processes. In either ITO or BPO, the outsourcing relationship goes further than just substituting for an internal IT service and a contractual relationship is sought where the service provider assumes responsibility for one or more of the organization's IT or even business functions (Hoecht, 2002). In this case, the relationship includes the transfer of resources of the outsourcing organization to the external service provider and involves a long-term commitment with a detailed legally binding contract. Significant organizational changes are needed as the role of the internal IT department changes form being a supplier of its own services to assuming the function of a controller and broker of IT and/or business services. A very high level of trust is required for such relationships as the risks involved are substantial. Because of the long-term timeframe, the level of resources committed and the emphasis on cost efficiency, a bureaucracy-based approach to relationship management and management control is often pursued. This is not always the best fit to the task, and leads to disappointment on both sides and further enforces the desire to impose a high level of management control.

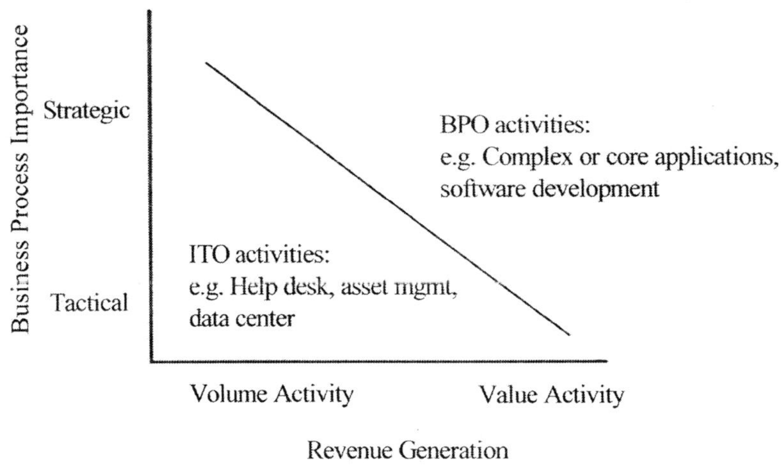

Figure 2. ITO vs. BPO: trade-off between process control and revenue generation (Saxton, 2003).

Research Methodology

The research methodology used for this case study research on outsourcing economics and innovation was a combination of academic literature review and structured primary research interviews with key banking and IT service delivery executives, enhanced with secondary research. The questionnaires for the case studies with the four banks chosen were guided questions, targeted to senior executives familiar with the outsourcing deal under discussion. Each case study had at least two sides to the story: interviews both with the bank and with the IT outsourcing provider.

The interviews, given the different geographies, were conducted by telephone with the most senior person available in regards to the respective outsourcing deal. Each participant was given the questionnaire in advance, and each interview lasted 30 – 45 minutes in length. Table 2 provides an overview of the four cases discussed below, with details on the activity outsourced and the size and length of the contract.

Table 2. Overview of Case Studies

Bank	IT Provider	Date Announced	Outsourced IT Activity	Size, Length of Deal
Deutsche Bank	IBM	September 2002	Computing data centers	Euro 2.5 billion, 10 year deal
JP Morgan Chase	IBM	December 2002	IT infrastructure outsourcing of computing operations, including all data centers, data and voice networks, and help desks.	US$ 5 billion, 7 year deal
ABN AMRO	EDS	August 2002	Wholesale Client Services (WCS)	US$ 1.3 billion, 5 year deal
CIBC	HP	September 2002	IT infrastructure, previously a joint venture of both companies	US$ 1.5 billion, 7 year deal

CASE STUDY DESCRIPTIONS

Deutsche Bank / IBM

In September 2002, Deutsche Bank awarded IBM the outsourcing contract to manage its computer centers in continental Europe, with activities starting in early 2003. The impact to the IT organization of Deutsche Bank is a transition of Deutsche Bank resources, systems and approximately 900 employees to IBM during the first quarter of 2003. Deutsche Bank also gains a new computing facility run by IBM in Rhine-Main region of Germany.

Deutsche Bank stated at the announcement that the objective was to reduce operating costs from outsourcing a sizeable portion of its European IT operations as well as to become more flexible in the use of its IT resources and ability to adopt new technologies. A spokesman for Deutsche Bank said in his interview that key to the deal was IBM's ability to update Deutsche Bank to state-of-the-art technology while offering it a utility model for purchasing IT resources. The spokesman commented: "This is being driven by our strategy to get rid of fixed costs [and] areas that we feel are not our core competencies." Deutsche Bank was impressed by IBM's e-business on demand technology, which would allow Deutsche Bank a more flexible answer to the changing financial services arena by integrating core business processes and systems. The bank expects to save $1 billion over the next decade through its outsourcing deal with IBM.

Deutsche Bank felt comfortable outsourcing its data processing operations because IBM and other IT services vendors have proven that they can provide sufficient uptime and security. IBM was seen as a strong partner to overall manage technological and operational risks and to ensure long term technological innovations. And IBM provided a valuable career perspective for Deutsche Bank employees through joining a global, well-respected IT-company.

From IBM's point of view, there were a number of reasons why IBM felt, together with subcontractor CSC, that it was a good match for Deutsche Bank's objectives in this activity. These include the fact that the IBM culture is fairly close to current Deutsche Bank corporate culture and that IBM's European coverage (in terms of geography and capital IT investment) minimizes risk for Deutsche Bank.

JP Morgan Chase / IBM

JP Morgan Chase outsourced its IT infrastructure of computing operations, including all data centers, data and voice networks, and help desks to IBM. The impact to the IT organization is a transition of 4,000 contractors and employees to IBM in first half of 2003. The IBM's "e-business on demand" utility cost model, plus service visualization via IBM's Utility Management Infrastructure, was key in the bank's decision to outsource, according to the managing director of the Enterprise Technology Services Group at J.P. Morgan Chase. In the current economic climate, he added, "it is more attractive for us to be on a more variable, pay-as-you-use structure instead of investing a significant amount of capital in bricks and mortar and hardware and software."

Technology investment is seen now in terms of governance, according to the Vice President (VP) of Financial Markets at IBM in the U.S., and outsourcing is a way to reallocate capital. The reason for this outsourcing trend, according to this IBM VP, is simple: "Trade volumes are down, assets under management are decreasing, and financial services companies are looking to exchange fixed cost for variable cost structures." IBM Research has created a service visualization capability to allow IBM to show the customer whether it is a business process or technology bottleneck that is causing the service problem.

ABN AMRO / EDS

ABN AMRO negotiated a contract with EDS to provision technology services and applications development in the major countries in which Wholesale Client Strategic (WCS) business unit operates. WCS provides investment-banking services to corporate, institutional and public sector clients worldwide. The technology benefit was a more cost-effective method to deliver services more efficiently.

The impact on the IT organization of ABN AMRO is the transition of several hundred employees to EDS, with certain core employees staying on the ABN AMRO side of the IT management. Under the five-year deal, EDS also allocates personnel resources and assigns several thousand employees to ABN AMRO sites in the Netherlands, United Kingdom or wherever necessary within the WCS organization. ABN AMRO's objective was not only IT cost reduction, which is important for serving the clients of ABN AMRO, but also a more flexible cost base.

An interview with the Executive VP for ABN AMRO's Wholesale Client (WCS) Strategic Business Unit led to a discussion of how strategic IT investment projects have been traditionally a very low percentage of the total portfolio. Once the group realized that many parts of the infrastructure were either discretionary or mandatory for business operations, they focused on how to reduce the total return to shareholders by cost transparency and accountability in the service delivery model. Transparency of costs and governance were some of the key drivers for the outsourcing activity. This was due to their performance culture and need to create management for value metrics by doing "smart sourcing" to control cost and risk more effectively.

EDS believes it provides value in these deals by way of its smart organization and shared services. For example, EDS is the fifth largest mortgage processor in the world. EDS sees cost and risk drivers for outsourcing in banking as cost reduction, core and supportive functions, Basel II and necessary performance metrics for the bank to measure transactions against service levels. EDS offers its "service dashboard" to enable companies to examine the benefits from the outsourcing activity. This dashboard monitors service and client satisfaction using different colors, e.g., green (good), yellow (fair), red (unacceptable), based on information from the client site. EDS defines cost, risk, leveraging of skills, and the format of reporting all to be concerns of ABN AMRO in this deal.

CIBC / HP

HP bought CIBC's 51 percent interest in the service provider INTRIA joint venture, given total control to HP as it already owned the other 49 percent. HP acquired in this deal approximately 1,280 IT professionals, related technology assets, and two data centers in Toronto, Canada. The benefit to CIBC is HP Services will provide to CIBC a single point of accountability for the services covered under the agreement, as well as consistent service levels, improved billing, and more predictable IT costs.

Not long ago, many financial services companies were poised to leverage their considerable IT experience and technology investment to provide services for outside customers. When it joined with HP to form the INTRIA joint venture marketing outsourcing services to companies in North America since 1998, CIBC seemed prepared not only to commit significant internal resources to IT, but also to leverage those resources to expand its business. With the new deal, however, CIBC not only is withdrawing from IT as a line of business, but also is pulling back from investing in internal IT resources as well. This direction is reflective of the entire financial services industry, which is taking a " back to basics" approach that focuses on core business areas and reduced spending.

A CIBC senior executive vice president and its chief information officer said the agreement "lets us focus on what we do best – providing our customers secure and reliable financial services." CIBC can now focus its capital and its management time on its core banking business, yet "our customers can rest assured that the IT infrastructure supporting our financial services will be managed by the experts from HP Services," he added.

The change in structure, from HP's point of view, was one of total cost of ownership (TCO), a calculation done based on a set period of time. The original joint venture was created to offset costs for CIBC, based on a direct return on investment (ROI) calculation. As time progressed, 90 percent of the transaction was actually service in the form of infrastructure and 10 percent was actually assets off the books. After a period of time, it was no longer a strategic advantage for CIBC to be in this line of business, and the shift in ownership of the activity occurred.

Analysis of Cost, Risk and Efficiency in Case Examples

Cost and Service Delivery

In their objectives of IT cost optimization, banks are approaching cost with a new service delivery paradigm. The concept of utility computing and treating technology resources as a pay-as-you-go deal is part of the draw for outsourcing deals such as J.P. Morgan Chase / IBM, as discussed in the case studies. Optimizing IT costs while at the same time preparing for the future can be achieved through a combination of initiatives: saving costs initially, turning fixed into variable costs and investing the freed budget for the future.

Table 3. Economic Incentives to Outsource from Case Studies

Incentives to Outsource	DB / IBM	JP Morgan Chase / IBM	ABN AMRO / EDS	CIBC / HP
Coping with Market Volatility	Interested in utility costing benefit	Interested in utility costing benefit	Reduce cost by changing to variable costing structure	Shift services and capital costs off books to service provider
Lack of Skills	Career path for staff	Not applicable (NA), as the JPMC Labs for IT R&D are well-known	Career path for staff	Shift staff to provider for improved services
Improve Budget Allocation	Better control of data center function	Control cost via std. operations	Reduce exposure to market fluctuations	Leverage investment by shifting assets

Table 3 summarizes the incentives to outsource for the four case studies in terms of Table 1 shown in the literature review. As previously shown in Figure 1, what has driven the need to outsource was tactical, volume activities that needed to have more cost clarity in their make-up. For example, IBM offers the two banks utility pricing so that they can use usage-based costing methods, for example, providing longer-term cost reduction as the banks can see where they are having the most variable costing.

Trust and Risk via Governance

Given that none of these case studies can be considered market-based patterns of transactions (Van der Meer-Kooistra and Vosselman, 2000), as that is not characterized by investment in specific assets, these outsourcing relationships can be governed by either a bureaucracy-based or a trust-based pattern. As we see from the literature (e.g., Van der Meer-Kooistra and Vosselman, 2000), a bureaucracy-based pattern is characterized by types of asset specificity that can be protected by contractual rules and high frequency of transactions. A trust-based pattern is characterized by a high degree of asset specificity and high interdependency between the parties, with activities and output that cannot be measured accurately.

Each of these cases shows dependency for both parties, appropriate commitments for long-term contracting including SLAs and other governance mechanisms, and some market efficiencies. The pattern of outsourcing relationship for these case studies shows an evolution from the traditional multi-year outsourcing bureaucracy-based pattern to a more hybrid interactive, market and trust-based pattern *with business process asset specificity involving human assets, physical assets and/or site assets as the governance driver*. In these cases, trust had already been established as all of these parties previously had outsourcing relationships.

With the exception of ABN AMRO who asked seven companies to bid, the other banks asked for limited bids mainly to the single outsourcing party.

Zaheer and Venkatraman (1995) propose that a greater level of business process asset specificity creates an increased requirement for governance to offset the dependence caused by such specific assets. Indeed, a higher degree of dependence due to higher investments made in business processes (e.g. human assets, physical assets and site assets) requires that the relationship include greater safeguards to make sure their transaction specific assets will not be appropriated opportunistically. Therefore, control, risk sharing and value via innovation from modularity and flexibility of infrastructure all require a strict governance structure, based on trust and reputations.

As shown in Figure 3, based on a presentation of the outsourcing deal by ABN AMRO, this is how the bank sees cost, control, risk sharing and value via innovation for the change in service delivery paradigm. Of these four elements, control of the service and risk sharing are placed after the cost element in prioritization from the bank's perspective. Value is again considered the innovation, from the ability to be flexible and modular with service growth.

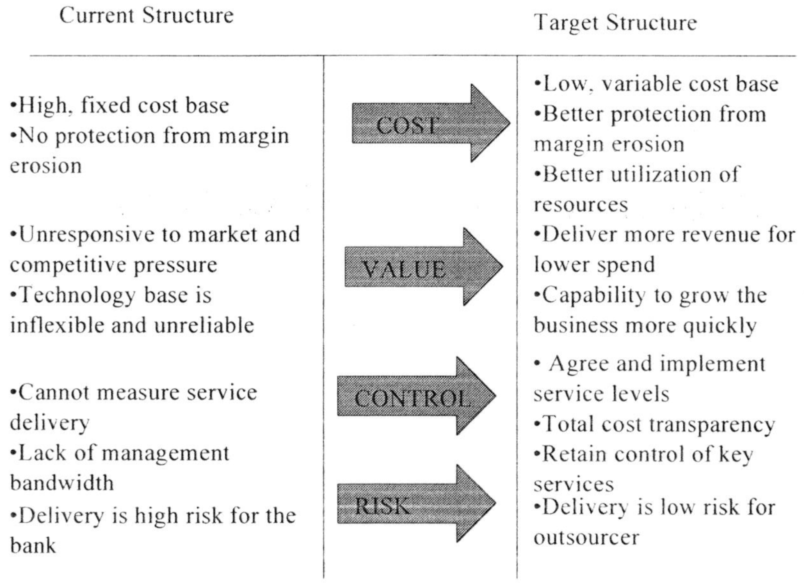

Figure 3. Service Delivery Paradigm Drivers (from ABN AMRO interview materials).

These recent deals have mainly emphasized the outsourcing of horizontal technology management functions, allowing financial institutions to more effectively manage scale issues through "services on demand."

Governance and Efficiency in the "Make or Buy" Paradigm

The TCE literature shows that supplier lock-in and switching costs of a long term IT outsourcing contract may disintegrate any supposed surplus from market efficiency (Mayer, 1999). Interestingly, this research showed that the banks involved define modularity (variability of IT costs) to be a precursor to flexibility to innovate, therefore achieving efficiencies in the market place. The investment in the IT service provider relationship is based on achieving that modularity, via these service delivery tools such as EDS' Service Dashboard, for which the bank could not do within its own governance infrastructure.

This research suggests that outsourcing of IT services can also be produced more efficiently if one of the parties invests in "transaction-specific" assets that cannot easily be put to other uses if the buyer/seller relationship breaks down. We suggest bargaining power in the relationship may be based on which side of the contractual relationship invests in these assets. Williamson (1985) uses the phrase "hostage taking" which could describe asset integration such as the integration of IT personnel into the outsourcing firm.

As these cases show, investments in asset specificity can take a variety of forms:

- *Site* or *location specificity*—one party locates its facilities in a favorable location to save on costs, such as the IBM / Deutsche Bank example;
- *Physical asset specificity*—investments are made in specialized equipment, such as a data center designed effectively in terms of capacity, for a particular customer such as Deutsche Bank in the Rhine-Main region of Germany;
- *Human capital specificity*—one or both of the parties develop skills or knowledge specific to their contractual relationship, as in the ABN AMRO case with WCS;
- *Dedicated capacity*—capacity is allocated to serve a customer who is large relative to market size, so that it would be difficult to find alternative customers, such as CIBC and HP Services; and
- *Brand name capital*—the parties must maintain the reputation of a shared brand name. Or in this case, given the publicity of the respective deals, the reputations of both parties are in the public eye as to the success of the relationship. This is the case for all four cases discussed above.

Contracts offer some protection for transaction-specific assets by tying the buyer and seller together for a specified period. However, bounded rationality precludes comprehensive ex ante contracting that specifies how the parties will behave in all possible circumstances. If contracts are inherently incomplete, parties may perceive potential gains from opportunistic behavior. As a result, attention must be focused on more complex (or internalized) governance mechanisms to fill gaps in the contract, settle disputes, and adapt to new conditions. Contracting parties may also make ex ante efforts to screen counterparties in terms of reliability or reputation, and/or design ex post safeguards to protect transaction-specific investments. As contracts become more flexible, they allow more potential for opportunism. Thus, asset specificity, combined with the potential for opportunism and bounded rationality, tends to move the efficient governance structure towards vertical integration on the spectrum. But bounded rationality tends to preclude organizations based entirely on markets or on vertical integration.

Ownership of Infrastructure and Property Rights Theory (PRT)

When asset specificity, bounded rationality, and opportunism make contracting problems severe, vertical integration may be needed to ensure that the value of transaction-specific assets is internalized. It can also allow for flexible redeployment of assets and personnel when the conditions surrounding the transaction change. But in these cases, contractually the human and capital assets outsourced may flow only to the IT service provider, such as in the IBM / Deutsche Bank and CIBC/HP cases.

Property rights theory (PRT), pioneered by Sanford Grossman and Oliver Hart (1986) and continued by Oliver Hart with John Moore (1990), begins with the TCE assumption that firm boundaries matter in situations where lock-in occurs due to long-term relationships and, because future is uncertain, cannot write complete long-term contracts. PRT therefore identifies each firm with the assets it owns and takes the view that asset ownership matters because owner has residual control rights. PRT then focuses on how ownership of physical assets, which gives residual rights of control over the assets, alters the efficiency of trading relations. PRT differs from the TCE in that it focuses on distortions in *ex ante* investments, in contrast to the TCE *ex post* haggling costs. PRT also assumes that efficiency losses are of the same nature in all ownership structures. That is, ownership of physical assets affects the parties' abilities to engage in opportunistic behavior not only in market transactions, but also within the firm.

When examining these cases using a PRT lens, ownership may be seen as a bargaining chip. When the IT service provider takes on board the human capital related to the capital equipment it is now managing, what happens if the contract fails? Do the personnel return to their original employer? The capital equipment may or may not stay on the books of the bank (each of these deals handles this differently), but the human capital has already been absorbed by the IT service provider into its own culture. In its complexity, ownership of the human resource is both *ex ante*, in how it removes the people from head count, and *ex post*, in haggling after the deal fails, to reacquire some of the human resources. The level of the outsourcing complexity in the transaction, which is associated with contractual incompleteness, will be the shifting parameter that may determine both incentive schemes and integration decisions.

This allocation of human capital, as well as location of capital assets *ex ante* and *ex post* of the transaction, starts to blur the firm boundaries in the complexity of the integration of resources within the long-term partnership. This is not the introduction of this concept to the industry, as banks have been using contractors for years to outsource specific elements of the bank's applications. These external contractors are considered part of the bank's IT team, and are treated as such in terms of access to information and input into IT strategy for their areas. Given EDS claims to be the fifth largest mortgage processor, what might this say about firm boundaries in terms of processing of information?

Implications on Firm Boundaries in Contracting

The rationale for IT outsourcing was given as reshaping the IT cost structure to make it more modular and flexible or variable. Banks foresee the strategic need for IT cost flexibility to innovate and respond to changing market conditions, addressing their sustainable competitive advantage in the market. Outsourcing capital-intensive production improves a firm's ability to respond in a flexible manner to technology change, to accumulate knowledge, to avoid inefficiencies and to compress time-to-market for products and services (e.g. D'Aveni and Illinitch, 1992).

Theories of firm boundaries give indication why certain activities might be candidates for outsourcing by stressing efficiency gains in terms of transaction and production costs. But what still needs to be addressed is how decisions on choice of outsourcing partner, based on the partner's dynamic capabilities (also seen as efficiencies), impact the dynamic capabilities and efficiencies of the outsourcer. This may be seen as a bit of a domino effect. It also may be an intangible, yet potentially measurable, component of the decision-making process of how a bank builds a relationship with an IT service partner.

The concept of having that flexibility to reshape assets is discussed in strategic management as dynamic capabilities (Teece, 2003). The roles played by both a bank and its IT service delivery provider, in how they invest in IT resources (asset selection) and how they financially allocate that resource (coordination of activities) internally and between parties, are a part of the discussion of dynamic capabilities. But these choices are also related to both the firm boundaries and the governance of the transactional exchange of those capabilities. This may be seen in how most of the banks in the cases used IT service delivery partners that they had established relationships with, as they may have already understood the dynamic capabilities and medium-term strategies of these parties. This may be examined by the author in a future research paper within financial services outsourcing field.

Implications to Outsourcing Contracts in the Industry

Financial institutions are finding that an alignment of business strategies, operational processes and IT investments is a key driver for operational efficiency and resilience. Many FSI, both in banking and insurance, have been embracing outsourcing as a catalyst for such alignment, either because the outsourced pieces already reflect a strategic business transformation or they reduce and bring flexibility to various fixed IT and operational expenses. This will lead, as shown by research from IBM in Figure 4, to a more utility-oriented computing service delivery model.

Twenty-one of 39 Fortune 500 banks, brokerages and insurance companies surveyed by Gartner Inc. in November 2002 stated their top reason for outsourcing IT was to focus on core businesses. Other factors that were cited included increasing shareholder value, improving corporate efficiency and reducing operational risk management (Mearian, 2003).

Banks are focusing on outsourcing for IT cost optimization to create governance for cost, control, risk and value, via the ability to be innovative. As shown from the case studies, IT cost optimization is actually leading to a new service delivery paradigm, allowing banks to provide innovation and value from flexible and modular service. Technology spending appears to be related to creating innovation through value and bringing benefits in cost and efficiency. And that efficiency is provided by trust and risk sharing in the IT service value chain between the partners, creating dynamic capabilities for the bank.

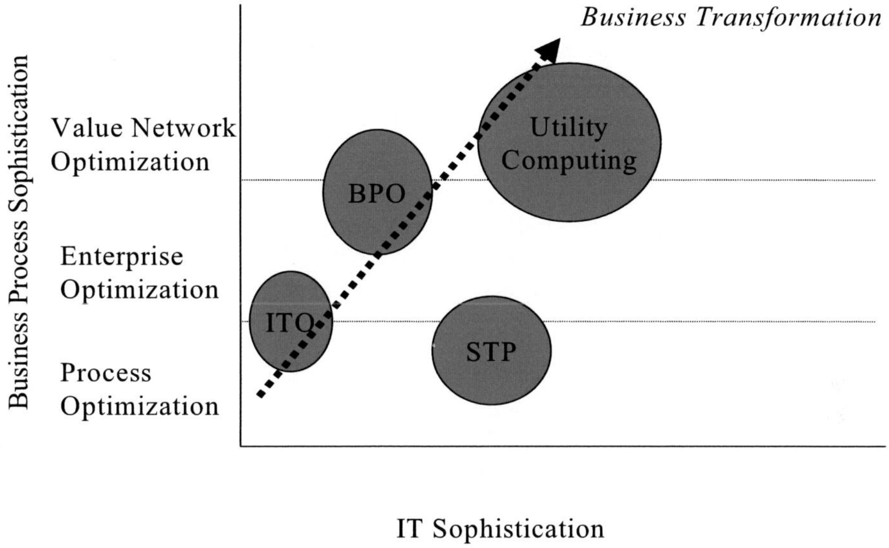

Figure 4. Evolution of service delivery, as a function of business process and IT sophistication (Saxton, 2003).

Limitations of the research include the select number of case studies of larger outsourcing deals. Outsourcing activities of smaller banks may provide additional insights. The future direction of this research is to include other financial service institutions (e.g. insurance and securities firms) to see how these trends compare across industries.

REFERENCES

Alexander, M. and D. Young, "Strategic Outsourcing," *Long Range Planning*, 29(1), 1996, 116-119.

Alpar, P, and A.N. Saharia, "Outsourcing Information System Functions: An Organization Economics Perspective," *Journal of Organizational Computing,* 5(3), 1995, 197-217.

Barney, J., "How a Firm's Capabilities Affect Boundary Decisions," *Sloan Management Review*, 40(3), 1999, 137-145.

Beath, C.M., Straub, D., "Managing Information Resources at the Department Level: An Agency Theory Perspective," in Proceedings of the Twenty-second Hawaii International Conference on Systems Sciences, Vol. III, Kailua-Koua, Hawaii, (January 1989), 151-159.

Corbett and Associates, "Outsourcing's Next Wave," Article written in 2002, available online as of May 28, 2003, at http://www.firmbuilder.com/articles/19/50/752/.

Datamonitor, *Outsourcing in Banks and Building Societies*, Report, 1994., *IT and Business Process Outsourcing in Financial Services*, Report, 2003.

D'Aveni, R.A. and Illinitch, A.Y., "Complex patterns of vertical integration in the forest products industry: systemic and bankruptcy risks," *Academy of Management Journal,* 37, 1994, 596-626.

Duncan, N.B. "Capturing IT Infrastructure Flexibility: A Study of Resource Characteristics and their Measure," *Journal of Management Information Systems* 12(2), 1995.

Frei, F.X., P.T. Harker, and L.W. Hunter, "Innovation in Retail Banking," The Wharton School, University of Pennsylvania, Working Paper No. 97-48-B, 1998.

Granovetter, M., "Economic Action and Social Structure: A Theory of Embeddedness," *American Journal of Sociology*, 91, 1985, 481-510.

Grossman, S.J. and O.D. Hart, "The Costs and Benefits of Ownership: A Theory of Vertical and Lateral Integration," *Journal of Political Economy*, 94(4), 1986, 691-719.

Hart, O.D. and J. Moore, "Property Rights and the Nature of the Firm," *Journal of Political Economy*, 98(6), 1990, 1119-1158.

Hoecht, A. "The Role of Trust in Strategic Sourcing Relationships," Working Paper from University of Portsmouth, presented at the EURAM conference in Stockholm, May 9-11, 2002.

Lacity, M.C. and R. Hirschheim, "The Information Systems Outsourcing Bandwagon," *Sloan Management Review*, 34(Fall), 1993, 73-86.

Lacity, M.C.; L.P Willcocks, and D.F. Feeny, "The Value of Selective IT Sourcing," *Sloan Management Review*, 37(Spring), 1996, 13-25.

Mayer, K., "Managing Buyer-Supplier Relationships in High Technology Industries," Ph.D. Dissertation, University of California, Berkeley, 1999.

Mearian, L., "Banks Pick Up the Pace of IT Outsourcing," *Computerworld*, 37(1), January 6, 2003, 6.

McFarlan, F. W. R.L. and Nolan, "How to Manage an IT Outsourcing Alliance," *Sloan Management Review*, 36(Winter) 1995, 9-22.

O'Heney, S., "Outsourcing is Hotter than Ever," *ABA Banking Journal*, May 1996, 44-50.

Roach, S.A., "Making Technology Work," Report from Economic Research Unit, 1993, Morgan Stanley & Co., New York.

Prahalad, C.K. and G. Hamel, "The Core Competence of the Corporation," *Harvard Business Review*, 68(3), 1990, 79-91.

Saxton, K., "Winning with industry value," presentation by Keith Saxton, Director, Financial Markets, IBM, *Dealing with Technology* conference, The Brewery, City of London, April 30, 2003.

Stalk, G., P. Evans, and L.E. Shulman, "Competing on Capabilities: The New Rules of Corporate Strategy," *Harvard Business Review*, 70(2), 1992, 57-69.

Teece, D., "Economies of Scope and the Scope of the Enterprise," *Journal of Economic Behavior and Organization*, 1, 1980, 233-247. "Explicating Dynamic Capabilities: Asset selection, coordination, and entrepreneurship in strategic management theory," presentation on 2 September 2003 at the Copenhagen Business School, Working Paper available at URL: http://www.cbs.dk/departments/ioa/research/Teece_Dynamic_Capabilities.pdf

Van der Meer-Kooistra, J and E.G. Vosselman, "Management Control of Interfirm Transactional Relationships: The Case of Industrial Renovation and Maintenance," *Accounting, Organizations and Society*, 25, 2000, 51-77.

Williamson, O.E., *Markets and Hierarchies: Analysis and Antitrust Implications*, New York: Free Press, 1975. *Markets and Hierarchies: Analysis and Antitrust Implications*, New York: Free Press, 1983. *The Economic Institutions of Capitalism*, New York: Free Press, 1985., "Opportunism and its Critics," *Managerial and Decision Economics*, 1993, vol.14, 97-107.

Wood, D. and D. Batiz-Lazo, "Corporate Strategy, Centralization and Outsourcing in Banking: Case Studies on Paper Payments Processing," *International Association of Management Journal*, 9(3), 1997, 35-57.

Zaheer, A. and N. Venkatraman, "Relational Governance as an Interorganizational Strategy: An Empirical Test of the Role of Trust in Economic Exchange," *Strategic Management Journal*, 16, 1995, 373-392.

INDEX

A

B

C

D

E

F

G

H

I

J

K

L

N

O

P

Q

R

S

T

U